A Horror of Great Darkness

Hitler and the Third Reich in the Light of Biblical Teaching

By Joseph E. Keysor

Published by

ATHANATOS
PUBLISHING GROUP

A Horror of Great Darkness

Hitler and the Third Reich in the Light of Biblical Teaching

By Joseph E. Keysor

Published by

ATHANATOS
PUBLISHING GROUP

A Horror of Great Darkness:
  Hitler and the Third Reich in the Light of Biblical Teaching

By Joseph E. Keysor

Published by Athanatos Publishing Group

ISBN: 978-1-936830-67-1

website: www.hitlerandchristianity.com

Copyright Info

We gratefully acknowledge permission to use more extensive quotes from the following two sources:

Luther, Martin. *On the Jews and Their Lies*. Translated by Martin H. Bertram. Luther's Works American Edition, vol. 47. Philadelphia: Fortress Press, 1971.

Wentorf, Rudolf. *Paul Schneider: Witness of Buchenwald*. Translated by Daniel Bloesch. Vancouver: Regent College Publishing, 2008.

Table Contents

Preface

There is a growing mountain of books about Hitler and the Holocaust, but very few of them have been written from an expressly biblical point of view. Of those that have, some of them have been only of a brief and introductory nature that precludes serious analysis.

This book attempts in some small way to remedy that deficiency. It approaches this highly important subject of modern history from the vantage point of belief in the Bible as the Word of God, so directly inspired by Him as to be not only spiritually but also historically and factually reliable, a sure guide both for this life and for the world to come.

I realize that such an approach will exclude my book from serious consideration in the eyes of many, and that even Christian scholars who privately believe in the Bible feel that matters of historical fact and interpretation should be presented in a professional manner according to which the direct discussion of biblical concepts is excluded from the outset. Their disapproval is not a matter of concern to me, although I regret, for their sakes, such self-imposed intellectual limitations.

It is my belief that biblical teachings apply directly to the issues of modern life, so much so that the exclusion of them impoverishes scholarship, and confines attempts at understanding to a lower plane far beneath what we as rational and spiritual beings should be capable of. It is my hope that this book will help, however inadequately, to a broader understanding of the eternal relevance of scriptural Christianity to modern life. It is also my hope that the book will help in some way to counter the false accusations against Christianity made by people who do not understand, and who may not want to understand, the deeply secular and anti-Christian nature of Hitler's ideology. It was not Christianity, but the rejection of Christianity, that opened the door to horrors unknown in the previous history of the world.

Introduction

In 1944 Alexander Werth, a correspondent attached to the Red Army, saw the Nazi death camp Maidenek shortly after its discovery. There were mounds of ashes containing human bones, charred remains on the floor of the crematorium, a trench full of naked corpses – it was an "unbelievable Death Factory," "vast" and "monumental." Werth sent a detailed report to the BBC, but they dismissed it as "a Russian propaganda stunt" and refused to air the story[1].

Not long afterward, invading British and American armies came across other camps. As more information was obtained, the full horror of the crimes of the Third Reich began to dawn upon the consciousness of the West. So great was the impact of these calculated, methodical and industrialized atrocities that they contributed significantly to the rise of post-modernism. Not only did nuclear weapons, napalm, pollution and the emptiness of modern life show that more scientific progress was not necessarily going to usher in a golden age; not only did two world wars explode the foolish modernist myth of civilization as unending progress; not only did continued advances in astronomy and physics demonstrate that science could not solve the riddle of the universe, but only introduced yet more and deeper unending riddles – in addition to all of these deadly blows to the pride of a once triumphant modernism, the crimes of Hitler and his myriad followers revealed the evil lurking behind the shimmering veils of "culture" and "civilization."

The Third Reich is a powerful testimony to the reality of evil. This evil did not end in 1945, and it has since appeared in various forms in other places – in Cambodia, in Rwanda, in Darfur, in Serbia, and even in the United States of America in our own day. The horrors of abortion clinics, where millions upon millions of helpless and innocent human beings have been arbitrarily labeled as inhuman and, like the victims of Hitler's death camps, legally killed in the name of a false philosophy of life, demonstrate the ongoing vitality of fascist principles. We can make a better world if we just eliminate all of those people who get in the way or who don't fit in. The Nazi death camp doctor Josef Mengele would have felt right at home in a modern abortion clinic, making his contribution to progress by killing babies. The spirit that animated Hitler and his followers has assumed different forms and disguises, but it is the same spirit nonetheless.

It was the belief of the "Enlightenment" that, by rejecting religion and tradition and relying on reason alone, mankind would be able to make a better world. This dazzling vision of self-reform and self-improvement by a

---

[1] Alexander Werth, *Russia at War 1941-1945* (New York: E. P. Dutton, 1964), p. 890.

i

humanity emancipated from God has proven to be a mirage, a delusion, a failure. The twentieth century, which – according to the dreams of secularists – should have been the most enlightened, progressive, and civilized period in history, turned out to be vicious, brutal, and bloody. Even in societies that escaped the devastations of war and totalitarianism, the humanist dreams of peace and material prosperity have proven to be strangely dissatisfying.

Is there something wrong with human nature? Can it be that deep down we are not really so good after all? How is it that human beings can even think of such acts as the Nazis did, let alone commit them? Moreover, it was in the heart of Europe that this occurred. We may secretly look down on Cambodia, Rwanda, the Sudan or Yugoslavia as backward and underdeveloped places (even if we don't want to admit it), but Germany was a land of science, philosophy, and music. It represented what was thought to be the very best of Europe's heritage. How could so many supposedly advanced people in a fully developed country have been so evil?

Countless books have been written in an attempt to unravel this dark and sinister riddle. The events of the Holocaust have been examined from every angle – historically, sociologically, philosophically, theologically – and no universally convincing answer has been found. It is possible that if a complete and definite answer ever were found it would not be believed, being so far removed from everyone's expectations. Nevertheless, the effort to understand continues, and the Holocaust has become an important field of study in its own right, established as a recognized field of research and scholarship in leading universities throughout the Western world.

The subject of the Third Reich continues to compel interest, as it points to the existence of a deeper and darker dimension to life which many would prefer to ignore. Unfortunately, it is a subject to which Bible-believing Christians have not made enough of a contribution. True, the world of academic scholarship is now so overwhelmingly secular that any excessively religious talk about the Bible, the teachings of Jesus Christ, sin, the spiritual reality of human evil and of Satan leads only to contemptuous dismissal by narrow-minded and ignorant people. Some Christian scholars who have found a cozy niche for themselves would damage their careers if they were too overtly religious and said too much about these subjects. In spite of modern secular bias, however, looking at some aspects of the problem of Hitler from a biblically Christian point of view (as I understand it) will I believe bring a new perspective from which to consider the spiritual darkness of the Third Reich.

It might also demonstrate the profound relevance of Christian doctrines not merely to personal salvation, but also to the current trends and problems of the modern world. Biblical teaching has much more to say about the modern age than many suppose, and when we try to shine the light of Scripture into the dark places of Nazi Germany, surprising shapes begin to appear – and this is not merely a historical question. Some aspects of Nazi ideology are highly relevant to us today, and we can see the failures of the German churches to oppose the lies of false worldly ideologies being reenacted in too many contemporary American churches. What a powerful temptation it is to avoid controversy and just be like everyone else. For this reason, conformity to the world and its false wisdom has always been a recognized problem for the church, not only in in Nazi Germany, but in the Roman Empire, the Middle Ages, and in our own time.

Modern secularism can tell us little about the Holocaust beyond the mere facts of what occurred. In a meaningless universe that somehow exploded out of nothing, all of life is reduced to a pointless adventure, snuffed out after a brief moment by death. Belief in the Judaeo-Christian God, however, gives genuine meaning to the terms "good" and "evil," and allows us to evaluate not merely the crimes of the Nazis, but the ideas behind those crimes, relative to a definite standard – a standard rooted, if Christianity is true, as I believe it to be true, in the very nature of the cosmos itself. Bizarre acts of senseless delight in cruelty that are totally inexplicable within a secular context have spiritual origins and so require non-material explanations.

Biblical teachings about the spiritual truths that govern the world and the reality of evil in the human soul are infinitely more relevant to an understanding of our world than are totally unsubstantiated pseudo-scientific speculations about multiverses or about a minute speck a micro-fraction of a centimeter in diameter that somehow exploded into an orderly cosmos governed by detailed and highly specific laws.[2] The Bible has much to say about important aspects of our existence that eternally transcend the exceedingly limited reach of the physical sciences and the clumsy groping of autonomous human reason.

It is commonly claimed, however, that religion is part of the problem, that the Bible itself teaches hatred of Jews and that centuries of "Christian" antisemitism were thus the direct result of orthodox Christian doctrine. It is also commonly argued that this religious antisemitism either led directly to the crimes of the Nazis or else contributed indirectly but significantly to them. "Without Christian antisemitism, the Holocaust would have been inconceivable"[3] – this view is by now standard in most attempts to unravel the riddle of Auschwitz and the myriad crimes of the Nazis, and is accepted as the norm in academic circles.

---

[2] Stephen Hawking and Leonard Mlodinow, *The Grand Design: New Answers to the Ultimate Questions of Life* (London: Bantam Books, 2011), p. 168. The exact size, according to Hawking, was "a billion-trillion-trillionth of a centimeter." He has not informed us how many angels can dance on the head of a pin.

[3] Dennis Prager and Joseph Telushkin, *Why the Jews? The Reason for Antisemitism* (New York: Touchstone, 2003), p. 87.

Christian philosopher William Lane Craig makes the valid point that when it comes to ridiculous ideas taken seriously by no one – such as, that Jesus Christ came from outer space – arguing is not an effective strategy: "If you argue with him, this gives the impression that his view is worth refuting and therefore has some credibility, which it does not."[4] While for the example he gives Craig's advice is sound, on the very different subject of the Nazis Christian indifference has been a mistake, and our passivity in this area has encouraged yet more and more extreme claims. Although there are some attacks on Christianity in this area that are so distorted, convoluted, and devious, that exposing all of their errors of fact and logic would be a complete waste of time, these issues are still worth responding to in a general way.

Instead of engaging in futile arguments with people who are not interested in seriously understanding both sides of a question, it might sometimes be better just to ask, "What do you think Christianity is? Do you know what Jesus taught?" and try to keep the conversation on a more basic level. Yet at other times some more information might be helpful – especially since those who have too much confidence in human reason are unaware of the extent to which it was thoroughly modern thinkers such as Wagner, Haeckel, Nietzsche, Hegel, Schopenhauer, Darwin and many others who most effectively articulated ideas that spread gradually through society and (along with complex social and historical factors) helped to make the Holocaust possible.

If Europe's intelligentsia had not turned away so dramatically from Christianity the Holocaust would never have occurred. It took the loss of God and the resultant ideas that people were essentially only beasts; that human life was a mere physical phenomenon of no great significance; that traditional ethics were unscientific and out-of-date; that struggle was the iron law of life; that we should get back to nature, and nature was remorseless conflict; that our life's meaning was found in the national group as determined by race; that the state was the highest source of law and authority – it took these and yet other sophisticated modern ideas to lay the foundations for crimes such as had never yet been seen.

It also took the blessings of modern technology which gave us more power than we know how to handle wisely, and exponentially increased the destructiveness of evil men without providing any compensatory moral safeguards. Indeed, what traditional moral safeguards did exist were systematically and proudly dismantled. Racism, virulent nationalism, imperialism, lofty philosophical schemes remote from the reality of individual suffering, denial of eternal realities, pride in the power and glory of man emancipated from God – it is here, in the foul morass of the innately sinful

---

[4] William Lane Craig, *Reasonable Faith: Christian Truth and Apologetics* (Wheaton, IL: Crossway, 2008) p. 328.

human heart, not in the Bible or in conventional beliefs about God, that the roots of National Socialism lie.

Before examining these and other ideas in a separate volume (tentatively titled *The Secular Origins of National Socialist Ideology*), we will need to explore the religious dimensions of this topic in this first volume. Because misinterpretations of what the Bible actually says are constantly used to link Christianity to the Holocaust, it will be necessary to establish the essential point that the Bible does not teach hatred of Jews. This will be the main focus of chapter 1, "The New Testament and the Jews." Biblical Christianity recognizes the common guilt of all in the death of Christ, insofar as he died for all, and the shared guilt of Pontius Pilate and the Gentiles is explicitly stated (Acts 4:26-27).

Chapter 2, "The Jewish people and their enemies," will consist of an examination of the problem of antisemitism. Who are the Jews? Where did they come from, what do they represent, and why have they been so widely hated, and for so long? What is this strange force of hatred that adapts itself to different circumstances over many centuries and geographical locations while retaining an inner continuity? Only the Bible taken as literal historical fact gives us an answer, without which there can be no real comprehensive understanding of the identity of the Jewish people, or of the anti-Judaism that continually arises against them. This will require discussing biblical teachings about sin and evil, including the higher and unseen spiritual powers of wickedness that so consistently intervene in human affairs. The invisible forces of evil are great and they are real, and without some recognition of this no deeper consideration of our subject is possible.

Many attempts to explain Hitler and the Holocaust today are based on the assumption that this spiritual dimension of reality is off-limits (being either non-existent, or inherently unknowable, or at least too subjective for authentic academic discourse). There is to be sure a place for the mere recording of historical fact, but for a deeper understanding of these questions we must enter into the realm of the human spirit – of beliefs, of emotional needs and aspirations, of things far above lifeless, petty and empty materialism. If this precludes scientific certainty, so be it. The methods of the laboratory are not suitable for this subject. We need an understanding that far transcends the lesser, easier and safer studies of inert material objects.

It is sad to see people trying to seriously discuss the Holocaust when they have no coherent concept of evil – when they adhere to a materialistic world-view that makes any real understanding or definition of evil impossible. If the universe just happened by accident and is composed strictly of matter and energy, there is no evil, other than what humans arbitrarily so declare because something seems bad to them. Hitler thought racial impurity, democracy, and the Versailles Treaty were "evils," and this seemed reasonable to him and to many others. Without God, there is no real good or evil, only changing human fads and fashions. Hitler made the very modern point in *Mein Kampf* that ethics had no enduring basis in reality, but were merely human inventions.[5]

Yet, belief in God is not in and of itself an easy solution, and often merely introduces new problems of its own. For this reason we will need to study religious anti-Judaism at some length in chapter 3 ("The problem of 'Christian' antisemitism"). Even if it can be shown that the New Testament is not inherently anti-Jewish, as is often falsely claimed, the question still remains: how is it that those who claimed to believe in Jesus practiced hatred, lies, and cruelty against the people from whom Jesus emerged? Only by ignoring many fundamental doctrines about our calling and purpose as Christians in a fallen world. Evil in the name of Christ – whether against Jews or against anyone else – will bring heavy condemnation on the Day of Judgment.

Especially significant in this context is the problem of Martin Luther. Since this deeply spiritual man who did so much to deliver the church from harmful and unbiblical medieval accretions is constantly mentioned – and misrepresented – in discussions of the Holocaust, it will be necessary to consider his motives. It will also help to clarify this conversation if we understand the vast differences separating the 16th and the 20th centuries. Luther was not responsible for and had nothing to do with significant aspects of modern Germany's development. Moreover, the basic ideas of the Reformation had nothing in common with National Socialist ideology. Less important figures such as Augustine, Chrysostom, and others will also be mentioned in chapter 3 (I mean less important in discussions of antisemitism).

This chapter will also briefly look into the distinctly non-Christian antisemitism that emerged out of modern Germany's turning away from traditional Christianity. Kant, Fichte, Schopenhauer and others introduced new concepts of the Jews which were far more relevant to Nazi anti-Judaism than anything that emerged out of the Reformation. When Hitler wrote that the Old Testament was historically false and that Judaism was not even a religion at all,[6] he was in the tradition of Kant and the "Enlightenment," not of Calvin and Luther. The perceptions that Christianity was false and harmful to the German spirit, and that Christianity came from the Jews, were integral parts of National Socialist philosophy. This is clearly evident in Hitler's strangely neglected religious comments in *Mein Kampf*. Nietzsche's furious and hate-filled attacks on Jewish Christianity and his discovery of Jewish plots to corrupt society as elaborated on at length in *The Antichrist* will be mentioned in this context (though a more detailed analysis will have to be deferred to another time).

---

[5] Adolf Hitler, *Mein Kampf*, trans. Ralph Manheim (New York: Houghton Mifflin, 1999), pp. 287-288.

[6] Ibid., pp. 303-305. Hitler quotes Schopenhauer here.

The final two chapters will examine some questions of Hitler and religion in detail. This is now a post-Christian age and many people who have no understanding of what Christianity is are easily fooled by dubious arguments and by malignant anti-Christian propaganda. Wasn't Germany a Christian country? Weren't many Nazis "Christians or sons of Christians?" Didn't Hitler himself claim to be a Christian in a speech in 1922, a speech in which he referred to Christ as his "Lord and Saviour"? Didn't he promise to support the churches, and didn't many Christians and even church leaders support Hitler, or at least fail to oppose him? Surely if Hitler had been against Christianity the churches would have united against him, wouldn't they? Hitler even signed an official agreement with the Vatican. That (to some) proves Hitler was a Catholic, although it has never been argued that his agreement with Stalin proves Hitler was a Russian.

The great majority of Christians have no idea how popular and effective some of these arguments are. Based on ignorance of Christianity, of German culture and history and of Hitler's beliefs, they are commonly used to link the supposed irrationality of religious belief with the real irrationality of National Socialism. Those who fear that the greatest threat to America's liberty comes from religious conservatives do follow a sort of logic. It is a false logic that will quickly collapse before any informed analysis, but too little has been said in response, allowing for more and more reckless accusations (often inspired not only by ignorance, but also by hatred and fear of a religion that in its purest form holds people to strict standards of right and wrong).

Chapter 4 – "Hitler's religious, quasi-religious and anti-religious ideas" – will not attempt a comprehensive survey of Hitler's complete ideology, but instead will explore Hitler's rejection of Christian beliefs; his hostile statements about Christianity; and his advocacy of ideas unheard of for 1800 years and more after Christ. Hitler did sometimes refer to "god" and claimed to be doing the will of some kind of a "god," but his emphases on racial purity, life as merciless struggle, and German superiority (among other things) show him to have been speaking of something totally contrary to a conventionally Christian understanding. His comments about a "creator" or "creation" have led to hasty and ill-informed attempts to link Hitler to today's biblical Creationism, in which Hitler did not believe (we have already referred to his contemptuous dismissal of the Old Testament as a historically false book).

The failure to rightly interpret Hitler's religious comments has caused great confusion. Taking Hitler's condemnations of immorality and atheism in the wrong way are one reason why many on the left are afraid that if anyone like Hitler ever appears in America he will come from the "religious right" (while they ignore the dangers posed by the anti-religious left). I think that a secret fear of another Hitler is one reason why many American Jews timidly and irrationally support leftist secular candidates no matter what.

It will not be difficult to demonstrate that Hitler was deeply hostile to Christianity; that he never referred to many essential Christian doctrines; that he held many ideas contrary to biblical Christianity; that he was as far removed from the teachings of Christ as east is from west or as night is from day. But, this clarification is necessary. Without it, it will be impossible to understand Hitler's attempts to manipulate religion and use it to advance his own very different agenda. *Mein Kampf* contains some revealing comments about these subjects, more than is commonly realized. They have been consistently overlooked by historians who are not too concerned with Christianity and know little about it. These comments include Hitler's recognition of the obviously Jewish nature of Christianity and his plans for its replacement, by force if necessary, with new ideas.[7]

In chapter 5, "The Christians in the Third Reich," we will look at how the churches were affected when Hitler's anti-Christian ideas were put into practice. This should clearly reveal the true meaning of Hitler's vague comments about religion. It should also serve to clarify the nature of Christianity relative to Hitler's commitment to a new view of reality emancipated from traditional ethical and moral restraints. We will also need to consider some commonly raised questions. Why did the Christians support Hitler? Why did they so rarely speak out openly against him? How did they respond to increasing government pressure, and even persecution? Why didn't they speak out more for the Jews? Was this because the antisemitism supposedly inherent in Christianity led them to see the Jews as deserving of divine punishment? Because there is a spiritual kinship between religious faith and the need to blindly follow a Fuhrer? Or because keeping silent to save one's own skin is ordinary human nature which Christians should rise above but all too seldom do?

Apart from human weakness, the Protestant churches in Germany had been undermined from within for a century and more before Hitler by a new version of Christianity which denied the essentials of the faith and, while retaining much religious language, presented what was in fact a new religion. The deity of Christ, his sacrificial death and resurrection, the authority of the Bible, the realities of the Day of Judgment, Heaven, and Hell were denied or explained away by "scholars," "pastors," and "theologians" who called themselves Christians and were so considered by the world, but who robbed the church of its spiritual life and vitality and left it empty and helpless (with rare exceptions) before the far greater spiritual power of National Socialism.

Christianity is not defined by the churches of Germany, by German pastors and theologians who agreed with Hitler, or knew that he was wrong but did not want to go to a concentration camp. Nor is it defined by people who came along nearly two thousand years after Christianity began. It is defined by

---

[7] Ibid., pp. 454-455.

Christ, and by the teachings he gave to the apostles, as we have them in the New Testament. True, there are many lofty ideals presented there that Christians consistently fall short of, yet there have been many Christians in many countries over many centuries who have been sincere enough in their walk with Christ to be innocent of hatred, massacres, persecutions, and malicious lies. Such common and ordinary people are consistently overlooked by those whose hostility to Christianity leads to a highly subjective and often dishonest manipulation of evidence.

The early Christian writer Origen of Alexandria wrote, "A desire to know the truth of things has been implanted in our souls and is natural to human beings."[8] A natural desire to know the truth about the Holocaust, to understand the causes of one of the greatest catastrophes in world history, has occasioned a vast amount of words. Too many of them have been written by people ignorant of or even hostile to scriptural Christianity. Faithful adherence to the teachings of Christ, all of them, insofar as we are capable of it, and belief in his deity, sacrificial death, resurrection and return were not the cause of the problems we will now attempt to explore.

---

[8] Robert Louis Wilken, *The Spirit of Early Christian Thought: Seeking the Face of God* (New Haven: Yale University Press, 2003), p. 165, quoting Origen's *First Principles*.

Chapter 1. The New Testament and the Jews

For many centuries before Hitler, European Jewry suffered in varying degrees from religious antisemitism – and this tradition of Jew-hatred constantly comes up in attempts to explain the Holocaust. Nazi hatred and persecution are sometimes seen as merely logical continuations of what had gone on before. The "Christians" demonized Jews and killed them, or implied they should be killed, and the Nazis continued the process through to the end.

Others accept the fact that Nazi antisemitism was different both in degree and in kind from previous forms of anti-Judaism. They understand that never before had anyone tried to carry out the systematic extermination of the entire Jewish people; that the random massacres and sporadic mob attacks of the Middle Ages were significantly different from the industrialized and bureaucratized mass murders of the Third Reich; that Nazi ideology was composed of ideas that first became noticeable in the nineteenth century.

Even as some recognize obvious differences, however, they will still link Hitler's hatred to the earlier religious antisemitism, asserting that it was Christianity that created the reservoir of hate that Hitler was then able to exploit for his own very different ends. This "Christian" Jew-hatred is often claimed to be directly from the New Testament, which supposedly demonizes Jews as Christ-killers, children of the devil, deservedly under God's wrath. Thus, what is inconceivable to many ordinary Christians is now a common assertion in academic discussions of the Holocaust: that biblical Christianity, directly or indirectly but always significantly, had something to do with the horrors of the Final Solution.

The following quotation illustrates what is now a commonplace in Holocaust studies: in spite of undeniable differences between Naziism and Christianity, "Christian hostility toward Jews remains a factor essential for any sound attempt to explain how and why the Holocaust happened."[1] Such conceptions of some kind of a relationship between the Bible, traditional religious antisemitism and Nazism are now so widespread among non-Christians that I believe it is not possible to explore later modern and secular manifestations of Jew-hatred without first attempting to clarify this issue. This will mean defending the assertion that religious antisemitism was a direct

---

[1] Richard L. Rubenstein and John K. Roth, *Approaches to Auschwitz: The Holocaust and its Legacy* (Louisville KY: Westminster John Knox Press, 2003), p. 20. Later, discussing the origins of "Christian" antisemitism, the book presents "some of the points that are the most crucial for linking Jesus' demise with Auschwitz" (p. 34). Such thinking represents the mainstream of current secular scholarship. The book is recommended by the publisher as "a popular choice for college courses on the Holocaust and genocide."

violation of plain biblical teachings; that in no way, shape or form does the New Testament teach hatred of Jews or of anyone else.

Before approaching this point, it might be helpful to make a few general comments about the Middle Ages so as to put the cruelties of religious antisemitism in their proper perspective. For example, the Jews were often treated badly during that period, but then so were many others. Jews were massacred at times, so were others. The slaughters and atrocities committed by the Huns, the Mongols, the Vikings, and the various European rulers in their constant wars when Europe was supposedly united under one religion did not affect only Jews. It is not as if all Europeans lived lives of peace, ease, and prosperity while only the Jews suffered.

The history of the Jews in medieval Europe was not one of unrelieved massacres either. There were times and places where the Jews were tolerated, if restricted, and even given a measure of protection. Prof. Steven Katz points out in his in-depth study of the Holocaust that Jews were at times better treated, with more rights and privileges, than many of the peasants, "that medieval Jewry did have a life other than that expressed in pogroms and despoliations."[2] Another source says that until the First Crusade in 1096, "the situation of the Jews [in Europe] was tenuous but tolerable."[3] For yet further confirmation: "Until the eleventh century the Jews lived in moderate comfort in French and German cities."[4]

Jews were sometimes given a measure of autonomy within their numerous restrictions and at times managed to create a rich and thriving Jewish culture. Katz even gives specific examples of some medieval rulers who sought to protect Jews in their dominions (Emperor Henry IV, King Stephen of England, Emperor Frederick I and others). This is not to deny the many injustices, cruelties and horrors the Jews experienced. It is to say that oversimplifications do not help towards an understanding of later forms of anti-Judaism. In the attempt to systematically exterminate the entire Jewish people we have something new.

It is also worth pointing out that Jews are not exempt from human crimes, errors and sins, and even committed massacres against each other in Bible times when they were masters in their own land. For example, in the civil war that resulted from the attempt to punish the tribe of Benjamin for the death of the Levite's wife, over 65,000 Jews were killed by other Jews (Judges chapters 19-21). The Old Testament bears ample record to the sinfulness of the Jews.

---

[2] Steven A. Katz, *The Holocaust in Historical Context (Vol. 1)* (New York: Oxford University Press, 1994), pp. 307-308.

[3] Dennis Prager and Joseph Telushkin, *Why the Jews: The Reason for Antisemitism* (New York New: Touchstone, 2003), p. 79.

[4] Abram Leon Sachar, *A History of the Jews* (New York: Alfred A. Knopf, 1966), p. 185.

Didn't King Saul order the execution of 85 priests because Abimelech had helped David? Didn't Joab, David's general, kill 360 of Abner's men? When Absalom attempted to seize the kingdom from his father David there was a great battle in which Jews were slaughtering Jews. When Jehu seized the throne of Israel he killed Ahab's son Jehoram, and then proceeded to massacre all of Ahab's royal family – sons, grandsons, relatives, and even servants, and friends. He also killed all of the prophets, priests, and worshippers of Baal, and then murdered King Ahaziah of Judah and his brothers.

The history of Israel in the Hasmonean period in the century or so before Christ also has plenty of bloodshed. The Jewish king Alexander Jannai slaughtered thousands of his subjects. At one time he had 800 people crucified, with their wives and children killed in front of them as they were dying on crosses. Yet more Jews were killed in the civil war between Aristobulus and Hyrcanus. Rival groups of Zealots during the revolt against Rome fought each other. One Zealot leader, Menahem ben Judas, "launched a reign of terror," killing anyone who did not support his group or who showed sympathy to Rome.[5]

There was not merely bloodshed. The Maccabean leader John Hyrcanus conquered Idumaea on the east side of the Jordan and forcibly converted its inhabitants to Judaism. This act was repeated by his son Aristobulus I, the first of the Hasmonean monarchs (he reigned from 104-103 B.C.). Aristobulus conquered a region north of Galilee called Ituraea and also compelled its inhabitants to become Jews. There is no way of knowing how much more of this might have occurred had the Hasmoneans maintained sovereignty for a longer period.

Church historian Philip Schaff relates that Bar-Cochba, leader of the second Jewish revolt against Rome in the second century A. D., "caused all Christians who would not join him to be most cruelly murdered."[6] Schaff also makes the observation that after Bar-Cochba's failure and the final destruction of political Israel by the Romans, "the Jews had no opportunity for further independent persecution of the Christians." Prior to this time they had, of course, persecuted Christians to the point of imprisonment and even death.

Such events do not show a problem with Judaism, they show a problem with human nature. Emotional tirades against the wickedness of European Christianity by bitter and angry people fail to take the reality of human sin into account. Prior to the return of Christ himself, Christianity does not promise to

---

[5] Norman Gelb, *Kings of the Jews: The Origins of the Jewish Nation* (Philadelphia: The Jewish Publication Society, 2012), pp. 178-79, 210.

[6] Philip Schaff, *History of the Christian Church (vol. 1, Apostolic Christianity from the Birth of Christ to the Death of St. John A.D. 1-100)* (Peabody, Mass: Hendrickson Publishers, 2011), pp. 37, 38 (both quotes).

eliminate the evils of life. Cruelty and killing have been found in all parts of the world and in every period of history – and that "Christian" atrocities were sin, direct disobedience to plain Christian teachings, will be discussed shortly. First, though, we need to stress an important point: that Nazi antisemitism was radically different from anything that had ever been seen before.

At no time in the centuries of Christian cultural dominance did anyone attempt or even advocate the extermination of the entire Jewish people. Sporadic assaults by mobs or by vicious and brutal Crusaders were not carefully planned ahead of time by an efficient modern state. Even the dreaded Inquisition was not directed exclusively against Jews, and did not remotely approach genocide – but none of this has anything to do with the teachings of Christ. Neither does it have anything to do with the vast majority of Christians over the centuries that have been far removed from such wickedness.

Not only the results but also the motives of these two varieties of antisemitism were profoundly different. That Jews were plotting to rule the world; that they were corrupting the purity of Aryan blood, which was fatal to the German people as purity of blood was necessary to prevail in the struggle for survival of the fittest; that Jews were subhuman, vermin, plague bacilli; that they controlled the international banking system; that sickly Jewish values transmitted to Europe through Christianity had replaced healthy German paganism – these ridiculous ideas were unheard of before the modern era, and emerged out of various strands of modern secularism. Some of those strands go back as far as Kant and the "Enlightenment," and can be found in the lofty ideas and imposing rhetoric of Germany's finest philosophers.

But what about the accusation that the New Testament itself teaches that Jews are children of the devil, under the wrath of God, making biblical Christianity itself responsible for all of the blood shed in the name of Christ? That this is not the case can easily be seen by a consideration of relevant biblical passages, as well as by a consideration of the lives of great numbers of ordinary Christians who have never harmed a Jew or wanted to.

Following are some commonly alleged examples of New Testament anti-Judaism. I should add that I take these narratives of Christ's death to be accurate and literal historical narratives of what actually took place.

When Pilate saw that he could prevail nothing, but that rather a tumult was made, he took water, and washed his hands before the multitude, saying, I am innocent of the blood of this just person: see ye to it (Matthew 27:24).

This is commonly used to show that the Jews, not the Gentiles, were responsible for the death of Christ. To quote Steven Katz again, it has been "recognized by almost every Christian commentator on Matthew from patristic to modern times"[7] that this passage emphasizes the guilt of the Jews.

Somehow all of those commentators neglected to read Acts 4:26-28, which says that "both Herod, and Pontius Pilate, with the Gentiles, and the people of Israel, were gathered together" in the crucifixion of Christ. The reference to the Gentiles here refers to the Roman soldiers, who could have come from any part of the vast Roman Empire – but there must also have been non-Jews among the spectators who joined in the mockery of a king dying on a cross.

There are Christians who have not failed to notice Pilate's obvious guilt. Justin Martyr wrote in the second century A.D. of "the conspiracy which was formed against Christ by Herod King of the Jews, and the Jews themselves, and Pilate, who was your procurator among them, with his soldiers."[8] He says "your procurator" in this quote as the work, the *First Apology*, was dedicated to the Roman emperor, the Senate, and some Roman notables. Justin thus links them to Christ's death.

Matthew Henry wrote in the eighteenth century that "Both Jews and Gentiles were obnoxious to the judgment of God, and concluded under sin, and Christ was to be the Saviour both of Jews and Gentiles; and therefore Christ was brought into the judgment both of Jews and Gentiles, and both had a hand in his death." Henry also notes that Pilate found no fault in Christ, knew that the Jewish leaders were moved by envy, and yet delivered an innocent man to be tortured to death for the sake of expediency. Such an act of cruel and cowardly injustice cannot be wiped away by a gesture of hand-washing and a declaration of innocence. In Henry's words, "What nonsense was this, to condemn him, and yet protest that he was innocent of his blood! . . . Though Pilate professed his innocency, God charges him with guilt, Acts 4:27 . . . it is not so easy to transfer the guilt of sin as many think it is."[9]

To say that the New Testament blames only the Jews for Christ's death is now a common misconception on the part of people who are basically ignorant of what Christianity teaches on this vital subject. They only repeat what they have heard somewhere, or else have read the Bible without comprehension, eager to find fault and not even wanting to genuinely understand.

---

[7] Katz, *Holocaust in Historical Context*, p. 356.

[8] Justin Martyr, *The First and Second Apologies*, trans. Leslie William Barnard (Mahwah, NJ: Paulist Press, 1997), p. 50.

[9] Matthew Henry, *Matthew Henry's Commentary on the Whole Bible: Matthew to John (vol. 5)* (Peabody, Mass.: Hendrickson Publishers, 1991), p. 340, both quotes.

Then answered all the people, and said, His blood be on us, and on our children (Matthew 27:25).

It is true, some of those with the name of "Christians" have applied this to the Jewish people as a whole – were they right in doing so? When shortly after the Exodus from Egypt the Israelites murmured and said "Would to God we had died by the hand of the Lord in the land of Egypt" (Exodus 16:3), God did not honor their request, bring them back to Egypt and slay them there. When later the Jewish people received the report of the spies about the greatness of the Canaanites, they despaired and said, "Let us make a captain, and let us return into Egypt" (Numbers 14:4). God did not honor that statement and hearken to their request, bringing it even upon those who were not present and had no knowledge of what was occurring.

God's eternal purposes are not swayed by our rash and foolish words and bad mistakes, and nowhere do we see the apostles preaching that the Jews are henceforth and forever under an iron and eternal curse. Those who had directly participated in Christ's crucifixion were shown their guilt (Acts 2:23), but even they were offered forgiveness of sins and the promise of eternal life. Moreover, Paul teaches in Romans chapter 3 that all of us, Jews and Gentiles, are alike under condemnation for sin – "There is none righteous, no, not one . . . For all have sinned and come short of the glory of God."

Incidentally, "all the people" in the verse cited above means "all the people who were present before Pilate at that time" not, as someone ominously suggested, all Jews, everywhere, forever. If in a Holocaust survival narrative we read that someone was hiding from "the Germans," this does not mean all Germans everywhere in the world. It refers to those Germans specifically who were involved at that place and at that time. Luke 23:27 tells us that "a great company of people" followed Christ wailing and lamenting as he carried his cross to Golgotha. Must they be placed under some curse also?

But, "The Jews killed Christ! Death to the Jews!" was used as an incentive for violence and slaughter. I wonder how many drunken peasants who went on murderous rampages using such words had even read the Bible. Those miserable evildoers and enemies of Christ certainly had no understanding of the following points, well known to all who actually read and believe in the Bible:

[1] That Christ laid down his life voluntarily (John 10:17-18).

[2] That this was part of God's predetermined plan for our redemption (Acts 2:23).

[3] That Christ on the cross said "Father, forgive them; for they know not what they do." Our calling as Christians, as followers of Christ, if we really are

6

followers of Christ, is to be agents of reconciliation, not of wrath, and those who do evil in the name of Christ will receive a heavy condemnation on the Day of Judgment (I Peter 4:14-17).

[4] That, as Christ died for the sins of the world, anyone who sins in any way, however small, is directly involved in his death (I John 2:2). Arthur Pink wrote, "He was bearing *our* sins in His own body on the Tree (I Peter 2:24). He had taken our place and was suffering, the just for the unjust."[10] Or, as Martin Luther said, "when you firmly believe that his wounds and sufferings are your sins, to be borne and paid for by him," then you can "cast your sins from yourself and onto Christ."[11]

Since this concept is so often misunderstood, it is appropriate to give a couple more quotations. Francis Schaeffer, a well-known modern American evangelical author, raised no eyebrows when he wrote "I say the world killed Christ because not only the Jews were responsible, but Roman power and all mankind as well. Gentile and Jew alike, represented by the Jewish Sanhedrin and the Roman procurator, killed Jesus Christ. Rebellious mankind, you and I, killed Jesus Christ." [12] That this is not the result of a special post-Holocaust sensitivity can be seen in the words of the grand old eighteenth-century Wesley hymn "And Can it Be?", a hymn still sung in many churches today – "Died he for me who caused his pain? for me, who him to death pursued?" Writing in the 17th century, the great Puritan John Owen stated the obvious fact that the Jews and the Romans killed Christ.[13] Every serious Christian knows that if we had been there we too could easily have cried "Crucify him!"

[5] That if God did not spare the natural branches (the Jews), but broke them off because of their unbelief, we need to remember that we Christians too can be cut off, if we do not continue in God's goodness (Romans 11:17-21).

[6] That those who are guilty of "hatred . . . wrath . . . murders . . . shall not inherit the kingdom of God" (Galatians 5:20-21). It doesn't matter if they were baptized, went to church every day, took communion, or talked about Jesus. Murderers and liars ("The Jews need human blood for their Passover celebrations!") "shall have their part in the lake which burneth with fire and brimstone: which is the second death" (Revelation 21:8).

---

[10] Arthur W. Pink, *The Seven Sayings of the Saviour on the Cross* (Hyderabad India: Authentic, by arrangement with Baker Books, 2010), p. 77.

[11] Martin Luther, *A Meditation on Christ's Passion: Devotional Writings I*, trans. Martin H. Bertram (Philadelphia: Fortress Press 1969), p. 12.

[12] Francis Schaeffer, *No Little People* (Wheaton, IL: Crossway, 2003), pp. 95-96.

[13] John Owen, *The Holy Spirit: His Gifts and Power* (Ross-shire, Scotland: Christian Heritage, 2007), p. 124.

[7] That our calling as Christians is not to be agents of God's wrath (Romans 10:15).

[8] That it is those who have tasted the truths of the Christian religion and then fall away who "crucify to themselves the Son of God afresh" (Hebrews 6:4-6), not those who simply reject Christ in open unbelief. To say that the Jews who reject Christ continually crucify him thereby has no biblical basis. If it did, it would apply equally to the whole world, including many in the Christian churches who are still asleep in their sins and who (if the truth were known) have never known Christ.

A high-ranking church official in Slovakia is reported to have told a Jew in 1944 that "All Jewish blood is guilty. You have to die. This is the punishment that has been awaiting you because of that sin" (the crucifixion of Christ).[14] We can't blame secular historians too much if they take such wicked and ungodly statements by cruel and heartless people at face value (though often said historians are willfully ignorant). That the New Testament blames only the Jews for Christ's death is now a standard theme that finds its way even into what purport to be secular histories of the Third Reich.

Bare narratives of historical facts without an understanding of the biblically spiritual dimension have a real but nevertheless limited value. We certainly cannot expect an objective description of these higher themes from historians who praise Marx as a great revolutionary thinker while ignoring his venomous, secular, atheistic anti-Judaism and then point the finger at Christianity. They do this because they prefer for various reasons to discredit the Bible whenever possible. When Marx described Polish Jews as "this filthiest of all races," motivated by a "passion for greedy gain," and wrote elsewhere that "Money is the jealous God of Israel, beside which no other God may stand,"[15] he only revealed his complete ignorance of the subject (as of so many other subjects). The crucifixion of Christ was not relevant to the new antisemitism that emerged out of the so called Enlightenment – and Marx, because of his reliance on reason alone, was to a significant extent a product of the "Enlightenment," in spite of his many false and irrational ideas.

---

[14] Prager and Telushkin, *Why the Jews,* p. 152.

[15] Ibid., pp. 125 (first two quotes), 124 (third quote). This source also presents a quote from Hitler in which he seems to acknowledge Marx's anti-Jewish essay (p. 125).

Ye are of your father the devil, and the lusts of your father ye will do (John 8:44).

This is commonly pointed to in order to show that Christianity teaches Jews are children of the devil, but we see from earlier in the passage (8:37) that Jesus was speaking to those who were plotting to kill him. Someone has claimed that the idea of the Pharisees wanting to kill Jesus was implausible, but didn't Isaiah say that there were murderers in Jerusalem (Isaiah 1:21)? Didn't some Jews want to kill Moses (Exodus 17:4)? Some Jews (not all Jews), wanted to kill Joseph, David and Jeremiah.

Few would deny that even Jews can be capable of murder, but what Christ says here applies to all murderers. Catholics, Protestants, Jews, Buddhists, Muslims, atheists – all murderers are children of the devil. Mothers who want to kill their own child because it interferes with their personal freedom are also children of the devil, as are the doctors and nurses who assist them, as are their husbands or boyfriends who consent. People who think God is pleased by acts of violence are children of the devil – although the authorities of the state such as the police and the military do have a divine commission to keep the peace, a divinely sanctioned power of the sword for just and necessary purposes (as we see in Romans chapter 13).

This was never meant to condemn all Jews for all time, and has not been read in this way by great multitudes of sincere Christians who understand Christ's commandments about how we should live and deal with unbelievers. Nor did Christ's wise and just condemnations of the Pharisees place them outside of the common boundaries of a shared humanity. Jesus did not persecute them or even resist them, and confined his opposition to words and to teaching. That the worst instances of "Christian" antisemitism emerged centuries after Christ, even a thousand years and more, should be enough to explode the myth that biblical teaching in and of itself is inherently anti-Jewish.

. . . for ye also have suffered like things of your own countrymen, even as they have of the Jews: who both killed the Lord Jesus, and their own prophets, and have persecuted us; and they please not God, and are contrary to all men . . . for the wrath is come upon them to the uttermost (I Thessalonians 2:14-16).

This sounds very bad, but Paul says that the Thessalonians have suffered the same things from their own countrymen. The Bible is very clear – Jewish sin is human sin, and we are all guilty of it. Moreover, Jesus said "Inasmuch as ye have done it unto one of the least of these my brethren, ye have done it unto me." This means that those who kill any Christians, whether in the Roman arena or in the Nazi concentration camps, or in the Soviet Gulag, have done it unto Christ, and are guilty of his blood.

"He that is of God heareth God's words: ye therefore hear them not, because ye are not of God" (John 8:47).

In support of the charge that not ignorance of the Bible but rather the Bible itself really is part of the problem, it will be pointed out that Christ said the Jews could not understand his word because they were not really of God. This statement of Christ's to the Jewish leaders is a general truth that applies to all mankind, not only Jews. It applies to anyone, Jew or Gentile, who hears the words of Christ and rejects them. Unfortunately, it applies to many in the church as well who have a name of being Christians in the world, but who deny basic teachings about the deity, sacrificial death, and resurrection of Christ – and all the while imagining themselves to be "Christians," even "pastors" and "theologians."

If biblical teaching is of God, then those who refuse to hear it are not of God. This does not mean that they are to be cruelly treated, persecuted, or sent to death camps. It is the common description of unbelieving humanity, and applies equally to Jews and to Gentiles. Paul teaches in I Corinthians (chapter 1) that the world in its wisdom cannot know God, and that basic Christian beliefs are foolishness to the natural mind. If Christians imagine that they are supposed to reach out to such people, Jews or non-Jews, with hatred they have neither seen Christ nor known him.

. . . Satan entered into him [Judas Iscariot] (John 13:27).

It has been claimed that Judas is the symbol of the Jew for many Christians, but this is not at all the case. When it comes to Christian images of the Jew, anyone who is really serious about the Bible thinks of Abraham, Moses, David, Solomon, Joseph, Mary, John the Baptist, Peter, John, and Paul as well as of Judas. When sincere Christians consider the Jewish people, Judas is not the first person that instantly comes to mind.

It is unfortunate that when Hitler and the Nazis repeatedly made statements directly related to the Darwinian concept of life as a struggle for survival of the fittest, it is often claimed that such statements were taken out of context. Such care and concern for accuracy and objectivity are all-too-often conspicuously absent when it comes not to defending Darwinism but to criticizing Christianity. That the Bible is not inherently antisemitic can easily be seen from the vast multitudes of Christians over many centuries who never harmed any Jews. We have not seen crazed mobs of Baptists, Lutherans, Methodists, or Catholics rampaging through Jewish neighborhoods in America wreaking mayhem and shouting "Death to the Jews!"

This is not unique to America either. In many Western countries strongly influenced by Christianity Jews have been tolerably well (if not perfectly) treated. No countries in Nazi-occupied Europe were more helpful to the Jews than Norway, Denmark, and Holland, with their strongly Protestant backgrounds. There was a distinct lack of enthusiasm for Nazi antisemitism in Italy as well. Even in Germany itself before World War I, Jewish culture flourished to a great extent and many Jews were proud of their German cultural heritage.

Nevertheless, religiously motivated crimes against the Jews over the centuries have contributed to lasting misconceptions about Christianity – misconceptions that have been aggravated by harmful comments Christians have made. Since these are commonly pointed to as examples of how Christianity really is inherently antisemitic, we will need to examine them. That will require a more careful explanation of antisemitism, its nature and its origins, in another chapter. Unfortunately, there is a great deal of ambiguity about what Christianity is. This needs to be looked into before exploring more deeply the ungodly and wicked nature of "Christian" anti-Judaism.

In a book about Marxism, historian Eric Hobsbawm makes some comments about the decline and fragmentation of that ideology which describe very well the decline and fragmentation of Christianity. He says that what was once considered standard or "orthodox" Marxism has disintegrated into a variety of conflicting interpretations. As a result of this "disintegration of orthodoxy" "the line between what was Marxist and what was not grew increasingly hazy." There has been such a "decline of authoritative interpretation" that the nature of Marxism itself has become unclear.[16]

The same is true of Christianity. We now have Christians who believe evolution is a scientific fact and Christians who believe (as I do) that it is a false, ugly, and destructive pseudo-philosophy. We have Christians who consider abortion and homosexuality to be acceptable and moral, and Christians who (rightly, in my view) consider those practices to be naked evil. There are Christians who believe that Jesus is the best but not the only way to God, and Christians who believe (in agreement with scripture) that there can be no salvation outside of Christ. There are Christians who believe the Bible has scientific errors, and Christians who (like myself) believe it is infallible and divinely inspired even down to the facts and details.

More examples could be given, but the point is obvious. The word "Christian" has now become so vague and nebulous as to mean little or nothing. There are even Christians who use biblical terminology and write

---

[16] Eric Hobsbawm, *How to Change the World: Tales of Marx and Marxism* (London: Abacus, 2012), p. 371 (all quotes).

inspiring religious books but deny or question key doctrines and have smuggled in (often dishonestly) a great deal of secular philosophy. This is often called "neo-orthodoxy" and has gone a long way towards undermining the foundations of what used to be biblical Christianity. Such subtle mixtures of Christianity and philosophy are especially confusing to unbelievers, who rightly reject a fake religion that is historically, scientifically and factually false, but somehow "spiritually" true in a never-never land of useless pseudo-intellectual theological word games.

Apart from the problem of defining just what Christianity is (and this modern confusion goes back to the 19th century and greatly complicates discussions of Christianity in Germany), the discussion of "Christian" antisemitism is yet further complicated by the fact that there are two Christian churches. One is the physical, visible church. It appears outwardly to all. It has buildings, seminaries, churches, congregations, leaders, even theologians and writers of many books. Its members call themselves Christians and are so considered by the world, all on the basis of appearance only. Whether they truly want to follow the teachings of Christ is irrelevant.

The invisible or spiritual church on the other hand is composed of those who are in Christ, who have the Spirit of Christ and who believe that Christ is what the Bible claims him to be: God come to earth in human form, born of a virgin, teaching the way to God, dying on the cross as a sacrifice for the sins of the world, and rising from the dead. This includes Christ's ascent into heaven, whence he will return as God manifest to judge the world. All of this is taught by a divinely inspired scripture, infallible and inerrant, without which we Christians have no sure teaching and no certain hope.

There is obviously some overlap between the visible and the spiritual churches, but there are also those who are in the physical church but not in the spiritual one. They may have abandoned many or all essential doctrines and invented what is in fact a new religion dishonestly using borrowed Christian language to express what are in essence secular ideas; they may be theoretically orthodox and have a great knowledge of doctrines but the Spirit, the life, the vitality is not there. As Paul said, if I have all faith and all knowledge but do not have love, my Christianity is worthless and vain (I Corinthians 13:1-3).

Even the most mature and discerning Christian cannot tell in every case who is in which group. Nor can we tell how those who appear to be clearly in one group may change over time. But, the fact that there are these two broad groupings is amply testified by many scriptures. James 1:22-23 is one: "But be ye doers of the word and not hearers only, deceiving your own selves." He further elaborates on those who are hearers of the word but do not do it, and speaks of those who seem to be religious, but their religion is vain (v. 26). He also says that "faith without works is dead." There are plenty of dead

Christians in their boring and lifeless churches today, just as there were in Nazi Germany.

II Peter 2:1-2 speaks of false prophets and false teachers who claim not merely to be Christians but want to be leaders in the church, yet deny God, and use dishonest words, "by reason of whom the way of truth shall be evil spoken of." Romans 8:9 says "if any man have not the Spirit of Christ, he is none of his." We read of knowledge, faith, and good works that are of no value (I Corinthians 13:1-3); of apostles, church workers, and ministers who claim to be ministers of Christ, ministers of righteousness, but are false and servants of Satan (who can disguise himself as an angel of light) (II Corinthians 11:12-15). Christians are supposed to be salt, but we read of salt that has lost its savor and is *good for nothing* (Matthew 5:13). Of how many Christians and churches today might it be said that they are good for nothing? Then there are the false prophets who disguise themselves as sheep but in fact are wolves, who do great things in the name of God but will be rejected by him on the Day of Judgment (Matthew 7:15, 21).

That many who are in the churches and seem to be Christians in the world's eyes are not even Christians at all in God's sight is not merely an evasive tactic as some have claimed, a raising of the bar by arbitrarily defining Christianity in such a way as to escape from honest criticisms. That there is a lot of falsehood and spiritual deception in the churches is not merely an example of the "no true Scotsman" fallacy but has been carefully addressed by numerous Christian leaders over the centuries.

Augustine wrote of wolves in the church. John Bunyan wrote in *Pilgrim's Progress* of a tree that seemed fair without but was rotten within. In a sermon preached in Scotland in 1741 ("The Kingdom of God") evangelist George Whitefield warned his hearers "A man may be a member of the purest church, a man may be baptized, do nobody harm, do a great deal of good, attend on all the ordinances of Christianity, and yet at the same time may be a child of the devil." He tells them that if they have a form of religion yet do not have the righteousness of Christ in their souls all of their good deeds are nothing but filthy rags. As to those who claim to be Christians but live lives of wickedness, uncleanness, drunkenness, adultery, "Surely, without repentance, you will be lost – your damnation slumbereth not." [17]

Some comments from Whitefield's contemporary John Wesley have the same import. To someone that asserted "I am a Christian," Wesley responded: "*A Christian!* Are you so? Do you understand the word? Do you know what a Christian is? If you are a Christian, you would have the mind of Christ; and you would walk as he also walked . . . Are you inwardly and outwardly holy? I

---

[17] D. Macfarlan, *The Revivals of the Eighteenth Century (Particularly at Cambuslang) With Three Sermons by the Rev. George Whitefield* (Glasgow: Free Presbyterian Publications, 1988), p. 43, both quotes.

fear, not even outwardly."[18] John Wesley had frequent disagreements with people who claimed to be Christian but gave not the slightest evidence of it.

If we want to understand the relationship of Christianity to antisemitism to and the Holocaust, we need to remember that there are many different kinds of Christianity, and many different kinds of Christians. To begin with, we need to distinguish between Christians who are making a sincere effort to follow the teachings of Christ and those who consistently disregard his words. Any teacher can tell the difference between students who on the one hand are making a reasonable effort but make ordinary mistakes, and those on the other hand who make no real effort, and continually make significant errors because they do not care. God also can – and does – make such a distinction. Then there are students who physically assault the teacher and burn the school down. They are not hard to recognize.

What, then, is Christianity? Admittedly, there are widely diverse answers to this question, but profound ignorance of what Christ taught, and of what people who sincerely try to follow Christ believe and hope to accomplish, has vitiated countless secular attempts to relate Christianity in some significant way to National Socialism. To attempt a complete definition here would be too much of a digression, but this essay is based on a conception of Christianity that includes the following points. Even if I cannot arbitrarily decree what Christianity is or is not to the satisfaction of all, I can at least make my own approach clear.

First, mere references to "God . . . the Lord . . . the Almighty . . . Providence" are not necessarily evidence of Christianity or even of Christian influence. German thinkers in the nineteenth century who rejected the Bible still used such terms as "divine . . . God . . . the Almighty . . . Providence," but in a very different context and for very different ends. To give only one example, a pantheistic view of God that saw the whole cosmos as a unified divine organism, understood by reason alone without divine revelation and operating according to scientific law, was one source of ideas about "the Divine" or "the Almighty" in nineteenth-century German thought. This has confused people who have no knowledge of the Bible and no knowledge of German intellectual history. The gods of Kant, Hegel, Haeckel, Wagner and many others were very far removed from the God of Scripture and antithetical to Him.

Second, there must also be an inerrant scripture, a Bible inspired by God, true in every aspect, factually and historically as well as spiritually. If we don't have an accurate and wholly reliable Word of God we have nothing. Those who say the Bible is a useful guide only when it speaks of spiritual truths like the love or mercy of God, but false when it speaks of the creation, or the flood,

---

[18] Iain H. Murray, *Evangelicalism Divided: A Record of Crucial Change in the Years 1950 to 2000* (Edinburgh: The Banner of Truth Trust, 2000), p. 159.

or the miracles of Jesus, or is ambiguous about the resurrection, the virgin birth of Christ, and so on, have grounded their religion firmly on fiction. Many of the German Christians who followed Hitler did not believe in the Bible, but saw it as a merely human book, full of mistakes and errors. Hence their faith had no foundation.

Thirdly, it is a common misunderstanding (both inside the church and out of it) that those are Christians who merely agree to some doctrines; engage in religious activities; were born in a certain geographical area; or say the right religious words. This shows a profound ignorance of biblical teaching (and such ignorance is now the norm in discussions of Christianity and the Third Reich). The Bible does teach that we are saved by faith alone, not by our good works, but if we really believe Christ was God in the flesh, we will attach great importance to what he said. Living faith (as opposed to what the Bible calls dead faith) requires a deeper, inner life of the Spirit. This is explained by many biblical passages, and those who think that forgiveness through faith in Christ gives people license to hate, lie, murder, steal, get drunk, or live effortless lives of ease in stupid indifference need to be mindful of Revelation 22:12, where Christ says "And, behold, I come quickly; and my reward is with me, to give every man according as his work shall be."

Finally, and above all, there must be a fully biblical understanding of Christ – not as an Aryan, possibly the son of a Roman soldier from northern Europe; not as a mere human being with a very high level of God-consciousness; not as an antisemitic mortal who died in the fight against Judaism; not as some sort of strange spiritual being that maybe was born of a virgin, maybe not, that maybe rose from the dead, maybe not – but as the earthly manifestation of the hidden mystery of God. The source of eternal life made manifest, pre-existent before the foundation of the world, the remote and incomprehensible Supreme Being operative in the material world, the Christ of authentic Christianity is the whole Christ as presented in the historically accurate Scriptures. This includes his birth, life, teachings, death, resurrection and final return as described in the literal truths of the four gospels and as explained by the apostles, no more, no less.

All of this includes the deepest regard for Christ's teachings as being infallible and from God, a subject of which too many today are lamentably uninformed. For example, in his attempt to analyze the relationship between National Socialism and Christianity (an attack on Christianity cleverly disguised as objective scholarship), Richard Steigmann-Gall refers to Nazis who "adhered to all the requisite criteria for Christian religiosity – church attendance, baptism, communion."[19] Has this man ever read the Sermon on the Mount, or Paul's Letters to the Romans or to the Corinthians? There are indeed

---

[19] Richard Steigmann-Gall, *The Holy Reich: Nazi Conceptions of Christianity, 1919-1945* (Cambridge: Cambridge University Press, 2004), p. 6.

Christians whose conception of Christianity runs along those lines, who conceive of their religion as "orthodox notions and opinions" or "a constant course of external duties"[20] but Jesus did not say "Blessed are those who go to church," or "Blessed are cruel and vicious people who were baptized as infants." William L. Shirer's sarcastic comments about German generals and pro-Nazi businessmen who were "upright Christians" or "God-fearing men all"[21] reflect only his own misunderstanding and ill-informed bias.

It seems to be something of a fad now for anti-Christian historians of the Third Reich to speak of the "piously Protestant" regions that voted for Hitler, of "Protestant Prussia," of "Protestants" who abandoned the traditional faith to follow policies first cooked up by secularists and undreamed of in previous centuries. Maybe they think Frederick the Great, the thoroughly secular and unbelieving King of Prussia, was a devout Protestant Christian who began his day with prayer and Bible study and based his numerous wars of glory and conquest on the Sermon on the Mount. But, we understand that the dominant climate in academia today is one of ignorance, bias, and even hostility to Christianity – to the detriment of historical fact and objective analysis.

Too many people judge Christianity by its worst and least serious adherents, by people who openly rebel against the teachings of Christ and live lives not of human fallibility, but of open wickedness. Christianity can be made to look very sordid indeed if we consistently ignore the myriads of ordinary people who have sincerely tried to follow it. Of course, we can't blame the unbelievers for their ignorance when we Christians have failed so dismally to draw a clear line of separation between faithfulness to Christ and unfaithful worldliness, and have so diluted and obscured the Gospel message.

Given the repeated claim that the Nazis emerged in "Christian Europe," it should not be amiss to point out that, according to the standards of biblical Christianity, there has never been a genuinely Christian nation, let alone a Christian continent. There are countries and cultures which have been deeply influenced by Christianity, and received many benefits from it, but Christ said "Enter ye in at the strait gate . . . Because strait is the gate, and narrow is the way, which leadeth unto life, and few there be that find it" (Matthew 7:13-14).

"Few there be that find it." There has never been any country since the beginning of Christianity in which the majority of its citizens, especially those in power, were dying to self, taking up the cross, and walking in the way of Christ according to the Scriptures with the aid of the Holy Spirit. There have

---

[20] Henry Scougal, *The Life of God in the Soul of Man* (Ross-shire Scotland: Christian Heritage, 2005), p. 42.

[21] William L. Shirer, *The Rise and Fall of the Third Reich* (New York: Simon & Schuster, 2011), pp. 660, 665. Shirer's sad misrepresentation of Luther will be discussed in chapter 3. In many other respects his work is a useful introduction to the history of Third Reich.

been countries where there has been a higher degree of Christian influence, but they were not Gardens of Eden or Utopias, and remained liable to the many sins and evils inevitable in this fallen world. Poverty, injustice, alcoholism, crime, racism, hatred, ignorance, immorality – these will be present with us throughout this age and the Bible has never promised otherwise.

Prominent Christian pastor and writer D. M. Lloyd Jones stressed this point:

> A Christian state is impossible. All the experiments have failed. They had to fail. They must fail. The Apocalypse alone can cure the world's ills . . . You can never Christianize society. It is folly to attempt to do so. I would even suggest that it is heresy to do so. Men must be 'born again'. How can they live the Christian life if they have not become Christians? . . . the idea that you can impose a Christian life or culture upon non-Christian people is a contradiction of Christian teaching.[22]

Lloyd-Jones recognized the importance of legitimate reform and acknowledged that Christians can and should work for the betterment of society, but we cannot expect to have the impossible. It was Hitler, Stalin, Mao, Lenin, Castro and Pol Pot with their grandiose dreams who thought they could reorganize society according to their liking, instead of limiting themselves to what is truly possible in a fallen and sinful world. They tried to put themselves in the place of God, the infallible all-knowing geniuses who thought they knew the real plan for paradise on earth.

This still leaves us with the problem of supposedly Christian antisemitism. If it is not taught by the Bible, if it is indeed contrary to the Bible, how can it be explained? This is not a simple subject, and will require examination in the following two chapters. Chapter 2 describes anti-Judaism in general as a result of sin and evil in opposition to God's revelation and work. Chapter 3 presents anti-Judaism as a lamentable perversion and distortion of Christianity, unhesitatingly condemned by all serious followers of Christ.

---

[22] D. M. Lloyd-Jones, *The Puritans: Their Origins and Successors* (Edinburgh: The Banner of Truth Trust, 1987), p. 344.

Chapter 2. The Jewish People and Their Enemies

What is this strange and persistent power or spirit of Jew-hatred which has manifested itself over many centuries in many different guises, yet still retains an inner consistency? In a religious period such as the Middle Ages, it assumes a religious character. In secular periods, it adapts itself to the reigning ethos and stirs up bad will against the Jews among people who could not care less about the Bible – and whatever the motive, the end result is that harmless and innocent people are made to suffer and die.

In the Soviet Union, the Jews were obstacles to the international unity of the proletariat. In the "Enlightenment," they were obstacles to the emancipation of the mind from religious dogmas. In Nazi Germany, they defiled the blood purity of the German race, thus weakening it in the struggle for survival of the fittest. It is an insufficiently known fact that the Jews were also blamed for introducing through Christianity values contrary to nature and to the heroic paganism of the pre-Christian German spirit.[1] In our own day, now that the crimes of the Nazis have so thoroughly blackened old-fashioned antisemitism, a completely irrational and even malicious bias against Israel piously disguises itself as a tender concern for "justice" and "rights" for the poor innocent Palestinians that is strangely indifferent to other parts of the world.

Any serious attempt to understand the Holocaust must concern itself with the larger phenomenon of antisemitism in world history, and any serious attempt to explain antisemitism must at some point try to deal with the primary question "Who are the Jews?" Regrettably, some don't consider the question answerable or even worth considering. They are the people for whom the religious dimension is only a delusion. They believe that life as we know it came about as the result of impersonal chance. Matter and energy are, they confidently assert, the ultimate realities, and any spiritual or religious questions have no basis in fact. They have set the boundaries of reality to their own personal satisfaction, and anything that might lie beyond those boundaries is rigorously (maybe even fearfully) excluded.

If there is no God; if reality as we know it just sort of exploded into its manifold and intricate variety by blind chance, then there is no explanation for the Jewish people. There is also no comprehensive and convincing explanation for anti-Judaism either. If God did not make a covenant with Abraham and did not deliver the Jews from captivity in Egypt or give his laws to Moses on

---

[1] The idea of Judaism's unhealthy influence through Christianity on Germany and on Europe can be found in various forms in the works of Schopenhauer, Wagner, H. S. Chamberlain, Nietzsche, Haeckel, and others, and will be explored in the second volume of this study, God willing.

Mount Sinai, all of the biblical history of the Jews is a myth, or a kernel of history shrouded in myth, acceptable only insofar as parts of it can be corroborated from more reliable secular sources. Both the Jews and those who hate them are pointlessly living out their empty misunderstandings, all of them prisoners of some kind of damaging irrationality.

Who are the Jews, and how did they come into being? In the materialist scenario, no one knows. How did they alone survive over thousands of years when all of the other ancient peoples and cultures vanished or were altered beyond recognition? How did the Jews come to articulate ideas of God, religion, morality, and ethics that contributed so greatly to the foundation of Western civilization? The materialists have nothing worthwhile to contribute to this discussion, and hence all of their attempts to explain antisemitism in terms of ordinary human understanding necessarily fall short. Economic, social, psychological or historical factors by themselves are too limited, and leave fundamental questions permanently unanswered.

If we want to understand anti-Judaism and especially if we want to understand the Holocaust (insofar as such understanding is possible), we must have a deeper and higher understanding of the Jews and the nature of Judaism. If we want to have that, then we must bid farewell to those who obstinately deny the existence of life's spiritual dimensions. Imprisoned in their self-imposed limits, the scientific (or not-so-scientific) materialists can exclude God and the invisible spiritual realms if they want, but they have no comprehensive explanation for the astonishing history of the Jews or for the hatreds that have dogged them, and never will.

It is disappointing to see people trying to discuss antisemitism and the Holocaust without understanding who and what the Jews are. Conventional academic historiography as well as scientific methodology are irrelevant here. They cannot provide any meaningful insights into these questions. There are other ways and other dimensions of knowing, and a grasp of nuclear physics or of a lot of sociological and historical data are not fundamental here, they are irrelevant. Scientists, either real scientists or so-called social scientists, scholars and historians, may consider themselves the experts who have the last word on all important subjects, but their methods are wholly inadequate to understanding antisemitism in its various forms (and to an understanding of many other important aspects of life as well).

It might be useful at this point to refer to the inflated claims of some scientists to be the sole arbiters of reality. They sincerely believe that if they cannot recognize something, no one else can either. There is real wonder in the truths of science, but there are vast dimensions to the human experience that extend far beyond those truths. Quantum mechanics, relativity, the second law of thermodynamics, Newton's law of gravity – these are of no use to us in approaching problems of human nature and behavior. Those who go farther and farther into the strange realities of the subatomic world or into the vast reaches of outer space are making no progress at all towards an understanding of mankind if in all of their efforts they deny eternal spiritual verities. For those of us who believe there is a God, a God who not merely created the world but is active in it and even communicates with us in various ways – for us, the questions of Judaism and of antisemitism take on an entirely different dimension inaccessible to fossilized secularists.

If there is no God, all of Judaism is completely nullified as a useless fantasy – but if there is a God, and a personal God who created us with our unique capacities for reason, communication, and understanding, why should he not communicate with us? And if he does communicate with us, he does it in his ways and in his times, not according to our demands or expectations. This could include revealing himself not as a blaze of divine glory that would terrorize us all into forced and groveling submission, but in more indirect ways, suitable to our limitations. More specifically, if there were a man of great faith named Abraham, and if God revealed himself to Abraham in a unique way and promised to make him the father of a great nation, the scientific materialists might not like it, but they have stepped outside the laboratory now and have nothing but their personal beliefs, without evidence, to offer.

If this same God were to faithfully keep his covenant with Abraham and preserve his descendants, the Jewish people, through all of the many years and dramatic events of their subsequent history, he would have the right and the power to do this. If, moreover, God were to not merely preserve the Jews, but were to use them as a human means of revealing himself to the world, speaking to them through Moses and the prophets, and through those prophets to us, ensuring that their words were faithfully and accurately written and preserved for future generations, he would have the right and the ability to do so.

That, of course, is a lot of "ifs." That those possibilities are not at all contrary to reason rightly defined, and in fact go much farther toward an explanation of life and the cosmos as we daily experience them than do any theories restricted to matter and energy alone, is a subject that has been written on by many others more effectively than I can do here. Suffice it to repeat that, if the Bible is not true, there is no understanding of the Jewish people or of their experiences in history. If on the other hand the Bible is true, we have a coherent explanation for the Jews, as well as for the strange hatreds that have doggedly pursued them.

The orthodox Christian and Jewish explanation of the origin and nature of the Jews is that in their beginnings the Jews were a genuinely chosen people, uniquely selected of God. This does not argue for any innate moral or intellectual superiority on the part of the Jews. The Jewish scriptures amply record the sins, disobedience, ignorance, and rebellion of the Jews. That they came into being as a nation, were used as a means of revelation, and have survived to this day is attributable solely to God. It is nothing but his grace and his mercy that used the Jews so mightily in the past, and have preserved them to this very day. And, if God were to use the Jewish people as preparation for his own entrance into our fallen state in the person of Jesus Christ, to show us the way to God and to open that way for us, then the mystery and the purpose of the Jews is taken yet further, and is central to the Christian faith.

Who, then, are the Jews? Orthodox Jews and Christians who actually believe their respective Bibles part company when it comes to Jesus Christ, but we can agree that God made a covenant with Abraham; that in faithfulness to his covenant God increased and preserved the Jewish people; delivered them from captivity in Egypt in the manner literally described in the historically accurate book of Exodus; appeared to Moses on Mount Sinai, and gave him divinely authoritative laws, as truthfully recorded in detail in that same book. Something happened on Mount Sinai – that "something" was that God appeared to Moses. This divine origin of the Jewish people is also the first cause of all manifestations of anti-Judaism.

Those who assert that the Jewish identity is a merely human invention have exactly zero empirical evidence to support their arbitrary and dogmatically certain decrees. If they really want to go by facts and science alone, as they claim, let them adhere to their own standards and not pretend to speak with any degree of certainty on subjects for which they have no basis other than their personal beliefs and preferences. For those of us who believe in the Bible, contrary to the misguided values of this spiritually backward and dark age, the ultimate origins of Judaism are the manifestations of God to Abraham, Moses, and others. Dogmatic modernists may respond *"We* can say that *you* are wrong, because we have the certain truth that there is no certain truth (except for what we happen to feel good about), but *you* can't say that *we* are wrong, because that would be narrow-minded, arrogant and intolerant. There is nothing we dislike more than intolerant people who contradict us and refuse to accept our obviously superior views. We are so intelligent!" Let them argue as they like. That God appeared to Abraham, to Moses, and to the prophets as recorded in the Bible is central to an understanding of the Jewish experience in world history.

God established the Jews in the land which he had promised to Abraham, and dealt with them as he dealt with no other people on earth. Many times he chastened them because of their wickedness, yet in faithfulness to his promise he did not forsake them, although many times they forsook him. This seems impossible, unreasonable, irrational, and even ridiculous to many, but many things that seem impossible and ridiculous to independent human reason are not at all impossible or ridiculous, given the presupposition that an inconceivably vast and powerful spiritual being exists behind the cosmos of outward appearances. Such a being would necessarily operate on a plane far above ordinary human comprehension. We might also add that merely because a thesis is rejected, even ridiculed by many, does not mean it is necessarily false. This is especially true in our day of pop philosophy and pop science.

How, then, can antisemitism be explained in the light of this understanding of Judaism? To begin with, there are countless examples in world history of ethnic rivalries. People of different languages, skin colors, ethnic groups, classes, religions or nations have often practiced hatred and cruelty to one another. This is nothing surprising or new, and is attributable to the fact that human nature is not basically good, as some people fondly dream. It is basically flawed and sinful – therefore such negative characteristics as ignorance, fear, revenge, hatred, and love of violence and destruction are inevitable parts of human history. Berdyaev writes that evil comes out of the primordial and irrational abyss at the base of life.[2] It manifests itself in myriad ways – not only in open violence and cruelty, but in complacency, vanity, deceit, cowardice, love of power, in the whole spectrum of human vice and error from the subtlest unseen movements of the heart to the worst atrocities.

A substantive explanation and defense of the biblical teaching of original sin, that we are inherently and innately flawed from birth, would take us too far afield from the present topic. It should be pointed out, however, that there is no other credible explanation for the human delight in evil that is one of the most striking features of the Nazi era. That human beings should relish cruelty for its own sake defies secular understanding. How could impersonal evolutionary selection possibly account for such a phenomenon, or for the many other aspects of human consciousness that have nothing whatever to do with mere survival? Those who today regard themselves as enlightened, and who brag and boast of our potential without God, have a deficient understanding of the nature of the human soul.

What shall we say of someone who kidnaps a little child and kills it? Does this have an evolutionary explanation? That there is such a thing as real, objective evil, understood in contrast to the real, objective goodness of God, and that some people love evil, and hate good, because they are themselves evil, in darkness, and in love with darkness – this is a spiritual reality as real, and more real, than any scientific law. Behind Hitler and his followers, at the very heart of Naziism, was a deeper hatred of life, of people, of morality. Adolf Eichmann said that "he would leap laughing into the grave" because of the "extraordinary satisfaction"[3] he derived from having killed five million people. Who can explain this with no concept of sin? Without coherent concepts of good and evil, who can convincingly say that this was wrong? If

---

[2] Nicolai Berdyaev, *Christian Existentialism: A Berdyaev Anthology,* trans. Donald Lowrie (New York: Harper Torchbooks, 1965), p. 188.

[3] William L. Shirer, *The Rise and Fall of the Third Reich: A History of Nazi Germany* (New York: Simon & Schuster, 2011), p. 978 (citing Nuremberg testimony).

life is gratification of the will-to-power, what could give someone a greater sense of power than having the lives of millions at one's command?

Recognizing some spiritual truths is essential to a deeper approach to the Holocaust. Apart from sin and evil, there is no other explanation for someone grabbing a baby by the feet and smashing its head against a wall (unless we want to abandon all morality whatsoever). Unfortunately, there are many whose imagination completely fails before these questions. Their simple logic is based on a trivial understanding of the human personality and of the problems of life. They have difficulty in recognizing, and hence in confronting evil – not only in studies of the Holocaust, but in understanding the issues of our own day. They have been misled by the mistaken idea that people are only the products of their environments, that social existence alone determines consciousness. Thinking that the solution to social problems lies in government welfare programs or educational reforms, they search in vain for safe and ordinary explanations for extra-ordinary phenomena.

Human evil does not confound biblical understanding, but rather confirms it. This human tendency to evil works itself out differently in different circumstances, according to realities of time and place, according to countless historical, social, and cultural factors, but it is the same underlying sin. Thus, any approach to understanding anti-Judaism in general and the Holocaust in particular is and must be informed by our understanding of human nature. Are we products of matter, chance, and energy only, governed by natural law, or is there something transcending all of that, an inner force and reality unknown to conventional science? Is morality a merely human invention, as Hitler claimed in *Mein Kampf*, and as Nietzsche claimed in *The Genealogy of Morals*?[4] This was also one of Richard Wagner's ideas, though he may have expressed different things at different times.[5] In fact, it is a standard theme of secularism, since all secularists must hold to such a viewpoint if they reason consistently from their starting point of a strictly material universe.

If we accept and believe and understand by faith that morality has its origins in the eternal and unchanging nature of a holy and righteous God, then we can begin to understand sin as transgression of God's law. If we understand human nature as innately and naturally opposed to God's truth and God's law, then we can begin to coherently explain the various manifestations of cruelty, lies, ignorance, hatred, and callous indifference that are recurring themes throughout the whole of human history. That we as people are alienated from higher truth, and that what we need is not glorification of self, reverence for

---

[4] Adolf Hitler, *Mein Kampf,* trans. Ralph Manheim (Boston: Houghton Mifflin, 1999), pp. 287-288, and Friedrich Nietzsche, *The Genealogy of Morals,* trans. Horace B. Samuel (Mineola, NY: Dover Publications, 2003), pp. 3, 44-45, and much of the rest of the book.

[5] Bryan Magee, *Wagner and Philosophy* (London: Penguin Books, 2001), p. 56.

self, indulgence of self, but rather a denial of self, and a subordination of self to God – these are higher and healing insights that emerge from the denial of the modern myth of innate human goodness.

It should also be pointed out that the modern rejection of and even contempt for the teaching of original sin was shared by the Nazis. Alfred Rosenberg wrote in the *Völkische Beobachter*, the official Nazi Party newspaper, ". . . we reject the idea of burdening German youth with inferiority complexes from an early age. We do not want to evoke in it an awareness of its sinfulness, but values of its character."[6] What upright secularist could find any fault with this? A quote from an SS journal gives us a fuller explication of Nazi doctrines: "The abstruse doctrine of Original Sin, whence the need of salvation is said to arise; the Fall – and indeed the whole notion of sin as set forth by the church, involving reward or punishment in a world beyond – is something intolerable to Nordic man."[7]

A major cause of differing varieties of antisemitism and of the Holocaust was not the various economic, political, or sociological circumstances, as important as they were. A major cause was innately sinful human nature that responded to those external circumstances in a manner totally unpredictable by any scientific or sociological law. It is a very bad mistake, one could even say a stupid mistake, to argue that because Newton discovered the law of gravity, therefore the entire universe was merely a mechanism governed only by natural law (which Newton of course never maintained, being a strong believer in the existence of a divine governing power). The human soul is subject to spiritual principles and laws, to higher realities invisible to those who refuse to accept them.

A noted expert on Nazi Germany wondered what was the wellspring of Nazi violence. Some of it, he said, had to do with Hitler's charisma. Inflammatory antisemitic writing had something to do with it. Nazi parades, songs and banners excited foolish and empty people (many of them well-educated). The defeat of Germany in World War I is mentioned – but these and other external causes, important though they were, do not really answer the question. Yes, there were important social factors. Yes, there was also the problem of secular philosophies that justified cruelty and war as natural and condemned kindness and pacifism as weakness, and so legitimized our basest instincts. But only sin can explain the love of fighting, violence, and war that have appeared in all parts of the world in all periods of history. Human sin and

---

[6] Rudolf Wentorf, *Paul Schneider: Witness of Buchenwald*, trans. Daniel Bloesch (Vancouver: Regent College Publishing, 2008), p. 150 (quoting the April 28, 1934 issue of the paper).

[7] Dean G. Stroud, *Preaching in Hitler's Shadow: Sermons of Resistance in the Third Reich* (Grand Rapids, MI: William B. Eerdmans, 2013), p. 20 (quoting Michael Burleigh's *The Third Reich: A New History*).

evil are the raw materials of antisemitism, and were the essential motivation of the perpetrators of the Holocaust.

Sin and evil lay behind other aspects of Naziism in addition to antisemitism. Rocks, tables, mice and apes do not need meaning, hope, and purpose – but people do. This is because we have souls derived from the breath of God – and when our hearts are alienated from God by conceit and ignorance, then we seek meaning and purpose in the wrong way and in the wrong place. We seek justice, but do not know what it is. We try to do right, but do wrong without even knowing it. We are lost and groping in darkness, seeking false solutions to non-existent or to misunderstood problems. We condemn what is good, praise what is evil, and seek happiness in things that cannot last.

In the biblical world view, then, we have three basic principles of the human spirit that allow us to study all of the numerous manifestations of anti-Judaism closer to their single source. First, we have the divine origin of the soul, which accounts for our consciousness, our cognitive capacities, our virtues and our vices in a way that nothing else can. Second, we have the corruption of the soul by the fall of Adam and Eve – an historical event as real as the battle of Gettysburg. This corruption includes ingenious creativity in badness and real pleasure in what is false, wrong, and destructive. Third, we have the necessity of divine rules and guidelines. Within these rules we can find inner peace and fulfillment. Outside of them, we can become slaves to a broad range of emotions, from conceited and complacent apathy and stupidity to aggressive commitment to evil.

There is much evidence to support the assertion that a big part of the problem is human nature itself. If for example a major cause of the Holocaust were human nature (not simply German nature), then we would expect to find similar manifestations of Nazi-like evil in other parts of the world and at other times of history – and that is precisely what we do find. What objective thinker can fail to note the similarity between great crowds in European cities joyously hailing the outbreak of World War I in August 1914, and crowds of Germans deliriously hailing Hitler? Many isolated and random criminals today would be glad to join a movement or a party that, in exchange for adherence (or even merely lip-service) to some simple points would allow them to gratify their criminal impulses to the fullest extent.

Seemingly normal people turning into crazed killers? That was witnessed in Rwanda, where there was also a state-organized attempt to consolidate its power by first demonizing a vulnerable minority (the Tutsis) and then making a sustained and pre-planned effort to wipe that minority out (we recall Turkey and the Armenian genocide here). Cruel and senseless medical experiments and needless massacres carried out on a subject population seen as inferior? That was done by the Japanese in World War II. What if the Nazis were able to carry out basic human evil to farther limits because German society was more technologically advanced, and more corrupted by life-destroying philosophies?

Brutal acts inflicted on helpless and innocent people? That occurs all over the world every day. There is a profound kinship between the random sadistic crimes of individuals today and those of Nazi death camp guards; between Hitler and Mussolini, Lenin, Stalin, Mao, Castro, and even Napoleon (though of course there were differences). Hitler was in many ways unique, but he and his criminal followers did not come from another planet, and their traits can be seen all over the globe in various historical periods. Historian Paul Johnson notes significant similarities between Hitler and Mao, for example. This goes far beyond such obvious points as "They both killed lots of people," and extends to concepts of nationalism and the nature of government. Johnson refers in this context to Mao's "national socialism."[8]

Cramming people into trains and sending them on long journeys with inadequate food, water, and sanitation? That was done in the Soviet Union. Causing mass devastation and death in the pursuit of a senseless, unrealistic ideology, one that included racism and the desire to eliminate entire ethnic groups? That was done in Pol Pot's Cambodia. There are some striking similarities between Pol Pot and Hitler – and pointing out differences does not obliterate similarities. One biographer of the Cambodian dictator writes that "Pol Pot defies analysis," and in that context presents some of the same questions about his motives and personality that have baffled biographers of Hitler.[9]

Developing a totally false philosophy of life, arbitrarily classifying people who do not fit in with that philosophy as less than fully human, and then slaughtering them in the millions legally, and with a clear conscience? That is happening in our own day. A philosophy of total freedom to enjoy oneself without obligations and commitments to morality, to family and to motherhood are combined with a belief that people are only highly evolved animals to produce the abortion holocaust. Now once again millions of helpless and innocent people are being killed in the name of a better society, and most of the people who look back at the Holocaust and mouth their empty words "Never again" don't really care. This, along with the dismal failure of the world to stop other massacres and atrocities, makes the slogan "Never again" basically meaningless.

We flatter ourselves that we are basically good, but how many of us would also follow a leader if he offered us real hope of relief from prolonged

---

[8] Paul Johnson, *Modern Times: The World from the Twenties to the Nineties* (New York: Perennial Classics, 1992), pp. 197-198.

[9] David P. Chandler, *Brother Number One: A Political Biography of Pol Pot* (Boulder, CO: Westview Press, 1999), p. 5. The preference for dark skinned, ethnically pure Cambodians over lighter, racially mixed Cambodians, as well as hostility to alien ethnic groups like the Vietnamese, were parts of the Khmer Rouge's Nazi-like mixture of socialist, communist, and nationalist principles.

suffering? How many of us would look the other way and say nothing when strangers were taken away? How many of our neighbors that seem like ordinary people could come to delight in exercising power over others if only given the chance? And what is true of individuals is true of society as well. How much of our democracy and our civilization depends on stability and prosperity? Take those away for a long enough period of time, and anything can happen. This is true of the USA as well. Does anyone imagine that there are no people in America who would be capable of the worst cruelties, given the opportunity? Sometimes we may even see a little bit of Hitler in ourselves.

Returning to the causes of anti-Judaism, many peoples have experienced persecutions of many sorts because of the fact of sinful human nature. One thing that makes the Jews unique in the world when it comes to suffering is their extraordinary longevity. Other groups have vanished, but the Jews have survived. This has exposed them over much longer periods of time, and over much wider geographical areas, to many of the evils others have experienced in a much more restricted way – and why have the Jews alone had this longevity? Because of God's faithfulness to Abraham. It is God's will alone that has preserved the Jews, and will continue to preserve them.

This first reason for the uniqueness of antisemitism (ordinary human sin magnified by longer existence and greater geographical distribution) is also related to the second. Just as God's purpose for the Jews created and preserved them, it also separated them morally, ethically, and spiritually. Many times they forsook the one true God and adopted the false practices of their neighbors, for which they were often punished – but when the Jews could not and would not accept the false gods and customs of the ancient world and fully merge with their host nations, they aroused the animosity of pre-Christian opponents of Judaism. Pharaoh and Haman, who wanted to slaughter the Jews; Nebuchadnezzar, who was enraged by the defiance of Shadrach, Meshech, and Abednego; the Roman historian Tacitus and Apion the Greek writer, who objected to the Jews' failure to conform and were angered by perceived Jewish rejection of their society; Antiochus Epiphanes, the Hellenistic monarch of Syria who sought to destroy Judaism in the second century B.C. – they at least cannot be blamed on Christianity.

Along with human sin and God's separation of the Jews, a third cause for antisemitism is what Judaism in its purest and most fundamental form actually represents. That there is a God; that he is a moral God of laws that we need to obey; that he is a personal God who is concerned on an individual level with what we say and do; that we are not autonomous agents who find our greatest happiness in doing our own thing, but are morally obligated to do good and avoid evil; "Thou shalt, thou shalt not, because God has said" – these ideas in and of themselves arouse the hostility of ignorant and evil people.

That rebellion against God should find expression in hatred of the people most responsible for introducing the idea of the one true God is not surprising.

This is why the nineteenth-century French socialists were so hostile to Judaism. They did not care about the death of Christ on the cross. They did not believe in Christ and he was nothing to them. It was their dream of man's independence from God that led them to hate Judaism, of which many examples could be given. The idea that people who reject religion are therefore automatically logical and rational is a self-pleasing illusion.

An in-depth study of antisemitism states that the myth of the Jews dominating the world was first introduced "not by racists, fascists, or Nazis, but rather by socialists in nineteenth-century France." One example is the paranoid and irrational secular socialist fanatic Alphonse Toussenel, who wrote in 1845 that "Europe is subject to the domination of Israel." Another is Pierre Proudhon, who stated in 1847 that the Jews poisoned everything and should be expelled or exterminated. "The Jew is the enemy of the human race,"[10] he claimed in his left-wing wisdom. Karl Marx had such a deep hatred of the Jews – expressed in his venomous book *On the Jewish Question* – because Judaism completely nullified his idle fantasy of a human paradise erected without God. It was Jewish evidence of the truth of God's existence that aroused Marx's ignorant hatred. This is why the officially atheistic Soviet Union sought to eliminate Judaism. Secular leftists as a group are much more likely to be hostile to Jews and to Israel today than are people who believe in the Bible. This is because their entire world-view, and all of their hopes and dreams of a worldly utopia, are contradicted by biblical Israel.

It has been claimed that antisemitism was more virulent in Germany because of the stronger influence of religion there, whereas France and England had been more inoculated by secular values. Yet, given the intensity of antisemitism in nineteenth century France, the Jews there seemed more at risk than they did in Germany.[11] Voltaire, a pioneering secularist, despised Jews, and their emancipation led to increased hostility both from traditional forces of the Church and royalist circles, and from the newly emerging left. The obvious fact that in America today the forces of the left are far more hostile to Israel than are conservative Christians should not need to be explained.

In England, one reason for the lack of antisemitism was not the advance of secularism but rather the vitality of the Evangelical churches. Their strongly held and deeply personal religious beliefs (as opposed to the deadness of a state church in Germany) in no way led to widespread British antisemitism, and even mitigated against it. Kant, on the other hand, who has been called the

---

[10] Dennis Prager and Joseph Telushkin, *Why the Jews? The Reason for Antisemitism* (New York: Touchstone, 2003), pp. 127 (all quotes in this paragraph).

[11] Richard L. Rubenstein and John K. Roth, *Approaches to Auschwitz: The Holocaust and its Legacy* (Louisville KY: Westminster John Knox Press, 2003), pp. 71-72.

greatest thinker of the "Enlightenment," was hostile to Jews, and helped to establish a new approach to the Jews that was based not on belief in the Bible, but on rejection of the Bible. Also, the main themes of Hitler's *Mein Kampf* were deeply secular, as will not be hard to demonstrate in a later chapter, in spite of vague and nebulous statements about some sort of a "god" that strangely seemed to be interested only in the German people but not in the rest of the world. Hitler's "Creator" or "Almighty" needs to be understood in the context of German philosophy, being closer to Schopenhauer's impersonal cosmic Will or Hegel's World Spirit than to any recognized religion.

I confess I am tempted to feel resentment toward those who seize on every opportunity, every nuance, to blame Naziism and the Holocaust on Christianity, but do not have the ability to recognize the virulent and hateful antisemitism that emerged out of the rejection of Christianity. They claim to be rational, but in fact are motivated by deeper motives that they do not even recognize themselves. Perhaps one of the reasons they are so eager to discredit Christianity is because of their guilty consciences and their sinful lives. Some people go on and on about Luther and Christian antisemitism while totally ignoring the new secular antisemitism that was much closer to Hitler both psychologically and chronologically because they have a dominating inner need to try and discredit Christianity.

A fourth reason for anti-Judaism is that people with strict moral lives, an emphasis on family, on diligence both in daily work and in the life of the mind, will over time rise perceptibly above the common level. This the Jews have repeatedly done. In times of peace and prosperity this is not so much of a problem, but when people are really suffering, the better position of those above them can attract hostility. This is even true among people of the same group – and how much more true is it of outsiders and aliens?

Yet one more reason for antisemitism needs to be discussed. It is one that is not supposed to be even mentioned in many circles, and the mere introduction of this topic will lead to an instant loss of credibility with many in our pseudo-sophisticated modern age – yet, if we are going to understand Hitler's antisemitism (and all other forms) from a biblical point of view, it must not be avoided. This reason is incomprehensible to many who have attempted to analyze the Holocaust, but do not want to consider one of the most important aspects of the problem.

Both the Jewish and the Christian scriptures teach that there is a higher spiritual dimension of evil that is active in human affairs. There are great forces of darkness in the world, often expressed in the masses of isolated and disconnected wrongs, but at times concentrated and channeled into broad movements of great destructive power. Unseen powers and kingdoms of darkness actively exploit human ignorance, fear, sin, and unbelief. These forces have been, and continue to be, actively engaged against all of humanity, but especially against the Jews.

They are engaged against the Jews for two reasons. The first reason is the fact that the Jews were in the past so greatly used of God to shine his light into the world – and, as Jesus said, those that are in darkness hate the light. The second reason is that God has a further work for the Jews still to be accomplished, a work that the forces of evil and their human servants are struggling mightily to thwart. It is claimed by some Christians that, since the advent of Christ, the Jews no longer have any significance as a people, that they have been replaced by Christians in God's plan for the human race – but how do they explain the strange survival of the Jews? How do they explain the events of 1948, of 1967? If they think God had nothing to do with all of that, just what sort of a God do they believe in? A theoretical God who is not active in human affairs?

Returning to the subject of invisible spiritual powers of evil, these have a head, a ruler, identified in Scripture as an angel that rebelled against God and was cast out of paradise. This spirit of resistance to God's truth and to God's holiness we identify as Satan. Of course, there are those who do not want to hear about this, but we must leave them in their proud complacency. Perhaps later something will serve to waken them from their sleep. For the present, if consideration of this topic means contemptuous dismissal and banishment from serious consideration by the devotees of a now diseased and dying "Enlightenment" "rationalism," that can't be helped.

That Satan is active in the world is a biblical principle which enables us to see the Holocaust in a completely different light. For the devil, the prince of darkness, the death camps were a masterpiece of creativity, a matter for self-congratulation, a successful reversal of God's plan for humanity as revealed by Christ in the Sermon on the Mount, and as revealed to Moses in the Ten Commandments. The fiendish cruelties that baffle conventional secularism are more easily comprehended if we consider that "the whole world lieth in wickedness" (I John 5:19); that men whose minds were alienated from God were so corrupted by vain philosophy as to believe that the perishing of weak human animals was natural, normal, and healthy. Thus our innate propensity to sin was inflamed and encouraged by a reasoned denial of all ethical restraint.

Over the fiery darkness of the Holocaust were the presiding shadows of Satan and his demons – and isn't this one reason, perhaps the main reason, that the terrible figure of Hitler continues to arouse such interest, even fascination? His life is a clear indication of a reality beyond what we can immediately see. He gives us a sense of something larger at work above and behind all of the vast complexities of ordinary historical study. There was a greater power behind him – and the inability to come to terms with this is one reason why secular attempts to understand Hitler provide a lot of interesting information, but in the end inevitably come short and leave us no wiser than we were before. The higher dimensions of life, for good or for evil, are far different from what most expect, which is why reality continues to elude our misguided and simplistic projections and explanations.

How many times has the latest Hitler book promised important new insights, and then only given us the same information for the *nth* time? As useful and important as academic history often is, too many otherwise well-educated and knowledgeable people do not want to or cannot conceive of the reality of evil forces of which Hitler and his followers were only servants. This has led to foolish comments about "the banality of evil," as if the Holocaust, its perpetrators and the invisible spiritual powers behind them were "banal"; as if tossing babies out of upper story hospital windows into trucks below were "banal." So what if Eichmann looked ordinary in that Israeli courtroom and didn't have horns, fangs and a tail? In his years of hiding he had been carefully practicing anonymity. Someone could I suppose look at Einstein in his bathrobe brushing his teeth and write a super-intelligent essay about the banality of scientific genius.

Revelation chapter 12 teaches that "the great dragon . . . that old serpent, called the Devil, and Satan, which deceiveth the whole world" has a special animosity towards the Jewish people. The Bible describes him as "The prince of the power of the air, the spirit that now worketh in the children of disobedience" (Ephesians 2:2). This spirit can move not only individuals, but also groups and nations according to principles of falsehood and error. Satan presides over "the rulers of the darkness of this world," and directs "spiritual wickedness in high places" (Ephesians 6:12) by which the seekers of utopia are deceived in their blind attempts to create a better world – and it is too little understood that Hitler and his followers were trying to create a better world.

Those who rightly sense something working behind the scenes of great affairs, steering them and guiding them as if according to plan, mistakenly look for human agency. There is something working behind the scenes, but it isn't "the Jews," or "the capitalists," or some other elite group. It is "the spirit that now worketh in the children of disobedience," guiding them and moving them according to their changing situations and circumstances. This explains similarities of purpose and method among those who have no immediate connection. Isolated geographically or socially, they share the same spirit and work towards the same ends.

These directed spiritual and cultural currents (of which most are blissfully unaware) are not outside of God's higher overruling providence. The rise of modern Germany from obscure beginnings to great heights of power was not unknown to God. Neither was Hitler unknown to God. He could have struck Hitler dead at any moment, yet allowed him to work for a time. There was a limit, however. Hitler was not allowed to win the war, and in due time his power was brought down. It was brought down by the ordained forces of government, according to Paul's teachings in Romans chapter 13, and not by humanly devised assassination plots with exactly zero biblical justification.[12]

Historian Ian Kershaw states in his biography of Hitler that the failure of an assassination attempt in 1938 was due only to "pure luck." Hitler finished a speech and left a meeting ten minutes before a bomb exploded right behind where he had been standing (eight people were killed and sixty-three injured). There was (according to Kershaw) "nothing providential or miraculous about it," only "mere chance."[13] However, at least three other assassination attempts also failed, and by the narrowest of margins. In 1943, a bomb was smuggled onto Hitler's private plane. It somehow failed to explode – an examination of the retrieved bomb afterward showed that the detonator had malfunctioned. Another attempt to get at Hitler the same year failed when he left an exhibition hall after a mere eight minutes, preventing a suicidal mission by a German officer with bombs in his coat. The nearly successful attempt of July 20, 1944 failed because someone moved the briefcase containing the bomb minutes before it exploded. Also, the conspirators did not have time to set the timer on a second device and so failed to put it in the briefcase. If they had, the power of the blast would have been doubled and Hitler would almost certainly have been killed.[14]

Two of those failures were the result of Hitler's deliberate policy of making abrupt schedule changes for security reasons, but the other two were not. And even so, four failed attempts that we know of – is that really a matter of nothing but "luck" or "chance"? Or is it possible that the limits to Hitler's evil had been set, so that he could not be killed before a certain time, and could not continue to work after a certain time? For a historian to state categorically that this is not possible is to transgress his limits as a historian, and make authoritative pronouncements on a subject far beyond his field of expertise. We need much more than mere knowledge of historical facts, even lots of historical facts, to tell us if such things are the result of chance, or of some higher, hidden causality.

Sin and evil, whether in people or in higher and unseen spiritual powers, are the ultimate sources of antisemitism, as well as of all the other problems and

---

[12] It is too little realized that, since Hitler responded fiercely to the failed assassination attempt, the plot caused more suffering and bloodshed, not less. Thus the conspirators achieved the exact opposite of their intended result. It should also be remembered that if the plot had succeeded before the battles of D-Day or Stalingrad, and Himmler and Goebbels had remained in control, the attempted extermination of the Jews could have ended in the fall of 1945, or the spring of 1946. This Christian hero-worship of the conspirators is, to my mind, contrary to the Spirit of Christ and to Scripture.

[13] Ian Kershaw, *Hitler* (London: Penguin Books, 2008), pp. 546 (all three quotes).

[14] Shirer, *The Rise and Fall of the Third Reich,* 1020-22, 1051-52 (all three incidents).

miseries of life. This explains the underlying consistency of the undying hatred of Jews that adapts itself effortlessly to different situations. From ancient Greece and Rome, to the Middle Ages, through the centuries and up until the present day, it is the same sin, the same evil. This helps to understand not only the Holocaust, but also a serial killer, a child molester, a rapist, and all of the other evils in the world, of which the Holocaust is a single and great concentration. In fact, without wanting to minimize the terrible greatness and uniqueness of the Final Solution in any way, we can I think safely assert that all of the evil that was done there was only a small percentage of the sum total of misery that has afflicted mankind since Cain slew Abel.

The Bible presents the world as a dark place. We referred earlier to the statement in I John that "the whole world lieth in wickedness," and John also states in the opening verses of his Gospel that God's truth in Christ is light shining in the darkness of the world. Peter refers in his letters to the corruptions and pollutions of the world, to the filthy conversations of the wicked, and to believers as having been called out of darkness into the light. Paul describes the Third Reich well in the third chapter of Romans, when he refers to those who are "swift to shed blood: Destruction and misery are in their ways." Their mouths are full of lies and poison and "the way of peace they have not known." Whoever says that the Bible presents a shallow and optimistic view of life should stop speaking of things they know nothing about.

All of these and yet many other evils mean people are open to the designs and manipulations of Satan. Of course, in this technologically advanced but spiritually backward day and age many people will unhesitatingly dismiss such an idea, but if we consider that there are spiritual, non-material powers of wickedness exercising great (though not complete) power over human affairs, some important parts of the Hitler riddle start to fall into place. The most detailed sociological, historical, philosophical, or economic studies will never come even close to explaining his extraordinary rise. Maps telling us what percentage of the vote Hitler received in which region in 1932, interesting though they may be to some, will never explain the mystery of Hitler. His strange power and his malevolent and destructive hatreds fall well outside of the conventional boundaries of historiography laid down in academia. Surely something so extraordinary, so far beyond ordinary human comprehension as the Final Solution, must also have a cause that is extraordinary and equally far removed from human comprehension.

From the scriptural point of view, the main reason Hitler hated the Jews and sought to destroy them was because he was fighting against God and serving the devil – but this does not mean we can just explain Hitler by saying "The devil made him do it" and leave it at that. He was a willing and eager servant of Satan, and will be held accountable on the Day of Judgment for all of his thoughts, words, and deeds. Moreover, evil adapts itself to different situations, whether in Europe or in Asia, in the twentieth century or the twelfth, as circumstances require. Thus, even if we accept the reality of Satan and spiritual evil as the primary motivating force behind Hitler, we can still study the history of Germany and see how human ignorance and sin served evil in that specific context.

The existence of Satan and of evil is not a simplistic answer that cancels out earthly, visible reality. We can say that a serial killer is motivated by sin and evil, possibly even possessed by demons, but still the police have their task of studying clues and searching for suspects. We can say Hitler and his mindless minions were motivated by sin, yet still we can and should consider the history of the period, the emergence of new ideas and of social forces that caused evil to take the forms that it did. Sin and evil do not eliminate our need to search for understanding. Rather, they add another dimension that greatly complicates the issue – and does it need to be pointed out that those spiritual forces of wickedness did not disappear in 1945 but are still with us today? They do however assume different guises, and this too is a matter for careful study.

One of the most important factors in the emergence of National Socialist ideology was human philosophy. How often it is mistakenly assumed that rejection of God and reliance on reason alone mean that one's philosophy is necessarily rational. That one can deny divine revelation in the Bible and rely only on human understanding, yet still arrive at totally false and irrational conclusions is amply demonstrated by a study of German philosophy in the nineteenth and late eighteenth centuries. This will be examined later in other chapters, but it might be worth glancing ahead here.

People in the past with a misguided religious mindset could say "The Jews are torturing communion wafers" and today we scorn their empty stupidity. Those with a misguided secular mindset however could argue with equal depth of insight that the Germans needed to ensure the purity of their racial qualities, but the Jews were polluting them by interbreeding, and so fatally undermining the German race in its struggle for survival. Deluded apostles of autonomous human reason liberated from religious dogma could argue that life was a pitiless struggle in which traditional morals were useless and out of date; that the perishing of the weak by conflict, disease, or famine was normal, a part of natural law from which not even humans were exempt; that proud and warlike cruelty and the pitiless destruction of the weak were "strong" and "healthy," while those who adhered to outdated and unscientific conventions of justice, kindness, mercy, morality and forgiveness, were weak and corrupted by Judaism through Christianity. These and yet other "humanist" ideas did much to cultivate the soil for Hitler in the century and more before he came to power.

The ways in which humanist philosophy led to new and more virulent forms of antisemitism unheard of previously; in which it legitimized callous indifference and brutality, devalued the human soul, and delegitimized centuries of arduously developed social mores in search of a new morality; the way in which it exalted nation and race in such a way as conclude that the Jews were a threat to national survival – these and other related points are not difficult to substantiate. Suffice it to say for the present that the reality of evil was exalted and intensified by certain forms of modernistic humanism, the inevitable result of pride on innately sinful people who were far too intelligent to believe in God. They believed primarily in themselves, which is never an adequate basis for an understanding of higher truth.

One could go on in this vein at great length, but the point is clear. The Holocaust is not a German problem or a Jewish one, it is a human problem, and the fault lies within us. Never before in the history of the world has there been such a calculated, massive, organized, bureaucratized and industrialized expression of evil. As long as our civilization stands – which may not be too much longer – Auschwitz will be regarded as the single most potent symbol of human cruelty, an undeniable proof that there truly is such a thing as evil. But, this evil is not confined in time or space. It exists potentially in every human heart – and this evil is the main reason for antisemitism.

We keep hearing about what a cultured nation Germany was – too few consider that German culture was a big part of the problem. It was German thinkers in the century and more before Hitler who rejected Christianity and sought to invent their own moral world – a world in which good came to be viewed as evil and evil came to be viewed as good. It was their broken moral compass that pointed down a road that in the end led to the gas chambers. It has been said that the Germans were the best educated nation in the world – but what did that education consist of? The belief that we were nothing but animals? That the individual should be subordinated to the state? That the superior northern Europeans dominated the world by right of the natural law of force? That Christianity was outdated and unscientific, and that the struggle for survival of the fittest left no room for false notions of kindness, mercy, forgiveness, and pity?

Jesus said that Satan was a liar and the father of lies, a truth amply illustrated by the sordid history of modern man emancipated from God. The false philosophies presented by a host of pretenders to wisdom are completely useless in finding the hidden and higher meaning of life. They are of some interest today when it comes to understanding the illusions of modernism, in identifying the forms and pressures of the age, and in exercising one's own understanding by interacting with the thoughts of others, but their fine words left people in Germany hungry and starving spiritually, longing for meaning, for purpose, even for struggle and for sacrifice. Hitler understood this far better than do many today who think everything will fall into place of its own accord if we only give people sufficient education and meet their material needs.

One obstacle to an understanding of Hitler is that in certain low and cunning ways he was far smarter than the people who try to analyze him. That some of Hitler's most basic ideas were not found in the gutter or in rubbish bins but had been expressed in identical or similar forms by doctors, scientists, so-called philosophers (who might better be called misosophers), journalists, educators and other assorted intellectuals should raise serious questions about the entire modernist project. Hitler was a very modern man who sensed the weakness of the churches and the hunger of people for something to believe in, and he played on their deepest needs like a concert pianist.

Materialism is a great spiritual darkness that leaves its adherents helpless and vulnerable to forces they neither see nor comprehend – yet wickedness, cruelty, immorality, delusions, and lies are not "theist" or "atheist." They are human, and are found across the whole spectrum of ordinary human activity, from left to right, from atheist to theist. An obvious example of theistic wrongdoing is religious antisemitism. If, as I have asserted, anti-Judaism comes from sin and evil, what of the "Christian" antisemites? What of people who are supposedly Christians but use the name of Christ to justify persecution of Jews? Aren't Christians supposed to be lovers of God and followers of Christ? Since some understanding of the problem of religious antisemitism is helpful to an awareness of the radically different secular motivations of the Nazis, this question requires further examination.

Chapter 3. The Problem of "Christian" Antisemitism

During World War II, a church dignitary refused to help some Jews unless they converted to Christianity.[1] If he had read the parable of the Good Samaritan more carefully, he might have realized that the Samaritan did not inquire about the religious affiliation of the wounded man before giving him aid. Probably the Samaritan recognized the wounded man as a Jew and helped him regardless of the traditional enmity between their peoples. When Jesus said we should love our neighbor as we love ourselves he did not mean "except for Jews," or "except for people who do not agree with us about religion."

Beyond merely treating the Jews like anyone else, Paul teaches that we should have special regard for the Jewish nation, because "unto them were committed the oracles of God" (Romans 3:2), oracles that are vital to the Christian religion. Moreover, we know that Christ was born into a Jewish family and circumcised on the eight day according to the Law of Moses, with a sacrifice offered by his parents on his behalf in Jerusalem also according to that Law. When Christ appeared to Paul on the road to Damascus he spoke to Paul in Hebrew (Acts 26:14), and the earliest Christians were Jews. What to do with the first non-Jewish Christians was something of a problem that had to be resolved by a church council.

What reasons are there, then, for Christian antisemitism? It has been asserted that Christians see the Jews as a threat because their unbelief calls the legitimacy of our faith into question; that we need the support of the Jews to authenticate our faith, and that their continued existence in unbelief is "intolerable" to us. As elementary as that logic might seem to those who are unfamiliar with biblical teaching, it is not the real issue. That human nature, whether Jewish or Gentile, is fundamentally alienated from God and cannot believe without the gift of faith, is a basic Christian concept (I Corinthians 1:17-29). Those who do not understand this lack faith. They also do not believe or understand the Bible, which says that when their time has come God will give it to the Jews to believe (Romans 11:11, 25-26).

The fact that the Jews or anyone else, even our closest friends and family members, reject Christianity is not a stumbling block to the serious Christian. Concerning the Jews, Paul plainly teaches us that the Jews will not believe until the appointed time – yet their unbelief, until such time as God chooses to turn them, is "the riches of the Gentiles" (Romans 11:12). As such it is part of God's providence. This could very well mean, that if the Jews as a nation had from the start accepted Christ, they would have had a natural human tendency

---

[1] Dennis Prager and Joseph Telushkin, *Why the Jews? The Reason for Antisemitism* (New York: Touchstone, 2003), p. 152.

to be proud of their elite status. Gentiles, conversely, would inevitably have considered themselves to be second-class citizens, and would hence never have been able to fully enter into the blessings of grace.

Whatever the proper understanding of that verse might be, the Jewish rejection of the gospel was in no sense a hindrance to the spread and to the establishment of Christianity. The message of Christ does not depend on and has never depended on such merely human authentication. The real origins of Christian antisemitism, as was elaborated on in the previous chapter, are not in simple insecurity, but rather in human sin and evil. These can flourish behind a facade of religiosity, and have been active in various forms in the church from its first beginnings until today. They will remain active until the end of the age and the return of Christ. Thus it is not in the Bible, but in disobedience to the Bible, that we need to search for a solution to the problem of Christian antisemitism.

"But the Jews rejected Jesus!" So have many other people also rejected Jesus. We also who now call ourselves Christians rejected Christ before we came to believe, and are no better than anyone else (Ephesians 2:3). Historical instances of antisemitism, pogroms, lies, and many evils committed against the Jews are thus testimonies not to Christianity, but to the failure of "Christians" to understand their calling. If that means much of church history has been a failure, so be it, but let us not forget the myriads of ordinary and unremembered Christians who have been sincere enough in their walk with Christ to be far removed from massacres, cruelties, and hatreds. They, too, are part of church history.

Anti-Jewish aspects of medieval Christianity such as the Crusader massacres, charges of Jewish ritual murder, or torturing communion wafers (desecration of the host) did not even appear until a thousand years and more after Christ. Prager and Telushkin report that "The first accusation of ritual murder was made in 1144," and the first recorded accusation of "host desecration" came in 1243 (this was 28 years after the Fourth Lateran Council declared the doctrine of transubstantiation to be official church teaching).[2] Surely if such things were endemic to Christianity they would have appeared long before that. They have exactly zero biblical basis, and emerged only in a time of great spiritual darkness, ignorance, and superstition.

Ridiculous medieval stories about a Jew who stabs a communion wafer but converts to Christianity when he sees blood flowing out of it have no place in hundreds of volumes by countless Christian theologians, commentators, pastors, and devotional authors. Even Luther, who is constantly pointed to, wrote literally dozens of volumes of collected works in which the Jews are not relevant and not an issue. Weird stories of saints, legends, and miracles were one of the abuses the Reformation sought to correct. No Protestants, in spite of

---

[2] Ibid., pp. 81, 86, 87.

38

our many and obvious failings, have ever been concerned with sacred communion wafers, as they have no biblical basis.

When writing about communion, Paul was not concerned about communion wafers being tortured. He was concerned about people partaking of communion unworthily, making themselves guilty "of the body and blood of the Lord" (I Corinthians 11:27). Here it is not Jews, but rather people with the name and appearance of Christians, that according to Scripture are guilty of Christ's death. If anyone crucifies Christ afresh it is not those Jews (or anyone else) who merely deny Christ (as I also denied Christ for many years) – it is those who partake of communion unworthily, or who have had some experience of the truth of Christianity but then fall away (Hebrews 5:4-6). The attribution of Christian anti-Judaism to the belief that Jews crucify Christ afresh just by existing in unbelief has nothing to do with serious Christian doctrine or practice.

How many of the things that occurred in the medieval period were nothing but sin and evil in Christian disguise! That people should be forced to convert on pain of death makes a mockery of every single scriptural teaching about baptism. When the Ethiopian eunuch requested baptism, Philip said to him, "If thou believest with all thine heart, thou mayest" (Acts 8:37). That forced baptisms should later be upheld as binding was the result of ignorance of biblical Christianity, even of salvation itself. Jews, Buddhists, Hindus, Muslims, even atheists will I believe fare better on the Day of Judgment than people who use the power of the church and the name of Christ to perpetuate such sin, ignorance, lies and evil. Far from justifying them, their use of Christ's name will I believe bring them greater condemnation.

But what of certain medieval regulations against the Jews that are said to have been copied by the Nazis? Does that show a Christian influence on Naziism – or does it show the same underlying force of evil, hatred, and lies working both in a deeply corrupted and worldly Christianity in the Middle Ages and in secular ideology in our own times? The second alternative means that many who had the name of "Christian" were spiritually akin to the Nazis (lacking of course modern technology and ideology). This they will find to their sorrow on the Day of Judgment, when it will be evident that using the power of the church and the name of Jesus Christ to persecute Jews (or anyone else, including dissenting Christians like the Waldensians or the Albigensians) was in fact sin against God. Such things should reflect only on the deluded people who practiced them (many of whom probably never even read a Bible), not on those who do not practice such things because of the genuineness their faith.

Prager and Telushkin's detailed study of antisemitism lists 10 parallels between church laws against the Jews and Nazi laws[3] – yet other parts of

---

[3] Ibid., pp. 88-89.

medieval Europe lacked such laws, and not a single one of the examples given comes from Protestant countries after the Reformation. That the Church of the Middle Ages with its pomp, glory, wealth, pride, power and cruelty had strayed very far from the teachings of Christ is a regrettable fact which we do not have to try and cover up or explain away. We may point out though that persecution of Jews has nothing to do with the ordinary lives of countless Christians, in many countries over long periods of time, and that it is a direct denial of many biblical teachings. We may also point out that none of those restrictive medieval measures came anywhere close to the worst Nazi excesses, which were totally unimaginable in the Middle Ages. Apart from undeniable similarities, there were also profound and equally undeniable differences in motivation and in end result.

A better understanding of the contested relationship between religious and Nazi antisemitisms will have to follow a closer examination of the latter. For the present, let us remember that Jews polluting the blood purity of the Aryan race was not a concern of traditional religious antisemitism. Neither was the belief that the Jews, through Christianity, had corrupted Europe with false values that were contrary to nature and harmful to the German nation in its struggle for survival. These and still other ideas foundational to Nazi antisemitism emerged in the nineteenth century and can be related to various trends, including German forms of Romanticism, social Darwinism, modern nationalism, even to the seemingly remote philosophies of Kant, Hegel and Fichte. They are related not to the Bible, but to the turning away from the Bible that was such a profound characteristic of much nineteenth-century thought.[4]

Let us also be sure not to forget the millions of ordinary Christians who never harmed Jews or anyone else, but sought rather to live lives "unblameable in holiness" as the Bible says we should do. Myriads of Christians have never concerned themselves with the ignorant lies and wickedness mentioned above. They have sincerely tried to follow the teachings of Christ – not to perfection, we all fall short, but well enough at least to avoid slaughtering or torturing people, or spreading hateful and ignorant superstitions and lies.

There were even such harmless Christians in the Middle Ages. The Jewish experience in Europe during that period was not one uninterrupted pogrom, and at some times Jewish culture was able to reach a high level of development (as was elaborated on in chapter 2). One reason for this is that there are certain limitations inherent in Christianity which ensured that a systematic attempt to slaughter all of the Jews could not and did not occur in the medieval period. One limitation was the Christian concept of government

---

[4] If someone wants to jump straight from Luther to the Holocaust while at the same time simplistically misrepresenting the nineteenth century as a time of only progress for Jews in Germany, this can only be described as propaganda, not history.

40

as ordained by God to keep the peace and punish evil. This very limited understanding of the role of government had nothing to do with modern totalitarianism.

Hitler's belief that one purpose of the Nazi state was to maintain the racial purity of the German people so that it could prevail in the struggle for survival[5] was – needless to say – unheard of in previous centuries. Rulers in the Christian understanding were themselves subject to a higher law. This belief, while it did not suffice to eliminate all injustice and bring paradise on earth, was a real and widely believed restraint. A situation in which the word of the Fuhrer was the highest law would have been inconceivable.

Another limitation was Christian morality, which teaches that we will be held accountable for our actions on the Day of Judgment, and commands us to treat others as we would like to be treated ourselves, to forgive, to not take vengeance. Many people did not take such things seriously, and did whatever they pleased, but many did. They had a legitimate fear of God that was completely absent from modern secular ideologies.

Yet a third limitation was concepts of the Jews. Along with the distorted idea of Jews as permanently under God's wrath and deserving his punishment, there was also an understanding that the Jews would as a nation someday be restored to God's favor (Romans 11:23-24); that they were the people of the prophets and merited respect for that reason (Romans 3:3); that their continued existence in affliction and exile was a fulfillment and a confirmation of prophecy. Though not always perfectly understood or followed, these ideas did ensure that the Jews were not considered as subhuman vermin and enemies of the human race.

A Danish Christian wrote in a church newspaper in 1942, "We do not step into the breach for the Jews because they are human beings of some special worth, but because they are human beings and because God has commanded us to treat human beings in a humane way."[6] This is authentic Christian teaching. Incidentally, I don't remember ever having read of any Darwinists under Nazi occupation protesting Nazi policies because of their belief in the theory of Darwinism.

Let us also remember that basic biblical teachings of salvation that apply to everyone universally are not antisemitic, nor do they necessarily lead to antisemitism. Saying for example that Jews cannot earn forgiveness of sins and salvation by keeping the law of Moses or by following religious rules, that none of us earn our way into heaven by our good deeds, is not an attack on or a dismissal of Jewish law either (as some have mistakenly claimed). Paul

---

[5] Adolf Hitler, *Mein Kampf*, trans. Ralph Manheim (Boston: Houghton Mifflin, 1999), pp. 199, 403.

[6] Kevin Spicer, ed. *Antisemitism, Christian Ambivalence, and the Holocaust* (Bloomington, IN: Indiana University Press, 2007), p. 22.

teaches plainly that ". . . the law is holy, and the commandment holy, and just, and good" (Romans 7:12). The problem is not with the Law, which is an expression of God's character – it is with us, who are incapable of keeping God's laws as we ought.

The idea of the Old Testament Law as a curse is not antisemitic either, as has been claimed, but comes from Moses, who said "Cursed be he that confirmeth not all the words of this law to do them" (Deuteronomy 27:26). The claim that Christians entirely repudiate Jewish law or think God gave the Jews the law as punishment for their sin is a misreading of Christian teaching, even if some confused pastor or misguided theologian may have made that claim. The laws that God gave to Moses on Sinai are an expression of God's holiness. Paul describes Moses' face as shining with light, a peculiar form of antisemitism (II Corinthians 3:7).

God's holy laws given to Moses and faithfully preserved for us in the Bible inevitably condemn us in the end, as we naturally and necessarily fall short of God's perfection. Nevertheless, substantial parts of the Jewish law are confirmed and reestablished in the New Testament. We are not saved by keeping the law but, once saved, we have an obligation to follow the law and to repent if we fail (except in the case of dietary or ceremonial laws, which have been expressly set aside). That Christians can just "believe" and then do whatever they please with no regard even to the 10 Commandments is an unfortunate misconception of salvation by faith that directly contradicts many plain scriptures.

But doesn't Christianity assign an inferior status to Judaism? The Bible teaches that salvation is found in Christ alone. As has already been said, that can hardly be called antisemitism which applies equally to the entire human race without exception. It even excludes many who have the name of "Christian" yet do not know Christ and have none of his Spirit. Replacement theologians who feel that the church has taken the place of the Jews should still look on Jews as human beings like anyone else, not as vermin to be exterminated. Their loss of a special place does not deny their humanity, but should merely put them on the same plane as all other non-Christians.

It is true that Christians claim to have a higher and fuller revelation of God in Christ, and "a better covenant, which was established upon better promises" (Hebrews 8:6). However, many Jews (if they are not wholly secularized) *also* claim to have a better covenant than non-Jews, including Christians – yet they still feel an obligation to treat those outside of their Mosaic covenant as human beings. To look at it another way, denying that Jesus was born of a virgin; that he was God come to earth in human form; that he died on the cross for the sins of the world and rose from the dead – these are legitimate belief statements, not expressions of anti-Christian "hate." Neither is affirming those Christian teachings hatred toward the Jews, Moslems, Buddhists, atheists, or to the "liberal" "Christians" who deny them. It is not reasonable to link every denial or criticism of Jewish teaching to pogroms and to Hitler.

But doesn't Christianity teach that the Jews are under divine punishment for the rejection of Christ, that God's will is for them to suffer, and that those who make them suffer are thus doing the will of God? This is a complex problem, and requires some examination. Moses wrote in the Torah that if the Jews obeyed God and kept his commandments, he would bless them in the land, and establish them there (Deuteronomy 28:1-14). He also taught, however, that if the Jews did not keep God's commandments he would punish them, and in the end cast them out of the land and scatter them abroad (28:64) where they would be afflicted and oppressed by their enemies.

This prophecy was fulfilled twice, in the destruction first of the northern kingdom of Israel, and then in the southern kingdom of Judah. As we read in the prophets, these disasters were sent by God – not because of minor shortcomings, but because of open and prolonged wickedness and a persistent refusal to repent. Christians can hardly be blamed for seeing Israel's destruction by the Romans as yet another fulfillment of this prophecy – and if, according to their own prophets, the sins of the Jews led to a short expulsion by the Babylonians, how much greater sin must have been required to bring about a much longer exile?

To say that their expulsion from the land is a sign of God's disfavor is obvious, and consistent with Judaism itself. However, that the Jewish people survived and returned to their biblical homeland is a clear sign, or should be, to all Bible-believing Christians, that God is still at work with the Jews. Nowhere outside of the Jewish community is support for Israel stronger in America today than among Bible-believing Christians. Even in the early 1700s Jonathan Edwards was writing that, according to biblical teaching, ethnic Israel would someday be restored to its ancient homeland.[7] This does not, by the way, mandate complete agreement with all Israeli policies, since even in the Old Testament era there were wicked or misguided Jewish rulers.

Returning to the subject of the destruction of Israel by the Romans, Jesus taught submission to and cooperation with the authorities. If the Jews as a nation had followed the teachings of Christ in this regard, there would not have been two rebellions against Rome, and they would not have been cast out of the land. Thus it can be said that the rejection of Christ and his message was a direct cause of their later rebellion and expulsion. We do not have to imagine any sort of mystical blood curse on the Jews, but can attribute their disaster to

---

[7] Iain Murray, *Jonathan Edwards: A New Biography* (Edinburgh: The Banner of Truth Trust, 1988), p. 49 (citing Edwards' "Notes on the Apocalypse" in the Yale Edition of *The Works of Jonathan Edwards*, vol. 5, 1977, p. 135). Murray states that Edwards' view of unfulfilled prophecy "in its main outline . . . corresponded with beliefs which had been general among the Puritans," p. 49.

the inevitable and natural results of their own actions and unbelief. We can see Moses' prophecy of suffering and destruction as having found fulfillment in the destruction of Israel and in the subsequent Diaspora, a direct result of the judgment of God, yet brought by the Jews upon themselves by their blind folly of rebelling against Rome in disobedience to the commandment of Christ.

It will be claimed that this can justify Nazi crimes as being God's deserved punishment – but the Assyrians and the Babylonians, expressly designated in Scripture as agents of God's wrath, were violent, proud and cruel men. God can if he chooses execute wrath by withdrawing his hand and abandoning people to the wicked. That has nothing to do with our calling as Christians and does not make acts of evil less evil. It is not our mission to persecute anyone, Jews not excepted. Those who thought otherwise were deeply deceived. We are not called to be agents of God's wrath, to be condemned in turn for our own crimes. That is not for us who name the name of Christ. Christians are called to be agents of reconciliation, not of wrath. Let evildoers like the Assyrians and the Babylonians be instruments of God's wrath – that is not our place or our calling. We read in Obadiah that even those who rejoiced in the afflictions of the Jews and took advantage of them were themselves condemned.

A second reason that punishing Jews is not God's will for us as Christians is that the Bible teaches in Romans chapter 11 that God has not cast away the Jewish people. He has yet a purpose for them, as we can see in their survival and in their miraculous return to their biblical homeland. Let us participate with God in this rather than fight against it, and consider that the final restoration of the Jews will be a blessing for us as well (Romans 11:15).

Third, as has already been said, Jewish rejection of Christ is human rejection, of which we also as individuals were guilty before we came to know Christ. So, we are no better than they, and were also ourselves children of wrath and under condemnation, "by nature the children of wrath, even as others" (Ephesians 2:3). Or, as Paul says in Romans, ". . . we have before proved both Jews and Gentiles, that they are all under sin; as it is written, There is none righteous, no, not one" (Romans 3:9-10).

Fourth, we are expressly warned not to be high and mighty against the Jews. If Gentiles who are genuinely in Christ (not merely everyone who has the name or appearance of "Christian") are like branches that have been grafted into the covenant of God's promise, and the Jews have been broken off because of unbelief, we need to be careful lest we too be broken off. "Be not high-minded, but fear: For if God spared not the natural branches, take heed lest he also spare not thee" (Romans 11:17-24). Jesus said if we do not forgive others God will not forgive us. We have no claim to God's mercy if we deny it to others.

Fifthly, God is able to graft the original branches back into the tree. We can already see this at work, as more Jews are seeing that faith in Christ as the Son of God does not nullify Judaism but rather fulfills it. It is our part as Christians to support this process, encourage it, and participate in it, not to oppose it. We do not hinder God in any way by opposing his workings, but we do hurt ourselves.

These points are not merely theology or empty God-words. On the contrary, they explain why so many Christians have held to the literal truth of biblical teachings about Christ and his salvation, yet have never been enemies of the Jews. Mindful of the biblical teachings just stated, they have tried to treat the Jews as they would like to be treated themselves, and have even shown respect to the Jews as the people of the prophets and of the Messiah, who will someday be turned to Christ.

As to those who see their calling as Christians to be one of cruelty, lies, and murder, Christians may have wrong ideas about various things, including Jews, because we are fallible humans. There comes a point, however, at which repeated mistakes and sins become not human error but open wickedness and defiance of God. We cannot always tell exactly where that line is, but God can. Those who are serious about Christ, if they persist in the straight and narrow way that Scripture sets before them, will be kept safe from such evil by the providence of God. Also, let us not forget that if we do not have charity towards others, our Christianity is in vain, as Paul warns us in I Corinthians 13.

Much of orthodox, biblical Christianity is unnecessarily confused with antisemitism and unjustly linked to the Holocaust. Scripturally-based Christians do claim to have a fuller revelation and do see Christ as the fulfillment of Old Testament laws. Yet, we recognize our spiritual debt to the Jews, and remember that Paul said the Jews were "beloved for the fathers' sakes," even though they were enemies of the Gospel (this at a time when Christians were being actively persecuted by the Jewish leadership) (Romans 11:28). We (many of us) believe God has a further work to do with the Jews; and we recognize that the Jewish rejection of Christ is human rejection, which places Jews who reject Christ on the same plane of unbelief as everyone else (including many so-called Christian "churches," "pastors," "scholars," and "theologians" who also reject the claims and deity of Christ, in spite of their fake religious rhetoric).

Neither is trying to bring the Christian message to Jews antisemitic, a means of eliminating the Jewish people spiritually. Jesus said we should go and teach "all nations," not "all nations except the Jews." In witnessing to Jews we are treating them as we treat others, sharing a message which is for everyone (although of course that message can be shared in the wrong way, and in the wrong time). And many Jews will testify that coming to believe in Christ does not require the forsaking of their Jewish heritage or inevitably lead to assimilation with the Gentile world.

It should be added that when Paul says "to the Jew first, and also to the Greek" (Romans 1:16), he is not saying that Jews are more important than others, or that Christians get more points with God if they can effectively witness to Jews. Paul meant "first" chronologically – Christ came first to the Jews, and the gospel message came first to the Jews. Often Paul would go to the synagogues of the Jews first and bring his message there – but if the Jews rejected the message, then it was brought to others. All of these topics have been greatly obscured by those who call themselves Christians, yet deny the authority of the Bible and many essentials of the faith.

It would be good if we could stop here and move on to the next chapter examining Hitler's exact relationship to biblical Christianity, but unfortunately we need to look at some specific Christians whose names constantly come up in discussions of "Christian" anti-Judaism: John Chrysostom and Martin Luther. We can also mention some more peripheral figures such as Ambrose, the 4th century bishop of Milan, Augustine, and Adolf Stoecker, Protestant chaplain to the Kaiser's imperial court.

Concerning Ambrose, when the Roman emperor Theodosius ordered a bishop in another part of the empire to pay for the rebuilding of a synagogue that had been burned in his bishopric, Ambrose objected, and put pressure on the emperor to rescind his order, even to the extent of refusing to perform a Mass while the emperor was in attendance. Ambrose argued that since the synagogue was "a house of impiety" and "a home of unbelief," Christians should be under no obligation to rebuild it.[8]

Just as one Jew who owns a bank does not prove that Jews control the world's economy, so Ambrose does not stand for or represent the myriads of Christians who never burned a synagogue or wanted to. Even in that time, many synagogues were left unmolested. As to Ambrose being a "saint," that is for God to determine. Jesus said "Many that are first shall be last and the last first." Great saints in the world's eyes may appear differently in the last day when all secrets are revealed. As to him being a "father" of the church, I don't think it is reasonable to call those men "fathers" when they came along hundreds of years after the church had begun. Anyway, God is supposed to be the Father of the church, and Jesus said "Call no man father," for God is our Father.

Parenthetically, a Christian place of worship was recently burned in Israel.[9] I doubt that the Israeli government has offered to pay for the damage (nor should it). If such an offer were made by the government, more likely than not

---

[8] Prager and Telushkin, *Why the Jews?*, p. 79.

[9] "Israeli Messianic congregation building burned down," *israel today*, Friday Jan. 18, 2013; http://www.israeltoday.co.il/NewsItem/tabid/178/nid/23628/Default.aspx; accessed February 2014.

many Jews, even religious leaders, would object to government funds going to restore a Christian place of worship. This is not to justify Ambrose. It is to say that we are dealing with ordinary human nature here – a problem to which not only Christians are liable. My own belief is that if the emperor wanted to rebuild the synagogue that was his concern, and withholding communion not because of major sin and unbelief but because of matters of policy was wrong and unbiblical. Church leaders, like major figures in the Bible, can err.

Concerning Chrysostom, he is not a major figure in the history of Western Christianity. If it were not for his frequently quoted attacks on Jews he would be (for many Christians) nothing more than a name in history books. Unfortunately, in his *Eight Orations Against the Jews* he spoke of Jewish synagogues as cursed places, fortresses of the devil, worse than whorehouses, dens of criminals, and pits of destruction. He described Jews as less than beasts, assassins of Christ, and objects of God's anger whom it was the duty of Christians to hate.

"Chrysostom" means "golden-mouth," and at other times speaking on other subjects Chrysostom may have been eloquent by human standards. He has been highly praised by some as an eloquent theologian. On the other hand, we read in I Corinthians chapter 13 that charity (or love toward others) is patient and kind, and without charity eloquence is worthless. We also read in James 3:10, 17: "Out of the same mouth proceedeth blessing and cursing. My brethren, these things ought not so to be . . . the wisdom that proceedeth from above is first pure, then peaceable, gentle, and easy to be entreated . . . . "

I don't know what Chrysostom's problem was, but I suspect he was trying to sound like some of the Old Testament prophets who also brought very strong denunciations against their own people. For example the prophet Isaiah, moved by the Spirit of God, referred to the Jewish people as "a sinful nation, a people laden with iniquity, a seed of evildoers . . . rulers of Sodom . . . people of Gomorrah" whose hands are full of blood and whose worship of God is vain (Isaiah 1:4,10,13,15). No one has as yet been crazy enough to link these and many other prophetic indictments of Jewish sin to later antisemitism and the Holocaust.

It may be that Chrysostom thought he was imitating Christ's denunciation of the Pharisees – but Christ and the prophets spoke not from human anger, but righteously, according to the truth of God. I don't think that can be said of Chrysostom. And, Christians are entrusted with the gospel of reconciliation, not a message of wrath. True, Christ spoke very strongly against the Jewish religious leaders (not against all Jews), but he had an authority no one else has ever had. It is significant that none of the apostles ever tried to imitate Christ in this respect.

Chrysostom has done some damage to the image of Christianity, but his approach was not that of the apostles (as anyone can see who at least tries to read the Bible objectively). His approach was also not that of great numbers of

Christian writers whose works have been far more influential than those of Chrysostom. Augustine, Pascal, Wesley, Bunyan, John Owen, Richard Baxter, Jonathan Edwards, Calvin – none of these writers (or many others) have made such angry tirades against the Jews. Even Luther did not mention the Jews in the vast majority of his voluminous works (excepting of course countless references to Old Testament teaching in support of the Reformation). He was not overly concerned about them for most of his career.

Christian writers do of course make theological statements about salvation through Christ which are disagreeable to those Jews who do not accept Christ, but this is not antisemitism – just as a Jew saying "Christ did not die for the sins of the world and did not rise from the dead" is a legitimate belief-statement, not an expression of hateful anti-Christian bigotry. It is tempting for some to try and link all criticisms of or disagreements with Jews to the Holocaust, no matter how remote, but those who have studied the emergence of National Socialist ideology recognize that its foundational ideas were rooted firmly in the nineteenth century, and they came from people who did not believe in the Bible.

Chrysostom's writing on this point is very far from representative of biblical Christianity as it has been practiced by vast multitudes of Christians over nearly two thousand years. It is, I believe, therefore inaccurate to state that "the most thoroughly anti-Jewish positions were advanced by the church's greatest saints and most rational thinkers."[10] That the Jews were a plague bacillus, germs that should be exterminated; that the Aryans were the master race and had a mission to lead mankind on its onward and upward progress – these and other Nazi ideas had never been previously advocated by any reputable Christian authors. It took the modern age and emancipation from religion for enlightened human reason to arrive at that stage of sophistication.

Augustine's name comes up less frequently as he has never been convicted of hateful rantings against the Jews. His ideas on the subject serve to show the innate restraints that operated on those who seriously believed in the Bible and tried to live by it, and which successfully mitigated against the later excesses of the modern secular and anti-religious age. The source just cited conceded that "Augustine could not withhold all affection for the Jewish people, because God's work of redemption had been carried on through their history, culminating in the crucifixion and resurrection of Jesus."[11] This is in complete agreement with what Paul says in Romans 3:1-2, 9:4-5, and 12:28.

Vague statements such as "Augustine considered the Jews instruments of Satan" should be not be repeated or accepted without documentation, as many

---

[10] Richard L. Rubenstein and John K. Roth, *Approaches to Auschwitz: The Holocaust and its Legacy* (Louisville KY: Westminster John Knox Press, 2003), p. 53.

[11] Ibid.

such things are circulating now that someone read somewhere or heard somewhere with no understanding of Christian teachings of sin and evil. Also, some statements about the Jews and evil seem worse than they really are to those who do not understand that identical statements can be and are made about mankind as a whole. For example, Augustine did believe that the Jews' refusal to acknowledge Christ was spiritual blindness – yet the Bible and Augustine assert that this is true of the entire world outside of faith in Christ. It does not apply to Jews alone, though it may be applied to Jews in a way that sounds bad if understood by those ignorant of Christian teaching to apply to Jews only. Augustine wrote at length about the sin and evil in his own soul.

If Augustine taught that the continued existence of the Jews in exile was a testimony of God's judgment against them (in agreement with Deuteronomy 28:63-66), yet he did not teach that it was our duty as Christians to be harsh and avenging angels of God's wrath. He understood that we ought to treat Jews as we would like to be treated ourselves, Christ's commandment to us for all, and try to influence them for Christ.[12] The Jews have had and still have a unique role to play in the providence of God, but at bottom they have the same sin and the same need for salvation as anyone else.

Such was Luther's earlier position, but unfortunately he lapsed into hostility towards the Jews late in his life (most notably in his oft-quoted tract *On the Jews and Their Lies*). In so doing, he greatly confused the question of biblical Christianity's relationship to antisemitism, and gave a lot of ammunition to those who want to argue for the Christian influence on the Holocaust and for the inherent anti-Judaism of biblical Christianity. Because of Luther's emphasis on Christianity based on the Bible alone and because of his great historical influence, his errors concerning the Jews are taken as proof of a flaw inherent in Christianity itself (as if the flaws and mistakes of David, Solomon, and other biblical characters much greater than Luther were indicative of flaws at the heart of Judaism itself).

A major figure in the history of Christianity and one whose best spiritual writings have been helpful, even deeply influential to me and to many others, Luther's importance requires a deeper examination of exactly what it was that he had against the Jews. I make no apologies for this lengthy digression, as without a proper understanding of Luther it will not be possible to grasp the extent to which Hitler and the Nazis were driven by modern motives chronologically and philosophically distant from the 16th century, from the Protestant Reformation, and from biblical Christianity as a whole. A few cut-and-paste quotes from Luther were useful to the Nazis, but Luther's reasoning was alien to them (popular misconceptions and accusations notwithstanding).

Luther's main concern as a reformer was not with the Jews. They do not figure in his most important Reformation writings, and if he had died just a

---

[12] Ibid., p. 54.

few years earlier before he wrote his notorious tract near the end of his life his name would not even come up in these conversations. That Luther had a life-long obsession with Jews is one of the many errors or falsehoods circulated about him. Neither is this necessarily contradicted by Luther's early comments about Jews in his "Lectures on Romans" of 1515-1516, or some lectures on the Psalms from about the same period. That the Jews were in sinful alienation from God by their rejection of Christ was also said of mankind as a whole. That the entire human race is under the same condemnation for sin apart from faith in Christ was a fundamental point of Paul's (Romans 3:9-11), and of the Reformers. The main thrust of the Reformation, and Luther's greatest achievements, had nothing to do with "the Jews."

The widespread failure to understand what Luther hoped to achieve is regrettable (especially on the part of those who claim to be historians). The *95 Theses* were not an "attack" on the Catholic Church, but a respectful attempt to reform it. Luther's complete break with the Church of Rome came later. Luther did not object to the selling of papal indulgences because he was upset by some Catholic "bogeyman," but because he thought it morally wrong and biblically false to tell people they could purchase forgiveness of sins. The Reformation was not just a "misunderstanding" that could have been resolved if people had calmed down and discussed things reasonably. There were central and unavoidable conflicts about salvation and the nature of the Gospel itself that could not honestly be papered over. Many of those same issues are still vital today, though in different ways, and if we think we can leave the Reformation emphasis on the Bible alone and salvation through Christ alone behind us, we are making a bad mistake.

Luther was concerned first and foremost not with the Jews, but with freeing the church from doctrinal and ceremonial encrustations that had no biblical basis. This meant repudiating many Church practices that were either superfluous or directly contrary to the Bible. It meant denial of the Church's authority to dictate interpretations of the Bible, and emphasized individual liberty of faith and conscience. This emphasis on spiritual liberty and independence of thought contributed greatly to the development of Western democracy. Everyone who believes we should not all be required to automatically submit to one particular church as the sole representative of truth is in agreement with one of Luther's most fundamental points. Luther was a crucial figure in the emergence of Europe from the medieval period.

In his book *Civilization: The Six Killer Apps of Western Power*, historian Niall Ferguson comments in various places on the positive effects of the Protestant Reformation. For example, he credits the rise of modern Western civilization to both the Renaissance and the Reformation.[13] This should be a

---

[13] Niall Ferguson, *Civilization: The Six Killer Apps of Western Power* (London: Penguin Books, 2012), p. xv.

commonplace, but unfortunately it isn't. Ferguson also states that Luther's religious revolution preceded and "unintentionally begat" the intellectual revolution which followed. "Because of the central importance in Luther's thought of individual reading of the Bible, Protestantism encouraged literacy, not to mention printing, and these two things unquestionably encouraged economic development (the accumulation of human capital) as well as scientific study."[14]

Ferguson also refers to higher literacy rates brought by Protestant missionaries. This was not merely cultural imperialism either. I once asked an educated African if he would like his country to return to the culture it had before the Westerners came – he laughed.   Lamin Sanneh, a Gambian theologian, has some worthwhile comments on the importance of literacy often brought first by missionaries who devised writing systems, grammars, and dictionaries for previously illiterate peoples, and who did not just impose Western values but brought many benefits.[15] They taught people to read and write with no guarantee that this knowledge would be used only to teach Christianity.

Even those who directly link Luther's anti-Judaism to later developments in German history can still see his larger significance. The previously cited work on the Holocaust by Rubenstein and Roth, while strongly condemning Luther's attitudes toward the Jews, has this to say: "Luther did as much to discover the new world of the spirit as Columbus did to discover the territorial New World. If, as many historians and sociologists of religion maintain, the modern world is in large measure an unintended consequence of religious and cultural forces arising out of the Protestant Reformation, Luther can be seen as one of its seminal creators."[16]

The revolutionary idea that people could approach the deepest questions of life on an individual basis, apart from outdated medieval Church dogmas and unthinking obedience to Church leaders, "personalized faith . . . . Protestant faith emerged with the breakdown of the old medieval order and hastened the new social order."[17] This was a bright light for much of Europe that remarkably revitalized Christianity. Historian Robert Wistrich, while severely criticizing Luther, also recognized the importance of "his devastating assault

---

[14] Ibid., p. 67, 263.

[15] Lamin Sanneh, *Whose Religion is Christianity? The Gospel Beyond the West* (Cambridge: William B. Eerdmans Publishing, 2003), see especially chapter 2 ("Christianity Reappropriated: The Bible and Its Mother Tongue Variations").

[16] Rubenstein and Roth, *Approaches to Auschwitz*, p. 57.

[17] David F. Wells, *No Place for Truth or Whatever Happened to Evangelical Authority?* (Grand Rapids, MI: William B. Eerdmans Publishing Company, 1993), p. 88.

on the corruption, falsehoods, and superstitions abounding in the papal Rome of his day."[18]

It has been said that the Reformation sundered Europe's spiritual unity, but who needs a unity of so-called faith that has to be enforced by Inquisitions, torture, and murder? We are told that the Reformation led to many religious wars – what do people think Europe was before the Reformation? Have they read any history at all? Why does it need to be explained that there were countless wars in Europe for two thousand years and more before the Reformation, and that the Thirty Years War – constantly presented as an example of religious strife – was indeed sparked by religion, but quickly became an old-fashioned dynastic power struggle with Catholics aiding Protestants against their Catholic rivals?

One historian wrote of the violence that afflicted Europe before religious conflicts were mitigated by secularism. Is that why the twentieth century was the most peaceful century the world has ever known, because of the blessings of secularism? Consideration of these subjects is vastly complicated by those whose devotion to their materialist ideology makes it difficult for them to discuss religion objectively. Is it rational to blame Christianity for poison gas, napalm, and all of the other weapons of modern destruction? It was not Christian teaching that transformed war from a limited affair of the battlefield to something vastly greater, more vicious and destructive. Is it not in fact ridiculous for people who flatter themselves on their objectivity to give science credit for all of the advances of modern technology, yet exempt science from any blame for its abuses?

Another historian spoke of the Reformation and Counter-Reformation eras as a terrible period in which people and books were burned "regularly." Solzhenitsyn wrote in his *Gulag Archipelago* of the vast numbers of books and manuscripts destroyed by the KGB. The Nazis too burned books, all of this in the twentieth century. It is true of course that the Reformation was a time of deep religious conflict, but at the spiritual center of that conflict was the vital and necessary question of liberty. Are we to be in spiritual subjection to an authoritarian church-state structure which tells us what to believe and demands unthinking and unquestioning obedience? Or are we to seek out our own understanding and believe as seems right to us? This was at the heart of the Reformation – and docile obedience to Rome in the sixteenth century would not have ushered in a golden age of peace anyway. Conflict is endemic to human existence, and appears in every age, every civilization. This is due to human sin and disobedience to God, not because conflict is "healthy" and "natural," as dogmatic modernists like Haeckel and Nietzsche confidently asserted.

---

[18] Robert S. Wistrich, *Hitler and the Holocaust* (New York: Modern Library, 2003), p. 13.

There are some who feel that Darwin and his leading German apologist Ernst Haeckel are more relevant to an understanding of Hitler than are people who actually believed that God was watching what they would do, and would send them to hell if they were liars, thieves, drunkards, adulterers and murderers.[19] It is not hard to understand why some might think that the idea of people as animals locked in an endless struggle for survival is more helpful to an understanding of Hitler than the idea that there would be a resurrection from the dead, that we would arise to stand before God and give an account for our lives, after which we would be admitted to an eternity of paradise or condemned to an eternity of torment. Does anyone want to claim that Hitler believed in such religious concepts? Even mentioning the word "Hitler" in that context is ridiculous.

Returning to the subject of the Protestant Reformation, we need spiritual liberty, and the liberty brought by the Reformation to think and to believe freely was a very important reason why science and learning flourished in northern Europe as they did nowhere else in the world. John Montgomery has written an entire chapter on the relationship of science to Protestantism, and effectively refutes charges of Luther being hostile to science, or opposing Copernicus' theory.[20] There are no negative comments from Luther on the theory after 1543, when Copernicus *De revolutionibus* was first published, and Luther's friend Philip Melanchthon and other second generation reformers came to support Copernicus (as Montgomery also shows). They were deeply involved in the beginnings of the coming scientific revolution. Secularists like to talk about the persecution of Galileo – as a non-Catholic, I feel that has nothing to do with me, and nothing to do with Christ or the New Testament. Also, many people, not only Luther and not only Christians, found the new idea of the solar system hard to accept at first.

Neither was Luther hostile to the life of the mind. When he said that Madame Reason was the devil's whore, he was not speaking of the power of reason by which we learn languages, analyze a logical problem, design a building, or seek a cure for illness. He was speaking of reason in opposition to God, and the many ways it seeks to escape from God. Luther was a deeply

---

[19] See for example Jerry Bergman, *Hitler and the Nazi Darwinian Worldview* (Kitchener, Ontario: Joshua Press, 2012) . . . Daniel Gasman, *The Scientific Origins of National Socialism (*New Brunswick USA: Transaction Publishers, 2004) . . . and Richard Weikart *From Darwin to Hitler: Evolutionary Ethics, Eugenics, and Racism in Germany* (New York: Palgrave Macmillan, 2004). Weikart has the useful insight that Hitler's ethics were not based on the Bible as the Word of God, but on the supposed benefit to German racial health and dominance. Gasman demonstrates conclusively that many of Haeckel's ideas were close to or even identical to Hitler's.

[20] John W. Montgomery, *In Defense of Martin Luther: Essays by John Warwick Montgomery* (Milwaukee: Northwestern Publishing House, 1970), chapter 2 "Luther and Science."

learned man with a thorough grasp of the philosophical and theological controversies of his day, and was not in any sense the coarse buffoon or comic strip character some have tried to make him out to be. His best works have a deep spiritual power conspicuously absent from too many Evangelical authors today.

Much has also been said about the Protestant work ethic, without appreciating that it is general Christian teachings of the purpose of life, accountability to God, the need to be sober, diligent, kind to others, obey the laws, be faithful to one's spouse, avoid drunkenness and crime, and to treat others as you would like to be treated that contributed greatly to the political, scientific, and economic advance of the West. Even a noted secularist like the biologist Jacques Monod recognized that the emergence of modern science only in the "Christian West" and nowhere else might be attributable to some extent to the character of the Christian religion.[21] And, while basic Christian truths are neither Catholic nor Protestant but biblical, it was Luther and the Reformers who made these truths more accessible to many people in a real and living way, apart from the dead hand of superstition, relics, saints, and endless burdensome regulations.

In this context Ferguson quotes a Chinese scholar's recognition of Christianity's foundational importance to Western culture: ". . . we have realized that the heart of your culture is your religion: Christianity. That is why the West has been so powerful. The Christian moral foundation of social and cultural life was what made possible the emergence of capitalism and then the successful transition to democratic politics. We don't have any doubt about this." Ferguson quotes another Chinese academic to the effect that "such concepts as freedom, human rights, tolerance, equality, justice, democracy, the rule of law," and other positive aspects of Western civilization were incomprehensible without the "Christian understanding of transcendence."[22]

For much of Europe, the modern understanding of these qualities was developed according to Protestant concepts of freedom of thought but within the immeasurably vast metaphysical framework of eternal biblical truth. That life has a higher purpose; that there are objective standards of right and wrong; that we will be held accountable in the next life for how we lived in this one; that there is a personal God and that love, rationality, and humanity are not merely unexplainable materialistic accidents but are related to the origins of the cosmos in God – these and other related concepts enlarge and enrich the

---

[21] Jacques Monod, *Chance and Necessity: An Essay on the Natural Philosophy of Modern Biology*, trans. Austryn Wainhouse (New York: Alfred A. Knopf, 1971), p. 174. Monod thinks this was "perhaps" and "in part" due to the Church's distinction between the sacred and the profane, meaning that the mysteries of nature were not sacred and off-limits, but open to investigation.

[22] Ferguson, *Civilization*, p. 287, all quotes.

soul, and add new dimensions to life. They are "truths of infinite moment . . . the highest themes which can challenge an immortal mind."[23] This contrasts vividly with the emptiness and pointlessness of modern materialism, a poisonous soul-deadening fog that stifles the human spirit and warps our highest aspirations. No wonder modern art, literature, and music are so ugly and inferior. No wonder the modern age with its precious and vastly overrated scientific progress has produced marvels of death, destruction, and inhumanity unknown in the entire previous history of the world. Progress – but in which direction?

D.M. Lloyd-Jones wrote that "the Protestant Reformation liberated men and taught them to think for themselves."[24] This is not to say that the Protestants were always the good guys. Nor is it to deny the many problems and evils of Western society. Unlike the fantasy of Marxism based on its imaginary historical analysis, the Bible does not offer the delusion of paradise on earth. It recognizes that there will be sin and evil until Christ returns, but it gives a higher moral standard, a hope, and a purpose that significantly impacted Western civilization for the good. Luther had a great deal to do with this.

It is no coincidence that the Jews were well (if not perfectly) treated in every single country that emerged out the Reformation. Even in Germany before the catastrophe of the First World War, the Jews had established deep roots and made great social and cultural progress. This was true to such an extent that many Jews were proud of their German cultural heritage. A Reform Jewish prayer book published in Germany in 1818 even went so far as to remove all prayers for a return to Israel, and for the Messiah to come. "They were fully content as Germans and could fulfill all their national aspirations as Germans in Germany,"[25] and had no further need of Israel or of a Messiah.

The worst excesses of secular anti-Jewish ideology that emerged in Germany in the nineteenth century and were foundational to Naziism came not out of the Reformation, but out of the widespread repudiation of Christianity that characterized a significant part of European culture in the beginnings of the modern era. They are more related to Hegel, Fichte, Schopenhauer, and even to Kant than they are to the Reformation. When Hitler wrote in *Mein Kampf* that the Jews had no concept of an afterlife and were nothing but materialists[26] he was elaborating on a theme introduced by Kant, not by Luther. We have seen in chapter 2 the intense hatred of Jews that emerged out

---

[23] Philip Schaff, *History of the Christian Church (vol. 1, Apostolic Christianity from the Birth of Christ to the Death of St. John A.D. 1-100)* (Peabody, Mass: Hendrickson Publishers, 2011), p. 741.

[24] D.M. Lloyd-Jones, *The Puritans: Their Origins and Successors* (Edinburgh: The Banner of Truth Trust, 1987), p. 218.

[25] Prager and Telushkin, *Why the Jews?*, p. 202.

[26] Hitler, *Mein Kampf*, p. 306.

of French secularism and socialism, and was expressed by people who did not believe in or care about Luther or the Bible. Their hatred of Judaism was due to the fact that its most fundamental teachings denied their delusional faith in human reason and progress.[27]

Francis Schaeffer writes, "For a long time Reformation ideas formed the basis of North European culture, and this extended to include that of the United States and English-speaking Canada, etc."[28] This does not mean that those countries were free from common human evils, or that all of the people in them were devout, Bible-believing Christians. It does mean that deeply influential concepts of God, his laws, and the afterlife provided a framework within which individual liberty could flourish along with respect for law. Because of the Bible, there was a sane balance between the social obligations and the political rights of the individual.

Remarkably, noted historian Robert Conquest devotes a chapter of one of his books to explaining how democracy became established in the West without even recognizing Christianity as an integral part of that. He sees religious truth as being related to fanaticism, irrationality, and the excesses of modern secular ideologies, and claims they all spring from the same root of irrationality. He equates the Bible and Marxist dogma as sacred texts to be followed by people in need of absolute truths and final answers. He equates 17th-century English religious extremists and Byzantine mobs fighting about religious issues with Nazis and Communists.[29]

What Conquest and others who share his now common views fail to recognize is that there are infinite and eternal differences between the Absolute Truth of God revealed in Jesus Christ and the Bible on the one hand, and the "Absolute Truths" of modern secularism as revealed to Marx, Lenin, Hitler, Darwin, Stalin and Mao on the other. In placing all sure conviction of truth – except for his own – under the same condemnation, Conquest fails to differentiate between "Do unto others as you would have them do unto you" and "We are liberated from God's law and can create our own paradise here in this life without him."

The Christian idea of Truth is very far from contradictory secular concepts that bubbled up out of the malodorous swamps of German secularism and denial of God. That we have immortal souls and are only being tested here for a short time on earth is a very powerful motive for the elevation of the

---

[27] See Prager and Telushkin, *Why the Jews?* chapters 10 ("Secular Antisemitism: The Enlightenment") and 11 ("Leftist Antisemitism"). That people can totally reject the Bible yet still hate Jews for other reasons is too hard for some people to grasp.

[28] Francis Schaeffer, *The God Who is There* (Downers Grove, IL: IVP Books, 1982), p. 108.

[29] Robert Conquest, *Reflections on a Ravaged Century* (New York: W.W. Norton, 2001), pp. 40, 51-52, 55.

individual personality above the demands of the state and of society. The loss of the sense of the divine origin and eternal destiny of the human soul is one of the main starting points for fascism, which in the end inevitably subordinates the individual to the group (since there is nothing higher than the group, personified by the state).

Alcide de Gasperi (a victim of Mussolini and later leader of Italy's first postwar government in 1945) rightly said: "The theoretical and practical principles of fascism are the antithesis of the Christian concept of the state, which lays down that the natural rights of personality, family, and society exist before the state."[30] Or, as Nicolai Berdyaev put it: ". . . the Christian ethic is more individual than social; for the human soul is worth more than all the kingdoms of this world."[31] Human worth as derived from God was an essential concept in the development of Western society. Its disappearance contributed directly to the horrors we are trying now to understand.

This is hard (if not impossible) for many limited modern thinkers to grasp, especially when they have come to think of the religious impulse in and of itself as false, irrational, harmful and potentially dangerous. When a highly praised historian writes that the vicious and brutal secular mass murderer and tyrant Lenin had a zeal for humanity comparable to some Christian saints, we realize how remote much of our modern intelligentsia is from a fair understanding of Christianity. Since when does the "love of saints" have anything to do with Lenin's police state, his secret police, his executions? To say that Lenin was animated by the same spirit and zeal which motivated a true man of God is an amazing statement by someone who obviously has no understanding of Christ's teachings, or of the many Christians who have followed those teachings well enough to live common, peaceful and ordinary lives far below the exalted vision of the ivory tower historian.

Paul Johnson recognizes that Lenin's methods "corresponded in a curious way to the Marxist perception of the world." [32] Curious, that an avowed Marxist should look at things in a Marxist way. A true man of God, according to the Bible, unlike Marx and Lenin, does not aim to bring about paradise on earth. He does not think that human reason is a sufficient guide, or that dictatorship of the favored group will bring peace on earth (after all of the enemies of human happiness have been crushed like insects). The Bible-believing Christian knows that full happiness cannot be obtained in this life

---

[30] Paul Johnson, *Modern Times: The World from the Twenties to the Nineties* (New York: Perennial Classics, 1992), p. 579.

[31] Nicolai Berdyaev, *Christian Existentialism: A Berdyaev Anthology,* (New York: Harper Torchbooks, 1965), p. 196.

[32] Johnson, *Modern Times,* p. 64. Johnson even admits that Marx recognized the necessity of and advocated the use of "revolutionary terror" to destroy the old society and establish the new, and quotes Marx to this effect (p. 66).

due to the sinfulness of human nature, and so looks for the final resolution of all injustice in the world to come. Only the most fanatical secularists with their man-centered, self-centered world views are vain enough to believe that they can reshape humanity according to their theoretical blueprints, and that their opponents can be slaughtered in the millions without a qualm for the sake of an imaginary future happiness.

Linking Lenin to Christians rather than to Marx's hateful intolerance shows – in my view – a sad disorientation. Both Marx and Lenin were fanatical and intolerant atheists. Both had a burning zeal to destroy the status quo, and build their fantasy world on the ashes. Both had contempt for those who contradicted them; were separated from reality and ignorant of human nature and real-world economics; and relied on dictatorship to impose their solutions (which they knew would never be accepted otherwise). Marx's famed dictatorship of the proletariat was not just a theory or words in a book. He rightly understood that religion, capitalism and private property would never be eliminated without it.

Both Marx and Lenin had contempt for democracy, and both made the ludicrous claim that their nonsensical theories were "scientific." Finally – and this is their deep spiritual kinship with Hitler – both thought they were the saviors of mankind, and those who disagreed with them were enemies to be destroyed. Yes, they had differences, and Lenin adapted Marx to a different situation, but in spirit Lenin, Marx, and Hitler all thought they could remake the world according to their liking, in defiance of God and his laws. Their deluded theories – all of them predicated upon a rejection of the Bible – brought misery and ruin to countless millions.

Can some people really not see the difference between adherence to the truth of Christ, and adherence to the useless fantasy of a paradise established after private property and religion have been abolished by the dictatorship [!?] of the proletariat? No, they can't see the difference. To them, Christ's heavenly kingdom as exemplified by the Sermon on the Mount is comparable to the earthly kingdom of fanatics like Lenin, Hitler, Mao, Stalin, and Castro, men who wanted to exterminate or enslave the worthless wretches that dared to oppose the future happiness of mankind as dreamed of by them in their infallible wisdom. It is with good reason that Thomas Oden contrasted modern arrogance with Christianity's sane and realistic preference for "modest, incremental shifts toward proximate justice" instead of "totally revolutionary redefinitions of the universal human order. This requires a scaling down of social planning and a scaling up of personal accountability."[33]

Biblical Christianity as revived by the Reformation (however imperfectly) was foundational to Western democracy, individual liberty, and the

---

[33] Thomas C. Oden, *Requiem: A Lament in Three Movements*, (Nashville: Abingdon Press, 1995) p. 126.

subordination of the state to a higher law. It also helped to restrain (if not to eliminate) sin, which is why in our post-biblical age we are now having an explosion of such evils as crime, drugs, homosexuality, pornography, abortion and general immorality – and, not coincidentally, a huge increase in the power of government with a corresponding loss of individual rights. There's no need to mention the Crusades or the Inquisition here either. They had nothing to do with the teachings of Christ, and have nothing to do with the vast majority of Christians who have ever lived.

This benign influence of biblical Christianity was greatly facilitated by Martin Luther – and his writings had such a deep and rapid impact because of the many spiritually liberating and healing aspects of the biblical teachings that he drew attention to. Nevertheless, he has been criticized by Christians for such statements as "sin boldly," and for offering an extreme guarantee of salvation no matter how much we sin. Those were reckless comments in private writing however, dashed off I suppose in haste and under pressure, not at all representative of his best and most widely circulated works – and which of us have not written or said things we should not have? In his *Commentary on Galatians* and in his *Preface to Romans*, to name only two works, Luther states very plainly, at length and in depth, that faith in Christ does not give us license to sin openly, that our acceptance by God in Christ should not make us consider sin to be a slight thing. "God always hateth sin," Luther wrote, and stressed that our forgiveness in Christ should make us want to avoid sin and resist its innate and natural workings, not to acquiesce tamely in it.[34] To my mind, Christians who have not read Luther's theology should not criticize it.

Jesus said that as we judge others, so will we be judged. We would not want others to judge us by our worst mistakes, our most foolish and hasty comments, but by everything, good and bad, on balance. Seen in this light Luther was wrong on occasion, sometimes badly wrong, and by no means to be put on a pedestal, but he was very right on others and had overall a very positive impact on the development of church history. To this day people study his writings on the authority of the Bible, our condemnation for sin, and our salvation in Christ alone with profit and deep edification – and they do this while recognizing Luther's various mistakes.

But, unfortunately, Luther attacked the Jews. For this reason he is regularly mentioned in discussions of the Holocaust. An objective examination of Luther's life and work however, including his comments about Jews, will show his ideas to have been very different from the bizarre secular ideologies of the 19th and 20th centuries. Personally, I think Luther's fall into the sin of anger and bitterness against the Jews towards the end of his life can be

---

[34] Martin Luther, *Martin Luther: Selections from His Writings*, ed. John Dillenberger (New York: Anchor Books, 1962), pp. 151-152 (from *A Commentary on St. Paul's Epistle to the Galatians*).

compared to David's sin with Bathsheba. David, a far greater man than Luther, fell into a far more terrible sin with no extenuating circumstances. The prophet told David, and David admitted, that he had had Uriah killed and stolen his wife. This sin was not quickly done either in a moment of passion, but was maintained over a period of time.

What would we think of someone who dismissed David because of his fall and gave no credit to his other qualities – or used David's sin as proof that there was something innately wrong with Judaism? It is amazing that a great man of God like David could fall as he did, but that does not negate his overall achievement. I believe the same can be said of Luther. It is sad that a great man like Luther should stumble and fall flat on his face, but that is not the whole of the story. Some comments that a Russian scholar, Yuri Yarim-Agaev, made about Solzhenitsyn are very relevant here:

> I feel it somehow wrong to start talking about one of the greatest men of the 20th century by discussing a rather inconsequential mistake of his old age. We should define first the broader context of his life and achievements. We should judge him first and foremost by his deeds, which had a great effect on our civilization, not by the quotes from his little known works, which barely had any influence.[35]

It will be said that Luther's tract was far from inconsequential, that it had tragic results – but I will argue and attempt to establish elsewhere that the unique manifestation of evil that was the Holocaust first began to assume a vague form in the ideas of the nineteenth and late eighteenth centuries. Luther's tract *On the Jews and Their Lies* did not have a great influence on Protestant Christians, most of whom never bothered with it. John Wesley and John Bunyan, two highly influential figures in English Protestantism, benefitted from Luther and were even significantly influenced by him, yet had no interest in his then obscure tract about the Jews. If they had read it, they would have easily recognized that Luther was wrong.

Many serious Christians have studied Luther carefully and been influenced by him, while at the same time disagreeing with him on various important issues (such as church polity, infant baptism, the significance of communion, predestination, or other points). Many of them have not even looked at *On the Jews and their Lies*. I read Luther off and on for years and never heard of the tract. When I first heard of it I did not believe it, it was so different from the important works of his I had read. Reading it for the first time was a cause not of influence but of disappointment at Luther's decline in his senescence.

---

[35] Jamie Glazov, *High Noon for America: The Coming Showdown* (Brantford, Ontario: Mantua Books, 2012), p. 105.

Secularists may find it hard to understand that people can esteem Luther (at his best) as a great man of God, and yet be totally uninfluenced by his tract against the Jews. There was high drama in the spiritual contests of the Reformation, and Luther's powerful indictments of a corrupt ecclesiastical establishment, as well as his sometimes extraordinarily deep biblical teachings, had an impact few other single individuals have ever had. Were it not for the unique historical developments of the 20th century (for which few will blame Luther), his anti-Jewish comments would be forgotten by all but Luther scholars, a matter of complete indifference to many Christians who can continue to benefit from his extremely influential Reformation writings on the importance of the Bible alone, not man-made traditions, as the rule of faith and practice.

In II Samuel the prophet Nathan says to David that because of his sin with Bathsheba, he had "given great occasion to the enemies of the Lord to blaspheme" (12:14). The same can be said of Luther. By his sinful attacks on the Jews he gave great occasion to the enemies of biblical Christianity, and enabled them to portray the teachings of Christ and the apostles as part of the problem. Those who have read Luther's most important Reformation writings will readily see, however, that the sound biblical principles he espoused were not related to evils that were to emerge hundreds of years later from ideas and circumstances with which Luther had nothing to do. Too many comments about Luther are written in hostility to Christianity and out of an eagerness to find fault.

The main focus of the Reformation was not "the Jews," and to claim that Protestants were significantly influenced by Luther here is a serious misrepresentation (in the section on the Christians in the Third Reich it will be argued that the failure of the German churches to speak out for the Jews is attributable to various reasons, including simple fear, not a tract of Luther's). Anabaptists were more harshly treated than Jews in the Reformation and Counter-Reformation, and their views were considered to be more of a threat to the church and to society than was Jewish failure to accept the New Testament. But, some people who write about this are not really interested in historical fact.

As has already been said, if Luther had died earlier (say, in 1542 instead of 1546) we would not need to be discussing this obscure tract, which (to my knowledge) was endorsed by no other Protestant leader and was considered extreme even in Luther's day. But, let's look at *On the Jews and Their Lies* more carefully, and see what Luther actually said. To begin with, it is essential to stress what he did not believe. He did not believe that the Aryans were the master race, destined to rule the world. He did not believe that the Germans in Europe should be united into a single giant state that would dominate all of its neighbors. Modern German nationalism did not exist in Luther's time. Germany was divided into many small states, cities, principalities and

61

kingdoms, and national unification lay in the distant future. In this respect as in others, we can agree with the historian who said that the "remote religious cultures and hierarchical politics of the Reformation" could not be directly connected to the Third Reich.[36]

One writer who does his very best to pin as much blame for the Holocaust on Luther as he can concedes that antisemitism in Germany "grew rapidly during the Napoleonic era" and "became a forceful ideology in the 1870s."[37] This is blamed on the "Christian right" – yet it was not traditional Christianity but rather increasingly powerful forces of secularism that began to stress the then new and progressive idea of national unification early in the 1800s. The forces of conservatism were more likely to support the maintenance of the status quo and the existing divisions of Germany with its separate kingdoms than to advocate what was then considered progressive or even radical change. The growth of German nationalism was more directly related to romanticism and to idealist philosophy than to anything in the Bible (which attaches no importance whatever to nationalism).

It needs to be repeated that nationalism, which is now considered to be a concern of the right, was in Germany in the first half of the nineteenth century considered to be progressive and democratic. National unification meant the end of numerous small reactionary and autocratic governments, and – it was anticipated – would hasten the establishment of democracy and freedom of thought. This included of course freedom to criticize the churches and Christian teaching, and the increase in open rejection of Christianity directly paralleled the rise of the completely unbiblical phenomenon of extreme nationalism. The authority of the churches – both Catholic and Protestant – was greatly weakened in this period and in the succeeding decades before 1914. During the same period, nationalism increased in vehemence as people turned more and more to the nation for meaning, hope, and inner fulfillment. Luther would have rightly called such an emphasis idolatry.

Attempting to explain the origins of the Holocaust, Weiss examines Luther's psychology, his conversion, his inner turmoil, devoting more than ten pages to Luther because of the Holocaust which happened four hundred years later, while Ernst Haeckel, the social Darwinist who had many ideas close to and even identical to Hitler's, is mentioned twice in the index and gets approximately one paragraph. We find German racial superiority and life as merciless struggle in Haeckel, not in Luther. Nietzsche is mentioned (according to the index) only once in the entire book, and that in passing – Nietzsche, who said the weak and the inferior should be exterminated;

---

[36] Richard Evans, *The Coming of the Third Reich* (New York: Penguin, 2005), p. 2.

[37] John Weiss, *Ideology of Death: Why the Holocaust Happened in Germany* (Chicago: Elephant paperbacks, 1997), p. viii (both quotes).

Nietzsche, who said that sympathy for the weak was worse than any vice; Nietzsche, the arrogant elitist who proclaimed the natural rightness of slavery and declared that people of lofty spirits (like himself) should have contempt for the common herd; who decreed dogmatically that war was good and strong and healthy and preferable to the peace of the weak (a view not exactly supported by his own somewhat less than dazzling record of military heroism in the Prussian army).

These are only a few of the ideas that, taken in context and in writings completed and published or prepared for publication by Nietzsche himself, link him directly to the Third Reich. Much more could also be said about Gobineau, Fichte, Hegel (the father of modern totalitarianism), Kant, Wagner and others. For the present, suffice it to say in this paragraph that Hitler visited the Nietzsche archive more than once, not any memorials or sites honoring Luther. That Jewish Christianity had corrupted Europe was a Nazi theme we find in Nietzsche's *Antichrist*, not in Luther – but Nietzsche's message of self-glorification and total freedom is music to the ears of modernists, while Luther's doctrine of the need for repentance from sin and belief in God is anathema. This means that Luther gets raked over the coals for comments irrelevant to his main life's work, while Nietzsche gets a free pass for the most inhumane and brutal ideas ever presented in the guise of philosophy (ideas that are consistently evaded and whitewashed by his often less than fully objective admirers).

How we approach these questions depends on our presuppositions. People who share Nietzsche's belief in the absence of God and his resulting egotistical emphasis on the primacy of the self assume that basic ideas which are true and good cannot possibly have anything to do with Hitler's ideology, which was wrong and bad. At the same time, they see National Socialism as harmful and irrational, and Luther's basic beliefs in the existence of the biblical God as harmful and irrational, and so find it very easy to make a connection. On the other hand, those who consider Nietzsche's views to be wrong, destructive, and bad can easily link him to Hitler. And, sharing Luther's basic understanding of a God who can be understood through the Bible, they can easily see that – in spite of Luther's glaring faults – he did not contribute to the emergence of National Socialism. Many people have linked Hitler more to later German philosophy than to Luther.

Unfortunately, some are more interested in discrediting Christianity through Luther than in understanding the environment out of which Hitler actually emerged. We are none of us after all detached and purely objective thinking machines who consider only the facts without being influenced by our presuppositions – and those presuppositions are not always known to us. There are those who do not want to consider the possibility that the denial of traditional religion and the reliance on human reason alone may have been a mistake. Hence, the many profoundly secular emphases in so much of Hitler's ideology must be ignored, minimized, or explained away while religion is attacked with relish instead – and this by people who brag and boast of their self-authenticating rationality.

It has often been observed that philosophy did play a role in fertilizing the soil for Hitler. For example, the importance of Fichte, Hegel, Herder and others to the emergence of modern Germany is a commonplace of intellectual history. This seemingly abstruse topic is of more relevance to the Holocaust than many realize. When Hegel posited that there was a vague spiritual force working through history to bring about cultural progress, and that that this force used national groups – first the Greeks and the Romans, and now the Germans – he laid the basis for the increasingly extreme belief that the German race was responsible for the future advancement of mankind. In order to fulfill this higher purpose and to remain in touch with the higher power, the Germans needed to be authentic, pure, and free from foreign influence.

The cultural and racial purity of the German people came to be seen increasingly over time as vital to the future well-being of the human race. This was a foundational element of the proto-Nazi Folkish movement (as exemplified by Lagarde, Langbehn, Wagner, and H. S. Chamberlain, to name only a few). Such ideas were of course inconceivable in a more traditionally Christian context, and there is hence more than a little truth in the statement "The primary cause of Naziism lies in philosophy. Not economics, not psychology, and not even politics."[38] And, we might also add, not in Luther's (and many others') desire to get free of dead medieval dogmas. The source just cited goes on to state that "National Socialism was first a philosophy of life believed and advocated by highly intelligent men and women. Professors, public intellectuals, Nobel Prize-winners [the author names three, two of them in physics and one in literature] – all powerful minds working at the cutting edges of their disciplines."

A different author, a historian of science who does not blame National Socialism on Luther's magic power, refers to the "pliability of even so-called intellectuals" and their susceptibility to Nazi ideology. He further observes: "The readiness with which large numbers of physicians, jurists, scientists, and other academics lent themselves to the abominations committed under the last of these [referring to Nazi schemes for race purification] show [sic] that

---

[38] Stephen R.C. Hicks, *Nietzsche and the Nazis: A Personal View* (Loves Park, IL: Ockham's Razor Publishing, 2010), pp. 10-11 (both quotes this paragraph). This is not by the way a Christian book, and Luther is mentioned and quoted only once, towards the end. Hicks is more interested in criticisms of Nietzsche. While highlighting important differences between Nietzsche and the Nazis, Hicks notes profound similarities as well, including: hostility to capitalism, democracy and liberalism; the belief that war and violence were natural and healthy; an emphasis on will, instinct, and feeling over reason; and an elitist contempt for the masses. Much more needs to be said about this elsewhere.

scientific literacy by itself provides no immunization"[39] – meaning immunization against irrationality. The claim that religion is irrational and hence a source of danger while science is rational and hence a bulwark against extremism and fanaticism is a claim unsupported by a full consideration of empirical evidence. The belief that those who reject religion and rely on reason alone are therefore automatically rational and objective is a potentially harmful fantasy.

There is much more to Christianity than the Crusades, witch burnings, and the Inquisition, and people who constantly point to those as evidence of religious fanaticism while ignoring a much greater weight of contrary evidence are driven not by pure reason and logic, but by other motives. Nowhere is this more evident than in discussions of the purported origins of National Socialism. Some people seem to be unaware that Germany was considered among the world leaders in science and technology in the late nineteenth century, and that German culture in the fifty years before Hitler came to power is not represented in general histories as built solidly on belief in the Bible or other principles of the Reformation.

Writing in the 1920s, the Italian Marxist Antonio Gramsci referred scornfully to "orthodox religion, which has by now quite shriveled up."[40] He was speaking of his own country, but the same could have been said of Europe as a whole, Germany not excluded. Speaking of Italy, I hope no one has had the temerity to blame Mussolini's thoroughly modern and secular national-socialist-fascism on Catholicism. Gramsci also wrote of the disintegration of the old social order (both political and religious) and of the opportunities this offered to revolutionary new ideologies introducing a "new conception of the world" which included of course a "new morality" as well. These *new conceptions of the world* with their *new moralities*, whether of Communism on the left or of fascism on the right, emerged out of the fogs and mists of modernism, not out of Lutheranism, general Protestantism or Catholicism.

Great changes profoundly influenced Germany in the centuries following Luther, and to automatically link him to everything that followed is historically illiterate. For example, the charge that Luther was the originator of German nationalism fails to take into account the many historical and cultural changes that facilitated the emergence of virulent German nationalism in the 19th century. The Reformation was international in scope, and while Luther did write against ecclesiastical abuses in Germany – he was after all a German – his critique had such a wide resonance because it dealt with biblical and

---

[39] Gerald Holton, *Science and Anti-Science* (Cambridge, Massachusetts: Harvard University Press, 1993), p. 181.

[40] Antonio Gramsci, *The Antonio Gramsci Reader: Selected Writings 1916-1935* (New York: New York University Press, 2000), p. 213 (first quote), p. 192 (last two quotes).

European, not merely German issues. The fanatical and irrational nationalism of the 19th and 20th centuries has no biblical basis, and emerged after and because of the rejection of higher biblical authority.

Luther was in no sense of the word a modern nationalist. His *Address to the Nobility of the German Nation*, which someone ominously linked to modern German nationalism in a book on the Holocaust, did not call for the Germans to unite on the basis of race and become a massive power that could dominate Europe and seize more territory. Germany at that time was divided into hundreds of small kingdoms, cities, and other political entities, and this was no problem for Luther. His concern was ecclesiastical, and his intent was to inform German rulers that they did not need to submit to the dictates of the papacy. Luther's most fundamental ideas were not uniquely German or nationalistic. That is why they so rapidly took root in many countries outside of Germany. It would help if some people would learn more about Luther before analyzing him and his influence. When Luther spoke about serving "his beloved Germans" he was not talking about twentieth century issues of political unification, racial preservation, conquest and domination. He was talking about spiritual things, especially about a spirituality liberated from medieval errors, without blind and forced subservience to often corrupt and cruel ecclesiastical authorities.

In the above mentioned *Address*, which can be linked to Hitler only by first ignoring its contents and second by jumping over more than four hundred years of German history, Luther offers twenty-seven ideas for reform. These have to do mostly with relations between the various German states and Rome. Church law, finances, ecclesiastical authority ("No one should ever again kiss the pope's feet"),[41] the marriage of priests (allowable), monasteries and masses, letters of indulgence, educational reform and the unjustified opulence of the nobility – the work has nothing to do with the Holocaust.

An obscure work of Luther's (*Dr. Martin Luther's Warning to His Dear German People*) had to do with Emperor Charles the V's threat in 1530 to eliminate Protestantism by force. Luther discusses refusal to obey the government in matters of faith; the possibility of resistance; the fault of the Roman Church in wanting to compel uniformity of faith; clarifications of the Protestant position; and many other issues of religion and society – not the Jews, not German supremacy, not political totalitarianism, not imperialism, racism or *Lebensraum*. It should not be necessary to state the obvious point that Luther was a man of the sixteenth century, not of the twentieth, and his main concerns were not those of the modern age.

Nineteenth-century German super-patriots like Heinrich von Treitschke made a lot of noise about Luther and tried to claim him, only because he was a great German and for no other reason. They had no interest in Calvin, many of

---

[41] Luther, *Selections from His Writings*, p. 441.

whose ideas were identical or close to Luther's, because Calvin was French (there is even a great deal of the supposedly Calvinistic doctrine of predestination in Luther's *Bondage of the Will*). Neither did those who in a totally different context later tried to puff up Luther into a great national liberator according to their own nationalistic fantasies have any understanding of or belief in the main ideas that motivated Luther. The drive to unify Germany politically under the aegis of Prussia came from a nationalistic love of earthly power and glory seen many times in history in many parts of the world. This was the result of human sin, not of Reformation principles.

The "German philosophers, politicians, and theologians who interpreted the Reformation as the first great expression of the Germanic soul"[42] at the same time rejected biblical Christianity and traditional religion – and that is true even of "theologians" who in Germany had long since abandoned belief in the Bible. Theological "liberals," who were often little more than Kantian and Hegelian philosophers dabbling in Romanticism and covered with a thin veneer of religious rhetoric, were delighted to take Luther's denial of Catholic dogma and go on to extend it in the name of spiritual liberty to the denial of biblical dogma as well. Hence their misguided devotion to the German nation, a devotion that was closer to Fichte than to anything in the Bible or in Luther, where the eternal destiny of the immortal soul is far more important than questions of national boundaries or of ethnic identity.

Some who have claimed that Luther was the father of German nationalism find support for their view in the writings of Treitschke and others – though many antiquated comments in other fields by those same boastful Prussian nationalists are now easily recognizable as simply ridiculous. Their comments about Luther's nationalism should be equally considered. That is after all a strange father that comes along nearly 300 years before his son is born (dating the emergence of modern German nationalism from around the beginning of the nineteenth century). It can safely be said that Napoleon had more to do with the emergence of the modern German nation than Luther did. That the German people, the *Deutsche Volk*, emerged out of the Reformation split between Protestantism and Catholicism, that Luther created the German people by his translation of the Bible [43] – these are the sort of extreme and ahistorical simplifications that greatly complicate these discussions. How did the modern French, Spanish, Italian, English and Russian nationalities and languages manage to emerge without a Luther?

Luther understood the basic biblical teaching that a Spaniard, a Frenchman, a Pole, or a Jew who dies and goes to heaven is better off than a German who dies and goes to hell, and (in agreement with Scripture) had not the slightest

---

[42] Weiss, *Ideology of Death*, p. 29.

[43] Eric Metaxas, *Bonhoeffer: Pastor, Martyr, Prophet, Spy – A Righteous Gentile vs. The Third Reich* (Nashville: Thomas Nelson, 2010), p. 20.

concept of *Deutschland über alles.* "Germany over everything" – this contemptible and dim-witted sentiment was the direct result of later idolatrous attempts to replace God with the nation, to find meaning and purpose in the nation. It was Fichte, not Luther, who advocated national unity on the basis of a common language transcending arbitrary political boundaries, and when the film director Leni Riefenstahl wanted to give her beloved Fuhrer a gift, she gave him Fichte's writings, not Luther's.[44]

Houston Stewart Chamberlain, an early supporter of Hitler whose ideas are commonly linked to National Socialism, a man who was praised in the Nazi press and by Hitler himself, made a few comments about the Reformation. He stated that the Reformation should be understood from the standpoint of German "national psychology," and in considering it we should "pay no attention to any dogmatic disputes concerning creed." This would have been a surprise to the people involved at the time. That doctrines of the papacy, the mass, the church, the interpretation of biblical teachings, and salvation were not important; that the real issue was merely "a revolt . . . of the Germanic soul against un-Germanic spiritual tyranny" – these are opinions of someone who was not approaching the Reformation from a Lutheran or from a Catholic standpoint.[45]

It is not difficult to imagine what Hitler's reaction would have been if someone had given him a book of Luther's stating that we were all (including Hitler) guilty of sin; that we were in danger of everlasting punishment in hell and there was no way we could earn God's favor by our good works; that our only hope was the work of Christ accomplished for us on the cross, as we read in the Bible which is the inspired and infallible Word of God; that all of the wealth and power and glory of the world mean nothing if in the end we are cast away by God and sent to a place of eternal torment. Hitler's reaction would have been at bottom that of any good secularist – disgust and contempt, amusement, or perhaps bored indifference.

Every sincere Catholic and Protestant of the 16th century would have instantly recognized the glories of modern nationalism as false. They would have unhesitatingly rejected the folly of Fichte's claims that our freedom lay in the Fatherland and our immortality was only the ongoing survival of our nation. For those people who have actually read with some understanding a

---

[44] Timothy Ryback, *Hitler's Private Library: The Books that Shaped his Life* (London: Vintage Books, 2010), pp. 122-123.

[45] Houston Stewart Chamberlain, *Foundations of the Nineteenth Century*, trans. John Lees (Lexington, KY: Elibron Classics, 2013) (chapter 6, "The Entrance of the Germanic People Into the History of the World"), p. 512. Significantly, Chamberlain passed quickly over the Reformation to discuss more important racial questions, including the shape of skulls, fair-haired Slavs, race mixture, and so on. Elsewhere Chamberlain explicitly condemned antisemitism based on "religious prejudice with its dangerous bias" (p. 338).

few of Luther's best and most important Reformation works, even the shorter ones, it does not require explanation that the National Socialist agenda or even simply modern nationalism in its political sense are nowhere to be seen. To claim that in Luther "Germanness and Christianity were effectively united"[46] is to miss the entire point of the Reformation and to completely mischaracterize his achievement. Many American Evangelicals today have little interest in or knowledge of the Reformation.

Neither did Luther believe that the Jews were plotting to corrupt the purity of Aryan blood so they could destroy the German people and rule the world. Isaiah chapter 60, as well as other Old Testament prophecies about a re-established Israel, were to the Reformers and to Catholics as well the inspired word of God. They foretold a time of universal peace when all of the world would be freely united in the worship of the one true God as manifested in Jesus Christ. To modern secular anti-Semites, on the other hand, such scriptures were only proof of the Jewish lust for world domination. Thus, H. S. Chamberlain could write of Isaiah 60, "absolutely forged, from the first to the last word, are such chapters as *Isaiah* lx., that famous Messianic prophecy, according to which all the kings of the world will lie in the dust before the Jews . . . ."[47] Hitler also referred to the Jewish "drive to seize world control," and stated that "Jahwe's prophecy is only an expression of this clear objective."[48]

Luther's conventional and traditional religious antisemitism was of the sort that did not, and could not, produce a Holocaust in the thousand years and more of European Christianity that preceded the Reformation. Many writers in the century and more before 1933 emerged from the "Enlightenment," from Romanticism, and from an overall turning away from traditional religion. It was their untrammeled human reason, emancipated from biblical teaching, that produced new ideas fundamental to National Socialism.

It has been said that Hitler quoted Luther – but Hitler quoted Torah as well, and used "an eye for an eye and a tooth for a tooth" to justify his invasion of Poland. In *Mein Kampf* Hitler referred to Luther only once, briefly, as a great reformer, along with Frederick the Great and Richard Wagner.[49] When Hitler

---

[46] Metaxas, *Bonhoeffer*, p. 91.

[47] Chamberlain, *Foundations of the Nineteenth Century*, p. 479 (chapter 5, "The Entrance of the Jews into the History of the West"). Two of the main themes in this chapter are: (a) the Jewish corruption of German blood through interbreeding, which led to decline in the crucial struggle for racial dominance; and (b) the insidious, harmful influence of Jewish values and ideas on European culture through the Semitic corruption of an originally Aryan Christianity. Chamberlain goes to some trouble to show that Jesus was an Aryan, not a Jew.

[48] Werner Maser, *Hitler's Letters and Notes* (New York: Harper and Row, 1974), p. 241.

[49] Hitler, *Mein Kampf*, p. 213.

analyzed the Jewish "problem" at length in his book, he didn't use any of Luther's main points – neither are Hitler's ideas of racial purity, Aryan supremacy, and Nature's ordained struggle for survival of the fittest to be found in Luther (or in Aquinas, Augustine, Melanchthon, or any other recognized and authoritative Christian teachers).

If some secular extremists seem to think that the sixteenth century is more important for an understanding of Hitler than the nineteenth century, my guess is that they are motivated by an emotional need to attack Christianity, not by reason, logic, facts or evidence. It is no surprise that Hitler specifically rejected religious antisemitism as inadequate. Criticizing the nineteenth-century Austrian antisemitism of the Christian Social Party he stated that it "was based on religious ideas instead of racial knowledge . . . If the worst came to the worst, a splash of baptismal water could always save the business and the Jew at the same time."[50] Like other secular anti-Semites – especially H. S. Chamberlain, whose ideas he often shared – Hitler thought traditional religious antisemitism was superficial and prevented a genuinely "scientific" understanding of the Jewish problem. He also stated in *Mein Kampf* that both the Protestant and the Catholic clergy were of no use in the struggle for German racial dominance in pre-World War I Austria.[51] Perhaps in this spiritually primitive technological age it needs also to be explained that biblical teachings are totally contrary in every respect to Hitler's mad dreams of racial purity. Only people who rejected the Bible and relied solely on their own wisdom would be foolish enough to concoct such theories.

A sincerely converted Jew was accepted by traditional religious anti-Semites, but not by the Nazis. Hitler was not concerned with out-of-date and unscientific religious ideas. He did quote the overtly anti-Christian Schopenhauer on the Jews, though, and used anti-Jewish ideas found in Kant, Richard Wagner, Houston Stewart Chamberlain, and other more recent antisemites. He certainly didn't quote the passage from *On the Jews and Their Lies* in which Luther referred to the Jews as a people of "great patriarchs, excellent kings, and outstanding prophets," honored and chosen by God "above all other nations on earth," entrusted with God's Word, and used to prepare the world for the coming of Christ.[52]

Neither did Hitler quote Luther's *Preface to the Psalms*, where Luther said "No books of moral tales and no legends of saints which have been written, or ever will be written, are to my mind as noble as the Book of Psalms . . . the book contains divine and helpful doctrines and commandments of every kind.

---

[50] Ibid., p. 119-120.

[51] Ibid., p. 109.

[52] Martin Luther, *On the Jews and Their Lies*, trans. Martin H. Bertram (Luther's Works American Edition vol. 47, Philadelphia: Fortress Press, 1971), p. 163.

It should be precious and dear to us."[53] The accusation that Luther despised the Old Testament is, like many other statements about him, wrong. Luther considered it to be the inspired Word of God, translated it into German, and appealed to it often to support his views in Reformation debates. We don't have to believe everything we hear about Luther.

In *On the Jews and Their Lies* Luther assumes the historical accuracy of the biblical narrative. He elaborates on the Exodus of the Jews from Israel at some length, and says that if need be God could have parted not merely the Red Sea, but cliffs of solid rock, and led the Jews through them, since it was absolutely impossible that the word of God should be false or fail.[54] This is completely opposite to Hitler's contemptuous dismissal of the Old Testament – he asserted that the Jews had never even had their own country, and had never been nomads either, but were merely parasites with no culture of their own.[55] Hitler's understanding of the Bible as being historically unreliable and a merely human contrivance is of course squarely in the mainstream of all respectable secular thought.

It also worth pointing out that the Reformation led to increased emphasis on Christianity's Hebrew roots. Luther supported Johann Reuchlin in his struggle to prevent the Talmud and other Hebrew literature from being banned and (like all of the other Reformers) constantly appealed to the prophets and other Old Testament writers to support their views on doctrine. It has been well said that "despite Luther's anti-Jewish outbursts, the Reformation he launched gave new emphasis to Christianity's Hebraic roots for the first time since the primitive church."[56] Luther would have readily accepted the modern American Christian writer A. W. Tozer's uncontroversial statement that the authentically biblical concept of God is derived from Hebrew and Christian sources.[57] Paul de Lagarde, on the other hand, a racist and nationalist writer in the late nineteenth century, "considered Luther the greatest German hero, who had erred only by preserving much that was Jewish and rotten in Christianity"[58] – this included the teachings of the Jew Paul.

The Confessing Church's unwillingness to adopt the Aryan Paragraph denying the right of anyone of Jewish descent to hold church office, while far

---

[53] Luther, *Preface to the Psalms,* in *Selections from His Writings*, pp. 37-38.

[54] Luther, *On the Jews and Their Lies*, p. 209.

[55] Hitler, *Mein Kampf,* pp. 303-304.

[56] Gene Edward Veith, Jr. *Modern Fascism: Liquidating the Judeo-Christian Worldview* (St. Louis: Concordia Publishing House, 1993), p. 52 (quoting Paul Gottfried's "Heidegger and the Nazis," *The Salisbury Review*, Sept. 1988, p. 35). Veith might have mentioned that Luther's finest and most influential works, works that were eagerly read throughout Europe, contained no such outbursts.

[57] A. W. Tozer, *The Knowledge of the Holy* (Colorado Springs: Authentic, 2008), p 5.

[58] Weiss, *Ideology of Death*, p. 139.

short of direct rebellion against Hitler, was still a clear statement of the essential humanity of the Jews, and struck at the heart of Nazi racial theory. Hitler himself recognized the Protestant rejection of his racial theories when he wrote in *Mein Kampf* that Protestantism failed to accept his analysis of the centrality of the Jewish racial problem.[59] And it is well known that the strongly Protestant heritage of Denmark, Holland and Norway did not at all incline people to sympathize with Nazi goals.

In spite of Luther's anger, in all of his years of primary influence when he had the ear of Germany and of much of Europe, he never publicly called for the killing of Jews, and did not write harshly against them. He has been accused either of engineering the expulsion of Jews from Saxony, or at least of not interceding on their behalf when the Elector of Saxony decided to expel them. "Engineering" and "not interceding for" are two very different things. I don't know if the accusation that Luther caused this can be substantiated. They had been expelled from other places, including Saxony (they later returned), before Luther was even born. Luther was not the close political advisor of Frederick, the Elector of Saxony (though Frederick acknowledged having been influenced by Luther's writings). Luther's failure to intercede (or even his "engineering") can be related to other ideas we need to examine, and does not necessarily have anything to do with Auschwitz. If it can somehow be shown that he specifically instigated this expulsion (which I have not yet seen), this was again conventional (though sinful and unChristlike) thinking that led to expulsions from Spain, England, France, and other parts of Europe – but never to attempted extermination. The Holocaust was a uniquely modern phenomenon, as is not hard to demonstrate.

So – repeating that this was in no way central to Luther's main goals – what was his problem with Jews? Part of it may have been related to his health. He had prolonged and serious health problems in old age, and I have seen in my own family how that can over time work significant personality change for the worse. One Luther biographer suggested that blockage by kidney stones could have led to uremic poisoning, which is medically known to have an adverse effect on the temperament.[60] D. M. Lloyd-Jones, who had medical training before going into the pastorate, wondered if health issues could have been behind Luther's hostile comments about Calvin and Zwingli, who agreed with him on many essential points.[61]

Historian Gordon Craig comments on Otto von Bismarck's increased irascibility, even vindictiveness, in old age, and stated that "his undoubted

---

[59] Hitler, *Mein Kampf*, p. 113.

[60] James A. Nestingen, *Martin Luther: A Life* (Minneapolis: Augsburg Books, 2003), p. 101.

[61] Lloyd-Jones, *The Puritans*, p. 227. He says, "I am not at all sure but that at that point one can almost invoke medical illness in the case of Luther."

political talents had been blunted increasingly in his last years and that his behavior had tarnished his earlier triumphs."[62] Luther had also been the object of intense hostility and bitter attacks over many years, which – combined with disappointment at the course of the Reformation – could have contributed to a darkening of his outlook. Other examples could be found in history of old men who fell far short of their best earlier achievements.

Looking more closely at *On the Jews and Their Lies* (which few have done), it can be said that much of the tract is merely mainstream Evangelical theology that many Christians have held without being hostile to Jews. For example, Luther argues at length and in depth about prophecies that point to the Messiah; the inability of Jews to earn God's favor by keeping the law; the fact that mere possession of the laws of Moses, circumcision, or physical descent from Abraham are no guarantees of God's favor; that God promised the throne of David would stand forever, and if Christ is not the Messiah than this promise has failed. He also has many biblical references to the sin and rebelliousness of Old Testament Israel to substantiate his point that being a physical Jew does not automatically confer special status in the eyes of God.

This was not merely a Jewish question. Luther also saw Catholic rules and regulations in the same light, and in this tract linked Jews, Catholics, Mohammedans, and even some Protestant sects as manifesting the same error – attempting to earn God's favor by obeying rules and commandments. What Luther called the Jewish error of failing to understand our inability to earn favor with God was also described by him as a human error, one that Luther himself had been trapped in for many years. In Luther's words, "They [the Jews] claim to be God's people by reason of their deeds, works, and external show, and not because of sheer grace and mercy . . . The Turks follow the same pattern with their worship . . . Jews, Turks, Papists, radicals abound everywhere. All of them claim to be the church and God's people . . . . "[63]

When Luther speaks of the Jews and the devil it is not realized that (in agreement with biblical teaching) he saw the devil as active in the world at large, and evil in human nature itself. Luther's statement "we *will* sin and evil, we *speak* sin and evil, we *do* sin and evil"[64] would sound very bad if applied to the Jews, but he says that of all of us, including himself. This is one reason why so many people are eager to discredit Luther. By seizing on and

---

[62] Gordon Craig, *Germany 1866-1945* (Oxford: Clarendon Press, 1978), pp. 170, 179.

[63] Luther, *On the Jews and Their Lies*, p. 175. "Radicals" is a reference to extreme Protestant sects.

[64] Veith, *Modern Fascism*, p. 92 (quoting *Bondage of the Will*). Veith contrasts Luther's *The Bondage of the Will* with Leni Riefenstahl's Nazi propaganda film "The Triumph of the Will" to show the gulf between Christian doctrine of sin and the Nazi (and Nietzschean) exaltation of human will.

magnifying his undeniable mistakes, they feel justified in ignoring his message (brought by many others as well) that we are not basically good, but are in need of the forgiveness for sin that is found only in Christ.

So, some comments in Luther's tract about Jews as evil were also applicable to humanity as a whole, and comparisons equating the Jews with the Turks, the Catholics, and even other Protestants occur here and there throughout the text. "Satan is the prince of this world,"[65] Luther rightly taught, and he was not just speaking of Jewish neighborhoods. Christians, as well as atheists, are liable to the devil's deceptions. But, when in his anti-Jewish tract Luther referred to Jesus' statement "You are of your father the devil" (John 3:39) and applied it to the Jewish people as a whole when Christ clearly meant a specific group, he erred in his understanding (as serious students of Luther have had no trouble recognizing). He erred on other points as well (as for example I believe he erred on the question of infant baptism and on the canonicity of the book of James). No one who rightly understood Luther would ever follow him blindly and claim that he was free from error, to be followed on all points without question.

Luther makes much of the destruction of the Temple and the nation of Israel by the Romans, arguing that this is a clear sign of God's disfavor. He gives this as proof that the Jews have been rejected by God and are no longer his people, supported with a quote from Hosea 1:9 – "Then said God, Call his name Lo-am-mi [not my people]: for ye are not my people, and I will not be your God." He forgot to quote verse 10, which plainly shows that this condemnation is upon a certain group of Jews at that time, not upon all Jews forever.

It has been claimed that, because Luther saw the destruction of Israel as God's wrath, he would have said the same of the Holocaust. Yet, Jewish thinkers have also seen the Roman devastation as the result of God's anger – in agreement with Torah, and with prophetic explanations of the destructions of the two kingdoms of Judah and Israel as the result of judgment on the Jews for their many sins. It is not the teaching of biblical Christianity, nor was it Luther's teaching in his many serious works written in his prime, that God has called Christians to be agents of wrath, or to be pleased when wrath comes, whenever and on whomever it may come.

As has already been mentioned, in the book of Obadiah the people of Edom were condemned because they rejoiced in the day of Israel's fall and spoke proudly in the day of Jewish distress, even though that Jewish affliction was directly related to God's anger. They seized Jewish goods, prevented people from escaping, and delivered those they managed to capture into the hands of their enemies. They are told, "as thou hast done, it shall be done unto thee: thy

---

[65] Luther, *Bondage of the Will, in Selections From His Writings*, p. 203.

reward shall return upon thine own head." Christians who rejoice in the suffering of others are very far from the Spirit of Christ.

Returning to Luther's tract, although in the abstract we can agree with many of the strictly theological arguments, much of it is marred by hostility. Saying, for example, that the Jews were blind and stupid fools to boast of their physical descent from Abraham[66] does not help to understanding – yet, in this tract Luther speaks in the same tone of other groups. He also speaks this way of himself and of Christians: "Oh, what do we poor muck-worms, maggots, stench, and filth presume to boast of before him who is the God and Creator of heaven and earth . . . we are but dirt and nothing in his eyes; all that we are and have comes from his grace and his rich mercy."[67] Such a view totally nullifies Aryan supremacy.

This last quote is a good example of Luther's persistent tendency (not noticeable in his best works in my opinion) to state a biblical truth in excessive language that alienates rather than persuades. Many more could be given. When Luther refers to Old Testament Israel as an evil whore and a slut,[68] he is referring with exaggerated and unhelpful rhetoric to a point that was often made by the prophets: "for the land hath committed great whoredom, departing from the Lord" (Hosea 1:2). Luther here refers to Deuteronomy 31:27, Psalm 95:10, and Isaiah 48:4 to substantiate his main point that merely being circumcised, having God's Word, and being physically descended from Abraham are not proofs of God's favor. Of course, the prophets were speaking by the Spirit of God, and not in fallible human anger as Luther was.

Luther called Rabbi Akiba, a renowned Jewish scholar of the 2nd century A.D., a simpleton and a fool for embracing Bar Kokhba as the Messiah and supporting him in the second revolt against Rome. This sort of rhetoric is not helpful, but it is striking that a renowned Torah sage should devote his life to study and then be so hopelessly mistaken about the Messiah. But, we read in Luther's writings – and in those of many other Christian writers – that human nature is innately sinful from birth, that the entire human race is in the same lost condition apart from God's grace, that ignorance and folly are not uniquely Jewish attributes but a part of the human condition.

This low (and biblical) view of fallen and sinful human nature was totally antithetical to ridiculous nonsense about "Aryan supremacy" or a "master race." Anyone who came up with such ideas in the sixteenth century would have been quickly dismissed as a nut. It took the modern secular age, with its belief in human reason emancipated from God and from the Bible, to come up with ideas of racial purity and Aryan supremacy that glorified man with no regard for our sin relative to God's righteousness. Luther and all Christians of

---

[66] Luther, *On the Jews and Their Lies*, p. 148.

[67] Ibid., p. 144.

[68] Ibid., p. 166.

the sixteenth century, Catholic or Protestant, could never have accepted Aryan supremacy. Only sophisticated moderns were stupid enough to follow it (this includes of course Christians of various sorts who abandoned plain biblical teachings in order to follow the world).

Contrary to what some have claimed, Luther was not upset because Jewish rejection of Christ was a threat to his conception of Christianity. Christians who actually believe in the Bible understand very well that the salvation of individuals or of groups is in God's hands. Luther stressed this repeatedly in other writings. In this tract, he also mentioned the destruction of the state of Israel and the subsequent dispersion of the Jewish people. This was to him proof, in agreement with Torah, that the Jews were no longer in God's favor. Luther was much more concerned with Catholic than he was with Jewish doctrinal opposition, as can easily be seen by looking at the contents of his writings as a whole. Jesus said, "No man can come to me, except the Father which hath sent me draw him" and "no man can come unto me except it were given unto him of my Father." That the Jews refused to accept Christ was to Luther the result of that same unbelief which Paul teaches is characteristic of the human race as a whole.

What really made Luther angry (as he explained at length in his tract) were insulting comments that Jews were reported to have made about Christ, Mary, and Christians in general. That Jesus was a sorcerer and servant of the devil who accomplished his miracles by magic; that Mary was a harlot and Jesus was born illegitimately; that Jesus was conceived while Mary was menstruating and hence was mentally defective; that Jews would spit on the ground or curse when they said the name of Jesus, or say "May all the devils take him" – these and other alleged comments provoked Luther's ailing and aged fury.[69]

It has been claimed in response to this that the Jews as an endangered minority would not have made such statements, but there is ample evidence to the contrary. To give only one example, a medieval Jewish parody of the life of Christ called the *Toldos Yeshu* claimed that Jesus was born after Mary was raped. In his *A History of the Jews*, Abram Leon Sachar wrote that, given the sufferings of the Jews in medieval Europe, it was "impossible for the Jews to regard the Prophet of Nazareth as other than the scourge of God, a fiend unmentionable." He then describes the *Toldos Yeshu* as "a collection of hideous tales purporting to be his [Christ's] life story, read eagerly during the Middle Ages by an embittered people . . . the response to centuries of persecution in the name of Jesus."[70]

---

[69] Ibid., pp. 256-257 and following.

[70] Abram Leon Sachar, *A History of the Jews* (New York: Alfred A. Knopf, 1966), p. 125.

There is a specific example in the tract. Luther claims that three learned Jews came to debate Scripture with him. He gave them "a letter of recommendation to the authorities, asking that for Christ's sake they let them freely go their way." Later, he heard that they referred to Christ as a "hanged highwayman," and added "Therefore I do not wish to have anything more to do with any Jew." This normal – though sinful – human anger has nothing to do with nineteenth-century philosophies of race.[71]

Maimonides referred to Jesus, said "may his bones be ground to dust," and then called him illegitimate (spiritually illegitimate, not physically, since his mother was a Jew).[72] This – as well as other comments from other sources, such as Paul of Burgos (Burgensis) and Anthony Margaritha – is not to justify Luther's anger. He should have realized the reasons for such hostility, and he should have remembered that Christ himself responded calmly when insulted. It is to say that Luther's motivation was very different from the secular antisemites we will examine later. The founders of the tradition Hitler emerged out of did not believe in the Bible, did not believe Jesus to be the Son of God, and cared little or nothing about these things.

Luther was also angered (again, as he says in *On the Jews and Their Lies*) by the common theme of usury, and by Jewish attempts to convert Christians. Again, this was a wrong reaction on Luther's part, but haven't some conservative Jews in Israel been very hostile to Christian missionary activity there? This was not one of Luther's main points, however. He spends more time stating that the Jews longed for their Messiah to return and destroy the Gentiles, as was done in the book of Esther. The identification of the Gentiles (including Christians) as God's enemies like Old Testament Amalek (Exodus 17:14-16) is an illustration of this: "a tradition settled into Judaism according to which the nations were of Amalek, the 'other' which was at war with Israel and with which Israel was at war." "Amalek came to personify the evil Other . . . [and] Christianity became part of Amalek's metahistorical reality."[73]

Rightly or wrongly, Luther perceived that Jews were hoping their Messiah would come and slaughter the Gentiles. He also claimed in *On the Jews and Their Lies* that "their Talmud and their rabbis record that it is no sin for a Jew to kill a Gentile . . . since they believe that they are the noble blood and the circumcised saints and we the accursed Goyim."[74] This could have been connected with assertions of Jewish superiority as seen in the tradition that "the people of Israel possessed a divine image of holiness that was unavailable to the rest of humanity . . . the image of Israel was holy while the image of

---

[71] Luther, *On the Jews and Their Lies*, pp. 191-192.

[72] Spicer, *Antisemitism, Christian Ambivalence, and the Holocaust*, p. 240, discussing Maimonides' *Epistle to Yemen*.

[73] Ibid., pp. 242, 239.

[74] Luther, *On the Jews and Their Lies*, pp. 156-157, 226.

others was impure and profane . . . the image of holiness which is special to the children of Israel alone." The idea that "the people of Israel alone were the holy image of God" [75] could easily have lent itself to misinterpretations of Jewish attitudes toward Gentiles.

This relates to popular superstitions about Jews poisoning wells or kidnapping children and killing them. Luther had some doubt about this, but thought it was possible.[76] This is an illustration of the conformity to the world that has been a problem with the church from the beginning and will be until Christ returns. How can we be free of cultural elements that have surrounded us since birth, but are contrary to Christianity? We grow up with them and they are widely believed – but they are wrong. Here we must die to self enough to transcend our environment, but that is never easy, and never fully attained in this life.

Jewish complaints about life in Germany were sarcastically dismissed – in Luther's view no one had asked them to come to Germany and if they didn't like it they should leave: "In addition, no one is holding them here now. The country and the roads are open for them to proceed to their land whenever they wish."[77] More significantly, Luther made some comments that are now commonly linked to Hitler. He said Jewish synagogues should be burned, that Jews should be forced to do manual labor, and that they should be subjected to other repressive measures.[78] This has even been called a "blueprint" for the Holocaust – as if anyone in the 1500s could have imagined Auschwitz and an international system of transportation to designated killing centers. Many of Nietzsche's quotes, taken at face value, are more relevant to the Holocaust than the complete works of all the Reformation authors combined.

Luther's worst comments have been constantly quoted, but what is almost never explained is that in the same tract Luther changed his mind, and said such measures would not accomplish anything, that the Jews should be expelled from Germany instead. In his words:

> In my opinion the problem must be resolved thus: If we wish to wash our hands of the Jews' blasphemy and not share in their guilt, we have to part company with them. They must be driven from our country. Let them think of their fatherland; then they need no longer wail and lie before God against us that we are holding them captive, nor need we then any longer complain that they are burdening us with their blasphemy and their usury. This is the

---

[75] Spicer, *Antisemitism, Christian Ambivalence, and the Holocaust*, p. 241, 256 (both quotes). Spicer is discussing traditional Jewish views of the Gentile world, both negative and positive.

[76] Luther, *On the Jews and Their Lies*, p. 217.

[77] Ibid., p. 265.

[78] Ibid., pp. 268-272, 285-286.

most natural and the best course of action, which will safeguard the interest of both parties.[79]

Now, this was sinful and wrong – "the wrath of man worketh not the righteousness of God" as it says in James – but it is very different from what Luther is usually accused of. This was the traditional sort of antisemitism that had led to the expulsion of the Jews from other countries such as England, France, parts of Germany and Spain, but never led to genocide – and, if the Jews had been expelled from Germany, it might have prevented the Holocaust.

Saying that rulers with Jewish subjects should act like a physician dealing with gangrene could easily refer to consistent and thorough expulsion, not to extermination. Even saying that the Jews should be harshly dealt with, as Moses himself dealt with rebellious Jews on more than one occasion,[80] could refer to a severity of complete expulsion, not to the death penalty. Christians and Jews often look to Moses for an example without thinking that we have his authority and trying to imitate him literally in totally different situations.

Significantly, in a number of places in his tract Luther expresses a milder opinion on how Christians should deal with Jews, meaning that his worst statements are not a matter of considered policy, but rather of Luther's anger increasing as he wrote. For example, elsewhere in the tract he wrote "We let them go their way and wait for their Messiah. Their unbelief does not harm us . . ." and also, "Thus we must let them go their way and ignore their malicious blasphemy and lying." This is followed by "the more one tries to help them [the Jews] the baser and more stubborn they become. Leave them to their own devices." He tells pastors and preachers to warn their parishioners "that they may be on their guard against the Jews and avoid them so far as possible. They should not curse them or harm their persons, however."[81] Such comments are completely ignored by people who seem not to have read the tract they are writing about.

Yet, Luther went farther, and wrote, "We are at fault in not slaying them. Rather we allow them to live freely in our midst . . . ."[82] He also spoke in this context of avenging the blood of Christ. All that can be said here is that Luther stumbled badly, but that in all of his earlier years of greatest influence he never advocated such things, they were not part of his life's work or purpose, and never became a part of mainstream Protestantism. In his whole life Luther never sought to enact a policy of killing. This is not representative of Christianity, Protestantism, or Lutheranism – just as the massacre of the Hivites by Jacob's sons Simeon and Levi in retaliation for their sister Dinah's defilement reflect only human sin and error, not any flaw inherent in Torah

---

[79] Ibid., pp. 287-288. Luther also refers to expelling the Jews on pp. 272, 276-277.

[80] Ibid., p. 292.

[81] Ibid., pp. 177, 191, 192, 274 (all four quotes consecutively).

[82] Ibid., p. 267.

Judaism. What Jacob's sons did was far worse than mere words that were never acted on, yet it does not prevent us from believing that God spoke to Jacob.

It is too easy to read these things looking backward from the Holocaust. When Luther wrote that the fact of Jewish expulsion from their homeland was proof of God's anger according to their own scriptures, and that this argument struck them to the ground like a thunderclap, meaning they had no valid answer to it, he was not speaking of dead Jews lying on the ground in the Holocaust. He is speaking of an unanswerable argument – and Moses did say that God would keep the Jewish people in their land if they obeyed him, but cast them out if they rebelled and refused to submit to correction. Too many people discuss Luther without even knowing what they are talking about. Highlighting this quote of Luther's, as if it had something to do with Hitler's social Darwinist, Wagnerian and Nietzschean dreams of purifying the race or crushing and dominating or even exterminating the weak without pity or mercy, is anti-Christian propaganda, not serious analysis.

We do not find appeals to Luther, to the Bible, or to Reformation theology in Nazi rhetoric about the elimination of the weak and the unfit, or about the necessity of dealing with the Jewish threat to Aryan racial purity. The Nazis did not build a Luther museum as they did for Nietzsche,[83] nor did the highly image-conscious Hitler pose for a photograph by a bust of Luther as he did for Nietzsche. It was after all Nietzsche who taught that the unfit should be exterminated, and that more power meant more happiness. "What is good? All that enhances the feeling of power . . . What is happiness? – The feeling that power is increasing . . . The weak and the botched shall perish: first principle of our humanity. And they ought even to be helped to perish."[84]

It was Gobineau who taught in the mid-1800s that racial purity was essential to national survival, and we do not find any Christian writers of the sixteenth century, Protestant or Catholic, stating that nature's weeding out of the unfit by harsh conditions of struggle was essential to continued development and advancement of the species. It was Hegel who taught that the great men of history were exempt from ordinary moral considerations and were perfectly justified in crushing the common and insignificant people beneath their feet, and it was Hegel who taught that we found our fullest freedom in obedience to the state, which was the agent of progress for some sort of vague and nebulous World Spirit.

---

[83] R. J. Hollingdale, *The Man and His Philosophy (Revised Edition)* (Cambridge: Cambridge University Press, 1999), p. 243. Hitler visited the museum a number of times.

[84] Friedrich Nietzsche, *The Antichrist,* trans. Anthony M. Ludovici (Amherst, NY: Prometheus Books, 2000), p. 4 (subsection 2, all quotes). These are just a few of the many Nazi-like ideas found in that book.

Conventional religious antisemitism, sinful and wrong though it was, never led to a Holocaust. It took modern technology and modern philosophy, including new forms of secular philosophical and biological anti-Judaism, to make modern horrors possible – and it should be pointed out that some quotes attributed to Luther may be completely fictional and should not be considered without proper documentation. Many fraudulent accusations have been made against Luther, who was a deeply hated man even in his own day. A purported statement of Luther's about drowning a baptized Jew may have never been made at all. The claim that Luther felt Jews could not convert as they were too completely controlled by Satan is easily refuted from comments he made even in *On the Jews and Their Lies*.

In the third paragraph of the first page of the tract, Luther stated that it was impossible for Jews to convert to Christianity. Yet, later in the tract Luther completely contradicted himself, and stated that Jews could be converted – meaning he did not consider them to be completely beyond the pale of humanity, as has been claimed. For example, he said "If this should move any Jew to reform and repent, so much the better," and "Whenever a Jew is sincerely converted, he should be handed one hundred, two hundred, or three hundred florins, as personal circumstances may suggest. With this he could set himself up in some occupation for the support of his poor wife and children, and the maintenance of the old or feeble." The last sentence of his tract is an expression of his hope for the conversion of the Jews.[85]

So many misconceptions of Luther are now so firmly rooted that only a careful reading of his best Reformation works (such as few are now capable of) is sufficient to remove them. Luther was not a coarse, vulgar, brutal man, but was a true scholar with a deep knowledge of Greek, Latin, Hebrew, philosophy, and the Bible. He has been accused of using a lot of scatological language, even by badly informed Evangelicals, but that is not at all true of his *Commentary on Galatians*; his *Address to the Christian Nobility*; his *Babylonian Captivity of the Church*; or his *Preface to Romans*, and other profound works. Ignorance of the Reformation and of its basic principles has become a hallmark of American Evangelicalism. Even some of Luther's shorter and more accessible works are too hard for many Christians today.

Eric Metaxas in a best-selling and widely praised Evangelical book ridiculed Luther and presented him as some kind of buffoon.[86] Yet, he praised Dietrich Bonheoffer as being theologically orthodox when even in Metaxas' book Bonhoeffer is directly quoted as saying that "I believe that with God it is such that all who loved each other on earth – genuinely loved each other – will

---

[85] Luther, *On the Jews and Their Lies*, pp. 137, 140, 270, 306.

[86] Metaxas, *Bonhoeffer: Pastor, Martyr, Prophet, Spy*, pp. 92-93.

remain together with God, for to love is part of God." Bonhoeffer then adds "Just how that happens, though, we admittedly don't know."[87]

This was written in a letter while Bonheoffer was a student pastor in Barcelona, and so might be considered as a youthful error (as if even student pastors should not be required to know basic doctrines). In the pages immediately preceding, however, Metaxas asserts that there was "never any kind of significant theological change" between these earlier views of Bonhoeffer's and his later ones, that "there was an orthodox theological foundation" to Bonhoeffer's theology in this earlier period, at the time of his statement that just to love someone was enough to get to heaven, somehow, we don't know how.[88]

More familiarity with Luther's basic Reformation principles of faith and salvation (which of course were not Luther's alone but were widely shared) would help to an understanding of Bonhoeffer's neo-orthodox theology, a theology that included denying the inerrancy of Scripture, as well as doubting the virgin birth and the resurrection of Christ.[89] These and numerous other doctrinal statements should prevent anyone from regarding Bonhoeffer as an Evangelical hero. There are numerous red flags in Metaxas' book, all of them ignored by Evangelicals who are more interested in hero-worship than in the sound biblical doctrines upheld in the Reformation.

It is true, things have changed in many ways since the sixteenth century. Even the world "Protestant" is dated. As one doctrinal Protestant said, "I am not protesting anything." The issues we face today are very different, but the ringing appeals of Luther at his best to the great truths of Romans are sadly lacking in the church today. If we consider Luther in his prime and at his best, not in an unfortunate old age, his deep spiritual insights reflect very negatively on today's increasing Evangelical deviations from essential doctrines.

Returning to criticisms of Luther, his call for the crushing of the peasant rebellion has been used to show that he was cruel and bloodthirsty, but his position was sound, even if his rhetoric was not. The rulers had every right to crush with swift severity a rebellion that was creating more evils than it opposed. What if someone had put Hitler to death after his failed putsch, or executed Lenin and Trotsky after their first failed attempt to overthrow Russia's newly-formed democratic government? How many lives would have been saved by some initial severity? Luther's language does show his consistent fault of stating a valid position in excessive and immoderate language.

---

[87] Ibid., p. 86.

[88] Ibid., p. 84 (both quotes).

[89] Dietrich Bonhoeffer, *Christ the Center,* trans. Edwin H. Robertson (New York: HarperOne, 1978), pp. 104-105, 112.

Earlier, Luther had written an *Admonition to Peace*, in which he admitted the legitimacy of peasant grievances and urged both sides (peasants and nobility) to avoid a conflict. In *Secular Authority: To What Extent It Should Be Obeyed* (published in 1523), Luther warned the nobles that they could no longer abuse the people as they had done for so long – "men cannot, men will not suffer your tyranny and presumption much longer."[90] He advised them to rule more reasonably, and wrote "drop your outrage and force, and remember to deal justly." He also said in this treatise that the secular authorities had no right to compel religious belief. "Heresy can never be prevented by force." The power of the state was ordained by God to deal with outwardly criminal acts, not to beliefs, a point Luther elaborates on at length – "for although all the Jews and heretics were burned, yet no one has been or will be convinced and converted thereby."

Many comments that have been made about Luther are simply false, and even ridiculous. His importance for later German history has been fantastically exaggerated. It is absurd to state that he permanently molded the German character to such an extent that he was personally responsible for what happened centuries later. One lengthy and detailed study of German history in the modern era doesn't mention Luther at all, though the index does have references to Wagner, Haeckel, Hegel, Nietzsche and Freud.[91] What did Luther have to do with the unification of Germany under Bismarck; the catastrophe of World War I and the failures of the German General Staff; the imposition by the Allies of an ineffectual and unpopular democracy; the economic problems of the 1930s?

It is said that it was Luther who taught the Germans docile obedience to authority. Apart from the fact that Christ and the apostles also taught obedience to the authorities and political submission to Rome, how did Russia, Spain, Italy, Japan, Cuba, Cambodia, and many other countries fall under cruel dictatorships without Luther's influence? The Germans who resisted Napoleon, or participated in the revolutions of 1848, or sought to overthrow the Weimar government and undo the Treaty of Versailles were not motivated by any Lutheran teachings of obedience. Incidentally, Luther taught that the authorities (ecclesiastical or civil) had no authority over individual belief, and had no right to compel anyone against their conscience. Luther laid his life on the line for this and risked death by his refusal to submit to authority over his personal faith.

In his otherwise useful history of the Third Reich, William L. Shirer completely contradicts himself when he states in the same paragraph that Luther taught "the supremacy of the individual conscience" while at the same

---

[90] Luther, *Selections from His Writings*, pp. 391 (first two quotes), and 389, 390 (last two quotes respectively).

[91] Craig, *Germany 1866-1945*.

time ensuring "a mindless and provincial political absolutism" by his "passion for political autocracy."[92] On the following page Shirer states that it was the catastrophe of the Thirty Years War that made "blind obedience" an integral part of the German character. Strong democracies emerged in nearly all of the Reformation countries and it is Hegel, not Luther, who provided theoretical justification for modern totalitarianism because of his emphasis on the supremacy of the state.

Although Shirer's book is in general an excellent work, and was rightly praised by a serious historian like H. R. Trevor-Roper, it is not invulnerable to criticism. Specifically, his sad mischaracterization of Luther shows only his complete failure to understand the Reformation. At the end of his autobiography *Twentieth Century Journey*, Shirer shares enough of his ideas about life to make it obvious that the principles of the Reformation were alien to him – but the same can also be said of other acclaimed historians of the Third Reich. Bias against and ignorance of Christianity are now standard features of secular history. Fortunately, Shirer's analysis of modern trends in the century or so before Hitler was vastly more acute. His overview of the ideas of Fichte, Hegel, Treitschke and Nietzsche as contributory to extreme nationalism, totalitarianism, and violence is in my view a useful contribution to the understanding of Hitler, in spite of its neglect of some other important figures.

Luther's doctrine of the "Two Kingdoms" differentiated between the spiritual realm of the church and the earthly realm with its political rulers appointed by God to maintain order (as also taught by Paul in Romans chapter 13). This has often been used to blame Luther for teaching submission to tyranny, yet Luther saw the earthly rulers as also under a higher authority, God's law, not as a law unto themselves. As it says in the Lutheran Augsburg Confession, "But when commands of the civil authority cannot be obeyed without sin, we must obey God rather than men (Acts 5:29)."[93] True, the teaching that God had ordained the authorities could be (and was) used as an excuse for doing nothing, but Luther's intention, teaching, and practice did not mean total obedience to any human government.

A letter of June 1939 from the local Gestapo headquarters to the church authorities of the Rhine province presents the criminal record of a Lutheran pastor incarcerated in Buchenwald, Paul Robert Schneider. According to this official document, Pastor Schneider was hostile to the state. He was accused (among other things) of calling National Socialism a work of the devil; making

---

[92] William L. Shirer, *The Rise and Fall of the Third Reich: A History of Nazi Germany* (New York: Simon & Schuster, 2011), pp. 91-92. John Montgomery's book *In Defense of Martin Luther*, cited earlier, contains a detailed response to Shirer's deep misunderstandings of Luther ("Shirer's Re-Hitlerizing of Luther," pp. 142-149).

[93] Veith, *Modern Fascism*, p. 63.

disparaging remarks about *Mein Kampf*; disobeying a Gestapo order forbidding him to preach in his own church; saying that "The brown crowd [the SA] does not belong in the church"; accusing the Reich government of falsifying the results of an election; and stating in a sermon that the German youth belonged not to Adolf Hitler or to Baldur von Schirach, but to Christ. An eyewitness account by a fellow-prisoner states that while in Buchenwald Pastor Schneider was given 25 lashes for refusing to salute the Nazi flag.[94]

Such a person is completely irrelevant to historians who will tell you everything you ever wanted to know about sports, the cinema, academia, and music in the Third Reich, but have little interest in the church, and no interest in a minor figure who publicly contradicted Naziism at the cost of his life. Paul Schneider died in Buchenwald, and not because of some undercover secret agent work, but because of his public testimony for Christ. This is perfectly consistent with Luther's own willingness to die rather than submit his beliefs to the dictates of the authorities – but it has little relevance to Germany in the 1930s and mobs of people excited about Hitler.

People don't understand the extent to which Lutheranism had ceased to be a dominant national force long before the 20th century. Does anyone try to interpret British policies in the 1920s and 30s in the light of Cranmer, Tyndale, Latimer, and Ridley, as if England hadn't moved on the in the subsequent 400 years? I haven't heard anyone blaming Luther for Germany's policies in the EU anyway. It does seem that some who enjoy linking Luther to the Holocaust are blissfully unaware of the trends of nationalism, romanticism, social Darwinism and idealistic philosophy that so profoundly altered German consciousness and brought it into the modern era.

About Luther and the Nazis, there has been a lot of what is really only anti-Christian propaganda which distorts the issues and obscures understanding. For example, to call both Luther and Hitler "characteristically German" is to say that ordinary and typical Germans were either power-mad dictators or Catholic monks trying to find peace with God by following the Bible as closely as possible. With the same logic, we could say that Richard Nixon, Martin Luther King, Elvis, and Walt Disney were all "characteristically American" – whatever that means.

Calling the Nazis "children of Christians" is the result of misunderstanding what Christianity is. Absalom and Amnon were "children of David," but his spirituality did not rub off on them. Does their wickedness nullify the Psalms? Christianity is supposed to be a matter of individual choice and belief on the part of children who may or may not grow up to follow their parents. Moreover, standard histories of Germany in the period between the two world wars do not show an appreciable number of devout, Bible-believing Christians

---

[94] Rudolf Wentorf, *Paul Schneider: Witness of Buchenwald,* trans. Daniel Bloesch (Vancouver: Regent College Publishing, 2008), pp. 325-328, 340.

filling Weimar literature, art, cinema, and theater with pious themes of repentance from sin and faithfulness to Christ in obedience to the Word of God. No book about Weimar Germany that I have ever seen stressed its biblical character. On the contrary, that period represents the quintessence of modernism and secularism.

To call Luther an ally of the Final Solution or to say that he anticipated the worst Nazi atrocities is to misunderstand the entire purpose and thrust of the Protestant Reformation, to which Jews were a minor issue. We shall later observe much more of Hitler in nineteenth-century secularists than in Luther – but it is fashionable to indict Christianity nowadays. Indicting the bizarre fantasies of secular reason liberated from biblical truth is not nearly so emotionally satisfying. That not religion but rather human reason without religion can lead to disaster is a very threatening concept to those secularist extremists who find it difficult to deal objectively with opposing points of view.

That Hitler was familiar with and admired Luther's writings is, I believe, a complete fiction. Hitler openly expressed hostility to Jewish inspired Christianity, as we shall see in chapter 4, and in his analysis of the Jewish "problem" Hitler relied on arguments and principles unknown to Luther. If anyone thinks Hitler had the slightest interest in Luther's main Reformation principles or his best writings they are invited to produce their evidence.

The notorious Nazi propagandist and Jew-hater Julius Streicher said at the Nuremberg trials "that he had never said anything about the Jews that Martin Luther had not said four hundred years earlier."[95] Who believes that the criminals in the dock at Nuremberg were upright men of integrity who took a bold stand for their convictions, instead of using lies and cowardly evasions to minimize or escape their guilt? The briefest glance at some of Streicher's comments is sufficient to expose his pitiful excuse – at least for those who have even a rudimentary knowledge of the principles of the Reformation.

Cohabitation with a Jew poisons Aryan blood? The Old Testament "impresses us as a horrible criminal romance . . . This holy book [which Luther considered to be the inspired and infallible Word of God] abounds in murder, incest, fraud, theft and indecency"? Jewish financiers stand behind wars and international conflicts? The supreme task of the state is to preserve the purity of the race?[96] Everyone who knows anything about Luther understands that Streicher inhabited another world, and appealing to Luther

---

[95] Prager, *Why the Jews?*, p. 90.

[96] "Julius Streicher," Jewish Virtual Library, www.jewishvirtuallibrary.org/jsource/Holocaust. (accessed January 2014). Streicher's views about the Bible are identical to those espoused by some modern secular extremists. This should give them food for thought, but of course it won't.

was just an evasive tactic. If Streicher had really been a follower of Luther he would have understood that his fantasy of Aryan supremacy was a useless lie.

Those who want to use Streicher to show a link between Luther and Naziism should consider that he also claimed the Nuremberg racial laws were no different than and had the same purpose as the Jewish laws concerning marriage in the Old Testament. If someone does not want to understand that the purpose of the Old Testament marriage laws was to preserve the Jewish faith, that sincere non-Jews were welcomed, and that racial purity was not an issue, then they are willfully ignorant. And, it is now even claimed that the Israelite invasion of the Promised Land and the massacres of the Canaanites were no different from what Hitler did. Many of those who want to discredit Christianity by linking it to Hitler have the whole Bible in their gun-sights, including Torah.

Nazi government-sponsored celebrations in 1933 of the 450th anniversary of Luther's birth do not show a devotion to Protestantism. Their complete indifference to salvation from sin through Christ as well as their emphasis on totally different Nazi doctrines reveal only a propagandistic attempt to broaden Hitler's appeal and nullify potential religious opposition. Stating that Hitler and Luther were profoundly alike does not reflect Protestantism, it reflects typical Nazi propaganda which (like many other Nazi claims) should not be accepted at face value (unless someone wants to believe that the blond, blue-eyed Aryans really are the master race).

It has been said that the Nazis announced that the *Kristallnacht* pogrom "was in honor of the anniversary of Martin Luther's birthday."[97] A different source says "the attack on the secretary of the German embassy in Paris merely provided the pretext for an operation that had been in the planning for some time."[98] Ian Kershaw notes that the date also coincided with the fifteenth anniversary of Hitler's failed putsch in Munich in 1923.[99] Referring to Luther was more likely either a sneer at the Christians with their Jewish-influenced faith, or an attempt to deflect criticisms, as the pogrom was by no means accepted by all Germans. Historian Martin Gilbert records that some Germans wept at this persecution of the Jews.[100] This is confirmed by Shirer who wrote that "many Germans were as horrified by the November 9 inferno as were Americans and Englishmen and other foreigners."[101]

---

[97] Prager, *Why the Jews*, p. 90.

[98] Bernt Engelmann, *In Hitler's Germany: Everyday Life in the Third Reich*, trans. Krishna Winston (New York: Pantheon Books, 1986), p. 125.

[99] Ian Kershaw, *Hitler* (London: Penguin Books, 2008), p. 455.

[100] Martin Gilbert, *The Holocaust: A History of the Jews of Europe During the Second World War* (New York: Henry Holt and Co., 1985), p. 70.

[101] Shirer, *Rise and Fall of the Third Reich*, p. 435.

Significantly, Shirer stated that no Christian leaders spoke out against the pogrom. For the most part he was right, and we should not try to whitewash the pitiful failure of the churches – but there was at least one exception whose name has not been completely lost to history. A Lutheran pastor named von Jan of Oberlenningen in Wuerttemberg denounced the pogrom from the pulpit, called it a crime, and said it was the result of "the great apostasy from God and Christ, arising out of organized anti-Christianity."[102] A few days later he was attacked by a mob, severely beaten, and thrown into prison. Such a minor incident is of no importance to historians of the Third Reich, and will not diminish their petty and spiteful potshots at a Christian faith they are literally incapable of understanding.

The number of authentic Christians who suffered under Hitler is small when compared to the attempted extermination of the Jews, but they serve to illustrate the complete incompatibility between the ideas of Hitler and those of biblical Christianity. That Christianity had no place in Hitler's ideal society is obvious to those who have any understanding of the teachings of Christ and the nature of the Third Reich. Christianity is inherently contrary to the false teachings of the world, whether of Hitler, of Stalin, or of post-modern secularists trying to bring about their own earthly ideals without regard for the Creator and his laws. And if persecution should come in our own time, will we surrender, as so many German Christians did, valuing this present age over the world that is to come? Do we truly believe that to die is gain, or do we only say it without really meaning it?

One could go on for pages elaborating on "the Luther problem," but the main points should be clear. There are other thinkers that deserve more attention, all of them closer both chronologically and spiritually to the Third Reich, none of whom shared Luther's main emphases, all of whom rejected the Bible and thought that human reason and feeling alone were sufficient guides. To make one final point, it should be well-known that the churches, both Protestant and Catholic, were on the periphery of the great events that shook Germany from 1914 until Hitler's coming to power in 1933. It is true, they could – and should – have said more than they did, but the driving forces of National Socialism were not susceptible to church control.

Traditional Christianity did not dominate nineteenth- and twentieth-century Germany. This does not need to be explained to anyone with a basic understanding of modern European cultural history. Even in the nineteenth century the churches (while still influential) had lost their former position and were not able to direct or hinder the main course of events in Germany. Hence a minor figure like Pastor Adolf Stoecker, the Lutheran chaplain to the court of

---

[102] John Conway, *The Nazi Persecution of the Churches 1933-1945* (Vancouver: Regent, 1968), p. 375.

the Kaiser, could be ignored were it not for the fact that he too has been accused of playing a significant role in the development of later tragic events.

Howard M. Sachar's generally excellent and informative history of the Jews states that it was Stoecker who made "social antisemitism into an increasingly formidable political issue in Germany . . . [and] awakened right-wing German politicians to the functional utility of antisemitism as a party issue."[103] If this is indeed the case it would make Pastor Stoecker an important figure in the history of the Holocaust – however, in a book of such size and scope as Sachar's, it is perhaps inevitable that some details might be overlooked, and Stoecker may not really have been so influential after all.

We are informed by Sachar that Stoecker's Christian Socialist Workers Party was launched in 1877, with the idea of weaning the workers away from Marxism and strengthening their commitment to the established order. It was, according to Sachar, "only in later years" that the party began to include the fight against "Jewish supremacy" as a means of increasing the party's appeal. However, we are also informed by Sachar that *Gartenlaube*, a family journal with a mass circulation, attacked Jewish corruption in high circles in 1874. In 1875, Franz Perot's articles in the *Kreuzzeitung* "produced a sensation" by denouncing Bismarck's ties with the Jewish banker Bleichroeder, as well as his supposedly Jewish economic policies (*Judenpolitik*). [104]

Sachar also informs us that in 1873 Karl Lueger, an Austrian politician and later mayor of Vienna, developed "a political campaign directed largely against Jewish financial power." Another Austrian anti-Semite, Georg von Schoenerer, is credited by Sachar with pioneering "many of the propaganda techniques later to be used by the Nazis . . . in promoting his agenda, Schoenerer was the first demagogue who understood the potential of antisemitism." [105] True, Sachar was talking about Stoecker's influence in Germany whereas Lueger and von Schoenerer were Austrians, but Hitler of course grew up in Austria and it was the politics of Lueger and von Schoenerer that Hitler discussed at some length in *Mein Kampf*, whereas Stoecker was not mentioned.

Kershaw states in his biography of Hitler that "Certainly he [Hitler] learnt from Lueger the gains to be made from popularizing hatred against the Jews."[106] Another historian, Paul Johnson, says that "it was the Pan-Germanist Georg von Schoenerer, who taught Hitler to place the solution to the Jewish problem in the very center of politics."[107] Actually, both of those men had an

---

[103] Howard M. Sachar, *A History of the Jews in the Modern World* (New York: Vintage Books, 2006), p. 245.
[104] Ibid., pp. 244-246.
[105] Ibid., p. 228, 252-253.
[106] Kershaw, *Hitler*, p. 42.
[107] Johnson, *Modern Times*, p. 133.

influence on Hitler's political development. His detailed analysis in *Mein Kampf* of the policies of those two Austrian leaders and their successes and failures,[108] as well as his later application of what he had learned from them, show that Hitler was in his rise a very shrewd political analyst, not simply a crazy man or a moron. Hitler's later strategy of trying to win the support of the churches (like Lueger) instead of antagonizing them and alienating many potential supporters (like von Schoenerer) can be clearly seen in the passage from *Mein Kampf* analyzing Lueger and von Schoenerer – but others also made significant contributions to the emergence of a new, radical anti-Judaism unlike anything that had been seen before.

Sachar informs us that in 1850, well before Stoecker, Paul de Lagarde described the Jews as "bacilli," "vermin," and "cancer," and called for their extermination. In that same year, Wagner published his attack on the Jews, "Judaism in Music." Wagner later wrote "I hold the Jewish race to be the born enemy of pure humanity and everything noble in it."[109] It was these and others like them who first laid out the ideas that were to deeply inspire Hitler (no matter where he first heard them), and if we want to understand Nazi racial antisemitism, Stoecker isn't of much help to us. George Mosse wrote that Stoecker's traditional prejudices against Jews "held little future promise," and were merely "a prop for the existing social order."[110]

Someone rather recklessly claimed that the study of modern antisemitism in Germany should begin with the court preacher Adolf Stoecker. No doubt it is warmly gratifying to some to believe that a Lutheran pastor is to blame – but actually, the history of modern antisemitism in Germany goes back at least as far as Kant, Fichte, and Schopenhauer, as other scholars and historians have recognized.[111] It was Kant and the many that were influenced by him who helped to introduce a new anti-Judaism based not on Christianity but on the rejection of Christianity. Fichte added a new and different emphasis influenced by the fervent German nationalism that emerged in the Napoleonic era. It was Schopenhauer who blamed the Jews for corrupting Europe through Christianity, a subject that provoked Nietzsche to vindictive blasts against Jewish-inspired Christianity in his book *The Antichrist* (written just before he went completely insane). These men and many others like them were not

---

[108] Hitler, *Mein Kampf*, pp. 97-103.

[109] Sachar, *A History of the Jews*, pp. 243 (Lagarde) and 248 (Wagner).

[110] George Mosse, *The Crisis of German Ideology: Intellectual Origins of the Third Reich* (London: Weidenfeld and Nicolson, 1966), p. 132.

[111] Two sources out of many that begin their exploration of modern German antisemitism well before Stoecker are Paul Lawrence Rose's *German Question / Jewish Question: Revolutionary Antisemitism from Kant to Wagner*, and Michael Mack's *German Idealism and the Jew: The Inner Anti-Semitism of Philosophy and German-Jewish Responses* (see bibliography).

concerned about God's anger on the Jews for the death of Christ, but had different motives entirely.

Gordon Craig blames both Treitschke and Stoecker for making antisemitism respectable in Germany in the later part of the nineteenth century,[112] but "Enlightenment" and idealistic philosophy had made new forms of anti-Judaism respectable among the German intelligentsia long before. And, we should point out that it was not Luther but Gobineau who popularized the idea that racial purity was essential in the struggle for survival. Some of Hitler's comments about racial impurity leading to the decline and fall of a nation are identical to Gobineau's, whose ideas were widespread throughout German racialist circles. Hegel has been accused of contributing to the idea of Jews as a "ghost race," obsolete and useless, totally irrelevant to the forward movement of history, contributing nothing but only feeding off of the host people.[113]

According to Craig, Stoecker's anti-Judaism was not racially based. This was not merely a subtle theoretical distinction, but rather a deep difference between traditional religious antisemitism and the more virulent modern and secular varieties. Some people have studied and emphasized the new secular anti-Judaism, both philosophical and later racial, that emerged out of German modernism, but too many have not. Religious people attacked the Jews, the Nazis attacked the Jews – what's the difference? The differences were very great.

Victor Frankl, a psychiatrist who was also a Jewish survivor of the Holocaust, wrote: "I am absolutely convinced that the gas chambers of Auschwitz, Treblinka, and Maidenek were ultimately prepared not in some Ministry . . . in Berlin, but rather at the desks and in the lecture halls of nihilistic scientists and philosophers."[114] We may want to question his use of the term "nihilist," since the scientists and philosophers he referred to had very strong ideals and ethical systems. Nevertheless, he has a serious point that merits careful consideration. There were some important thinkers whose ideas Hitler skillfully welded into a coherent ideology of racial supremacy emerging out of life as conflict. Luther was not one of them.

It might be helpful to point out that people can dislike the same thing for widely disparate reasons. For example, someone on the left might dislike George Bush II because he didn't deal efficiently with the crisis of Hurricane

---

[112] Craig, *Germany 1866-1945*, p. 154 (both references to Stoecker in this paragraph).

[113] Paul Lawrence Rose, *German Question / Jewish Question: Revolutionary Antisemitism from Kant to Wagner* (Princeton: Princeton University Press, 1990), p. 109, 112.

[114] Jerry Bergman, *Hitler and the Nazi Darwinian Worldview* (Kitchener, Ontario: Joshua Press, 2012), p. 148 (the ellipsis is Bergman's).

Katrina; because he didn't have enough compassion for the poor; because he was not serious about the problem of global warming; because of the war in Iraq. Others might care nothing about those issues yet still dislike Bush because of his failure to close the border to illegal immigration; because of his violations of civil liberties; because of his reckless and wasteful spending; because of his failure to take his conservative Christian base seriously, and so on. Similarly, Germans could dislike Jews for any one of a number of reasons, including religious ones, without feeling Jews were the enemies of the master race and should all be killed. There are Americans today who do not like illegal aliens and would like to see them expelled – but not sent to death or slave labor camps.

A more detailed discussion of the Catholic and Protestant Churches in the Third Reich will have to be deferred to another chapter. For now, several points might serve to summarize the discussion of Protestant antisemitism. The first point has to do with Hitler's views of Protestantism; the second has to do with the actual condition of the Protestant churches when Hitler came to power in 1933. The third has to do with what it was Christ actually taught. These elementary points are usually overlooked by people whose understanding of Christianity is tenuous at best.

Concerning Hitler's views, he made a few references to Protestantism in *Mein Kampf*, references which I have not seen discussed elsewhere. In one fairly lengthy passage, Hitler the church historian completely nullified the Protestant Reformation and Catholicism as well by claiming that all of the many profound and irreconcilable differences between them were nothing but a Jewish trick. He explained in this passage that whether the Protestants or the Catholics emerged victorious was irrelevant – what was important was the survival of the Aryan race. He concluded by stating that even devout Protestants and Catholics could unite by forsaking their blind theological quarrels and uniting in obedience to Hitler.[115] If someone is not capable of understanding that this reveals Hitler's contempt for traditional Catholic and Protestant forms of Christianity, what can be done for them? Perhaps we can best help them by directing the conversation into more edifying areas (such as, "What does any of this have to do with Jesus Christ? Do you know what Christ taught?").

Elsewhere in *Mein Kampf*, Hitler asserted that neither the Catholics nor the Protestants understood the all-important question of race.[116] He conceded that

---

[115] Hitler, *Mein Kampf*, pp. 561-565.

[116] Ibid., pp. 111-113. For a striking example of how (when not completely ignored) these ideas of Hitler's have been selectively used and distorted by those who want to link Hitler to Christianity, see Samuel Koehne's "Reassessing *The Holy Reich*: Leading Nazis' Views on Confession, Community and 'Jewish' Materialism," *Journal of Contemporary History* 2013 48: 423), pp. 432-433. This is a scholarly and

Protestantism was "a better defender" of Germany's racial needs – this with reference to its genesis (in Germany) and to its later tradition (liberal Protestantism's openness to new trends and its denial of traditional doctrines). As to Protestantism's German genesis, it spread so rapidly throughout northern Europe because Luther was dealing with biblical issues, not German ones. England and Switzerland quickly equaled Germany as sources of Reformation teaching. Of course, one could not expect Hitler to have any understanding of such things.

As to the Protestant liberalism's modern tradition, in the preceding century and more much of the church had moved away from biblical authority and was hence much more amenable to significant changes. Nineteenth-century theological liberalism opened the doors of the church wide to many secular influences. But, in spite of this, Hitler went on to stress that Protestantism still failed on the (for him) essential Jewish question. He even went so far as to say that Protestantism "combats with the greatest hostility" attempts to solve the imaginary Jewish problem "since its attitude toward the Jews just happens to be more or less dogmatically established."[117]

When Hitler wrote his book in the 1920s, some people (though not nearly enough) were saying Hitler was wrong. Some Germans were saying, as they were not able to do after 1933, that the Germans were not the master race and Jews were not the enemies of humanity. One such example was a professor named O. Baumgarten who published a book in 1926 asserting the incompatibility of Christianity and Naziism. The book, which stated that "The cross and the swastika are mutually exclusive," was sent to every Protestant clergyman in Germany.[118] Naturally Hitler would interpret any denial of the Jewish threat or rejection of his program as being "hostile."

Various statements in *Mein Kampf* show Hitler's belief in the uselessness of traditional religion. Regrettably, they are consistently ignored by those who prefer to focus instead on some vague Christian-sounding rhetoric from Hitler's speeches, all of which were made early in his rule when he was also talking about world peace and international cooperation. This was when Hitler was still consolidating his power and felt a need to deal cautiously with the churches, especially while President Hindenburg was still alive. One historian notes that Hitler "made more references to God and to Christianity during the

---

secular critique of some serious errors of fact and of method in Richard Steigmann-Gall's book *The Holy Reich,* including neglect of important contrary evidence.

[117] Ibid., p. 113. Given the torrent of accusations, many of them made by those who seem to have little familiarity with Hitler's ideas on these subjects, some repetition may be excused.

[118] Wentorf, *Paul Schneider*, p. 21. Baumgarten's book was called *The Cross and the Swastika*. Wentorf mentions in this context some other obscure Christian publications critical of National Socialism before 1933.

first eight weeks following his appointment as chancellor than at any time thereafter."[119]

Why did Hitler never make such soothing statements during the war years? The answer should be obvious, and will be obvious to those who are not absolutely determined, no matter what, to link Hitler to Christianity. Possibly the thought that Hitler was motivated by secular concerns is too disquieting. It is much safer and easier to attack Christianity. In fact, Hitler made a number of other comments directly denying Christian teaching in *Mein Kampf*, but we can examine them in chapter 4 of this study.

After Hitler's views of Protestantism, the second point to our summary has to do with the state of the Protestant churches in Germany in 1933, centuries after the Reformation. Every institution or movement will go through great changes in such a long period, though it doesn't seem to be obvious to many who have zero knowledge of church history. Of course, not everyone has to read up on church history, but then perhaps they shouldn't try to write about it either. As early as the 1670s, some German Christians were concerned that Lutheranism had stagnated, that it had become merely a matter of ecclesiastical authority and intellectual discussions of doctrine without life, power, light, or genuine spiritual experience. This led to the emergence of Pietism, an attempt to find a more authentic experience within the Lutheran Protestant tradition.[120]

Along with a dull orthodoxy and individual attempts to find a more authentic experience, a third strand of Protestantism emerged in the nineteenth century. This is generally called theological liberalism, and developed out of the attempts of many Christian leaders to compromise biblical teachings with what they took to be the equally important or even more important insights derived from secular philosophy and from science. It is too little understood by many that long before 1933 much of modern German Protestantism had gone so far from the teachings of Luther as to have become a different religion entirely.

In his book *Reasonable Faith*, William Lane Craig presents a brief but effective overview of the internal spiritual collapse of the German churches. He states "The flood of Deist thought and literature that poured into eighteenth-century Germany from England and France wrought a crisis in German orthodox theology."[121] No longer capable of defending biblical

---

[119] Dean G. Stroud, *Preaching in Hitler's Shadow: Sermons of Resistance in the Third Reich* (Grand Rapids, MI: William B. Eerdmans, 2013), p. 5.

[120] Peter Watson, *The German Genius: Europe's Third Renaissance, The Second Scientific Revolution, and the Twentieth Century* (New York: Harper Perennial, 2011), pp. 45-47.

[121] William Lane Craig, *Reasonable Faith: Christian Truth and Apologetics* (Wheaton, IL: Crossway, 2008), p. 342.

doctrines now judged contrary to reason, but unwilling to dispense with Christianity altogether, increasingly Christian leaders were willing to concede that the Bible was full of mistakes, errors, myths, and false teachings, but somehow contained some spiritual and ethical truths nevertheless. Such views quickly became dominant among official German Protestantism.

Significantly, Bismarck's *Kulturkampf*, the attempt to break the power of the Catholic Church in Germany, was not based on Lutheran biblical interpretations of salvation, church authority, and the Bible. It was because Catholic opposition to modern trends made the Roman Church into "the enemy of liberalism, of belief in reform, above all of opposition to the cultivation of the human intellect and spirit in civic society"[122] through modern education emphasizing science and the humanities. Also, after the assertion of papal infallibility by a Vatican Council in 1870, loyalty to the Pope was seen as incompatible to loyalty to the Kaiser and the newly formed German Empire. Protestantism, however, with its abandonment of traditional doctrines was seen as more amenable to progress.

Nineteenth – century Germany, far from being a Christian country based on the Reformation, was known throughout the Christian world as the leading source of new ideas of biblical criticism that denied the divine authority and truth of the Bible. Church historian Philip Schaff wrote in the nineteenth century that the "critical and historical rationalism which was born and matured in this century in the land of Luther" was based on "opposition to the supernatural and the miraculous."[123] Another writer states, "But how did theological liberalism come about? In order to understand this, we must go back about 250 years to Germany where theological liberalism was born."[124]

Schaeffer states in this context that already by the middle of the eighteenth century German universities had lost a living and vital Lutheran orthodoxy, and notes "In church history a cycle seems to recur: living orthodoxy moves to dead orthodoxy and then to heterodoxy."[125] This is not to deny that some genuine Christian influence remained – but Christianity was no longer intellectually dominant. The forces of theological conservatism fought a futile rearguard action, but powerful forces of change made the old-time religion seem less and less relevant to many. Those who did not abandon it altogether thought they could adapt Christianity to the new times. This would, it was hoped, make Christianity more acceptable to sophisticated modern man, but in

---

[122] Watson, *German Genius*, pp. 421-422 (both for the quote and for comments on the conflict of loyalty that follow).

[123] Schaff, *History of the Christian Church*, pp. 856, 858.

[124] Francis Schaeffer, *The Church at the End of the Twentieth Century* (Wheaton, IL: Crossway Books, 1994), p. 110.

[125] Ibid., p. 111.

the end this spirit of surrender and compromise contributed in no small measure to the pathetic collapse of the German churches.

So-called higher biblical criticism – inappropriately called a "science" – was based on the principle that the Bible was to be treated as an ordinary book, written by ordinary means, and hence vulnerable to distortions and errors. Theology became merely humanistic interpretations and explanations of what were once considered to be the eternal foundations of Christianity, and the Bible came to be studied as a cultural product of the times in which it was written. A "profound ideological and philosophical shift was taking place," and liberal theology "tended simply to follow the curve of secular naturalism."[126] It was not because of Luther that German "Protestant" "theologians" followed Hitler. They had been abandoning Reformation principles and following the world for a century and more before Hitler came to power.

This theological progressivism included among others the ideas that Jesus did not die on the cross, but only swooned and later revived; that the Jews had no divine revelation but invented a fictionalized history; that the Gospels were not accurate records of what Christ did and taught; that the most important thing was to be sincere (surely that would be good enough for a God of love); that the apostles did not receive their teaching from Christ but made things up as it seemed right to them. All of this, of course, used words about "Christ . . . faith . . . the Gospel . . . love . . . salvation . . . grace" in a manner very confusing to those who are ignorant of these issues and judge only by outward appearances. This has been aptly summarized by J. Gresham Machen, who wrote that modern theological liberalism is "a totally diverse type of religious belief, which is only the more destructive of the Christian faith because it makes use of traditional Christian terminology."[127]

People who like to imagine that Germany was a Christian country, "the most Christian country on earth," know little about the subject. They have almost certainly never heard of the eighteenth-century professor Herrmann Samuel Reimarus. This individual wrote a lengthy critique of Christianity, published after his death by the famed humanist Gottfried Lessing. This Deistic work denied the resurrection of Christ, the biblical miracles, and the Old Testament narratives. Reimarus claimed that Jesus failed in his earthly mission and was executed, after which the disciples stole his body and fabricated a story about a resurrection.

In the first half of the nineteenth century David Friedrich Strauss wrote a book, *The Life of Jesus* (*Leben Jesu*) (1835). He did not want to dismiss Christianity outright as a mere apostolic fraud like Reimarus did, so he

---

[126] Ibid., pp. 110-111.

[127] John Gresham Machen, *Christianity and Liberalism* (Charleston, SC: Bibliolife, date not given, reprint of the 1923 edition), p. 2.

invented the theory that the myths and legends of Christianity developed slowly and naturally over time. The resurrection of Christ never occurred, but it did have spiritual significance – as other myths also contained deeper meanings. Again according to Craig, "Strauss's work completely altered the tone and course of German theology."[128] Now German "theologians" did not have to worry about the mistakes, errors, contradictions, and seemingly unscientific parts of the Bible. They could concede all of that, and still speak about the Bible's religious and spiritual significance – but unfortunately, with the Christ of faith detached from the Christ of history, theology entered a never-never land of speculation grounded solidly on thin air. This led to "faith" in some idea of Christ without the certainty of a literal, factual, historical Bible, the "faith" that we find in Bultmann, Barth, Bonhoeffer and other popular modern theologians.

According to Francis Schaeffer, "Karl Barth's basic position was this: Of course, the Bible has all kinds of mistakes in it, but it doesn't matter; believe it religiously."[129] Bultmann was far more extreme than Barth, and openly described fundamental biblical doctrines as mythology. With this neo-orthodoxy, to quote Schaeffer again, "theology stepped from the solid earth of rationality into a land where anything can happen." As the nineteenth century progressed, liberal and neo-orthodox so-called theology not surprisingly turned out to be helpless before newer and more powerful ideas such as Hegelianism, Romanticism, Marxism, Darwinism, social Darwinism, Freudianism, and National Socialism.

Reimarus and Strauss were not isolated figures. They represented deep and broad trends. Traditional biblical Christianity became increasingly out of date, and more and more people looked not to philosophy but to science and theology. In the words of Alister McGrath, "As clerical power began to decline in the eighteenth century, Western society began to look to others for moral vision and intellectual inspiration. It found such leaders in the growing community of intellectuals."[130] Too many people talk about "Christian Europe" and "Christian Germany" as if the great movement toward secularism that began in the eighteenth century and became increasingly dominant in the 19th century had never occurred. McGrath continues,

> At some point, perhaps one that can never be determined with historical accuracy, Western society came to believe that it should look elsewhere than to its clergy for guidance. Instead, they turned to the intellectuals, who were able to portray their clerical

---

[128] Craig, *Reasonable Faith*, p. 347.

[129] Schaeffer, *The Church at the End of the Twentieth Century*, p. 115 (both quotes).

[130] Alister McGrath, *The Twilight of Atheism: The Rise and Fall of Disbelief in the Modern World* (London: Rider, 2004), p. 49.

opponents as lazy fools who could do no more than unthinkingly repeat the slogans and nostrums of an increasingly distant past. A new future lay ahead, and society needed brave new thinkers to lead them to its lush Promethean pastures.[131]

It is difficult to overemphasize the profoundly irreligious nature of the upper reaches of German intellectual society, though of course much traditional belief still remained. Hegel, Kant, Feuerbach, Schopenhauer and other leading lights of German philosophy were none of them believers in the truth of the Bible or of the necessity of faith in Christ for salvation of sin. Kant and Hegel have been called "Protestant" philosophers not because of their ideas, which were thoroughly unbiblical. They have been mistaken for Protestants because they were born and lived in a certain longitude and latitude; grew up in a vaguely "Protestant" milieu; stressed the beneficial effects of Protestant Christianity in Europe's cultural development; or had a great influence on later liberal Protestants who found human philosophy more inspiring than divine revelation – but no serious student of philosophy has ever claimed those men were devout Christians who believed that Jesus died on the cross so that they might be saved from their sins and escape God's justice on the day of judgment as the divinely inspired Bible taught.

When someone claims that Kant reaffirmed the Christian worldview in his philosophy, we may reasonably infer that he has no knowledge of Christianity, or of Kantian philosophy, or both. In a well-known essay *An Answer to the Question: What is Enlightenment?* Kant expressed deep hostility to unchanging divinely revealed dogmas as representing the immaturity of mankind. He saw eternal unchanging truths as fetters that hindered the free spiritual and intellectual progress of mankind. In *Religion Within the Limits of Reason Alone* Kant revealed his open disbelief in many basic Christian doctrines. The title itself is a denial of divine revelation as a source of knowledge. Because of the cultural constraints of that day Kant was compelled to say some nice things about religion from time to time, but at the heart of his philosophy is a rejection of the traditional concept of a personal God, and an affirmation of the power of autonomous human reason.[132]

Cultural historian Peter Watson illustrated the decline of religious influence with some revealing statistics. He stated that the percentage of theological books published in Germany fell from 46 percent of the total in 1625 to a mere 6 percent in 1800.[133] He also spoke of Romantic concepts such as (among

---

[131] Ibid.

[132] I hope to be able to describe elsewhere Kant's political authoritarianism, elitism, philosophical indifference to human suffering, and new forms of antisemitism, and to show that he articulated some potentially fascist trends albeit in embryonic form.

[133] Watson, *German Genius*, p. 56.

other things) that of the "outcast genius . . . rebelling against a tame and philistine society" or "martyrs, tragic heroes who fought for their beliefs against overwhelming odds" that could easily have been applied to Hitler by his admirers.[134] Peter Viereck's dated but still useful study of National Socialism sees German romanticism as more significant to the emergence of Nazi ideas than any sixteenth-century thinker.[135]

Along with other links between modern trends and Hitler, Watson mentioned "Hitler's affinity for Hegel."[136] This will seem incredible to those who think that the man who rose from nothing to lead one of the most advanced countries in the world was too dense to read a book, but there are numerous philosophical themes from modern German thought scattered randomly throughout *Mein Kampf*. For example, the importance of great men of history, as well as a belief in the possibility of unending human progress, were basic ideas of Hegel that found their way somehow into Hitler's book. This does not mean, of course, that Hitler was a scholar or an academic philosopher. Hegel's influence was widespread, and some of his more accessible ideas were easily popularized. Thus we find Goethe saying "God does not exercise influence on earth except through outstanding chosen men."[137]

This was one of Hitler's favorite ideas. Wherever he picked it up, it has nothing to do with Reformation doctrines. Hegel wrote that Alexander the Great, Julius Caesar, and Napoleon Bonaparte derived "their purposes and vocation" from the "inner spirit," and asserted that they represented "the very truth for their age, for their world." He went on to praise these "World-historical men . . . the Heroes of an epoch," and claimed that "their deeds, their words are the best of their time."[138] The deeds of these heroes, of course, includes the deeds of the many soldiers who carried out their acts and brought the great heroes' plans to fulfillment

Calling the words and deeds of those blood-stained conquerors and their minions and myrmidons, men drunk with their own glory and indifferent to the suffering they caused, "the best of their time" completely denies the Sermon on the Mount. Other Hegelian rhetoric also shows how, as in the Goethe quote, religious words like "God . . . divine . . . spirit" can be used in support of ideas

---

[134] Ibid., p. 198. The comparison to Hitler is mine, not Watson's.

[135] Viereck, Peter. *Meta-politics: The Roots of the Nazi Mind* (New York: Capricorn Books, 1965). Viereck emphasizes the importance of Richard Wagner as a source of Hitler's ideas.

[136] Watson, *German Genius*, p. 615.

[137] Ibid., p. 118.

[138] William L. Shirer, *The Rise and Fall of the Third Reich: A History of Nazi Germany* (New York 2011), pp. 110-111 (quoting Hegel's *Lectures on the Philosophy of History*).

antithetical to scriptural Christianity. The biblical emphasis on the vanity of human glory and its preference for God's work with common, ordinary, and lowly people completely nullifies both National Socialism and Hegel's conceited, useless and empty pseudo-philosophy as well (see for example I Corinthians 1:26-29, as well as Matthew 5: 3-12, to give only two of many possible examples). If we really want to understand the Third Reich we need to hear less about Luther and more about Hegel.

It seems to be a common claim that *Mein Kampf* consists only of gutter philosophy that Hitler got from newspapers, pamphlets, and half-baked conversations, yet ideas from some of Germany's finest minds are found there.[139] Hitler's desire to unite all of the Germans in Europe in one state, for example, is found in Fichte, one of the leading lights of German idealistic philosophy – not in any thinker of the sixteenth century. When Hitler wrote on the opening page of his book that Europe's Germans should be united in one state,[140] he was expressing a (to many) self-evident truth with respectable intellectual antecedents.

Hitler's belief in the necessity of racial purity for victory in the struggle for survival, as well as numerous other ideas, link him to significant trends in modern German, not Reformation, thought. For example, oneness with Nature in opposition to the falsehood of modern civilization was another theme of Hitler's that went back to the Romantics (though of course the pre-Darwinian Romantics had a different understanding of "nature" than did Hitler). Condemnations of Jewish materialism, a standard Nazi theme, point back to the "Enlightenment," to Kant, Fichte, and other secular antisemites. The extraordinary claim of Hitler's that Judaism was not really a religion at all is found in Kant,[141] and in many others who shared Kant's secular mindset. It is not found anywhere in the dozens of volumes of Luther's collected works. Neither is it found in any other traditionally Christian thinker. As has already been noted, Luther considered the Jewish scriptures to be the authentic word of God, translated them, and appealed to them for support of his Reformation ideas.

Significantly, while Hegel, Fichte, and others considered Christianity to be the highest manifestation of truth in its day, they also considered it to be merely a stage in an ongoing process of development. For them, the process of

---

[139] In his book *Hitler's Private Library: The Books that Shaped his Life,* Timothy Ryback has gathered credible testimonies that Hitler was a heavy reader from people who knew him at various stages in his life. Hitler also made some extended comments in *Mein Kampf* on the importance of reading. Hitler's political rivals consistently underestimated his intelligence and so do many scholars today.

[140] Hitler, *Mein Kampf*, p. 3.

[141] Immanuel Kant, *Religion Within the Limits of Reason Alone*, trans. Theodore M. Greene (Clermont Ferrand, France: Digireads, 2011), p. 78.

historical development that had led from the ancient civilizations of Mesopotamia, to Greece, to Rome and now to Germany did not stop in 1517 with the Protestant Reformation. The process continued, and traditional biblical teachings were not eternal truths, but rather were historically and culturally determined temporary "truths," good in their day, but representative of a lower stage of development. Truth was considered to an ongoing part of mankind's moral and spiritual development, discovered by autonomous human reason, not given by divine revelation as Luther and all of the Reformers understood it to be.

"To the Germans particularly – Hegel, Schopenhauer, Schelling, and Fichte – we owe the establishment of the basic evolutionary notion that Being is Becoming and that fixity is an abstraction or an illusion."[142] Unchanging truth and divine laws which we were required to obey were considered to be barriers to further growth and development, and when German philosophers of the 1800s spoke of the social benefits of Christianity they were referring either to past achievements, way stations on the road of progress, or else to the need for common people to have some kind of ethical base derived from tradition, because the masses were incapable of attaining to higher philosophy. Luther was praised for rejecting medieval Catholic dogmas, but was also considered to have set in motion a process of spiritual liberation that continued after him.

One German author who was popular in the 1890s, Julius Langbehn, called for not one but three reformations. Luther's was the first; the humanist Gotthold Ephraim Lessing's was the second (in the eighteenth century); the third was to be based on "art, not science or religion," as "the higher good, the true source of knowledge and virtue." Rembrandt was for him the symbol of the artistic integrity which alone could save the German people. He mixed his passion for art with "nationalism, faith, intuition, and philosophy,"[143] and was a leading figure in the racist, antisemitic and nationalist Folkish movement which is commonly seen as a precursor in some important ways of National Socialism. Parenthetically, it may be recalled from a few pages previously that it was Lessing, Langbehn's second great reformer, who published Reimarus' account of Christianity as a fraud.

Since we are constantly hearing about Luther's influence on a supposedly Christian Germany, it might not be amiss to point out the deep hostility to Christianity that emerged in Germany with the so-called Enlightenment. For example Kant saw traditional religion as immaturity, and rejected relying on sacred books and religious authorities for the answers we were supposed to find for ourselves by the exercise of reason. He described religious dogma as

---

[142] Jacques Barzun, *Darwin, Marx, Wagner: Critique of a Heritage* (New York: Doubleday Anchor Books, 1958), p. 52.

[143] Watson, *German Genius*, pp. 432-433 (all three quotes).

"the ball and chain of his [the believer's] perpetual immaturity."[144] He did not believe Jesus Christ was God come to earth in human form, was born of a virgin, and died on the cross as a sacrifice for our sins.

Kant expressed himself in mild terms, but opposition to Christianity increased over time. Christian teachings of submission to even foreign authorities were anathema to the fiery nationalists who refused to submit to Napoleon as Christ and the early Christians submitted to Rome. Biblical teachings were completely contrary to the lofty philosophical programs of German idealistic philosophy. Schopenhauer openly rejected divinely revealed religious doctrines as childish superstition. Later in the century, Ernst Haeckel, Germany's leading Darwinist, ridiculed Christianity – and these men were only the most visible representatives of broad and deep cultural currents.

People who claim that Germany was a Christian country are ignorant of both Christianity and Germany. A darkening paganism intensified over that unhappy land with each passing decade. As German nationalism and racialism increased in intensity along with the growing industrial and military power of the new Germany, the Jewish aspects of Christianity drew increasingly unfavorable attention. Lagarde, Langbehn, Wagner and many others saw Christianity as unGermanic. Some of them rejected it altogether, while others tried to salvage something by inventing an Aryan Christ, and purifying Christianity of its Jewish influence (it was claimed by some that Christian ideas had originated in India but were contaminated by Jews).[145]

Comments from this period about Jewish control of Europe sound like the mutterings of a lunatic in a padded cell, until we realize that Jewish influence meant also Christian influence – and Christian influence meant all of the developments of democracy, liberalism, and capitalism which had emerged (as they saw it) out of Christian influence. That all of these unhealthy modern developments were the result of Semitic Christianity, in contrast to the proud and free simplicity of the noble pre-Christian Germanic pagans, was a basic theme of Wagner's. It was also a common theme of many other nationalist romantics, racists, and anti-Semites, of whom Wagner is only an example.[146]

This hostility to Christianity reached a high point in Nietzsche, who blasted Christianity as a Jewish trick, a system of cowardly lies devised by devious

---

[144] Immanuel Kant, *An Answer to the Question: What is Enlightenment?*, trans. H. B. Nisbet (London: Penguin Books, 2009), p. 2.

[145] The idea that the Jewish people originated in India goes back to the ancient Greeks – see Josephus, *Josephus: The Life & Against Apion*, trans. H. St. J. Thackeray (Cambridge, Mass: Harvard University Press, 1966), p. 235.

[146] While we can be thankful for the work that has been done on the Darwin-Hitler relationship, the many non-Darwinian aspects of National Socialism have deep roots in German romanticism and idealistic philosophy.

Semites to ensnare stronger peoples with a fake slave morality. In Nietzsche's words,

> . . . the Christian Church as compared with the "chosen people," lacks all claim to originality. Precisely on this account the Jews are the most *fatal* people in the history of the world: their ultimate influence has falsified mankind to such an extent, that even to this day the Christian can be anti-Semitic in spirit, without comprehending that he himself is the *final consequence of Judaism.*[147]

This quote, incidentally, explains how Nietzsche could say so many bad things about Jews yet condemn antisemitism in others – they had the wrong kind of antisemitism. Christian antisemitism was for Nietzsche a pathetic joke – condemnations of Jews by people who were themselves infected with Jewish values but didn't even know it. This included much outwardly secular philosophical antisemitism as well, for Nietzsche saw even German philosophy as infected with Christian concepts of "truth."

Nietzsche had his own private brand of Jew-hatred, and so made negative comments about other anti-Semites who did not measure up to his standard. One of their faults was their failure to recognize the Jewish nature of the Christianity Nietzsche so frantically hated: "the category of men which aspires to power in Judaism and Christianity – that is to say, for the sacerdotal class . . . What is Jewish morality, what is Christian morality?"[148] – one could go on and on. "We should feel just as little inclined to hobnob with 'the first Christians' as with Polish Jews: not that we need explain our objections . . . They simply smell bad."[149]

It is regrettable that some people whose hobby is attacking Luther, and other people who want to protect Nietzsche's reputation as the First Philosopher of atheism, do not pay more attention to the *Antichrist*. The book has been consistently misrepresented, but it should be studied carefully by those with an academic interest in the origins of National Socialism (not by anyone seeking a better understanding of Christianity or of life, though). The book says a great deal about the climate out of which Hitler emerged – and Nietzsche was not the lone ranger some mistake him for. In many ways he only presented a more extreme form of ideas advocated by others, and was not completely detached from his age.

It is assumed by many that since Nietzsche's basic idea of rejecting God is rational and good, he cannot possibly have any connection with Hitler's ideas,

---

[147] Friedrich Nietzsche, *The Antichrist*, trans. Anthony M. Ludovici (Amherst, NY: Prometheus Books, 2000), pp. 30-31 (section 24) (emphasis Nietzsche's).

[148] Ibid., pp. 31-32 (section 24), p. 33 (section 25).

[149] Ibid., p. 70 (section 46) (the ellipsis is Nietzsche's).

which were irrational and bad. Since Luther's basic ideas of a personal God who manifested himself to us in Christ and in the Bible on the other hand are widely considered to be irrational and bad, the connection to Hitler is much *easier* and also more *personally gratifying* for *subjective* and *emotional* reasons. People want to discredit the world view Luther so effectively represented at his best and in his prime – so they are less inclined to be objective when discussing him.

Alfred Rosenberg's state-approved book *The Myth of the Twentieth Century* had an understanding of Christianity very close and in some respects identical to that which Nietzsche presented in *The Antichrist*. That Christianity was an invention of the apostle Paul; that sin, judgment, and punishment in hell were fictions opposed to a "healthy" view of life; that Christianity had a false system of ethics – these and other ideas of Rosenberg's show the relevance of Nietzsche's critique of Christianity to an understanding of the Third Reich.[150]

Nor will it suffice to say that Hitler disavowed Rosenberg's book. He frequently disavowed extreme acts and statements by his supporters while doing nothing to prevent them. Rosenberg's book was official Nazi doctrine, and criticism of it was forbidden. Hitler appointed Rosenberg to important positions and consulted with him on important issues. Moreover, while Hitler could afford to dismiss some of Rosenberg's wilder flights of mythology, he would never have permitted the book to be published as an official statement of Nazi doctrine if it had directly contradicted him on any important point.

Studying the Reformation will not help us to understand Hitler. German culture before World War I was thoroughly up-to-date artistically, philosophically, scientifically, musically, culturally – and it is striking, the extent to which some of Hitler's most fundamental ideas can be made to fit within the guidelines of some of the most representative trends of modern rationalism.[151] Take for example *utilitarianism*: the criterion of the rightness of an action is not some divine law, but whether or not it facilitates the survival and expansion of the German race. There is also *empiricism*: does not empirical evidence gathered from the scientific observation of nature teach us that the weak and the unfit are remorselessly weeded out, and this is healthy, beneficial, and necessary to the advancement of the species? Let us not forget *positivism*: ethics and other lofty ideas are merely products of the human

---

[150] For a brief summary of Rosenberg on Christianity see Watson, *German Genius*, pp. 620-621.

[151] I have taken the following four basic concepts from F. A. Hayek's *The Fatal Conceit: The Errors of Socialism* (Chicago: University of Chicago Press, 1991), p. 61. Paradoxically, a rationalist emphasis on reason alone can lead in the end to some very irrational ideas, as well as to the idea that reason itself is secondary to will and to instinct.

imagination, whereas reality is found in "exact scientific truth" and "cold logic."[152]

Finally, there is *rationalism*: a right understanding of human life comes not from some higher external source, but is discoverable by the autonomous human mind unaided. We rely solely on experience and thought to arrive at truth. This detached and objective observation of the world around us teaches us that it is only normal for the sick and the weak and the less fit to perish. This is natural and healthy, and people who see it as cruel are weaklings.[153] This philosophy of Hitler's did not come from the gutter, either – unless we want to consider Nietzsche, one of modernity's most revered philosophers, or Ernst Haeckel, Wilhelmine Germany's leading Darwinist, and many other respected German opinion makers as having written from there.

Nietzsche asserted with complete certainty and confidence in his own intuition that kindness and pity for the weak were unhealthy and sick: "On the whole, pity thwarts the law of development which is the law of selection. It preserves that which is ripe for death . . . Nothing is more unhealthy in the midst of our unhealthy modernity, than Christian pity."[154] This is why Nietzsche said "The weak and the botched shall perish: first principle of our humanity . . . What is more harmful than any vice? – Practical sympathy with all the botched and the weak – Christianity."[155]

What should be one of the most disturbing things about Hitler, but is often missed, is the extent to which he was in the beginning a very logical man. He reasoned soundly and in a straight line, to the outermost limit, from widely accepted and respected (though false and ugly) presuppositions. Captain Truman Smith, who was stationed at the American Embassy in Berlin as an assistant military attaché, had a lengthy private conversation with Hitler in 1922. He wrote of the meeting afterwards, "Have rarely listened to such a logical and fanatical man . . . In private conversation he disclosed himself as a forceful and logical speaker, which, when tempered with a fanatical earnestness, made a very deep impression on a neutral listener."[156] No flags, no parades, no songs, no theater – just ideas and logic that were very convincing to lost, bitter and unhappy people groping in darkness. Hitler's theatrics were important and effective, but secondary.

Too many people try to analyze Hitler without understanding the power and the cogency of his ideas. We can easily recognize them as being evil and destructive now, after the fact, but this was not evident to enough Germans at

---

[152] Hitler, *Mein Kampf*, p. 287.

[153] Ibid., p. 285.

[154] Nietzsche, *The Antichrist*, pp. 7-8, 9 (section 7).

[155] Ibid., p. 4 (section 2). Part of this quote was given earlier, but a little repetition of this neglected aspect of Nietzsche's thought will do no harm.

[156] Shirer, *The Rise and Fall of the Third Reich*, pp. 46-47, fn.

the time. If it had been, they would never have supported him. Hitler gave many people hope, meaning, purpose, a goal, a sense of worth, and they were starved for those things. Given the decades of failure of passive and dull liberal Christianity and the emptiness of modernism's claim that human beings were merely beasts in a pointless, cold and impersonal universe, Hitler was like a beacon of light in the darkness.

Hitler was far above "the wretched gabble of politics."[157] He transcended the "national egotism" of dull bourgeois complacency, and condemned the German bourgeoisie many times in *Mein Kampf*.[158] Hitler more than anyone else had "courage for the forbidden." He honored himself, he loved himself, and he understood that "One must be superior to humanity in power, in loftiness of soul, – in contempt." He rejected "indolent peace, [and] its cowardly compromise," and above all he provided the Germans with "The formula of our happiness: a Yea, a Nay, a straight line, a goal." He understood Nietzsche's teaching that happiness was power, and that sympathy for the weak was worse than any vice. It is not hard to understand why someone might think that Hitler, "feared" and "terrible," was the *higher type* of Nietzsche's dreams, a man without mercy and without pity, a man of "thunderbolts and great deeds."

It should not be necessary to point out that all of these ideas have nothing whatever to do with what Jesus Christ taught, and many Christians believe. Jesus said, "Straight is the gate and narrow is the way that leadeth unto life, and few there be that find it" – a plain enough teaching consistently ignored by people who so light-heartedly paste the label "Christian" on someone with no regard to what they might have actually believed. Erich Koch, for example, a high-ranking Nazi official and Gauleiter of East Prussia, is called a Christian believer merely because he said "I held the view that the Nazi idea had to develop from a basic Prussian-Protestant attitude and from Luther's unfinished Reformation."[159] The "unfinished Reformation" of course meant that people in

---

[157] See pages 1-5 of Nietzsche's *Antichrist* for all quotes and related ideas in this paragraph. The italics are Nietzsche's. Nietzsche's dictum that the superior man "must honor himself, he must love himself" (p. 1), is at the very heart of the Hitler problem. This is the antithesis of the Christian emphasis on self-denial, mandated by the fact that our ideas and desires are so often wrong.

[158] For some of Hitler's denunciations of Germany's cowardly, rotten, stupid, worthless bourgeois culture and government, see *Mein Kampf,* pp. 373, 386, 406-407, 452 and elsewhere. That Nietzsche had a low view of the German people is commonly used to distance him from Hitler, but Hitler also had a low view of the German people, and openly expressed his contempt not only for the bourgeoisie, but also for the masses.

[159] Laurence Rees, *Hitler's Charisma: Leading Millions into the Abyss* (New York: Pantheon Books, 2012), p. 102. Rees takes this from Richard Steigmann-Gall's

the 1940s could not be held to 16th-century conceptions of faith and biblical authority. Luther's departure from Catholicism was a step in the right direction, but only a step. Full liberation from religious dogma had yet to be achieved. Science and philosophy had revealed new truths since Luther's day, new truths on which National Socialism was held to be firmly based.

Asserting that such a statement makes one a Christian believer requires a blithe indifference to all biblical standards of what it means to be a Christian. It also ignores the fact that Nazis after the war were not truthful and upright people who frankly confessed to their deeds and motives. On the contrary, they consistently sought to minimize their guilt and justify what they did with pathetic excuses. And what does a Prussian attitude of militarism, territorial conquest, and love of power have to do with Christ, or with the millions of Christians who, in obedience to Christ, have never cared about those things? Saying "I have a Prussian-Protestant attitude and Luther took a step in the right direction" does not prove or show or indicate or even imply that one wants to follow the teachings of Jesus Christ as God come to earth in human form, so that he might escape the wrath of God and be accepted into heaven when he dies.

By rejecting more and more biblical dogma, including the deity of Christ, his sacrificial death, the day of judgment and so on, "Protestantism" progressed so far from its starting point as to be, in effect, a new religion using Christian language. It should also be recalled that in the early part of the nineteenth century in Germany the church was very closely allied to the state, and overt attacks on Christianity were considered to be unacceptable. Kant got into trouble with the King of Prussia for deviating too far from Christian orthodoxy. He meekly submitted, although he was in no danger of being sent to a concentration camp. It was some time before those who rejected Christianity felt able to criticize it directly. So, vague general comments in favor of Christianity that had nothing at all to do with the main points of philosophy really had little meaning.

It is only natural that a secular author should assume that every theologian was a "devout Christian." That a "devout" Christian pastor, theologian, or bishop might have denied the divine inspiration of the Bible and found it to be full of mistakes, errors, and legends; questioned the reality of Christ's resurrection; thought that the kingdom of God was to come in this life only, as the result of social action; believed in the theory of evolution; and found more inspiration in Kant and Hegel than in Peter and Paul – this is too hard for many to understand. It should be recognized that the decision of such people to follow Hitler was based not on Christianity, but on the abandonment of Christianity.

The Holy Reich, but since Steigmann-Gall has been shown to selectively manipulate quotes – see footnote # 116 on page 92 – it is possible this quote also is incomplete.

When historians who have no understanding of the Christian religion and of recent church history present National Socialist quotes from Protestant figures (or from Catholic figures) to show Christian support for Hitler, they do not understand that what they are presenting are views of those who, if they were not simply fooled in the early part of Hitler's career or cowed into submission against their consciences, had abandoned the foundational truths of biblical Christianity and replaced them with worldly philosophies. Such evidence often shows not the Christian influence on Naziism, but rather the forsaking of traditional beliefs by people who accepted many new ideas contrary to the Bible, but still derived comfort from religious language. In outward appearance they may seem to have been Christians, but in spite of their religious rhetoric their beliefs were from the world. They illustrate nothing more than the failure of people with the name of "Christian" to stand faithfully by their beliefs.

Not long ago, someone who was attacking Christianity found a Protestant pastor who supported the Nazis' euthanasia program. This pastor was given as an example of how evil the Christians were, and of how Christianity was related to Naziism. The fact that some Darwinists had been calling for such a program long before Hitler was not mentioned. In the same vein, Richard Evans mentions "Protestant charities" whose "doctrines of predestination and original sin" led them to welcome sterilization of the unfit.[160] He neglected to point out that such ideas were unheard of in preceding centuries. What reputable Christian has ever used the doctrines of original sin or predestination as an excuse for sterilizing people ? The worthlessness of individual human life and the denial of the significance of the immortal soul are secular concepts, not biblical ones. It was not until the advent of the modern scientific age, and especially the advent of Darwinism, that people began to dispassionately argue for forced sterilization, for the extermination of the weak, the sick, the handicapped, the mentally ill, even unborn or newly born babies.

The pastor just referred to was abandoning the Bible and following the world. His quote, if it is genuine, shows the evil of the modern ideas to which he was conforming, not the evils of the Christianity he was denying. This also applies to many other quotes by Christians that seem to show agreement with Nazi ideals. Such evidence only illustrates the weakness of people with the name of Christians who failed to stand against the world. It says in the book of James that the friendship of the world is enmity with God, and "whosoever will be a friend of the world is the enemy of God." But, we cannot blame secular historians too much for not understanding this when even many Christians pay little attention to it.

---

[160] Evans, *The Coming of the Third Reich*, p. 377.

Some Christians are seriously committed to following the teachings of Christ (however imperfectly), but others are not. For those who are capable of understanding that not all Christians are the same, we can say that there were different types of Protestants in the Third Reich. We can recognize among them: (a) theological liberals who had long ago decided to follow the world and effortlessly conformed to the new ideas; (b) conventional conservatives as well as old-fashioned liberals who resented Nazi attempts to control the church and sought to retain some autonomy, all the while asserting their loyalty to Hitler; (c) religious people of various sorts, orthodox and liberal, who knew that Naziism was wrong but kept their mouths shut and went along out of fear; and (d) Christians who (like many other people) simply had the wool pulled over their eyes by Hitler and did not know what he was until it was too late.

Finally, we should not forget (e) a very few rare individuals, both Protestant and Catholic, who publicly opposed National Socialism. They paid a very heavy price, and their names do not usually come up in discussions of the Third Reich. Few if any of those who so lightly criticize the Christians from their positions of comfort and safety would have done the same. I don't remember ever having read of any Darwinist opposition to Hitler.

We are constantly told about the churches who failed to stand against Hitler. We hear less about the university professors, scientists, physicists, philosophers and biologists who also failed to stand against Hitler. True, Christianity claims to be a higher truth revealed from above – but don't unbelievers also claim to have truthful insights into life and how it should be lived? It is not purported to be a truth revealed by God from heaven, but it is still truth to them – and their truth did not lead them to oppose Hitler. Did any professor of Kantian or Hegelian philosophy ever risk losing his job or being incarcerated by telling his students in class that "A study of Kant and Hegel will reveal to us that the Germans are not the master race, and the Fuhrer is not infallible"? No one has ever died or ever will die for Kant's imaginary and useless ethical system. And Hegel? Ordinary individuals had no place in his grandiose nineteenth-century Prussian hallucinations.

As for Christians in Germany who seriously believed in the Bible as the Word of God and did their best to base their lives on the teachings of Christ, what could they have done to stop Hitler? Are not abortion, pornography, homosexuality, and Darwinism totally contrary to a belief in the truth of the Bible? Many Christians in America today think those things are wrong, and yet nothing can be done to stop them. Does anyone believe that a few pastors preaching in 1930 could have prevented the rise of Hitler by saying "According to the Bible, what is important is where you spend eternity, not how great and powerful Germany is"? If many pastors had preached that, and many Germans had sincerely believed and understood them, that would have made a difference – but many such pastors and many such Christians did not exist.

109

Much more could be said about these things. For the present, we can conclude this chapter by emphasizing what should be an elementary and obvious point: the validity of biblical Christianity is not determined by the churches in one particular country in extremely unusual circumstances nearly two thousand years after Christ died and rose again. Christ's teachings to treat others like we would want them to treat us; to not be concerned with earthly power and glory but to seek the kingdom of heaven; to have a healthy and respectful fear of God who is aware of all of our deeds and even of the secrets of our hearts; to walk uprightly and soberly, mindful of our end in an eternity of heaven or of hell – these and other Jewish doctrines were anathema to the Nazis. They were also rejected by many with the name of "Lutheran" and "Christian" who in their hearts had surrendered to the spirit of the age, and retained only the outward forms of religion without the spirit or substance.

If those of us who believe in a resurrection from the dead, in a day of judgment in which the righteous will be received into paradise and the wicked will be eternally punished, and in the manifestation of God in Christ, as described in the Bible – if we poor Evangelicals and Fundamentalists are blamed for Hitler in this benighted age, while those who rejected the Bible and taught ideas very close if not identical to Hitler's are exonerated, that cannot be helped. Such is the way of this dark and sinful world. Too many people want to avoid or even hate the Christian message and are glad for any chance to discredit it, no matter how far-fetched. But, Christ has taught us how we should respond to falsehood directed against us for his sake.

Luther by his mistakes gave them some ammunition, but it should not be hard for a genuinely impartial observer to recognize the anti-Christian origins of the new ideas that Hitler so skillfully welded into a coherent and compelling ideology. Before we look into that, however, there are unfortunately two more barriers that must be overcome – profound misunderstandings of Hitler's relationship to Christianity, and serious misconceptions about the Christians who had to live under Hitler's tyranny. These will require examination in chapters 4 and 5.

Chapter 4. Hitler's Religious, Quasi-religious and Anti-religious Ideas

Imagine a high-ranking official in the former Soviet Union. He is a member of the Communist Party, attends meetings, participates actively, and has pictures of Marx, Engels, Lenin and Stalin on his wall. He calls himself a Communist and is so considered by others, yet he lives a privileged life of luxury while the common workers lead miserable lives. Is he *really* a Communist? The answer to that, of course, depends on your definition of Communism. For this reason, discussions of the genuineness of said official's Communism should have something to do with what the word "Communism" actually means. This requires at least some significant and informed reference to the writings of Marx and Engels.

Such elementary considerations seem to be lacking from many discussions of Hitler's relationship to Christianity. Can those who keep trying to connect Hitler's comments about "God" to Christianity summarize even briefly some of the main teachings of Jesus? That a poor beggar who dies and goes to heaven is better off than a rich man who dies and goes to hell; that God is aware of all that we say, think and do, and we will be held accountable for it in the world to come; that if our country is conquered by foreigners we should not be concerned about it and cooperate with them fully, as the spiritual kingdom of heaven is more important – does anyone imagine Hitler had any interest in such (to him) ridiculous non-Aryan teachings?

People who want to bring Christianity into discussions about the origins of National Socialism on the basis of Hitler's comments about "the Almighty . . . the Lord . . . Providence . . . Fate . . . " or whatever should be asked: "What do you think Jesus taught and represented? *Deutschland uber alles*?" Hitler made vague philosophical references to God, including a few to Jesus Christ (not all of them positive) – but mere references to some sort of God, or even to Jesus, are not proof of Christianity. Hitler's higher power, whatever it was, was not the God of Abraham, Isaac and Jacob. It was not the God of the Trinity, Father, Son and Holy Spirit. It was not the God of the Bible, a book written by Jews.

Hitler's "god" was a nebulous philosophical entity in the German tradition of Hegel's World Spirit, that used select people (the Greeks, the Romans, the Germans) to advance mankind. It was related to Fichte's Absolute, with its special bond to the German people. It was in some ways identical to Schopenhauer's vast and impersonal cosmic Will, ceaselessly striving and impelling conflict and change throughout creation. Needless to say, none of those men thought that the Bible gave us a true revelation of God's character.

All of them thought that higher truth was accessible to human reason alone, without divine guidance.

That Hitler's "Almighty" came out of this tradition does not mean Hitler was a philosopher. He did not need to be – although there is more German philosophy scattered throughout the pages of *Mein Kampf* than many realize. Ideas first introduced by philosophers became over the decades part of the general vocabulary and were frequently used even in newspapers and political debates to justify Germany's unique superiority and destiny. Such lofty concepts, now believed in by almost no one, had far more to do with the formation of the culture that Hitler emerged out of than did any authentically biblical teachings.

Gordon Craig gives a number of examples of Hegel's profound and far-reaching influence on German political culture before 1900. Germany's victory over France in 1871 was hailed as an example of higher ethical purposes accomplished by war, "a divine judgment" confirming Hegel's theory that "the leading state-personalities take their turn in being the embodiment of the dominant philosophy of the time."[1] In other words, Germany's defeat of France was an expression of higher philosophical and spiritual truth. Hegel's theory of the state as an instrument of higher progress and hence reigning supreme over divisive individualistic tendencies was also widely accepted and, according to Craig, had a profound influence on German political realities.[2]

It is worth stressing what should be an obvious point – that the mere use of the words "God," "divine," or "Almighty" is no proof of Christian influence. Francis Schaeffer wrote,

> . . . no word is as meaningless as is the word 'god.' Of itself it means nothing. Like any other word, it is only a linguistic symbol – g-o-d – until content is put into it . . . no other word has been used to convey such absolutely opposite meanings. The mere use of the word 'god' proves nothing.[3]

It can be used to represent either concepts derived from the Bible, or contrivances of merely human philosophical ingenuity predicated upon rejection of the Bible as a false book.

In Hitler's case, god-words are confusing to people who interpret them with no knowledge of their use in the unbiblical context of nineteenth-century German secularism. It is hard for them to understand that people could

---

[1] Gordon Craig, *Germany 1866-1945* (Oxford: Clarendon Press, 1978), p. 35 (both quotes).

[2] Ibid., pp. 47-49.

[3] Francis Schaeffer, *He is There and He is not Silent* (Carol Stream, IL: Tyndale House Publishers, 2001), pp. 12-13.

completely reject the Bible as an authoritative to guide to life, emphasize science and human reason, be profoundly humanist in their approach to life, and yet still have some awareness of a higher spiritual reality. Traditional religion was rejected, but religious ideas and words were retained and recycled with entirely different meanings. This common phenomenon can be observed not merely in German Romanticism and Idealistic Philosophy, but also in the doctrines of liberal Protestantism.

The problem of understanding Hitler's religious comments is further complicated by his lack of sincerity. So many people now take (or pretend to take) all of honest Adolf's religious rhetoric at face value. He promised to support the churches – but failed, somehow, to keep his word. He made a few nice general statements about the importance of Christianity – most or all of them in the early part of his rule when he was not yet firmly in control. He was supported by many with the name of "Christian" – but how many of them did not know what Hitler really stood for?

Someone like Hitler had never appeared before in the history of the world, and many people – not only Christians – were deceived by him. Skilled diplomats and people who had devoted their professional lives to politics and to international relations were also fooled by Hitler. Hitler was a genius at lying just like Einstein was a genius at science. True, there were plenty of danger signals, but many people just could not imagine what they meant. Of course, if the Germans could have foreseen what Hitler would do to Germany he would have received no support.

Many Christians who supported Hitler had no real spiritual discernment, but were merely cultural Christians. They had been baptized into the Lutheran and Catholic Churches as infants, did not read or believe in the Bible, went to church two or three times a year if at all, and had no real commitment to the teachings of Christ. Many who were more serious believed that the Bible was full of mistakes and errors. They had vague religious ideas, what we now call "theological liberalism," but were more concerned with political security, national honor and economic stability than with the Sermon on the Mount. This can be true of even more orthodox Christians, whose sound doctrines have unfortunately not led them to a higher spiritual life.

It is commonly argued that if Hitler had been against Christianity, then the Christians would have opposed him – but they did not. Ergo, National Socialism must at the very least have been compatible with religious teachings. This plausible-sounding reasoning shows a great ignorance of the state of the churches in Germany. Not only in 1933 but for a century and more before, the influence of the Churches (both Protestant and Catholic) had been declining in Germany. The fervor of the Reformation had long since faded away and degenerated into a dull and lifeless orthodoxy, or to a new version of Christianity known as theological liberalism. This was at bottom primarily a mixture of Kantian and Hegelian philosophy, romanticism, science and other contemporary trends that used Christian rhetoric but denied the full deity of Christ, the authority of Scripture and other essential truths.

We also need to consider the many Germans, Christians and non-Christians, who kept silent out of fear. How many of them knew Hitler was wrong but did not want to be attacked and beaten by Nazi thugs or sent to a concentration camp? Even before 1933 opposing Hitler could be a dangerous thing to do. Germany's large and well-organized Communist Party, the largest in Western Europe, quickly disappeared after Hitler came to power. Millions of former Communists who managed to avoid a concentration camp cooperated and went along to save their own skins. Christians should have been different, but – with rare exceptions – they were not.

Someone might wonder what any of this has to do with a Palestinian Jew and his twelve disciples. Serious attempts to address such a question are always absent from contrived, elaborate and fundamentally distorted attempts to present Hitler as religious in a conventional sense. Has anyone ever been able to point to one teaching of Christ's that Hitler followed? Hitler and his literally devilish ideology represented a complete denial of the Sermon on the Mount, as well as of the Ten Commandments.

Getting back to the question of what it means to be a Communist, those who for some reason wanted to link someone to Communism often found it easy to do so. "He signed a petition put up by a Communist front group . . . he said something positive about Karl Marx and even criticized economic inequalities in society . . . he marched in a demonstration organized by known Communists," and so on and so forth. Similarly, people who want to connect Hitler and Christianity for their own personal reasons have various bits of evidence to point to. "Here's a photograph of Hitler walking out of a church! Smoking gun!" How accurate such accusations are is a different question entirely.

Basic ideas of National Socialism were unheard of for 1800 years and more after the appearance of Christianity, and first emerged along with the increasing secularization of Europe in the nineteenth century. Such concepts as the central importance of race; people as animals in a life of merciless struggle; the superiority of blond, blue-eyed people over those beneath them on a hierarchical scale established by success in the harsh and amoral battle for survival; the need to establish national identity on the basis of race, and to consolidate all members of the same race into one state; Christianity as unscientific, and separating us from nature with unnatural values of pity and mercy; Christianity as essentially Jewish and hence out of character with a mystic Germanic nature – these and other essential ingredients of National Socialist ideology were first dreamed up by people who openly rejected historic and traditional Christian teachings.

One would think this might give some cause for reflection on the part of those who keep trying to paint Hitler as a fanatic from the "religious right," but, unfortunately, this is not the case. There are serious historians who have discussed the question of relationships between National Socialism and the ideas of Hegel, Fichte, Schopenhauer, Gobineau, Wagner, Nietzsche and others, including even Kant (who introduced new antisemitic concepts based not on belief in the Bible, but on rejection of the Bible). Some recognize that National Socialism was very much a modern phenomenon, but still there are those who persist in pointing the finger at Christianity.

Who are these people and what are their motives? Some are eager to find some way of discrediting the claims Christianity makes upon them and pointing at Hitler is one way to do this. Obviously, any religion that leads to such evil does not require much consideration. Some are merely ignorant. They know little about the Third Reich and less about Christianity and are just repeating something they heard somewhere. Others are knowledgeably ignorant. They have a lot of facts and information but still judge by outward appearances without any real discernment and have little or no spiritual understanding. This includes some well-known academic historians.

Some are only making propaganda. They may or may not even believe their accusations, but they have found that using Hitler as evidence that Christianity leads to political extremism is useful to their larger aim of marginalizing Christianity and excluding it from the public sphere. They have a secular, anti-Christian vision of an ideal society, and anything that allows them to identify religious believers as potentially dangerous fanatics is useful to them – never mind if it is true or not. Some people are I think inspired by malice and hatred of Christianity – and their influence has been more far-reaching than many Christians would like to think.

A good example of an extended attack on Christianity disguised as scholarship is Richard Steigmann-Gall's *The Holy Reich*.[4] This book has had some impact and its arguments using every religious comment by any Nazi as proof of Christian influence are now being quoted in other supposedly more objective histories. *The Da Vinci Code* inspired many Christian refutations, but *The Holy Reich* did not. Perhaps if Christians ever heard of it they assumed it was too ridiculous to dignify with a response. After all, if anyone makes a serious effort to read the four gospels and sees anything of Hitler there, they are – in my opinion – incapable of rational thought on this subject.

Such indifference or silence on our part is a mistake. It has only encouraged yet more and more extreme and even wild accusations. For example, in addition to claiming that church membership and infant baptism are proofs of Christianity (in complete ignorance of what the New Testament teaches on this), Steigmann-Gall goes so far as to assert that Hitler "regarded Christ's struggle as direct inspiration for his own" and claims "Hitler insists that

---

[4] Richard Steigmann-Gall, *The Holy Reich: Nazi Conceptions of Christianity, 1919-1945* (Cambridge: Cambridge University Press, 2004).

Christianity is at the center of Nazi social thought" and "regards the teachings of Christ as direct inspiration for the 'German' socialism advanced by the party."[5]

What sort of a mindset would make this extraordinary assertion with no reference at all to what Christ said and taught, or to beliefs that many common and ordinary Christians have sincerely tried to follow? The idea that National Socialism originated in Roman Palestine could revolutionize Hitler studies, if enough people with knowledge of Hitler could be found to believe it. Far-out as they may sound, such direct assaults on Christianity cannot be safely dismissed as mere eccentricities. The Bible says "Do not let your good be evil spoken of," and we do not do the cause of Christ any favors by tamely acquiescing in such propagandistic misrepresentations.

A detailed analysis of all of the errors, distortions and serious omissions of fact in *The Holy Reich* would take a large volume. If Steigmann-Gall's book were devoted to anything other than making Christianity look bad, its academic and intellectual defects would have long since banished it from serious consideration. Powerful trends of secularism that preceded National Socialism by more than a century are ignored or lightly skipped over. The basic teachings of Christianity are ignored. Deep contrasts are missed, Hitler's lies are presented as truths and slight resemblances are trumpeted as proofs. Yet, in spite of its many serious flaws, the book is agreeable reading to those who want to view religious belief as irrational and potentially dangerous.[6]

Such increasingly common mischaracterizations of Christianity are nothing new. They have been going on since the first Christians were accused of atheism, subversion, cannibalism and immorality. We have to expect such misrepresentations from a world that is by nature averse and even hostile to Christian teachings. They are a violation of the ninth Commandment not to bear false witness against our neighbor – but Christ has taught us how we should respond to false accusations.

---

[5] Ibid., pp. 27, 46 (both quotes).

[6] The book has been praised by a number of sources, but some have noted its many blunders and flawed methodology. See for example Manfred Gailus ("A Strange Obsession with Nazi Christianity: A Critical Comment on Richard Steigmann-Gall's *The Holy Reich*"); Ernst Piper ("Steigmann-Gall, *The Holy Reich*"); and Irving Hexham ("Inventing 'Paganists': A Close Reading of Richard Steigmann-Gall's *The Holy Reich*"), all in "Nazism, Christianity and Political Religion: A Debate," *Journal of Contemporary History* 42, no. 1 (2007), 5-7. See also this same journal for Samuel Koehne's "Reassessing *The Holy Reich*: Leading Nazis' Views on Confession, Community and 'Jewish' Materialism" (2013 48: 423).

There are those who have a more intellectual approach. They recognize obvious differences between National Socialism and Christianity, but see these as being on the surface. Underneath external differences there is – they claim – the same religious insistence on dogma, on Absolute Truth, on the rightness of one's cause. There is the same inability to relax comfortably in the tolerant acceptance of just about anything in the supposedly morally neutral worldview of scientific naturalism (though its vaunted neutrality quickly gravitates to non-scientific moral notions of what is and is not acceptable).

People who argue in this way are, I suspect, incapable of recognizing or admitting that the modernist project of building society without Christian teachings, on human reason alone, was a colossal blunder. It was after all autonomous human reason, free from religious restraint, relying on science and philosophy, on human wisdom, that dreamed up basic ideas that Hitler later so skillfully blended into his highly toxic ideology. It must be very threatening to some, to have to consider the possibility that rejecting Christianity and relying instead on science and philosophy, or merely intuition, does not lead not to a calm and rational society where everyone exists together in cosmic harmony, happily believing that we are all nothing but accidents in an essentially silent and impersonal universe.

A mere fifty years ago there would have been no need for a careful examination of the relationship between Hitler and Christianity. It used to be generally understood that Christianity had a generally beneficent influence on society. It was readily apparent that the ideas and the practices of Hitler had nothing to do with, and were in fact directly contrary to, all of the most essential aspects of Christianity. Now, however, in this new dark age with its intensifying hostility toward and ignorance of the historic Christian faith, those who hate and fear Christianity are increasingly voluble in their attempts to link it to Hitler. The fact that Hitler (along with Lenin, Mao, Stalin and Pol Pot) was as far removed from the Sermon on the Mount as it is humanly possible to get is of no importance to them.

"Germany was a Christian country . . . the Nazis were Christians or the sons of Christians . . . Hitler supported the churches and the churches supported Hitler . . . Christians have always hated Jews . . . Hitler called himself a Christian once in a speech in 1922" – how often these dubious arguments come up in attempts to explain Hitler. They sound very plausible to some who seem to have acquired their reasoning habits while growing up watching television. Their capacity for analytical thought is limited, their knowledge of German intellectual history ranges from slight to nil, and the same can be said of their understanding of basic Christian teachings. For them a propaganda photo or a political statement by Hitler are incontrovertible proofs – at least when it comes to religion.

People do not accept Hitler's word about other topics so lightly. No one with any credibility is saying "Poland attacked Germany first and Germany responded in self-defense. How do we know this? Hitler told us so! He said so himself!" It is not simply that some people are stupid (though that may be a factor). It is also true that many find it very easy to believe anything bad about religion – hence, there is some need for a Christian response to charges which, though false and ridiculous, have gained significant ground.

Christians are unaware of the extent to which it is now generally assumed that there is some kind of significant connection, direct or indirect, between their religion and the crimes of the Nazis. Hitler is commonly thought to have emerged from the "religious right," and this is one reason for the increasing suspicion toward those who speak of using the state to impose a conservative moral agenda. Even those who recognize many glaring differences between biblical doctrines and what went on in the Third Reich still feel that the religious impulse must have had something to do with it, even if indirectly.

Where did Hitler's ideas come from? The question is not merely an academic one. Apart from a general desire to understand the origins of the Second World War, Hitler's ideology is a central concern in some contemporary debates. This is not a matter of historical analysis only, but is still strikingly relevant to us today. If for example National Socialism can be convincingly shown to have been influenced by Darwinism, even if only partially, that is a powerful argument against the theory of evolution. It is not of course a scientific argument that bears directly on the truth or falsehood of the theory, but it is an ethical argument. Should we believe in and should we teach our children a theory that is potentially so detrimental to the common good?

If, on the other hand, National Socialism emerged out of a fundamentally religious, non-scientific approach to life, one stressing faith and authority over reason and evidence, that is a strong argument against religion. It shows the danger of needing something to believe in apart from detached and logical scientific objectivity. It places the Nazis among the ranks of true believers, people who can't think for themselves but need someone else to give their lives meaning and purpose and tell them what to believe. Plus, Hitler did often refer to God and claim to be doing the will of God – isn't this a clear example of the dangers of religion?

Leaving the contested subject of Hitler and Darwin for another time, it should take only a page or less to clarify the nature of Hitler's relationship to biblical Christianity. It should be sufficient to point out that Hitler followed none of the teachings of Christ and that no foundational Nazi doctrines are found anywhere in the New Testament. Yet, it is not sufficient. Some people need to be reminded of the spiritual, chronological, geographical and psychological distances between Roman Palestine and modern Europe. They also need to have it explained to them that all the basic ideas of National Socialism are false by elementary biblical standards.

Since we will never be able to properly approach Hitler and the Holocaust as long as we labor under misconceptions about Hitler's attitude towards Christianity; and since too many have unnecessarily complicated this issue with false accusations and overly clever innuendoes, it is necessary to look more carefully into the relationship (or lack of relationship) between Hitler's ideas and biblical teachings. The first thing we need to consider is the many points of essential Christian doctrine that Hitler and his many followers never mentioned and didn't care about. This should be self-evident, and it is self-evident to people who know something about what Christianity involves.

Has anyone ever claimed Hitler believed Christ lived a sinless life and gave us true teachings from God (which teachings we are supposed to make an effort to follow)? That he died on the cross as a sacrifice for the sins of the world? That the Bible teaches us about Heaven and Hell and we believe it as God's inspired and infallible Word?

Even a glance at *Mein Kampf* shows that Hitler had a very different understanding of reality. For example, in only the first four pages of "Nation and Race" (vol. 1 chapter 11),[7] we find the assertion that National Socialism is based on obvious truths. One of these "truths" is that "Nature" eliminates the weak by a process of ruthless competition – a process that leads to the higher development of various animal species. Only weaklings see this as harsh and cruel – it is just the way things are. When this is understood as applying to people, a significant part (but only a part) of the riddle of the Holocaust is solved.

We also read in this same place that when higher forms of a species breed with lower or less well-developed forms, this leads to weaker offspring and undermines the natural process of development. It is expressly stated that human beings are subject to this law of nature and cannot rise above it. People who believe that we as human beings are exempt from this iron law of struggle are deceived by Jewish delusions (this refers to the Jewish and Christian belief in a divine creation that sets man apart from the animals). Man is not apart from or above Nature's law of struggle. This is scientific truth, and ethical or moral ideas that are not based on this truth are merely human inventions that have no basis in reality.

Especially noteworthy in this lengthy passage is the belief in the vital importance of blood purity for victory in the struggle for survival. Hitler states that the Germanic inhabitants of the New World will remain masters of the continent as long as they do not suffer from blood defilement by breeding with lesser human species. This is of course pure and unadulterated Gobineau. It was the Frenchman Arthur de Gobineau who (in the mid-nineteenth century)

---

[7] Adolf Hitler, *Mein Kampf,* trans. Ralph Manheim (Boston: Houghton Mifflin, 1999), pp. 284-287.

came up with the theory that race was the key to history; that racial purity was essential to mastery, and that racial impurity led to decay and decline.

One writer asserts it is unlikely that Hitler had ever paid any attention to Gobineau's "complex" book – as if white racial superiority were rocket science – but then quotes an extended passage from *Mein Kampf* that sounds exactly like Gobineau, and says "Such words could almost be Gobineau's own."[8] He also gives examples of how Gobineau's writings were published in the Third Reich and even used in schools. Another writer dismissed Gobineau's theories as "arcane," and they certainly are arcane today – but they were not arcane in nineteenth-century Germany. They were well-known among extreme racists and nationalists and taken as self-evident fact, vital to Germany's continued ascent.

Richard Wagner met Gobineau in the 1880s and was sufficiently taken with his ideas to publish some essays on Gobineau, and even translated some of his writings. Ludwig Schemann, a member of Wagner's circle, established the Gobineau Society in 1894 and worked diligently to spread the word about the vital necessity of racial purity to continued German dominance. Gobineau also had some influence in the United States. For example, Madison Grant's *The Passing of the Great Race; or, The Racial Basis of European History* (1916) is in many respects merely an extension of Gobineau. Like Gobineau and like Hitler, Grant thought that the Nordic race was responsible for the best of the great world civilizations, including those of Persia, India and China. He believed that the superior white race would lose its domination if it fell prey to blood contamination.

Historian George Mosse wrote that "Gobineau set the stage and supplied the props"[9] for a new ideology emphasizing the centrality of race. This, of course, is not to blame Hitler and the Holocaust on Gobineau. The seething hatreds that emerged out of the radicalizing effects of the First World War and Germany's subsequent problems would have been inconceivable to Gobineau, who lived in a much more civilized era. Gobineau is merely one factor in a complex equation. Other ideas were also necessary ingredients of Hitler's National Socialist potion. It is to say that Hitler's worldview was not a biblical one. In fact, a mere portion of one single Bible verse completely nullifies the entire National Socialist ideology: God "hath made of one blood all nations of men for to dwell on all the face of the earth" (Acts 17:26).

Hitler's worldview – and he did have a worldview – was a profoundly modern one. The ideas briefly mentioned above seemed self-evidently true to a significant percentage of the German intelligentsia in the decades before

---

[8] Michael D. Biddis, *The Father of Racist Ideology: The Social and Political Thought of Count Gobineau* (London: Weidenfeld and Nicolson, 1970), p. 259.

[9] George L. Mosse, *The Crisis of German Ideology: Intellectual Origins of the Third Reich* (New York: Grosset & Dunlap, 1971), p. 90.

World War I. They were based not on the Bible, but on rejection of the Bible – a book which was of no importance to Hitler when writing *Mein Kampf*. Thus it is surprising to read Timothy Ryback's assertion that Hitler was "versed in the Holy Scriptures."[10] In support of this, he referred only to a book called *Words of Christ* (*Worte Christi*) found among the scattered remnants of Hitler's library (many of the volumes had been given as gifts and showed no signs of having been read). He said elsewhere, in a magazine article, that the book showed signs of being much handled – by whom he couldn't say – but was (unlike some other heavily marked books in the Hitler collection) unmarked except for a short penciled line by one passage: "You should love God, your Lord, with all your heart, with all your soul, with all your spirit: this is the foremost and greatest commandment. Another is equally important: Love your neighbor as you would love yourself."[11]

Does anyone claim that Hitler believed and practiced that? If he had, the entire history of Europe would have been unimaginably different. Furthermore, people who are seriously interested in the Bible read the book itself, not a miscellaneous edited collection of some sayings of Christ. They also read other books explaining biblical history and teaching. They do not contemptuously reject Old Testament history as completely false, like Hitler did in *Mein Kampf* when he dismissed the entire biblical history of Israel as fictional.[12] Not surprisingly, Ryback says nothing about any other Christian books in his detailed comments about the surviving books from Hitler's collection.

Frederick Oechsner, a German correspondent for UPI, was able to survey Hitler's libraries in Berlin and Berchtesgaden before the war.[13] Estimating the collection to have about 16,300 books, he divided it into categories. The largest was military books, approximately 7,000. Many of them "especially on Napoleon's campaigns," were "extensively marginated" by Hitler. "Those which were not available in German Hitler has had translated." Oechsner further observed that "Hitler has read many of them [the military books] from cover to cover." Hitler did visit Napoleon's tomb on his trip to Paris, by the way, demonstrating a more than passing interest in the man who in some important ways strikingly resembled him.

---

[10] Timothy Ryback, *Hitler's Private Library: The Books That Shaped his Life* (London: Vintage Books, 2010), p. xiii.

[11] Timothy W. Ryback, "Hitler's Forgotten Library: The Man, His Books, and His Search For God." *The Atlantic Monthly*. May 2003.
http:www.fpp.co.uk/Hitler/library/Atlantic_Monthly.html; accessed April 2014.

[12] Hitler, *Mein Kampf,* p. 303.

[13] Ryback, *Hitler's Private Library*, pp. 117, 257-261 (all quotes this paragraph). There is no exact date given. Ryback only says "A few years later" after another visitor's report from 1935.

Next were books on architecture, painting, theater and sculpture (about 1,500). Hitler is well-known to have had an interest in architecture and painting at least. There were works on spiritualism and astrology and "photographs of stellar constellations on important days of his life. These he has annotated in his own handwriting."[14] Oechsner noted many books on nutrition and diet, as well as about 400 books on the Roman Catholic Church. These included charges of immorality in the priesthood and illustrations of the power of the papacy with comments like "Never again" and "This is impossible now" written in the margin.

Many of the books (from 800 to 1,000 by Oechsner's estimate) were popular fiction, including romances, detective stories and American Indian adventure stories. Books of sociology were included. Except for the books on Catholicism just referred to, there was no mention made by Oechsner of religious books. No Aquinas, no Augustine, no complete sets of Luther or Calvin with Hitler's comments in the margin, no histories of the Reformation, no biblical commentaries or histories, no devotional books on prayer or the inner life.[15]

Of course, one journalistic report is hardly the last word on the subject. Oechsner may have missed some important books, or Hitler may have had some more personally important books elsewhere (the library having been arranged with a view to public image). Whatever the case, there is no evidence whatever that Hitler had the least knowledge of or interest in important biblical teachings even in a general way, let alone to the extent of being "versed" in them. He does have an occasional Bible quote in *Mein Kampf*, but only commonly known verses like "casting pearls before swine" or "a camel going through the eye of a needle." Hitler's book also contains a few references to Goethe and Schiller, but no one has ever claimed Hitler had a deep knowledge of those writers. Serious comments, or any comments at all, about the day of judgment, eternal life, forgiveness of sins through belief in Christ, God's concern for us as individuals, sanctification, justification, predestination, or any other important aspects of Christian doctrine and practice are all completely lacking in Hitler's speeches and writing.

Some references to Christ as an Aryan (with a human father of course) who was "liquidated" by the Jews in his heroic fight against Judaism do not show Hitler had any understanding of biblical teachings about the nature of Christ.

---

[14] Ibid., p. 258-259.

[15] My personal belief is that more of Hitler's inner life can be found in Nietzsche's *Antichrist* than in any other single book – a book that says the weak and the unfit should be exterminated; that pity and mercy are vices; that Christianity is a Jewish plot to enslave stronger peoples with a false slave morality; that the Jews are masters of decadence and behind all forms of decadence.

We are talking about commitment to important doctrines, not about any and every use of the word "Jesus" in whatever context. Some will say those doctrines are really not essential to Christianity, that it is enough just to "believe" in Christ in some ill-defined way. There are even theologians and church leaders who detach religious faith from biblical teaching and would support such a claim. Of course, anyone is free to define Christianity however they want, but the basic message of historic, biblical Christianity, Protestant, Catholic, or Orthodox was of no interest to Hitler.

Furthermore, apart from endless debates about what the essentials of Christianity might or might not be, the Bible is clear. Referring to a long list of sins including hatred, wrath and murder, it says that "they which do such things will not inherit the kingdom of God" (Galatians 5:19-21). We read in Revelation that "the abominable, and murderers . . . and all liars, shall have their part in the lake which burneth with fire and brimstone: which is the second death" (21:8).

It doesn't matter if Hitler publicly claimed to be a Christian once in over twenty years of speechifying. It doesn't matter if he used such words as "God," "God's will," "the Lord," or "the Almighty." Every time Hitler used the word "God" in whatever context he was breaking the Third Commandment which says we should not take God's name in vain. Nor does it matter if he promised to support the churches (which promise he broke), or if he signed an agreement with the Vatican (which he also broke). It doesn't matter if he was born in a supposedly Christian country or baptized as an infant. According to biblical Christianity, he will stand before God and receive a just sentence for everything that he said, thought and did. Paul's Letter to the Romans tells us what Hitler will receive on "the day of wrath and revelation of the righteous judgment of God." Then there will be "tribulation and anguish upon every soul of man that doeth evil" (2:5, 9).

Yet, while Hitler's beliefs were very far removed from biblical Christianity and in fact totally opposed to it, there were religious elements in National Socialism. They were so important that it might almost be said that Hitler was trying to found a new religion. He himself referred to National Socialism as a spiritual movement, a spiritual revolution, a philosophy that would save the world – or at least that elite part of the world that was worth saving.[16] And Hitler was justified in calling his ideology a philosophy (he even used that word, "philosophy"). It was not philosophical in the academic sense, but it presented a coherent world view of life as struggle in which the best and the strongest emerged triumphant and needed to be careful to maintain their dominance.

Historian Paul Johnson wrote, "the decline and ultimately the collapse of the religious impulse would leave a huge vacuum. The history of modern times

---

[16] Hitler, *Mein Kampf,* pp. 516, 446, 373.

is in great part the history of how that vacuum had been filled."[17] There is more than a little truth in this. The emptiness of modernism, including the false, destructive and ugly beliefs that we are just animals existing for no reason in a strictly materialistic universe, did leave a void – but the innately human religious impulse did not disappear. People's natural and healthy needs for higher meaning and purpose, even for struggle towards a worthwhile goal, were redirected and found a new outlet. Thus Naziism – like Marxism, and like other secular schemes for bringing an earthly salvation to mankind – did have a religious dimension. The trivial secular vision of life as the mere enjoyment of peace, self-satisfaction and pleasure in conditions of material sufficiency, as if people were no more than hamsters in a cage, however nice that cage might be, will never meet our deepest psychological and spiritual needs.

The extent to which Naziism was a coherent and all-embracing philosophy of life with a genuine spiritual dimension based on over a century of German culture is not always sufficiently appreciated. Hitler's ideas were to a great extent a substitute for rejected and discredited Christianity, and their acceptance was only possible in a society that was spiritually empty (and America today is increasingly a spiritually empty country also). This emptiness left many with a thirst for meaning that made them vulnerable to Hitler. It was the same emptiness that left others who were not followers of Hitler so strangely weak. Their inability to act or even to perceive what was happening greatly facilitated Hitler's rise.

Yes, Hitler was an opportunist who was willing to adapt to circumstances in pursuit of his long-range goals. Yes, there was a marked will-to-power, political deviousness, theatrical appeals to the masses – but all of that found expression within a definite framework of thought and was aimed at definite ends. That framework was suitable to that time and place and was in fact a consistent philosophy designed to replace the supposedly outdated and unscientific religious values of a bygone era.

So, there were counterfeit religious aspects to Hitler's ideology. It offered a new Promised Land – Germany; a new Chosen People – the Germans; a new concept of sin – racial impurity; a new means of cleansing from sin – eugenics and extermination of unfit elements. There was a new ethic – survival-of-the-fittest; a new paradise – the worldly kingdom of complete German domination; and a new revelation – the doctrines of Naziism, doctrines brought by a prophet chosen by "the Almighty" to deliver the German people from bondage. There was even a new concept of God – though this "god" was just a human philosophical invention. Sebastian Haffner, a German refugee writing in England during the war, even claimed that "Some intellectual Nazis actually

---

[17] Paul Johnson, *Modern Times: The World From the Twenties to the Nineties* (New York: Perennial Classics, 1992), p. 48.

play with the idea of deifying Hitler after his death and preparations to this end are already being made."[18]

This tendency is illustrated by the words of a Hitler Youth song: "We are the happy Hitler Youth; / We have no need of Christian virtue; / For Adolf Hitler is our intercessor / And our redeemer."[19] A speech given at a Nazi student rally contains these words: "National Socialism in all earnestness says: I am the Lord thy God, thou shalt have no other gods before me . . . ours is the kingdom and the power; for we have a strong Wehrmacht, and the glory – for we are again a respected nation." Heinrich Himmler toyed with the idea of placing Hitler among the German gods after his death and making him the head of a new German church.[20]

Those who contemptuously dismiss Hitler as merely a power-hungry nihilist will never understand him or the powerful nature of his appeal. He had a deep, dark and vast ambition – to remake humanity. Hitler sought to put himself in the place of God, to make himself the absolute arbiter of truth, of law, of life and death. He tried to take the fate of mankind in his hands, arrogated unto himself the highest allegiance of the German people, and worked diligently to replace Christianity with his own new ideas. To this end the Nazis on occasion borrowed Christian imagery. Christ driving the money changers out of the temple, the use of a Bible verse as the title of a painting of Hitler orating – these do not, as is sometimes claimed, show a Christian influence on the origins of Naziism. It shows Hitler as a rival to Christianity which he considered to be untrue and harmful to the German people in the struggle for survival.

This can be used to argue for the inherently irrational and even dangerous nature of religious belief. Even if it is conceded that Hitler did not believe in Christianity and was actually hostile to it, yet it will be said that he still appealed to the religious mindset and was to a significant extent religious himself. Such abuses – it is said – are inevitable among those who cannot be contented with the objectivity of materialistic scientific truth. Hence religious people are capable of all sorts of evils and atrocities, as is commonly claimed by the currently fashionable "new atheism" – and there is no denying that religion can be and has been abused. In the words of John Owen, a 17th-century English Puritan, "the more excellent anything is, the more pernicious the abuse of it. In all the world there is nothing so vile, as that which pretendeth to be God, and is not; nor is there anything else capable of so

---

[18] Sebastian Haffner, *Germany – Jekyll and Hyde: A Contemporary Account of Nazi Germany*, trans. Wilfrid David (London: Abacus, 2009), p. 20.

[19] Gene Edward Veith, Jr., *Modern Fascism: Liquidating the Judaeo-Christian Worldview* (St. Louis: Concordia Publishing House, 1993), p. 67, 68 (both quotes).

[20] Felix Kersten, *The Memoirs of Doctor Felix Kersten*, trans. Dr. Ernest Morwitz (Garden City, NY: Doubleday and Co., 1947), pp. 61, 110.

pernicious an abuse."[21] This applies not only to Hitler, but also to the so-called "Germanic Christians" who scrapped the Bible and eagerly followed Hitler as the bearer of a new revelation.

Hitler himself was aware of the religious dimensions of his program and wrote of it in *Mein Kampf*. "Any philosophy, whether of a political or of a religious nature – and sometimes the dividing line is hard to determine . . . a new spiritual doctrine . . . a new spiritual attitude"[22] – these and many other quotes that could be given show that Hitler was aiming at much more than merely political solutions to Germany's problems. This is one of the reasons for his hostility to Christianity – apart from its Jewish character, he saw it as a rival for the allegiance of the German people. Furthermore, the passage from which these quotes were taken speaks about the need to replace Christianity with the new philosophy, the difficulty of doing so, and the most effective strategy to bring about this end. We will examine this more closely later in the chapter.

So, is it religion that is the problem? Was the irrationality of Hitler the irrationality of religion and of religious people who need some "truth" to believe in, who need a savior of some kind, any kind, because they fear to confront reality? This is an increasingly common view, and it leads to claims that Hitler's rallies were comparable to religious revival meetings (as if George Whitefield, John Wesley, or D. L. Moody had anything to do with Hitler). It leads to claims that Germany's humiliation during World War I and its promised future resurrection under Hitler were "religious themes" comparable to the resurrection of Christ (as if Christ had had anything to do with national power and glory and was not in fact completely indifferent to such things).

If a basketball coach were exhorting his losing team during the half-time and telling them they could come from behind to win the game, someone might with equal justice call this an appeal to religious themes of humiliation, resurrection and redemption, or say that the enthusiasm of the crowd as the team came from behind to win was like the enthusiasm of a Nazi party rally. Whether or not such comparisons actually have anything to do with National Socialism is another question. But, if the motive is to discredit Christianity and belief in God, then we don't need to be too particular about such details. The vaguest or most tenuous seeming resemblance will do.

Some people are not capable of making objective comparisons between totally different and radically conflicting concepts of truth. When we read in a supposedly reputable historian that Hitler's speechifying against Jewish "maggots" can be compared to "revivalist intolerance," we have to conclude that said historian does not have the faintest idea of what a Christian revival is.

---

[21] John Owen, *The Holy Spirit: His Gifts and Power* (Ross-shire Scotland: Christian Heritage, 2007), p. 47.

[22] Hitler, *Mein Kampf*, p. 172 (all quotes).

He can lump diverse enthusiasms together under "emotionalism" without recognizing that there are good emotions and bad ones, positive and uplifting truths that benefit us and false "truths" that harm us. But, we understand that an ignorance of Christian teaching – along sometimes with outright malice – is one of the characteristics of this dark and spiritually underdeveloped age.

Such comparisons assume that Christianity is irrational, and Hitler was irrational, and that therefore they come from the same source and have the same character. The problem is that people who reject God and invent their own custom-made realities arbitrarily define rationality according to their own personal preference. Driven not by sober and detached logic, as they like to imagine, but by a deep hostility to God and to Christianity, people who compare Hitler's meetings to religious revivals do not know and do not want to know the difference between the teachings of Christ and a life devoted to following Christ, and the teachings of Hitler and a life devoted to following Hitler. The problem here is not stupidity, it is spiritual blindness.

This is not to deny of course that there have been real abuses of religion and attempts at religious revival that fall far short of Christ. There have been frauds and abuses in religion, in science, in politics and in every other human field of endeavor – but those who think that Hitler's appeals to hatred, fear, revenge, pride and national glory have anything to do with the Sermon on the Mount or the teachings of the apostles, need to think again (if they are capable of such a mental exercise). Hitler did manipulate and even imitate religion, and he appealed to people's innate need for higher meaning and purpose, just as a counterfeiter copies real money. It is because the money has value that it is counterfeited. Yet, before we excitedly jump to the longed-for conclusion that "religion is bad and religious people are potentially dangerous," we should recall that Lenin was an overt, declared, committed atheist who nevertheless resembled Hitler in many striking ways.

Both Hitler and Lenin despised democracy and destroyed struggling democratic governments. Both shared an unlimited thirst for power, saw themselves as infallible interpreters of a higher reality, and persecuted their enemies (real or imagined) with extreme cruelty. Both relied on force and brutality to eliminate opposition, had no respect whatever for the rule of law, and used all the rigors of a police state to impose their all-knowing wills – and both shed rivers of blood without a qualm. Finally, both thought – in agreement with Marx and myriads of lesser thinkers – that we could build our ideal society here on earth, even redefine human nature and create a "new man," all without God. The profound differences between Lenin and Hitler, and between Germany and Russia, make these higher parallels more striking. They transcend lesser differences.

Significantly, many of the imitations of religion found in National Socialism can be found in Marxism as well. Marx, the fanatical atheist extremist, also had a new chosen people – the proletarians. If Marx had ever had to spend much time with real workers he might have changed his mind. Too much time in the library was one of his many errors. There was a new paradise – his vision of a world without injustice and exploitation, after all of the enemies of mankind who saw things differently had been smashed by the dictatorship of the proletariat. There was a new concept of sin – exploitation – and a new personification of evil – capitalists. There was even a new revelation, one given to Karl Marx, who all by himself discovered the scientific laws of social development that had been concealed from everyone else since the dawn of human history.

A history of Russia relates that "the language of socialist revolution appealed to many ordinary Russians precisely because it resonated so strongly with religious notions of truth, righteousness, and salvation."[23] This same source further states that the Bolsheviks "often framed the socialist dream in sacred and messianic terms." Does this mean that Lenin and Stalin were not *really* atheists? But the new atheists who are getting so much publicity nowadays also have a firm insistence that their way is the right one; that they have the truth about life; that mankind is in danger but will be saved if we only hearken to them and follow their counsel. They also have strong ideas of what is right (Darwinism, homosexuality and abortion) and what is wrong (opposition to those things).

Concepts of truth, of right and wrong, as well as ideas for the improvement of society are innate. They are integral to the human experience, and can only be avoided by those who are content to merely exist on the lowest level with no thought at all for larger questions. People who deny the existence of God often paint with a very broad brush when it comes to condemning everyone who believes in God, but when it comes to the crimes of people who openly expressed atheism, materialism, confidence in science and hostility to revealed religion, then they bring out their microscopes and surgical instruments – or should I say their tap-dancing shoes?

The Bolsheviks were real atheists, hostile to God and to religion, but they were also human beings made in the image of God. No matter how hard we may try, we cannot escape our innate need for higher meaning, for justice, for something more than mere existence. The most doctrinally pure atheists today will find themselves falling into the same supposedly theistic tendencies as soon as they go beyond abstract arguments and begin to try and determine what is good for society, what injustice is and how to remedy it. When they go from the safe confines of academic debates to positions of real power, atheists have proven themselves to be more than capable of killing for their ideas – for the future good of humanity of course. Saving the human race is always a good

[23] Riasanovsky, Nicholas V. and Mark D. Steinberg, *A History of Russia* (New York: Oxford University Press, 2011), p. 485 (both quotes).

justification for the barbarism and inhumanity that every single atheistic regime has been notorious for.

Some people try to bring Calvin into this condemnation of fanatic adherence to "truth" – as if Calvin's Geneva had had concentration camps and secret police; as if Calvin had slaughtered, starved and enslaved millions; as if people were not free to leave Geneva at any time and go to another city in the same country (without having to worry about passports or visas, needless to say). Is it even possible to reason with someone who compares 16th-century Geneva to the Soviet Union or to Nazi Germany? The callous mass-murderer Lenin, seeking Marx's mirage of an earthly paradise, butchered more people in a single day with his famous "merciless mass terror" than were killed in Geneva in a century – and Genevan practices of capital punishment were the norm in Europe at that time. Lenin's practices were not the norm. Suffice it to say that the very great influence of Calvinism on England and America did not lead to the savage and fanatical atheistic and secular excesses of conceited moderns who thought that their own paltry intelligences were sufficient to work out the future happiness of mankind and remake the world without God.

Neither do Catholic and Protestant disputes about the eucharist in the 16th century or disputes about the Trinity in earlier centuries have anything to do with the problem of modern totalitarianism, or with the belief that it is legitimate to exterminate large numbers of people for the sake of a future imaginary happiness of mankind. That "warring theologians" should be compared to Lenin completely omits the fact that no "warring theologians" ever put into practice the horrors of the Soviet Union or the Third Reich. These sorts of comparisons are very wide of the mark and are motivated solely by hostility to religion, not by reason, logic, or objective consideration of factual evidence. Some historians seem to think that attacking religious beliefs that they do not understand is part of their professional calling.

It took denial of the immortality of the individual human soul to legitimize modern mass murders for the imagined good of mankind. The Huns, the Vikings and the Mongols enjoyed killing, but they weren't clever enough and educated enough to use philosophy to justify their bloodlust as a positive good, morally justifiable and beneficial. We must give modernity credit for modern crimes – unless, of course, our purpose is only to express our dislike for Christianity at every opportunity, whether appropriate or not. Likening Lenin to a religious fanatic is the kind of unhistorical bias which completely fails to comprehend that Christianity never in its many centuries of history produced someone like Lenin with a totalitarian state at his command.

Christianity is now routinely blamed for modern sins. One striking example is the accusation that plans for sterilizing physically disabled people, the mentally handicapped and criminals were welcomed by Protestant charities because of their beliefs in predestination and original sin. Of course, Christians know that the doctrine of predestination has nothing to do with sterilizing the unfit and was never used to advocate such practices in the many centuries of Christian teaching before the modern era. It was the modern rejection of these teachings and the belief that we were nothing but animals which made the idea of breeding people like animals, or preventing them from breeding (which was all part of the same program) seem plausible and respectable.

Too many people know little or nothing about Christian doctrines or the implications of those doctrines, as they have been elaborated on by reputable Christian thinkers. It was people who did not believe in the Bible that came up with the idea that people were essentially no different from animals and hence could *logically* and *reasonably* be treated as such. Some obscure religious-sounding quote from a Nazi-controlled journal written in favor of sterilization by someone who had abandoned biblical Christianity or who simply did not want to be put into a concentration camp (if such a quote could even be found) would not reflect in any way on basic Christian teachings.

Ian Kershaw states in his one-volume biography of Hitler that "there were strong feelings against euthanasia, particularly among those attached to the Churches."[24] The only public protests against euthanasia in the Third Reich were from religious leaders like the Roman Catholic Bishop Clemens Graf von Galen, or the Protestant Bishop Theophil Wurm. To ignore this is to cease writing history and begin writing anti-Christian propaganda. The Christian churches are not to be exempt from criticism, especially the churches in the Third Reich, but it should be honest, objective, and well-informed criticism. This is difficult for people who attack Christianity and then praise Marx as a great revolutionary thinker. His poisonous hatred of religion has had devastating consequences. It is no accident that in every single country where atheist Marxists have come to power Christians have been viciously and cruelly persecuted. Atheists have never been similarly dealt with on such a grand scale.

Sin and evil have been present in every civilization, whether in religious or in non-religious forms. However, it took the advances of modern technology to make undreamed of power available for evil men to use, and it took modern philosophy and ideology to legitimize pride and cruelty as if they were normal, natural and healthy. It is ironic that people (possibly suffering from intellectual and spiritual cowardice) will attribute modern advances to the rejection of religion, and then blame religion when their boasted modernity falls into a ditch (or maybe I should say when it falls into a mass grave full of naked corpses). Since fundamental human religious desires are innate, natural, normal and legitimate – including the need for meaning in life – attempts to eliminate religion have only led to badly manufactured replacements. In their intellectual arrogance and ignorance of human nature, those who seek to

---

[24] Ian Kershaw, *Hitler* (London: Penguin Books, 2008), p. 530.

eliminate Christianity are paving the way for new forms of evil and destruction.

Getting back to Lenin and Hitler, Paul Johnson makes a striking observation. "There is no essential moral difference between class-warfare and race-warfare, between destroying a class and destroying a race. Thus [with Lenin] the modern practice of genocide was born."[25] If Hitler saw history as determined by racial struggle (like Gobineau and many others); and if Lenin (like Marx) saw history as driven by class struggle; and if both sought to eliminate entire groups apart from any question of individual guilt or responsibility, what sort of people are they who willfully refuse to see a clear and obvious connection? This shows that in cruel and evil dictators we have a human problem, not a theistic or an atheistic one. We as people are capable of evil – and this same evil can emerge in secular or religious forms as the situation requires.

The Communists disguised their evils behind a lot of rhetoric about "justice" and "exploitation" that was very effective in deceiving dimwitted Western intellectuals. Hitler, on the other hand, was much more blatant, but the spiritual kinship between Communism and National Socialism, between people who rejected God and relied on their own differing but related human philosophies, was deep and profound. We can detect the baneful influence of Hegel behind these crazy modern theories. His concept of human progress as driven by the clash of ideas was reduced by Marx to a materialistic economic level and by Gobineau to a racial one, with devastating results Hegel could never have imagined.

Supposed contrasts between the right and the left are sometimes apparent than real. The Nazis stressed nationalism while the Communists stressed internationalism – all the while aggressively pursuing the national interests of Russia or of China. The Communists at first sought to eliminate private property while the Nazis did not, but both ideologies were hostile to free-market capitalism and felt that the state should have the final say in all important economic matters. It was no surprise that Stalin and Hitler were able to get along so well. The Nazis and the Communists in Weimar Germany had after all often co-operated to destroy democracy.

In contrast to overtly and officially atheistic Communism, we can accept that Hitler was some vague kind of theist – attempts to paint him as an atheist are not convincing. He often condemned atheistic Marxism and appealed to "Providence," "the Almighty," or "the Lord" to justify his actions. Yet, how much difference is there between a man who says "There is no god so I can do what I think is right," and a man who says "There is a god, but it is in complete agreement with my own ideas and goals and, in fact, is a human invention, so I can do whatever I think is right"? In denying the God of the Bible and making

---

[25] Johnson, *Modern Times*, p. 71.

man the center, there was a profound spiritual kinship between Communism and National Socialism. They both shared the same spirit of unbelief in the God of the Bible, and were fully confident in their reason and intelligence, and in their ability to remake the world. This kinship included hostility to and persecution of Christians, though Hitler found the much more important German churches to be useful to him politically, and so he did not seek to overtly destroy them as the Communists did the much weaker Russian and Chinese churches.

Parenthetically, Michael Burleigh sheds some light on Nazi hostility to atheism when he states that SS men were not allowed to call themselves atheists "because atheism betokened an unhealthy lack of community spirit and an equally unhealthy disbelief in life's higher purposes."[26] These "higher purposes" of course meant the exaltation of the German nation, the purification of the race, and the destruction of Germany's enemies, all for the sake of a larger common good. Atheists were supposed to be incapable of such high ideals, being concerned only with short term physical and selfish goals.

Referring not only to Communism and Naziism but also to the French Revolution and Mussolini's Fascism, noted Christian author D. M. Lloyd-Jones writes: "There is an element of worship in them, and also an apocalyptic element. They are not merely political programmes, there is something much deeper and almost demonic. This is true of Fascism as well as of Communism."[27] I suppose he says "almost demonic" because those movements were able to maintain a facade of rationality, at least in their beginning. In spite of their many differences, all of them were ideologies "in which men are asserting that they are the supreme authority" yet having distinct religious overtones.

Is this because religion is itself inherently bad, or is it because it is the way we are made? We as human beings need something more than mere existence. Those who reject God and the Bible will find something else to believe in. The spiritual dimension is an inescapable part of life, whether people recognize it or not – but spirituality is not necessarily good. It can be of truth and light unto life, or of lies and darkness unto death.

Some atheists like to imagine that by attacking Christianity they are helping to build a more peaceful and a more rational world. This is a bad mistake. The atheists are wrong, as they so often are when it comes to deeper questions of life. Speaking of nineteenth-century "progress," Jacques Barzun wrote: "No sooner, it seemed, had mid-century materialists destroyed the last remnant of belief in the hereafter than appeared Spiritualism, psychical research,

---

[26] Michael Burleigh, *Ethics and extermination: Reflections on Nazi genocide* (Cambridge: Cambridge University Press, 1977), p. 23.

[27] D. M. Lloyd-Jones, *The Puritans: Their Origins and Successors* (Edinburgh: Penguin Books, 1987), p. 333, 334 (both quotes).

132

Theosophy, Christian Science, Yogi, and innumerable shades of New Thought."[28] He might have added Communism, National Socialism, Social Darwinism, Freudianism, and the most trivial and mindless hedonism. People who reject God do not all of a sudden become personifications of pure reason.

When one set of spiritual beliefs and values is set aside, it will be replaced by others. Hitler is a good example of this. He sought not merely to make Germany a great power, expand to the east, or tear up the Versailles Treaty. His ambitions went far beyond mere politics. He wrote in *Mein Kampf* that he wanted to change Germany spiritually and create a new society based on a new idea of man.[29] Such radical innovations were only possible after the widespread rejection of Christianity – and Hitler was a radical, a revolutionary, not a conservative. There was a deep spiritual dimension to National Socialism, a hidden driving power completely concealed from those whose partial and dull or even false concepts of history confine them to the bare recording of material facts. To understand it even partially, there must be some awareness of dimensions to the human experience that today's intellectual elite are often sadly unequipped to deal with.

None of this reflects adversely on the Christian belief in God, as the God of the Bible is as far removed from the earthly imaginations of German romantics and philosophers as day is from night. Atheists have argued for a long time that God is only a projection of the human imagination, the wishful creation of our own longings. It is not hard to agree that this was in fact the case with Hitler. His concept of a "god" or "providence" that was concerned only with the Germans; that had ordained the struggle for survival of the fittest as the means of elevating mankind from its first animal beginnings to its highest point of development in the Aryan race; that had chosen him to bring Austria into the Reich, and deliver the German people from perishing in racial impurity; a God whose miracles consisted not of healing the poor, the blind, the lame, but of fulfilling German national ambitions – this concept of God was indeed only a projection of the human imagination. Marx's and Lenin's senseless and destructive fantasies about a classless utopia or an international proletariat united by class-consciousness were also such creations.

A good example of how a philosophical idea of "god" might be used in a manner far removed from Judeo-Christian concepts but easily compatible with National Socialism can be found in the writings of Ernst Haeckel, a leading biologist and Darwinist in pre-World War One Germany. Consistently with marked trends toward pantheism, Haeckel claimed that God was everywhere. He imagined that the universe was a "colossal organism" animated by a divine force that was not apart from and above nature, like the Christian God, but

---

[28] Jacques Barzun, *Darwin, Marx, Wagner: Critique of a Heritage* (New York: Doubleday Anchor Books, 1958), p. 105.

[29] Hitler, *Mein Kampf*, p. 634.

133

rather at one with nature. In Haeckel's words, "God is almighty; He is the single Creator, the single Cause of all things . . . God is absolute perfection . . . God is the sum of all energy and matter." Other comments reveal a belief that the Cosmos itself was God, a sort of pantheism that allowed for "the revival of many symbols of ancient German pagan religion and mythology."[30] This was passed off by Haeckel as scientific, the latest word in rational understanding of the cosmos. It is a common logical error of some scientists to assume that, because they supposedly rely on reason alone, all of their ideas about life are therefore inherently reasonable.

Haeckel, the perfect example of an acclaimed biologist hopelessly lost outside of his narrow field of expertise, was by no means the only German to use religious language in a thoroughly non-Christian context. The following quotation from Martin Bormann also shows a concept of "god" perfectly consistent with essential elements of secular humanism, not with the Bible. It comes from a circular sent by Bormann to party administrators in June of 1941 and shows how the Nazis used the word "God" to mean something very different from what might ordinarily be assumed.

> When we National Socialists speak of a belief in God, we do not understand by God, like naïve Christians . . . a human-type being, who sits around somewhere in space . . . The force of natural law, with which all these innumerable planets move in the universe, we call the Almighty or God. . . . The more accurately we recognize and observe the laws of nature and of life, the more we adhere to them, so much the more do we conform to the will of the Almighty.[31]

Since Bormann did not rise to his high position in the Reich by his creative independence of thought, such comments should be kept in mind when considering Hitler's and other Nazis' references to "the Lord" or "the Almighty."

Some other important points in the circular are: "National Socialism and Christianity are irreconcilable" . . . Christianity appeals to fear and ignorance while "National Socialism is based on scientific foundations" . . . the party must be "organized according to the latest knowledge of scientific research". . . science is a threat to religion . . . Christianity is an essentially Jewish religion that Germans have no need of . . . Christianity will disappear if children are not indoctrinated with it . . . God is not concerned with individuals . . . "we

---

[30] Daniel Gasman, *The Scientific Origins of National Socialism* (New Brunswick USA: Transaction Publishers, 2004), pp. 65, 67 (the last quote is Gasman's analysis).

[31] John Conway, *The Nazi Persecution of the Churches 1933-1945* (Vancouver: Regent, 1968), p. 384. See pp. 383-385 for the full text (*Nuremberg document* 075-D), and pp. 259-260 for the historical context.

National Socialists impose on ourselves the demand to live naturally as much as possible, i.e., biologically" . . . the influence of the churches "must be broken completely and finally."[32]

After a few days the statement, which was one of official policy from the Reich Chancellery, was withdrawn. Its excessive hostility to Christianity would, it was thought, hinder the war effort, and it seemed better to deal with the church problem later, after the war had been won. Nevertheless, it is a remarkable glimpse into the views of the party secretary and personal deputy of the Fuhrer. There is evidence to suggest that, had the Nazis won the war, the Christians in Germany would have been subjected to harsh persecution as Hitler sought the complete eradication of Jewish influence.[33]

While there was some dissension among party leaders about the best way to deal with the churches, what is important for us here is to remember that a God that is understood in terms of human reason and natural law without revelation is radically different from the Judaeo-Christian view – and "natural law" here should be taken to mean Hitler's concept of natural law as progress through struggle. As he said in *Mein Kampf*, nature develops higher life forms by ruthlessly weeding out the unfit. He included people in this of course, not merely animals, and this pitiless and impersonal process is referred to as "the divine will."[34] There are numerous quotes in *Mein Kampf* to the effect that the perishing of the weak and the victory of the stronger in the struggle for survival is the basic law underlying human existence. This was called "divine," yet was discovered by human reason, and worked according to what were thought at the time to be scientific principles.

Someone wrote that a reference by Hitler to obeying the will of God "reveals a more recognizably Christian conception."[35] The ancient Greeks and Romans spoke of the will of the gods, or of individual gods. The Homeric poems are full of references to the will of the gods or of a particular a god. Confucius spoke of "The Mandate of Heaven." The belief that there are divine powers and we are obligated to follow their will goes back to the beginnings of recorded history. When one takes a "will of God" that is not even remotely like anything mandated by the Bible, one that reflects the preoccupations of nineteenth-century would-be philosophers who dreamed up secular theories unheard of in over 1800 years of Christianity and then tries to link this to

---

[32] Ibid., pp. 383-385.

[33] Ibid., p. 292. In this chapter Conway describes the drastic measures taken against the Protestant and Catholic Churches in the Warthegau, the territory taken from Poland that was incorporated directly into the Reich.

[34] Hitler, *Mein Kampf*, pp. 286, 288, 132.

[35] Richard Steigmann-Gall, "Old Wine in New Bottles? Religion and Race in Nazi Antisemitism," in Kevin Spicer, ed. *Antisemitism, Christian Ambivalence, and the Holocaust* (Bloomington, IN: Indiana University Press, 2007), p. 297.

Christianity, one lays oneself open to the charge of being badly informed, or else of propagandizing without regard for elementary facts.

Hitler's statements about God represent not a Christian influence on National Socialism, but rather new concepts of God and of life that emerged out of the rejection of biblical teaching. To clarify this we will need to examine not only Hitler's unchristian and anti-Christian ideas, but also his expressed hostility to and contempt for Christianity as expressed in *Mein Kampf.* Nor were these ideas of Hitler's merely a personal invention or eccentricity. From the biblical God of the Reformation; to the weaker absent God of the deists; to the still weaker World Spirit of Hegel; to Schopenhauer's blind and impersonal Will; to Haeckel's (and Hitler's) "Almighty," that worked through and was understood by scientific laws, especially survival of the fittest; to the final disappearance of God as best exemplified by Nietzsche – the European cultural concept of God changed greatly, and concepts of ethics, truth, reason, and morality changed along with it.

Those philosophical inventions first sprang fully-grown from the brains of academic philosophers, flourished for a short time and then vanished. Hegel used to be considered the last word in philosophy. Now, he is hopelessly dated, and while some read him for his historical importance or for personal interest, virtually no-one believes in his Grand Cosmic Whatever. Almost no-one believes in Schopenhauer's Will or other such concepts now, but they did have a great deal of relevance in their day and traces of them are clearly evident in *Mein Kampf.*

There is not such a large gap between Hitler and earlier German philosophy as many believe. If we accept that there is a definite progress of mankind, one that is guided by a higher power understood by philosophy and human reason; if we consider that this progress is spearheaded by uniquely chosen nations, such as first the Greeks and the Romans, then the French, and now the Germans; if we accept that in order to remain in vital contact with this force the Germans need to keep themselves pure – first philosophically and culturally, then also racially – then we have at least started out in the general direction of National Socialism.

Of course, such a worldview has nothing to do respect for the individuals who are just insignificant parts of a grand cosmic process. It has nothing to do with love, pity, charity, mercy, and justice, or concern for the sufferings of others. It has nothing to do with the Bible either, and is in fact a denial of many of its fundamental teachings. Hitler had a vague notion of something he called "god," an indistinct higher power that conformed exactly to his wishes and allowed for many ideas that were directly contrary to Christianity. In describing those contrary ideas, the difficulty is in knowing where to begin. An entire book could be devoted to the purpose – an entire book of wasted effort. Those who have some understanding of what Christianity is and what Hitler was need no such evidence, while those who are resolutely determined to link

Hitler to Christianity in some way, any way, are adept at evading contrary evidence. They will continue on their merry way with a blissful disregard of facts, reason and logic – all the while flattering themselves for their superior rationality.

A photograph of Hitler coming out of a church; an army belt-buckle that says "God with us"; some words from a Hitler speech (often nothing but lies); praise from a politically motivated (or simply gullible) church leader when no one could imagine what Hitler would later turn out to be – these and other such examples of "evidence" do not prove anything.

Consider some of these ideas from *Mein Kampf*. Both here and elsewhere, in order to avoid a multiplicity of footnotes, I'll give the page numbers directly in the text, using the edition mentioned in the bibliography.

~ thanking heaven on his knees for the outbreak of World War I (161). Hitler also expressed his childhood happiness about the Boer war (158), and his "longing" for an end to the peace that preceded World War I (158). Didn't the Vikings and the Mongols love war?

~ national independence and honor as the loftiest and highest aim anyone can conceive of (177)

~ keeping the blood of the race pure as our holiest obligation (402)

~ racial impurity the original sin (249), with loss of paradise due to impurity of blood (296)

~ race at the center of life (403)

~ the fight for national survival outweighing all humanitarian principles (177)

~ the endlessness of human progress (295)

~ the creativity of the human mind our only hope and our salvation (446)

~ mankind raised above the animal world not by divine creation, but by human creativity, knowledge and inventions (445)

~ racial purity and selective breeding leading to higher forms of humanity (402)

~ elimination of the weak, the sickly and the unfit (404)

~ preserving and advancing the most highly developed members of the human race as our main goal (398)

It might also be suitable to add a quote from Goebbels to this litany of godless, stupid and wicked ideas. In a propaganda pamphlet of 1930 he wrote, "To be a Christian means: Love thy neighbor as thyself! My neighbor is one who is tied to me by his blood. If I love him, then I must hate his enemies."[36]

---

[36] "A Goebbels Propaganda Pamphlet, 1930," Louis Snyder (ed.,), *Documents of German History* (New Brunswick, NJ: Rutgers University Press, 1958), pp. 415-416.

Most people are capable of recognizing that these ideas did not come from Christianity. Fichte's intense nationalism and his fantasy about the pure German race being closer than other peoples to his higher philosophical reality are much more relevant to an understanding of the holiness of race and blood than anything in the Bible. There were, it is true, occasional feeble, insincere, and unconvincing Nazi appeals to religion for justification. In exactly the same way people today sometimes try to use Scripture to justify feminism, socialism, homosexuality or other modern ideas – not getting their beliefs from the Bible, but getting their ideas elsewhere and then seeking religious justification without regard for the Bible's plain and obvious intent.

Incidentally, sometime in the 1920s Joseph Goebbels wrote a novel that I have seen referred to more than once to support the theory of the Christian origins and nature of Naziism. In the novel the main character found the answer to Germany's problems in racism, antisemitism and nationalism, and stated that "The various churches have failed. Completely."[37] The book also contains the assertion that Jesus Christ was not a Jew. Another quote from the novel reads "Race is the matrix of all created forces . . . Reality is only the Volk [the German people]."[38] Since these reflect not Christianity but a denial of Christianity, and since Goebbels openly expressed his contempt for Christianity in his diaries (as we shall see shortly), it is unfortunate that we should have to deal with such trivial distractions. Borrowing the powerful and deeply symbolic Christ figure and adapting it to advance one's own program does not show the Christian origins of said program.

Returning to the subjects of Hitler's ideas as expressed above, it would be possible to balance all of them with contradictory Bible verses, but that really shouldn't be necessary. People who do not know that such beliefs have nothing to do with Christianity should do some more studying before they consider the subject. I would recommend reading at least the four Gospels, Acts and Romans (preferably in the more accurate King James Version rather than in watered down and sacrilegiously edited modern translations and paraphrases). Without going into a lot of detail, though, I would like to present a few Scripture verses.

We have already referred to Acts 17:26 (God "made of one blood all nations of men"). Romans 13:3-4 states that God's designated purpose for human government is to restrain and punish evil, not to exalt and magnify it.

---

[37] Steigmann-Gall, *The Holy Reich,* p. 21. The novel was called *Michael.* To completely ignore the open hostility to Christianity expressed in a well-known and accepted source such as Goebbels' diaries and then to build castles of speculation on far-fetched inferences from a novel is at best careless. At worst it is (to put it politely) disingenuous.

[38] Stephen R. C. Hicks, *Nietzsche and the Nazis: A Personal View* (Loves Park, IL: Ockham's Razor Publishing, 2010), p. 19.

And, most people would agree that Jesus' saying "Blessed are the peacemakers" is difficult to reconcile with enthusiasm over the outbreak of war. Even if war is regrettably necessary, we should never be joyful about it. I Thessalonians 4:3 states that God's will is our sanctification in holiness and righteousness – not preserving the master race or purifying German blood.

Hitler's frequently quoted statement about the state's obligation "to produce images of the Lord" (402) referred to preserving the purity of Aryan blood, hardly a biblical concept. The dream of breeding people like animals to produce the highest and best type shows the influence of racial theories that put people on the same plane as animals. This, of course, is the modern and secular concept of eugenics, not biblical Christianity. We could say that Hitler was a theistic evolutionist – except his "theism," as has already been said, was a very different sort of theism from what we find in Matthew, Mark, Luke, and John.

Inevitably, it will be argued that even Hitler's totally non-biblical theism proves the inherent dangers of religion. People who believe in God instead of reason, facts and logic are treading on thin ice, and find it easy to believe any weird theories. The obvious answer to this is, that Lenin and Stalin were open and avowed atheists, and they also accepted weird and destructive theories. They too stressed reason, science, and the reality of this life alone, yet their denial of religion did not keep them from going astray. Atheists can be just as selfish, blind and conceited as anyone else, even though they like to imagine that they are on a higher plane than the rest of us.

Anyway, indistinct religious comments have nothing to do with Christ – and Hitler's understanding of Christ was, as might be expected, a highly distorted one. He mentioned Christ seldom and obviously cared little about him. The rare references to Christ in *Mein Kampf* are noteworthy (they are almost always neglected in discussions of Hitler's religion). At one point, for example, Hitler referred to Christ as "the great founder of the new doctrine" (307). This curious circumlocution seems intended to try and say something complimentary about Christ without actually having to do so. Hitler expressed his view here that Christ – not God come to earth in human form – was killed by the Jews in an earthly power struggle. Christ's sacrificial death and resurrection, needless to say, do not enter into the picture. The death of a man who was after all only a mere mortal (probably with an Aryan father, maybe a Roman soldier) was not a motivating factor in Hitler's worldview.

The religious dimension of Christ's death was not a standard Nazi theme because such Jewish concepts as sacrifice and atonement for sin were not important to believers in Aryan supremacy. Though some propagandistic attempts were made to appeal to traditional religious antisemitism, Nazi hostility to Christ (though not overtly expressed in *Mein Kampf*) was common. One man recounted how he saw a Hitler youth tear a crucifix off of a classroom wall and toss it out a window yelling "Lie there, you dirty Jew."[39] Himmler was quoted as referring to "that Jew-boy, Jesus Christ," and saying "we shall cleanse the German people of the leprous sores of Christianity."[40] In spite of Himmler's occasional vague statements about respect for religion, SS-men were not allowed to attend church in uniform, hold positions of leadership in a church, or use religious symbols.[41] They were, for some reason, allowed to retain church membership, though any church which would allow an SS-man to remain on its membership rolls was very far from the New Testament ideal of the church as a gathering of believers from which open evildoers were to be excluded (I Corinthians 5:11-13).

Elsewhere Hitler referred to the new and unGerman doctrine of which Christ was the founder. He observed that the significance of Christianity lay only in morality, ethics, and culture (211). That Christ's main emphasis was ethics and morality was mainstream doctrine among German secularists and religious liberals. This is all that is left for those who deny the deity of Christ and the inerrancy of Scripture, and so have to try to explain Christ's life without reference to the miraculous or the divine. This view of Hitler's goes back to the so-called Enlightenment and is widespread today. There is nothing strange or unusual about Hitler's ideas here.

Not for the first or the last time we see Hitler's inner harmony with fundamental tenets of the modernist rejection of biblical revelation. Moreover, Hitler wrote elsewhere that Christ's emphasis on ethics, morality and love was completely false (without mentioning Christ by name). This is because the basic, underlying law of nature is that the strong survive and the weak die, and what is contrary to this is not real (286-287). It is struggle that leads to the development of higher species. This is the will of an impersonal higher power – and the idea that we can escape from or rise above this iron law of conflict, that there is something in us that transcends mere earthly nature, is "Jewish nonsense" (308). That included, of course, Christian nonsense, since the Semitic origins of Christianity were a common theme of the non-religious antisemitism of that period.

This passage is a direct denial of the biblical teaching of a divine creation of the human soul. It is directly related to Schopenhauer's idea that Jewish values working through Christianity had divided the unity of nature and separated man from the animals by its false teaching of the uniqueness of man. That we are essentially animals was a view shared by Hitler and by Schopenhauer. In the latter's words, "A man must be bereft of all his sense or completely chloroformed by the *Foetor* [odor] *Judaicus* not to see that in all essential

---

[39] Friedrich Reck-Malleczewen, *Diary of a Man in Despair,* trans. Paul Rubens (London: Duck Editions, 1995), p. 33.

[40] Kersten, *Memoirs*, p. 110.

[41] Veith, *Modern Fascism*, p. 66.

140

respects the animal is absolutely identical with us."[42] This was followed by a pioneering appeal for animal rights.

It is no accident that Hitler named Schopenhauer in *Mein Kampf* and quoted him directly on "the Jew" as the "great master in lying" (the only philosopher so honored).[43] This is an obvious compliment to Schopenhauer, as Hitler did not usually credit his sources. Hitler referred to Schopenhauer, who severely attacked traditional Christianity, as "One of the greatest minds of humanity." Like Schopenhauer, Hitler had no need of divine revelation. Schopenhauer is also (according to the index) the only philosopher referred to by name in *Hitler's Second Book*.

Hitler went on to describe the struggle for survival of the fittest as "exact scientific truth" (287). He claimed in this context that ethics as well as ideas that originate in feelings or emotional experience are not based on logic. Ideas that do not originate in objective truths of science derive only from men, and are nothing but the products of human imagination and creativity (287-288). This means of course that ethics do not have a transcendent source (that is, God) but are merely human inventions and have no higher existence apart from human imagination.

Many today would agree with this. Nietzsche made this obvious point – obvious to an atheist that is – in his *Genealogy of Morals*. Also in agreement with Nietzsche, Hitler claimed that traditional humanitarian ethics, derived from centuries of Christianity, were "absurd," chains to bind us with false conceptions of humanity (132). Hitler, in accordance with human reason and logic, acting on common principles accepted by respectable thinkers, broke those fetters with terrible results. My personal feeling is that Hitler understood Nietzsche and some necessary principles of secularism better than many people do today.

I was surprised (though I shouldn't have been) to find the identical sentiment about the non-reality of traditional ethics expressed by the Nobel prize-winning biologist Jacques Monod. Arguing that science was the only source of truth and that human ethics should be based accordingly, he asserts: "ethics, in essence *nonobjective*, is forever barred from the sphere of knowledge . . . [an] ethic of knowledge does not obtrude itself on man; *on the contrary, it is he who prescribes it to himself*."[44] Ethics do not have an

---

[42] Paul Lawrence Rose, *Wagner: Race and Revolution* (New Haven: Yale University Press, 1992), p. 94 (quoting Schopenhauer's "On Religion" in *Parerga and Paralipomena*).

[43] Hitler, *Mein Kampf*, pp. 305, 232. Schopenhauer is not directly named in the statement "one of the greatest minds of humanity," but is identifiable by the use of the same quote about Jews as masters of lying.

[44] Jacques Monod, *Chance and Necessity: An Essay on the Natural Philosophy of Modern Biology* (New York: Alfred A. Knopf, 1971), pp. 174, 177.

independent existence or source apart from ourselves. We invent them, they are solely products of the human mind, and have no scientific basis. This is not to say that Monod was identical to Hitler. It is to say that if we emerged by a natural process only, then it follows inevitably that ethics are merely human inventions and cannot be anything else.

Commenting on this quote, F. A. Hayek states that that "Monod is not the only biologist to argue along such lines."[45] Of course not. It makes perfect sense, if we accept the idea that the foundational realities of our existence are matter and energy, that science is the highest and truest form of knowledge, and that we came about by accident in a chance universe. Neither do Hitler's vague comments about God remove him from this equation. Although often pointed to as proof of Hitler's religious belief, his references to god, as we have seen, had to do with a severely limited entity, a human invention and perfectly consistent in many respects with scientific naturalism.

One of the many important aspects of the Hitler problem is his tendency to mix lies, truths and half-truths altogether. Sometimes he was very direct and said exactly what he meant. At other times, he skillfully lied, and said whatever was necessary to achieve a certain aim. When he spoke of respect for Christianity and the churches and promised to support them, the plain historical record easily shows this was a deliberate falsehood. His policy was to enslave the churches and reduce them to complete submission to the state.

When on the other hand Hitler spoke of some sort of higher power behind him, this was politically useful in that it augmented his aura of power, but it was not merely a tactic. Some will disagree, but I believe Hitler did imagine that there was some sort of force at work of which he was the instrument. These references to a higher power, however, even if sincerely uttered, serve to link him to something very different from Christianity.

Many educated people in the nineteenth century accepted the primacy of science over traditional religion and did not believe in or try to follow the Bible as divinely inspired, yet did not feel completely comfortable with rejecting God altogether. They tried therefore to combine both religion and non-religious knowledge. This was done in different ways, according to the relative weight given to one side or the other, but the idea of some sort of Something-Up-There that was referred to as "divine" yet understood within the confines of humanistic truth was quite common. Some sort of belief in god or at least some kind of spiritual reality was retained, but it was a human contrivance, adapted to suit the scientific (or nationalistic, philosophical or psychological) needs of people now separated from traditional dogmas, yet still in need of some sort of religious comfort.

---

[45] F. A. Hayek, *The Fatal Conceit: The Errors of Socialism* (Chicago: University of Chicago Press, 1991), p. 57.

It is to a large extent true, that "the God of the nineteenth century was materialistic . . . in the end most religious bodies gave in and absorbed the historical and scientific criticism of myths, religions, and dogmas."[46] This point is completely lost on people who seem not to have heard of nineteenth-century religious modernism, and so assume every reference to God points to Christianity. Christianity, however, has to do with Jesus as God and the teachings of Jesus, and when we find Jesus reduced to the status of a mere man about whom nothing can be exactly known because of the legendary nature of the four Gospels, it becomes apparent that we are talking about something other than historic, traditional Christianity.

This is especially noticeable in Hitler's references to Jesus Christ. According to him, Jesus Christ taught a system of imaginary ethics divorced from scientific reality. The origins of humanity were not from God, but rather from Nature's "ruthless choice" in weeding out the unfit (288). We do not dominate Nature, but are inescapably a part of it, and have only risen above the animals by our "knowledge of various laws and secrets of Nature" (287). It is not divine creation, but our intelligence that has raised us above the animals. Here we must note Hitler's profound and essential secularism. He was very far from being a creationist in the biblical sense. His speculations in *Mein Kampf* on the most advanced human types becoming "the sole ruler of this earth" (288) represent the dream of secular humanism – mankind independent of God.

Hitler's fascination with science is noteworthy here. He criticized the Catholic Church because its teachings conflicted with "exact science and research" (459). At one point Hitler even elaborated on the conflict between religion and science. He asserted that instead of remaining in its proper devotional or religious sphere, religion tries to apply its truths to the earthly realm. In this conflict between religion that has left its proper place and science, "victory will almost always fall to the latter" (268). Liberal Protestants had accepted long before Hitler that religion could not compete with science in the realm of fact and so retreated into a misty religious domain where things could remain spiritually true independent of and apart from reason.

This destructive separation of religion from reason, of rational arguments from faith, of the phenomenal realm of fact from a religious realm "off limits to reason"[47] goes back at least as far as Kant. In this context Hicks asserts that Kant's limitations on reason "more than anyone else's opened the door to the nineteenth-century irrationalists and idealist metaphysicians."[48] They in turn introduced new ideas of nation, state, ethics and antisemitism that were to have

---

[46] Barzun, *Darwin, Marx, Wagner*, pp. 90-91.

[47] Stephen R. C. Hicks, *Explaining Postmodernism: Skepticism and Socialism from Rousseau to Foucault* (Phoenix, AZ: Scholargy Publishing, 2004), p. 29.

[48] Ibid., p. 28.

very negative implications. In the Kantian tradition of lofty speculations increasingly separated from reality, they confused their imaginations with truth itself, and (with the help of numerous popularizers) did much to reorient the German people in the wrong direction.

These now antiquated philosophies came to dominate much of German so-called Protestant so-called theology in the nineteenth century, and in so doing moved the church onto the shifting sands of transient human wisdom. This is what Hitler meant when he complimented Protestantism as being more suitable for Germany than Catholicism because of its "later tradition" (112), a tradition of accommodation to secularism. The Catholics were doctrinally less flexible, yet, he condemned both Protestants and Catholics equally for failing to understand the Jewish question and the importance of racial purity (111). He also referred to the conflict between Catholics and Protestants as a Jewish trick devised to weaken the German people (561). This does not reveal a profound understanding of or sympathy for Christian teaching.

It has been said that Hitler did not criticize religion in *Mein Kampf* and it is true that we do not see there any long and extended denunciations or such frontal assaults as "Christianity is Jewish lies." This was Nietzsche's claim in *The Antichrist* – by no means an unheard of assertion at that time. Long before Nietzsche the fact of Jewish influence on Europe through Christianity was a cause for alarm among extreme German nationalists and other anti-Christian fanatics. Hitler was too much of a politician to say much about this in his book and speeches, yet his animosity did show itself in some parts of *Mein Kampf.* This has been too seldom remarked upon. Historians who were not Christians and ignorant of Christianity could easily miss them, or fail to see their relevance.

Before looking at *Mein Kampf*, it is worth referring to Robert Wistrich's useful summary of some of Hitler's private comments about Christianity. An invention of the apostle Paul that had undermined the Roman Empire and introduced an artificial and unnatural ethic of morality, Christianity had (in Wistrich's description of Hitler's view) "given birth to contemporary teachings of pacifism, equality before God and the law, human brotherhood and compassion for the weak."[49] These "had deliberately subverted the natural order"[50] by introducing Jewish values that led to domination of the strong and the healthy by the weak and the sickly.

While some have disputed the genuineness of these private comments of Hitler's (unjustifiably in my opinion), it is significant that they are in many important respects identical to those presented by Nietzsche in *The Antichrist*. In describing Hitler's ideas about Christianity as the "crude and malevolent

---

[49] Robert S. Wistrich, *Hitler and the Holocaust* (New York: Modern Library, 2003), p. 135.
[50] Ibid., p. 134.

rant of an unhinged mind,"[51] Wistrich was in fact accurately describing some of the ideas of Nietzsche as well. Hitler and Nietzsche would have agreed completely that "It was the Judaeo-Christian ethic that had alienated humanity from the wholeness of the natural order in pursuit of the 'lie' of a transcendent God."[52]

It has been observed that "one can find troubling echoes of a vulgarized and debased Nietzscheanism in the later diatribes of Hitler, Himmler, Bormann, and Rosenberg against Judeo-Christianity."[53] Was it really "vulgarized and debased"? Or was it Nietzsche straight, as he described Christianity in *The Antichrist*? I believe it was Nietzsche straight, and I would like if I may to add the parenthetical comment that this fact is not at all troubling to those who see Nietzsche's entire understanding of God, of Christianity, and of life to be merely one gigantic and destructive mistake.

Like atheist extremists today, Hitler had profound contempt for Christianity, but he did not declare it too blatantly. After all, even a common American politician will avoid antagonizing people unnecessarily about religion, and Hitler was after all a politician in his rise to power – yet, he did say plainly and directly (as we have seen) that Christian ethics were human inventions not based on scientific fact. That meant, if explanation is necessary, that Christianity (as well as the cultural ethos largely derived from it) was untrue. Man's deepest need for an authentic existence in harmony with nature was, Hitler thought, best met by National Socialism.

Far from being a complete repudiation of the "Enlightenment," National Socialism relied heavily on the use of reason in a way that actually makes sense if you accept a few false and ugly premises. Hitler stated that "If the National Socialist movement frees itself from all illusions . . . and accepts reason as its sole guide" it could succeed in revitalizing Germany (664). He was more logical than many realize and often reasoned in a straight and clear line – unfortunately, from the wrong starting points. National Socialism shared one of the "Enlightenment's" most cherished principles – the sufficiency of human understanding independent of divine revelation and God's law – and emerged out of a clearly discernible tradition of a century and more of secular thought.

It is a philosophical oddity, that people would deny divine revelation and claim that human reason alone was sufficient, then use that reason to arrive at the insufficiency of reason with a corresponding emphasis on will and on instinct (as the Nazis did). Following reason, they came in the end to the

---

[51] Ibid., p. 134.

[52] Ibid., p. 135.

[53] Jacob Golomb and Robert S. Wistrich, eds. *Nietzsche, Godfather of Fascism? On the Uses and Abuses of a Philosophy* (Princeton: Princeton University Press, 2002), p. 7.

conclusion that reason was not the sole or even the best means of arriving at truth. This was not of course unique to the Nazis, but was a vital element in the earlier Romantic reaction against the sterile, complacent, conceited and trivial rationalism of the smugly self-denominated Enlightenment. This is related to the Romantic emphasis on following nature, which by the way is not too dangerous if you are a poet like Wordsworth contemplating a lovely landscape – but what if nature is Darwinian conflict? Doesn't conformity to nature then mandate a new sort of ethic?

Such are the tortuous wanderings of minds separated from God. As an ancient philosopher once said, "there is nothing difficult about deducing a whole string of absurdities once a single absurdity has been conceded."[54] The Nazis followed some deceptive philosophical and pseudo-scientific lies to their natural conclusion. Thus the rationality that was so fundamental to the "Enlightenment" (and to the whole movement of European secularism) was one ingredient of National Socialism – rationality divorced from higher truths, and hence careening ever more wildly out of control.

Yet, there was also that religious or spiritual dimension. This strange combination of secularism and religion, of reason and belief, is one of the darker aspects of the riddle of Hitler. It was not inconsistent with a marked hostility to Christianity, and it will not be difficult to find such hostility in *Mein Kampf*. One example out of many that could be given is Hitler's condemnation of Christian missions. He spoke of the limited effect of the churches in Germany and said they had turned to foreign missions to compensate for their failures at home. While the Europeans are declining racially because of improper breeding, the missionaries go to Africa in search of converts, but only succeed in turning inferior but healthy people "into a rotten brood of bastards" (403).

That converting people to Christianity turns them into "rotten bastards" is hardly a ringing endorsement. Hitler went on to say that the churches should stop bothering the Negroes with teachings they neither wanted nor understood, but should devote themselves instead to maintaining the purity of the German race at home (403). This, as we see on the preceding page, included the forced sterilization of degenerate and depraved cripples and cretins (not most people's idea of the churches' mission).

Later Hitler complained about the Christianization of Europe, and blamed the loss of Europe's pre-Christian pagan religions on Christianity's intolerant fanaticism (454). Few people who accuse Christians of being intolerant are aware that they are repeating an argument of Hitler's. This common argument of secularists was also propagated by the notorious American fascist Ezra Pound. He claimed that "The greatest tyrannies have arisen from the dogma

---

[54] Aristotle, *Physics*, trans. Robin Waterfield (Oxford: Oxford University Press, 2008), p. 11.

that the *theos* is one,"[55] and then turned to Mussolini for warmth in his lonely modernism. Odd, how those who accuse Christianity of intolerance are often so intolerant themselves.

Hitler connected the "fanaticism" of Christianity with its well-known and undeniable Jewish origins, and noted that Christian "intolerance" was essentially Jewish. He expressed his "loathing" at Christianity's unfortunate appearance, and then stated: "The men who want to redeem our German people from its present condition have no need to worry their heads thinking how lovely it would be if this and that did not exist; they must try to ascertain how the given condition can be eliminated" (454).

He then proceeded to elaborate on how the power of Christianity in Germany should be broken: "A philosophy filled with infernal intolerance [Christianity] will only be broken by a new idea [National Socialism]" (454).

In the next paragraph Hitler calls openly for the persecution of Christianity:

> The individual may establish with pain today that with the appearance of Christianity the first spiritual terror entered into the far freer ancient world, but he will not be able to contest the fact that since then the world has been afflicted and dominated by this coercion, and that coercion is broken only by coercion, and terror only by terror (454-455).

Does this require any elaboration? The spiritual "coercion" of saying there is one God whom we must obey, while leaving people free to disagree, and the "terror" of a day of judgment that people were free to disbelieve in if they liked – these could only be broken by a different sort of terror. This meant in the end the Gestapo and the SS, even if Hitler could not have precisely envisioned the details when writing *Mein Kampf*. Why has this direct and open call to break the churches been missed by so many who write about National Socialism and Christianity? Perhaps they just assumed that Hitler's book was unreadable, and so never bothered with it.

Like other ideas in *Mein Kampf*, breaking Christianity was something that Hitler did not just talk about but actually sought to do. Why didn't the Christians pay attention to these words? For the same reason that many trained diplomats and professional politicians missed or did not take seriously many other things Hitler put in writing. They either did not read the book at all, or they read it without understanding; or, they understood Hitler's ideas in the abstract but never imagined they would actually be implemented.

As to the few Christians who may have read and understood this, what could they have done? Does anyone think a few sermons to an indifferent nation in the 1920s could have stopped Hitler and changed the course of world

---

[55] Veith, *Modern Fascism*, p. 44 (from Robert Casillo's *The Genealogy of Demons*, citing *Selected Prose of Ezra Pound 1909-1965*).

history? Many Germans in the Weimar era were more interested in Bert Brecht's *Three Penny Opera*, bicycle races, or the popular dancing girl Josephine Baker than they were in sermons based on the Bible. Have some of these people who like to talk about "Christian Germany" read a single book about the Weimar Republic?

Also, when Hitler's book was published and for some years thereafter, the National Socialist movement was still on the fringe of society. It did not seem very threatening and there did not seem to be much need for concern. When Hitler was catapulted to the forefront of a mass movement by the Great Depression, it was too late for anything but a powerful concerted action that none of Hitler's opponents were ever capable of. Some people who discuss these issues are very wise after the fact, but it is doubtful that they would have behaved any differently, had they been there.

A few other comments of Hitler's are of interest. Still in *Mein Kampf*, we note that he presented the very common humanist view that religion, if not true, at least has the merit of giving the common people some sort of guide, some basis for morality (267). Merely destroying traditional religion without having something to replace it with would end in nihilism or anarchy (267). In other words, it was not enough to destroy religion – something had to be there to replace it. Hitler had a lot of ideas about what that something might be. This included, of course, "morality" – morality that allowed for the extermination of multitudes of harmless and innocent people; for lying, exploitation and theft on a colossal scale; for unprovoked wars of aggression; for the breeding of future SS men in homes for Aryan mothers with no regard for family or marriage; and for extreme sexual promiscuity among Nazi youth.

Hitler's concept of morality was only that which (in his opinion) furthered the purification and domination of the Aryan race. It was only very superficially "bourgeois." Opposition to pornography, smoking, abortion or homosexuality had nothing at all to do with conventional morality, but were derived from Hitler's unique ideology. He had only contempt for conventional ethics and for the conventional religion from which those ethics were derived. The claim that Hitler somehow embodied middle-class morality is a surprising statement (we shall refer to some specific examples of his contempt for Germany's bourgeoisie shortly). Otto von Bismarck and Paul von Hindenburg were much closer to conventional middle class morality and, most would agree, they were far removed from Hitler.

He claimed that people were only Protestants and Catholics because of their upbringing, and that their deepest needs were unmet by the churches (85). This is in keeping with his comments about the general decline of religious influence in Germany before World War I (266). He noted the passivity of many Christians and commented that numbers of those who did not break away from the churches but remained in them were apathetic (267). The cultural Protestantism or Catholicism imposed on them in infancy meant little or nothing to many. To others it was more of a sentimental attachment only. Hitler (like many others, including concerned Christians) could see that the imposing edifice of religiosity in Germany lacked life and vitality – recognition of weakness in others was one of his special talents.

Many Germans – both inside and outside the churches – were empty and vulnerable, and Hitler craftily appealed to them. He did this so well that even today, after all that is known about Hitler, some people are still taken in. Those who prate of a "Christian" Germany that never existed have no idea how lifeless many German churches had become after decades of "theological" liberalism or of dead, spiritless orthodoxy. Hitler saw that emptiness, that need for conviction, for purpose, for sacrifice – and this was one of the main but not always sufficiently appreciated reasons for his rise. He filled a void created by well over a century of spiritual decline, and his calls for struggle and sacrifice deeply appealed to people who needed something more than mere existence. Contrary to the low expectations of some, people will not remain docile and contented if only their most basic material needs are met.

Hitler's real attitude toward Christianity – if confirmation is needed – is provided by Joseph Goebbels. He wrote in his diary:

> The Fuehrer spoke very derogatorily about the arrogance of the higher and lower clergy. The insanity of the Christian doctrine of redemption really doesn't fit at all into our time . . . It is simply incomprehensible how anybody can consider the Christian doctrine of redemption as a guide for the difficult life of today . . . A church that does not keep step with modern scientific knowledge is doomed. It may take quite a while, but it is bound finally to happen . . . The Fuehrer is an enthusiastic advocate of pure science . . . [56]

Goebbels also said in this same passage, "I have the greatest respect for the Fuehrer's tremendous intellectual achievement in all fields of knowledge."

German theologian Helmut Thielicke wrote of Hitler that "one had to look very closely and read his terrible book *Mein Kampf* very carefully to see the cloven hoof beneath the angel's luminous robes."[57] To describe Hitler's book as "luminous" and to claim that its blatant wickedness was difficult to see is a remarkable statement. The opening pages of one single chapter in Hitler's book ("Nation and Race," vol. I chap. 11) are full of lies and evil. Any pastor

---

[56] Joseph Goebbels, *The Goebbels Diaries 1942-1943*, trans. Louis P. Lochner (Westport, CT: Greenwood Press, 1948), p. 375. People who point to Goebbel's early novel *Michael* to show the alleged Christian qualities in National Socialism consistently fail to mention that the book is in fact an indictment of traditional religion as inadequate to Germany's real needs.

[57] Quoted in James Bentley, *Martin Niemoller* (London: Hodder and Stoughton, 1984), p. 43.

or theologian who could not clearly and easily see the godlessness there wasted his time in seminary, in my opinion – or perhaps this was just an excuse to justify failure to oppose Hitler from the start.

Yet, in spite of his contempt for Christianity's unscientific and Semitic character, Hitler considered his church policy carefully while writing *Mein Kampf*. In one lengthy passage, he asked if it were possible to exterminate "spiritual ideas" by force, and added that he had repeatedly considered this problem (170). It was of no small importance to him, and his conclusions are highly revealing, and essential for an understanding of his later church policies. This is one of the ideas in the book, like expanding to the east, that Hitler said, meant, and attempted to do – and Hitler specifically uses the word "religion" in this context – "If we ponder analogous cases, particularly on a religious basis" (170).

First, Hitler wrote that a spiritual idea such as Christianity could be eliminated by force only if every last exponent of the idea were destroyed. This would be harmful to the state, however, since "such a blood sacrifice strikes the best part of the people" (170). Hitler could not seek to directly exterminate the Christians as he did the Jews, because the Christians – using the term in the most general cultural sense – were of sound Aryan stock. They and their children were needed to build up the German nation, and could be tolerated as long as they posed no direct threat to the regime.

Secondly, Hitler correctly understood that overt persecution would only stir up sympathy for the movement being persecuted. This would serve in the long run to strengthen the churches (170). Creating heroes of the faith would have led to the exact opposite of the result Hitler sought to achieve. Therefore, he applied intense pressure, but selectively. He sought to eliminate the public influence of the churches, yet still permitted them to exist. On occasion he was able to yield on non-essential points, and curb the restraint of some of his more zealous followers.

Thirdly, Hitler wanted to win over people who were not fully persuaded of his program, and still had various degrees of attachment to the churches. He understood the importance of not alienating people unnecessarily, as we shall see shortly in considering his analysis of the failure of the Austrian anti-Catholic politician von Schoenerer. There were many people in the churches who were sympathetic to some of Hitler's aims, such as overturning the Treaty of Versailles, but were by no means enthusiastic Nazis. To have alienated them prematurely and unnecessarily would have been politically foolish, and Hitler was a very canny politician who made few tactical mistakes in his rise to power.

What did Hitler propose as a church solution then? First, a new idea must be provided to replace the old one. Second, there must be a steady and continuous application of force. People could not be allowed to propagate values directly contradictory to those of the state. While not subjected to direct lethal assault, the old idea must be restricted in every feasible way. "Only in the steady and constant application of force lies the very first prerequisite for success" (171). This is exactly the course Hitler followed in his dealings with the churches – drastically limiting them and, if need be, arresting or otherwise intimidating the few who were too outspoken, while at the same time indoctrinating the young with new values.

If, however, Hitler was so opposed to Christianity, why did so many Christians support him, some of them enthusiastically? Why did so many fail to oppose him? There were various reasons for this, but before considering them in a different chapter, it is necessary to respond briefly to four more points that are commonly raised in discussions of Hitler's attitude toward Christianity: (a) the accusation that he was a Catholic and his Concordat with the Vatican; (b) the support for "positive" Christianity in the Nazi party platform; (c) Hitler's many public statements about the importance of the Churches and his desire to support and work with them; and (d) a speech of 1922 in which Hitler not only claimed to be a Christian, but actually referred to Christ as his "Lord and Saviour." None of these will require lengthy analysis.

Beginning with the charge that Hitler was a Catholic, during his whole time in power he never mentioned the Virgin Mary, never participated in a mass, and never went to confession. He did not request absolution from a priest before his death. Moreover, he deliberately sought to destroy the Polish Catholic Church, which the Nazis persecuted with great cruelty. The Austrian Catholics fared better – after all, they were of Aryan blood and not inferior Slavic subhumans – but their Churches too were deliberately and systematically assaulted.

In 1941 the Austrian bishops made an official protest to the Reich Ministry of the Interior. They listed many grievances, including: the forbidding of all public celebrations of Catholic holidays; closure of higher educational facilities without judicial proceedings or justification; confiscation of nunneries and monasteries and forced eviction of their inhabitants officially described as "opponents of the state."[58] This was in a five page document, which included the statement that such actions were evidence of official hostility to the church, and not merely random incidents.

Much has been made by some of the Concordat Hitler signed with the Vatican in 1933. According to this agreement, the Catholic Church was to refrain from any political opposition to Hitler's regime while the Nazi government in turn would respect certain rights and privileges of the Church. This agreement, however, was broken many times in Germany (though not merely ignored as in Austria). Confiscations of Church property, persecutions

---

[58] Conway, *The Nazi Persecution of the Churches*, pp. 393-397.

of priests, banning of Catholic organizations were frequent. Catholic protests through official channels were completely futile.[59]

The Nazis made a lot of noise about Austria "returning to the Reich," but the Austrian Catholic Church was deprived of all legal status on the grounds that the Concordat applied to Germany, but not to Austria. Not surprisingly, when in 1937 the Pope issued an encyclical condemning Naziism (*Mit Brennender Sorge*), Hitler's response was not "The Holy Father has the power of the keys from Peter and we should submit." On the contrary, he sought to stifle it. Publication was forbidden, and those caught distributing it were arrested.

It has been claimed that Hitler was a "member in good standing" of the Church, and the question has been raised as to why he was not excommunicated. As to the latter, if the Vatican had excommunicated Hitler, it would have done great damage to the Catholic Church in Germany. Catholics would have either had to openly defy Hitler and face the fiercest and cruelest persecution, or they would have had to ignore the Pope. Rightly or wrongly, the Vatican decided that such a confrontation was not in its best interests.

As to being a member in good standing, I am not familiar with Roman Church law, but surely being a member "in good standing" must require more than merely paying a state tax but never being active or participating in the life of the church in any way, while at the same time persecuting and harassing it. If Hitler had officially renounced his church membership, it would have been much more difficult, if not impossible, for him to claim that his many actions against the Church were only responses to undue political interference.

After Hitler's Catholicism, the second issue is the Nazi party platform's endorsement of Christianity in point 24. This has occasioned some triumphalism from over-eager opponents of Christianity, who imagine it is documentary proof of the close relationship between Christianity and Hitler's fanaticism. Fortunately, it isn't a difficult point to deal with, as a number of points in that platform were never implemented at all and had nothing to do with what actually occurred after Hitler came to power. This is not to say that the platform had no relevance at all, but it was by no means a full description of what Hitler hoped to do or later did, and was ignored if situations no one had envisioned at the time of writing so required (the platform was first made public in early 1920).

Someone who based their understanding of the Third Reich solely on The Twenty-Five Points of the German Workers' Party would have some very strange ideas about Hitler's Germany. They would imagine that the national press was truthful (point 23); that the professional army had been disbanded (point 22); that political authority lay in a parliament (point 25); and that party

---

[59] Ibid., pp. 278-279 and p. 64.

membership was not a requirement for holding important government posts (point 6).

If some people would read more history before talking about Christianity and the Nazi party platform, they would find a number of economic points that the Nazis never even tried to enforce, such as: "Abolition of incomes unearned by work" (point 11); "nationalization of all businesses" (point 13); and the death penalty for profiteers (points 12 and 18). Shirer states that Hitler never intended to implement a single one of the economic planks, which were intended solely to attract votes.[60] This is not to deny that there was a socialist element in National Socialism. Hitler had the goal of ending class division and capitalist abuses – not by eliminating classes and capitalism altogether, but by uniting the classes in a racial community and subordinating the capitalists to the control of the state in the national interest. Capitalism was allowed to exist, but it had to be subservient to the state and contribute toward the collective good.[61] Nevertheless, economics was never one of Hitler's strongpoints, and when contributions began to flow in from big business, excessively socialist Nazis were brought into line.

If, like Nicolai Berdyaev, we define socialism as "the idea of regulating the social whole,"[62] then Hitler was a socialist, even if he only attempted to control capitalism instead of eliminating it. It should not be forgotten by the way that Lenin also allowed some capitalism to continue in his New Economic Policy. The fact that Lenin tolerated it for pragmatic reasons does not mean he was not still a socialist of a particularly deadly and destructive variety. Hitler did have some reason for naming his party a "socialist" workers' party, even if he did not conform to a strict definition of one brand of socialism. Nazis and Communists shared the belief that the economy was too important to be left to the vagaries of individual choice and the profit-oriented free market, and needed to be regulated by the state for the good of the whole.

The question of the socialist element in National Socialism is a good example of the problems involved in interpreting Hitler. People who think socialism is bad readily point to the socialist elements in Hitler's program, whereas people who think socialism is good deny that Hitler was a socialist at all. After all, if socialism is good and Hitler was bad, then he cannot have been in any way a socialist. It takes some objectivity to see that in some ways Hitler was not a socialist, but in other ways he was. Some comments in *Mein Kampf* about the sufferings of the workers and the worthlessness of the bourgeoisie sound as if they had been written by a Marxist.

---

[60] William L. Shirer, *The Rise and Fall of the Third Reich: A History of Nazi Germany* (New York: Simon & Schuster, 2011), p. 261.

[61] Hitler, *Mein Kampf*, p. 209.

[62] Nicolai Berdyaev, *Christian Existentialism: A Berdyaev Anthology,* trans. Donald Lowrie (New York: Harper Torchbooks, 1965), p. 311.

Hitler condemned various widely recognized problems of capitalism, including the poverty and injustice occasioned by capitalist greed. He denounced an economic system in which small craftsmen were dying out and workers were losing their independence, and also recognized the dismal living and working conditions, long hours and miserable wages that were the result of an economy based on selfishness and profit.[63] His solution was not to destroy capitalism and eliminate private property, but to bring them under the control of the state. This was not done, however, by following the extreme and unrealistic economic parts of the party platform. The platform was declared "inalterable" by Hitler to put an end to constant squabbling among party factions,[64] but it was far from "inalterable" when it ceased to meet Hitler's tactical requirements.

This is why attempts to use the party platform to show the Christian nature of National Socialism go so wide of the mark. Like the socialist planks, point 24 should not be simplistically taken at face value. A political platform after all does not always represent final policy even in ordinary politics, let alone with a devious man like Hitler. If someone looks only at a dubious political statement made in 1920 and ignores the Nazi government's sustained attempts over more than a decade to enslave the churches, what is to be inferred from that?

Even the term "positive Christianity" is more than a little dubious. What did it mean? It meant, as is perfectly clear from later developments, any form of Christianity, Protestant or Catholic, that was docile and obedient to Hitler. This especially included the new Germanic Christianity, which first emerged in the 19th century and ended in 1945 (it has not been heard from since). By no means an ad hoc contrivance of the Nazis but something with roots going back over a hundred years, this modern innovation sought to purge Christianity of its Jewish elements and adapt it to the needs of Aryan supremacy and German militarism. Jesus was converted into an Aryan, Paul was ignored or dismissed with contempt, most of the Old Testament was scrapped, and Christianity was reduced to whatever the unbelieving world would accept.

This sort of thinking is evident in the ideas of an important proto-Nazi, Houston Stewart Chamberlain. It was related to liberal "Protestantism" which denied the divine inspiration of the Bible and tried to reinterpret Christianity in the light of modern scientific and philosophical knowledge. Once the decision

---

[63] Hitler, *Mein Kampf,* pp. 234-235, 316, 317, 318. For comments on Germany's "rotten," "worthless," and "doomed" bourgeois society see pp. 406-407. That Nietzsche had a low view of Germans has often used to detach him from Hitler by people who fail to realize that Hitler had a low view of many Germans as well. The Nazi slogan "Germany awake!" (*Deutschland Erwache!*) meant they saw the Germans as sleeping.

[64] Kershaw, *Hitler,* p. 171.

is made to follow the wisdom of the world, there is no telling where it may lead. It can lead to Christian National Socialism, Christian Marxism (also known as liberation theology), Christian Darwinism, Christian homosexual rights, Christian feminism that supports abortion and lesbianism, Christian anything and everything. What this all has to do with Jesus Christ is a different question entirely.

Getting back to the subject of point 24, interpreting it requires some knowledge of Hitler and the Third Reich. For example, the religious plank of the platform demanded "liberty for all religious denominations in the state, so far as they are not a danger to it and do not militate against the moral feelings of the German race."[65] What did this mean? It meant, liberty for the churches "so long as they do not question Hitler in any way" (a danger to the state) "or fail to support him fully" (which would have militated against the moral feelings of the race as personified by himself). Later we will look at Hitler's real policy toward the churches – one of complete subordination of the church to the government.[66] We can agree with Wistrich's description of so-called positive Christianity as only a "cunning pretense" that concealed Naziism's "deep-seated rejection of the entire civilization that had been built on Judaeo-Christian ethics."[67]

Finally, point 24 states the party's opposition to "the Jewish-materialist spirit." What does this mean? Why did the Nazis constantly accuse the Jews of being materialists? How could anyone call the Jews, with their concept of the world as the creation of the one true God, "materialists"? What is materialistic about the Psalms, or the prophecies of Isaiah, or any book of the Jewish Bible for that matter? This was not a criticism from traditional religious antisemitism, nor does it have any biblical basis.

The accusation that Judaism was materialistic went much deeper than traditional objections to Jewish usury and love of money. This was an indictment of Judaism itself, as found in the Torah, and it goes back to the German "Enlightenment" and to Kant. It goes back to people who were not Christians and were not concerned about the death of Christ, but who disliked the Old Testament in and of itself and badly misinterpreted it. Kant should have been more modest and added the Old Testament to the many other important aspects of life confessedly beyond the limits of his comprehension, since he so abysmally failed to understand it.

---

[65] Louis L. Snyder, ed., *Documents of German History* (New Brunswick, NJ: Rutgers University Press, 1958), p. 395.

[66] For a detailed secular analysis of Point 24 showing that the fundamental Nazi emphasis was on race, not religion, see Samuel Koehne's "Reassessing *The Holy Reich*: Leading Nazis' Views on Confession, Community and 'Jewish' Materialism," *Journal of Contemporary History* 2013 48: 423), pp. 432-433.

[67] Wistrich, *Hitler and the Holocaust*, p. 132.

After Jacob the patriarch had his vision of a ladder that reached up to heaven, with God above it and angels ascending and descending on it, he made a vow, promising that if God would keep him on his journey, provide him with food and raiment and bring him home safely, he would give a tenth of all that he possessed to God, and the Lord would be his God (Genesis 28:12-22). To Kant this was a worship of God based not on spiritual freedom, but on a desire for material benefit.

This idea was reinforced by passages in Deuteronomy stating that if the Jews obeyed God, he would bless them in their land and they would prosper materially – but if they disobeyed him, they would be punished, and if they persisted in their disobedience they would be cast out of their land. These and other passages of like effect gave Kant and others the idea that the Jews served God for the sake of their own advantage and for no other reason. Needless to say, Kant did not believe that the Old Testament was the divinely inspired and inerrant word of God. Nor did he understand the essential true belief in God without which all merely external acts were rendered ineffectual.

Reasoning along these lines, Kant also asserted that the Jews had no real concept of an afterlife, and were concerned with this life only. In his words, "since no religion can be conceived of which involves no belief in a future life, Judaism, which, when taken in its purity is seen to lack this belief, is not a religious faith at all."[68] Once again, he revealed his ignorance of Scripture. It is true that we do not find the same emphasis on the world to come in the Jewish scriptures as we do in the New Testament, but to say that it is omitted entirely is a bad mistake. A few places that show Jewish concern for an afterlife are Daniel 12:2-3; Psalm 23:6; Psalm 9:17; Psalm 16:11; and Isaiah 65:17-18.

Some comments about Jews in *Mein Kampf* reflect Kantian and rationalistic, not traditionally religious anti-Judaism. When Hitler stated for example that Judaism was not really a religion at all, and that Jews had no concept of higher ideals, and even denied the existence of an afterlife, being strictly materialists,[69] Hitler was working within the well-defined tradition of secular anti-Judaism – a tradition within which Kant's modern philosophical and rational contempt for Jews was well-known. Antisemitic collections of hostile comments about Jews by leading thinkers made it possible for people to be influenced by them without having to wade through dense pages of difficult and totally irrelevant philosophy.

There is, regrettably, much more to the real nature of Hitler's views than a plank in a political platform or an agreement with the Vatican. Hitler also made some references to the churches and to Christianity in his speeches. For example:

---

[68] Immanuel Kant, *Religion Within the Limits of Reason Alone*, trans. Theodore M. Greene (Clermont Ferrand, France 2011), p. 78.

[69] Hitler, *Mein Kampf*, p. 306.

Christianity is the foundation of our national morality . . . to fill our whole culture once more with a Christian spirit . . . (February, 1933) . . . a really profound revival of religious life . . . The National Government regard the two Christian Confessions as the weightiest factors for the maintenance of our nationality . . . Their rights are not to be infringed . . . honest co-operation between Church and State . . . Christianity as the unshakable foundation of the morals and moral code of the nation . . . The rights of the Churches will not be diminished (March, 1933).[70]

Is it any wonder that many Jews in America today react reflexively and instinctively against the religious right?

The best way to evaluate such comments is to look at some other examples of Hitler's persuasive eloquence from the same period:

It is the sincere desire of the National Government to be able to refrain from increasing our army and our weapons . . . Germany desires nothing except an equal right to live and equal freedom . . . The German nation wishes to live in peace with the rest of the world . . . we are ready to cooperate with absolute sincerity (March 1933, before the Reichstag).

. . . our longing for peace . . . (May 1933) . . . We have declared a hundred times that we wish for peace (August 1933).[71]

It is now obvious that Hitler was talking about peace because he was in a position of weakness and did not wish to alarm his neighbors while he launched a rapid military build-up in preparation for war. The same is also true of the religious quotes. Although Hitler had become Chancellor he had not yet consolidated his power. In this critical transition period he did not need a lot of domestic conflicts and so found it necessary to tell gullible Christians what they needed to hear. Many of them were easily fooled. At the same time Hitler was talking peace while preparing for war, he was talking about the importance of religion publicly but telling his party leaders privately that "the unity of the Germans must be secured through a new *Weltanschauung,* since Christianity in its present form was no longer equal to the demands which were today made on those who would sustain the unity of the people."[72]

Significantly, all of these quotes come from the first months of Hitler's rule. He was not saying such nice things in the 1940s, when the pretense of pacifism was no longer needed and when the churches – insofar as they were not docile and obedient – were nothing but a minor nuisance. There was a speech before

---

[70] Adolf Hitler, *The Speeches of Adolf Hitler (April 1922 – August 1939) (vol. 1)*, trans. Norman H. Baynes (London: Oxford University Press, 1942), pp. 370-372.

[71] Ibid., (vol. 2) pp. 1016, 1018, 1080, 1085.

[72] Ibid., (vol. 1), pp. 377-378.

the Reichstag in 1939 in which Hitler responded to charges that the National Socialist state was hostile to religion. He claimed that there was religious freedom in Germany; that no one had been or would be persecuted because of their religious views; that no churches in the Reich had been closed, interfered with, or pressured.[73]

This speech has been pointed to as proof of the allegation that Hitler was not hostile to Christians and did not persecute Christians. He only persecuted Christians, it is claimed, if they made trouble for him politically, but he was not hostile to the churches. In the same way, we can prove that Hitler wanted peace, it was the Poles and the Jews that started World War II. How do we know this? Hitler said so himself! We have it in his own words. Reasoning along those lines, we can also prove that FDR was the greatest war criminal of all time and the Aryans are the master race – Hitler said so.

People who have not bothered to look at the historical record on this should not be talking too much about it. We do not have to prove that Hitler was to blame for the war with Poland – the facts are too well-known. Unfortunately, the facts about the Christians in Germany are not so well-known. Who cares about the many lesser religious groups that Hitler did not have to handle carefully and simply banned over the period of 1933-1938? Seventh Day Adventists; Bible Faith Fellowship; Free Pentecostalists of Berlin; Mission for Awakening in Germany; Bible Community; The Church of the Apostle John; God's Social Parish; New Salem Company; Union of Free Religious Communities in Germany; Bahais; Jehovah's Witnesses – these and yet other groups could be named, like Shepherd and Flock, or Christian Gathering.[74]

Who cares about the hundreds, even thousands of pastors and priests in Germany who were sent to concentration camps? We mentioned in the previous chapter a Lutheran Pastor, Paul Schneider, who died in Buchenwald. The Gestapo observed his funeral, noted who was present, and kept a detailed record of what was said. Church letters dealing with Pastor Schneider were intercepted and a Pastor Rolffs, who sought to raise money for the dead man's widow and children, was charged with violating #111 of the State Legal Code forbidding unauthorized fundraising. Although his trial was suspended for reasons that are not made clear, two more pastors – Karl Immer and Julius Vogt – were also harassed for attempting to help the Schneider family.[75]

---

[73] Ibid., (vol. 1), p. 401

[74] Conway, *The Nazi Persecution of the Churches,* pp. 370-374 (citing a Gestapo document).

[75] Rudolf Wentorf, *Paul Schneider: Witness of Buchenwald,* trans. Daniel Bloesch (Vancouver: Regent College Publishing, 2008), pp. 373-379. This source states that 200 pastors from all over Germany attended the funeral, as well as "[t]he whole Protestant and Catholic population" of the area where Schneider had served as a pastor before his final arrest. This display of public support for one officially labeled hostile to the state was disturbing to the Gestapo and was in fact a protest (p. 393).

The Gestapo was interested in the minutest details of church life, including the mandatory ringing of church bells on political occasions, ecclesiastical discipline of pro-Nazi church members and the posting of notices on bulletin boards. Hitler said in the same speech just referred to that "the priest as enemy of the German state we shall destroy." Those who know anything about Hitler and the Third Reich know that to Hitler an "enemy of the state" was anyone who failed to support him 100%. We shall examine his cruel policies toward the churches elsewhere.

There is yet one more speech of Hitler's which is often pointed to as proof that he was a religious man, and that therefore religion is bad and all religious people are dangerous. This speech, given in 1922, contains – as far as I know – the only documented claim Hitler made to being a Christian. Once in over 20 years of constant speechifying isn't much and it was never repeated, but since it is constantly brought up it needs to be examined.

Hitler said "my feeling as a Christian points me to my Lord and Saviour as a fighter . . . ."[76] Once again we have clear proof of Adolf Hitler's real, true, deep, sincere and genuine feelings. Before examining this, it should be pointed out that those who have any understanding of Christianity know there is much more to believing in Christ than spouting a few words about God, or occasionally quoting (as Hitler did) a few commonly well-known Bible verses. Abraham Lincoln quoted a verse, "A house divided cannot stand." This by itself does not prove Lincoln was a devout, Bible-believing Christian.

Jesus taught that trees are known by their fruits – good trees bring forth good fruit and bad trees bring forth bad fruit. Was Hitler's fruit good or bad? The fact that he mentioned Jesus a few times in his political career – especially when he wanted to pull the wool over the eyes of naïve and stupid Christians – will not help him on the Day of Judgment. Then he will be held accountable not merely for all of his words and deeds, but also for the secret thoughts of his heart.

No reputable Christian writer in nearly two thousand years before Hitler came to power ever said that it was the will of God for the master Aryan race to rule the world. Hitler thought that God needed his help to save the human race, but this had nothing to do with Christ. So what did Hitler mention Christ for then? People who think that Hitler was nothing more than a maniac forget that, in his rise, he was a skilled politician. He knew that General Ludendorff had strongly attacked Catholicism, and this led the general straight into the political wilderness. Richard Evans writes that Ludendorff's anti-religious comments in strongly Catholic Bavaria were "a certain recipe for political disaster."[77]

---

[76] Baynes, *Speeches of Adolf Hitler* (vol. 1), p. 20.

[77] Richard Evans, *The Coming of the Third Reich* (New York: Penguin, 2005), p. 201.

Hitler wrote at some length in *Mein Kampf* about the political importance of the churches. This is especially evident in his analysis of the reasons for the failure of Georg von Schoenerer, leader of the Austrian Pan-Germans before World War I. Parenthetically, since Schoenerer's followers addressed him as "Leader," which is of course "Fuhrer" in German, and since (according to one historian) it was Schoenerer who introduced the greeting "Heil!"[78], it would seem that late 19th-century Austria is more relevant than the Reformation to an understanding of Hitler.

Hitler approved of von Schoenerer's racism, antisemitism and German nationalism, yet also noticed his failure as a politician and his inability to achieve his aims. Although he praised von Schoenerer's ideas, Hitler thought he had made three important mistakes politically. One was his failure to get his correct theoretical ideas across to the masses. A second was allowing his movement to become bogged down in conventional parliamentary politics. The third was his attacks on the Catholic Church.[79]

Since this helps us to understand not only Hitler's politically motivated remarks quoted above, but also his overall policy toward the churches which he implemented after becoming Chancellor, it requires some attention. Schoenerer denounced the Austrian Catholic Church because it failed to support the ethnic Germans in the Austro-Hungarian empire in their struggle to resist Slavic domination. Its failure to stand for the rights of ethnic Germans (109) led Schoenerer to launch an "Away from Rome" (*Los-von-Rom*) campaign. Hitler considered this to be a bad mistake, as it caused the loss of much vital support. Schoenerer's opposition to the Catholic Church served only to alienate people who might otherwise have been useful to him (117).

This is contrasted with the policy of Karl Lueger, mayor of Vienna, and his Christian Social Party. Lueger, whom the young Hitler openly admired (55), was much more careful to manipulate existing social institutions instead of alienating them. Hitler noted how Lueger carefully won enough support from the clergy so that in the end the Church establishment had to follow (100). Luger was shrewd enough to work within the limits of what was possible (100) and gained valuable support for his Christian Social Party by avoiding unnecessary conflicts (119).

It might not be too much of a digression at this point to respond to accusations that Hitler's open acknowledgement of his debt to Lueger and his Christian Social Party is evidence of a Christian influence on National Socialism. Is it really necessary to explain that "Christian" in this sense was indicative not of devotion to the teachings of Christ as expressed in the Bible, but of cultural Christianity applied in its broadest and vaguest political sense?

---

[78] Ibid., p.43. Evans refers here to von Schoenerer's "avowed paganism and distaste for Christianity," p. 44.

[79] Hitler, *Mein Kampf*, pp. 97-123.

It is fairly not unheard of even today for European political parties to use the word "Christian" in their names – this is not indicative of biblical Christianity. And, Hitler's expressed debt to Lueger has to do with questions of political strategy that Jesus was not at all concerned with.

Hitler makes some criticisms of Lueger for failing to understand the racial problem, but he admired his political skill and his ability to manipulate the Church to his advantage. Hitler states that Lueger's success and Schoenerer's failure show the importance of not unnecessarily antagonizing potential allies (whether they be in the church, big business, or the military) – and he applied this lesson in his own rise. He modified his anti-Christian sentiments publicly – they were there in *Mein Kampf* but toned down, and few bothered to wade through the hundreds of pages of often (but not always) tedious verbiage. Hitler avoided unnecessary conflict, used some religious words, promised to support the churches, said something nice about Christian morality – all as a matter of political expediency. This lengthy passage shows his careful and informed approach to political strategy (97-123).

Hitler's vague comments about religion were merely a part of his political strategy, and the quote about Hitler's Christian "feeling" was a part of this. That it had nothing to do with Christian belief is easily evident from a superficial consideration of what Hitler actually said in the same speech. For example, in saying that Christ "was greater not as a sufferer but as a fighter," Hitler stated that Christ's driving the money-changers out of the Temple was more important than his death on the cross. He also said in this context that Christ died on the cross in order to fight the Jewish poison. This is not what Christians believe about why Christ died. Not a single one of all of the Christian denominations and groups in the world today would accept this – and of course the fact that Christ rose from the dead did not enter into the Hitler's mind. To Hitler, blood shed by German soldiers in defense of the fatherland was of greater importance than Christ's death on the cross.

Hitler also says in this speech that ancient Rome "was driven to its ruin through this same Jewish people." That the Jews brought down the Roman Empire seems totally ridiculous, until we consider that Christianity had been blamed for the collapse of Rome, and Christianity was a Jewish invention and a plot of the Jews. This charge was made and elaborated on at length by Nietzsche in his diatribe *The Antichrist,* along with deranged charges about the devious and corrupting influence of the Jews on society. It was a commonplace among secularists and nationalists in nineteenth-century Germany that Christianity had a destructive influence on society and the Jews were behind it. The idea that Jewish Christianity polluted the Roman Empire goes back to the French so-called Enlightenment.[80]

---

[80] Dennis Prager and Joseph Telushkin, *Why the Jews? The Reason for Antisemitism* (New York: Touchstone, 2003), p. 119.

That Hitler approached Christianity with his own racial and nationalist theories derived from elsewhere and firmly in place can be seen from a page of notes that Hitler made on the Bible in 1919. He refers in these notes to the Bible as a "Monumental History of Mankind"[81] – and the Bible is in fact a monumental history, monumental in its scope and in its influence. This does not necessarily mean it is historically accurate, however, and Hitler rejected the historicity of the Bible. This is clear from comments about the Jews never having had their own country and never having been nomads either.[82]

Hitler said of the Jewish religion that nothing in it was original, it was all stolen or borrowed (306). He added that the main purpose of Jewish law was to maintain the purity of Jewish blood (306). To Hitler, the Jewish religion was nothing but an ingenious trick (150), and the Jewish people at all times were never anything more than parasites (153). Do we need to say anything more about Hitler's view of the Old Testament? Instead of showing any real study of the Bible, these notes (one page in a lifetime) stress the fundamental conflict between Jew and Aryan (a modern German idea, not a biblical one).

Hitler also talked in this page of notes about "*purification* of the Bible" and a "[c]ritical examination of the *remainder*" [my emphases]. What was "the remainder"? Not much, as we can see from his comments above. The notes also contain the idea that "Privilege through strength [is] the basis of all Nature." This means that might makes right – not a teaching we see in the Sermon on the Mount or in the letters of Peter and Paul. This comes from biological racism and the concept of life as a ruthless struggle for survival of the fittest.

Those who understand something of the nature and spirit of biblical Christianity and who have some knowledge of what it is that Christ actually taught, will have no difficulty in perceiving the fundamentally and essentially anti-Christian and unbiblical nature of Hitler's ideology and practice. Unfortunately, before we move on to the subject of the churches in the Third Reich, yet one more aspect of the Hitler-and-religion question needs to be discussed – the Old Testament massacres of the Canaanites. Since this is now used by anti-Christ and anti-Christian propagandists to show the religious nature of Hitler's ideology as well as the innate badness of belief in God in general, some sort of response is necessary. We won't need to elaborate on the accusation that the Nazi racial laws were similar to the marriage laws of the Jews, since the latter allowed for marriage between people of different races and were concerned with religious belief, not with purity of blood.

Those who claim that what Hitler did to the Jews was in essence no different from what the Israelites did to the Canaanites are not being entirely

---

[81] Werner Maser, *Hitler's Letters and Notes*, trans. Arnold Pomerans (New York: Harper and Row, 1974), p. 283.
[82] see *Mein Kampf*, pp. 150, 301-306.

sincere in their professed concern for the importance of human life. They do not care about the millions of people slaughtered, starved and enslaved by Communism, nor do they care about the millions of unborn children foully slain in the name of a woman's alleged right to "choice." They really do not care about human life at all, and are only looking for excuses to justify their rejection of God.

Secondly, they do not – unless they are radically consistent pacifists – have any problem with the fire, death and destruction rained down on German and Japanese cities in World War II. The allied air forces probably killed more people in one or two bombing raids than were killed in the entire conquest of Canaan. This includes, of course, non-combatants – women, children, babies, old people indiscriminately massacred. Yet, this is accepted as a regrettable necessity, essential to ending the war, and the final responsibility is placed on those who started it.

So, total destruction is accepted as justified in this case – and does man have more power than God? Do we have the right to decree that destruction is the proper means to deal with evil so radical that there is no other way, but God does not? If the Old Testament is not the divinely inspired Word of God, then the Israelite conquest was at most an ordinary event such as has happened many times in the history of the world. If, on the other hand, the Old Testament is inspired and historically accurate, as I and many others consider it to be, then we have a situation in which God himself decreed such devastation, and with infinitely more wisdom and justice than Churchill and Roosevelt ever had.

But, it will be asserted, this means that religious fanatics can kill anyone because God told them to do it. We don't need to be any more concerned about this than we do about the possibility of the British or American air forces of today launching massive air raids on Vancouver or Stockholm. In the entire history of Christianity, and also in the subsequent history of Judaism, no one has ever claimed that they had a divine right and a divine presence comparable to that of Moses. Jews and Christians know very well that Moses had an authority we do not. Napoleon, Alexander, Julius Caesar, Genghis Khan, Attila the Hun – none of the great conquerors of history needed any religious beliefs to justify what was nothing more than a naked love of violence, power and human glory.

It may be true that any individual lunatic may claim God told him to kill the mailman, but this has nothing to do with the Judeo-Christian tradition. When we consider the sustained and persistent cruelties perpetrated in the name of modern ideologies, including the abortion holocaust, we realize that the greatest problems of the modern era have not been caused by those who make a sincere effort to follow the teachings of Christ.

Hitler asserted in *Mein Kampf* that his ideas of Aryan supremacy, racial purity and so on were "eternal truth."[83] Hitler was not simply an opportunist, but also had a vision of a pure, powerful, conquering, dominant humanity. This was derived from human wisdom unsupported by any biblical teaching. It was, as Paul said in the first chapter of Romans, worshipping the creature, Aryan man, the German race, above the creator. Hitler's ideal of humanity set free from moral restraints was completely antithetical to nearly two thousand years of Christianity. Why then did so many Christians – using the term very loosely – go along with Hitler and even support him enthusiastically?

---

[83] Hitler, *Mein Kampf*, p. 384.

Chapter 5. The Christians in the Third Reich

Introductory note – because of the complexity of the topic, this analysis will be divided into two parts. Part i will deal with questions of the church, its nature, purpose and place in German society. Part ii will consider Hitler's dealings with the churches.

i.

To many historians – I suppose we could say to most historians – the question of the churches in the Third Reich is not a significant one. When we consider the great events that shook supposedly civilized Europe to its foundations, Hitler's dealings with the churches seem like a very minor subject. This is especially true given the supposed irrelevance of Christianity to the modern world. And, of course, when we consider the sufferings and deaths of millions of people – most notably the Jews – a few thousand priests or pastors in concentration camps don't seem like very much.

Yet, on the other hand, there is more to this topic than meets the eye. A right understanding of the churches in the Third Reich not only can help us to a clearer understanding of the true nature of National Socialist ideology. It also provides a few rare examples of a commitment to higher truth that even the terrors of Hitler's concentration camps and secret police could not completely stifle. Moreover, there are questions of Christianity itself, what it means, and how its followers are supposed to act when confronted with the demands of a hostile totalitarian state. These issues are still of interest to those who want to be followers of Christ in the modern age. Now that the climate in America is becoming increasingly unfriendly to Christianity, those of us who claim to be followers of Christ can perhaps learn something from the experiences of the churches in Nazi Germany.

Regrettably, we cannot present a heroic picture of the churches boldly defying Hitler. The failure of Germany's religious institutions and the docility of the great majority of Germany's Christians (using the term "Christian" very loosely) are well known. Furthermore, there were "Christians" who were not merely docile and obedient – they openly embraced Hitler and his ideology, asserting that it was their duty as Christians to support the Fuhrer in his struggle to save the German race and defeat Bolshevism. They even went to so far as to claim that God had created the races, and it was their duty as good German Christians to keep the race pure.

It is not hard to see why people today consider such disgusting displays of cowardice and unbelief as evidence for the uselessness of Christianity – but there were a few notable exceptions. The isolated individuals who did defy the state raise profound questions about human nature, and even about the existence of truth itself. For example, on the night of November 9-10, 1938, the Kristallnacht pogrom swept Germany. In a state-organized explosion of official hatred, violence, arson and murder, Jews throughout Germany were subjected to a savage and a bestial barbarism that simple-minded nineteenth-century optimists hadn't counted on when they dreamed of building a better world based on reason, progress and science. A week later, on November 16, Julius von Jan, a Lutheran pastor in Oberlenningen, Wuerttemberg, directly denounced the pogrom from the pulpit. He was the only pastor in Germany to do so, as far as is known.

Basing his sermon on a text from Jeremiah – "O earth, earth, earth, hear the word of the Lord" (22:29) – von Jan referred to the fact that the nation of Israel had refused to hear Jeremiah's calls to national repentance and righteousness. Then he asked where were the prophets of God in Germany today, men who would call for justice and the right and condemn national sins? He stated that there were such men, but they had been sent to concentration camps or otherwise silenced.[1]

Von Jan referred to some unnamed church leaders who had been deprived of their incomes for speaking out against Nazi abuses, and then stated that there was a need for a day of repentance. He went on to refer explicitly to the pogrom, rightly understanding that safely vague generalities about sin and repentance were not enough. He denounced the murder of a Nazi official in Paris that provided the excuse for the pogrom, expressed concern for the victim, and then added: "But who would have thought that this one crime in Paris could be followed by so many great crimes in Germany?" People had been attacked, their houses of worship burned, their goods plundered, "simply because they belong to another race, and all this without anyone being held accountable."[2]

He stated that people knew the government was behind this, though they did not dare to say so, and stated that such criminality would bring God's judgment on Germany. He referred to the famous Bible verse, "Whatsoever a man soweth, that will he also reap," and said that the seeds of hatred being sown would lead to a harvest of horror. A few days later he was attacked by a

---

[1] Dean G. Stroud, *Preaching in Hitler's Shadow: Sermons of Resistance in the Third Reich* (Grand Rapids, MI: William B. Eerdmans, 2013), pp. 106-114. The sermon is given in full. Further information is also found in John Conway, *The Nazi Persecution of the Churches 1933-1945* (Vancouver: Regent, 1968), pp. 375-376. Conway gives the date as November 13th.

[2] Ibid., p. 112 (both quotes).

large mob, badly beaten and taken to jail. He was later sentenced to prison for the sinister crimes of "treachery" and "misusing the pulpit."[3]

What is the point of mentioning such an incident? It is not to avoid legitimate criticisms of the churches. To say, as someone did, that the churches defied Hitler is untrue. Such misrepresentations give Christianity a bad name. Neither is it to give Christians occasion for pride and hero-worship. Those who understand biblical teachings on the sinfulness of human nature have no need of heroes. The purpose is to present a manifestation of moral and spiritual truth from another realm unknown to those who have arbitrarily decreed that ultimate reality is only matter and energy. This example also shows what could have been the real antidote to Hitler, if only enough people had taken it.

That God will hold us personally accountable for our actions; that merely human success easily leads to destructive arrogance; that we need God's laws – these and yet other points in von Jan's sermon could have killed Naziism at its birth, if many people had believed in them. And, his prediction of God's coming judgment on Germany, ridiculous though it may have seemed to many at the time, was more than fulfilled, giving some comments in the sermon the status of possibly genuine prophecy.

Of course, we can't expect secular historians to pay any attention to such a trivial incident. It made no difference to the ultimate fate of the Third Reich. It was by no means representative of the churches as a whole. Von Jan was a lonely individual – but the incident is nevertheless highly significant. Who else in the entire Third Reich stood in a public place and openly denounced this crime? What mysterious and impressive power of conscience was at work in the man's heart, compelling him to stand alone and say what other people were afraid to say? This had nothing to do with survival-of-the-fittest. One reason people prefer to ignore this when they are interested in everything else about the Third Reich is because their extremely limited philosophies are completely incapable of taking such a phenomenon into account. It raises questions they do not want to have to consider. Perhaps they are afraid of the unknown, and do not want to change.

Some philosophers have determined in their supreme wisdom that there is no higher reality beyond that which they can immediately experience – or, if there is such a reality, we cannot understand or know anything of it. After all, if knowledge comes from experience, and that higher realm is beyond our experience, we can say nothing meaningful about it. Who are these elite thinkers and would-be guides of mankind that think they can arbitrarily declare the limits of our knowledge of reality according to their own imaginations? Do they represent such a high point of human intellect and experience that no one can go beyond them? "I cannot perceive it – ergo, no one else can either"?

---

[3] Ibid., p. 107.

What if that part of reality that we can all ordinarily experience is only the lesser part, the easier part? What if there is something that is inaccessible to ordinary thought and experience, but is not inaccessible if it decides to reveal itself through higher faculties of mind and spirit that far transcend mere physical sense? If this is the case, then we can enter into realms of feeling and knowing far above and beyond the pedestrian philosophers who think that they can confine human experience to the range of their speculative thoughts alone.

Hegel thought the invisible higher world manifested itself through the great thinkers (like himself) and the great conquerors. He thought that his philosophy as well as the kingdom of Prussia of his time were revelations of a higher invisible reality, at the cutting edge of human progress (a view few would share today). Schopenhauer thought that the ultimate reality beyond the world of sense and appearances manifested itself through music, that music was "the voice of the metaphysical will"[4] that underlay all of creation. Does this make Beethoven's Ninth Symphony a source of secret wisdom? Some might think so, though others could with equal justice make the same claim for poetry or painting. Can some hidden cosmic reality reveal itself somehow through Mozart but not through Klee or Kandinsky? Who says? The great philosophical experts who all by themselves determine what we can know about what cannot be known?

Hitler (like Hegel) thought the men of action driven by great ideas were the agents of some nebulous higher power that worked progress through strife and conflict. What if there is indeed some higher reality, but it manifests itself not in Alexander the Great, in Beethoven, or in Hegel, but in more simple people like von Jan? As much as some might dislike this idea, who are they to decide how something otherwise completely unknown to us might decide to manifest itself? To say "We cannot know it, but we can say it reveals itself in this way but not in that way" is ridiculous. To say "We cannot know it, but we can come closest to it in great music" is also ridiculous.

With complete certainty bordering on dogmatism they articulate highly sophisticated and intelligent mistakes. Just as our eyes do not have light within and of themselves but require illumination from an outside source to see, so also our minds and souls do not have light to perceive immaterial realities within and of themselves, and require light from an outside source. Without that external light, our minds are necessarily estranged from what is highest and best in the human experience. With that external light, that external reality that exists independently of and prior to paltry and merely human dreams about knowledge and experience, we can go far beyond arbitrary limits posed by people who sound very deep and complex but in fact do not know what they are talking about.

---

[4] Bryan Magee, *Wagner and Philosophy* (London: Penguin Books, 2001), p. 171.

Why did von Jan feel compelled at the risk of his life to speak simple truths unknown to ordinary human intelligence? Plain words of right and wrong can be more profound than winged philosophical flights that are purely imaginary. What if it is not music or science that give us a glimpse of the infinite, but rather men like von Jan? What if it is his words that reveal the unknown realm, that take us far away from the tedium of everyday reality up to deeper aspects of knowing off-limits to science and to merely human intelligence? If that is the case, all of modern philosophy crumbles into dust.

People are entirely too respectful of the great names of German philosophy. Kant, Schopenhauer, Hegel, Fichte, Nietzsche, Heidegger – who were they? What if they were all simply mistaken about the ultimate nature of reality? Their wisdom is that of the world which passes away. There is something more, beyond anything they could ever dream of – and if anyone wants to disagree, let them first confess that they are asserting only their own personal preferences, nothing more. They have too much confidence in their own limited intelligences, just like Kant and Hegel, sitting at their desks imagining that by speculative thought alone they could reach the farthest accessible limits and accurately delineate the highest truths available to us, as if their minds were the guides and compasses of reality. And how few people follow them now? What philosopher today would have such confidence in the power of merely imaginative speculation to unlock the secrets of reality?

At the close of his sermon, which in my view contains more wisdom than all of secular German philosophy from Kant to Heidegger combined and multiplied by a thousand, von Jan said: ". . . this confession of guilt of which people think they are not permitted to speak, has been at least for me today like the casting off of a great burden. Praise God! The truth has been spoken aloud before God and in God's name. Now the world may do to us whatever it wishes. We stand in God's hand. God is faithful."[5] He said this knowing what lay in store for him, but he was motivated by a love of truth and a strength of spirit completely incomprehensible to those who imagine that we are nothing but accidental little blobs of matter in a cold and silent universe with no higher purpose.

A second incident illustrates the same principle. Paul Schneider, a Lutheran pastor had been banished from his province by the Gestapo and forbidden to preach in his parish. He felt that the Gestapo had no jurisdiction over the church, and did not accept their authority over his preaching. He knowingly ignored their deportation order, returned to his church, preached a final sermon, and was arrested that same day. Having been detained twice before because of his "offences" against the state, he was sent to Buchenwald, where

---

[5] Stroud, *Preaching in Hitler's Shadow*, p. 114.

he was eventually murdered.[6] This act of principled disobedience, by the way, occurred in 1937, when the facts of the concentration camps and the consequences of defying the Gestapo were well-known.

Not satisfied with merely disobeying the Gestapo, Schneider felt obliged to explain his actions. He justified his refusal to accept the state's authority in a lengthy letter sent to the provincial governor, to the Interior Ministry of the Reich, and to the Reich Chancellery in Berlin. In this conflict, "Paul Schneider stands alone . . . We do not know of any statement made by the leadership councils of the Confessing Church from this time in which it wholeheartedly supports Paul Schneider . . . This failure will remain an agonizing question addressed to the Confessing Church."[7]

We should also mention Clemens August von Galen, the Catholic bishop of Munster. In August of 1941, he preached a very direct condemnation of the Nazi practice of euthanasia, the murdering of people considered to be unproductive and useless. He gave specific details of the program, and denounced its violation of the Christian ethic of the sanctity of life. Among many powerful and public denunciations in the sermon of the cruelty of this government practice, he also warned of the "punishment that the just God has to impose and will impose" on a people that rejects God's laws.[8]

One of the main points of the sermon was that "never and under no circumstances outside of war and justified self-defense is a human being permitted to kill an innocent person."[9] Why not? Because of God's law against killing. This is a motive that will impel a man to stand before the state and at the risk of his own life denounce the dispensing of useless people as if they were nothing more than old horses that could be gotten rid of when no longer needed. This is also a motive totally unknown to those gray, empty and shriveled spirits who believe that people are nothing but advanced animals who came about by accident. This is why few Christians but no Darwinists ever publicly protested Nazi euthanasia policies. Why should they? From a Darwinian point of view, the Nazi policy was very logical.

Galen also mentioned other Nazi violations of the Ten Commandments. "You shall have no other gods before me"? Germany was their god and Hitler was their messiah. "You shall not steal"? Confiscation of Jewish goods and businesses was mere theft. "You shall not commit adultery"? Nazi immorality,

---

[6] Rudolf Wentorf, *Paul Schneider: Witness of Buchenwald,* trans. Daniel Bloesch (Vancouver: Regent College Publishing, 2008).

[7] Ibid., pp. 270-274 (letter of principle) and p. 276-277 (all quotes). More will be said about the Confessing Church later. Briefly, it was composed of Christians who sought to avoid complete submission to the state and to maintain traditional creeds and worship, while at the same time affirming their loyalty to the state.

[8] Stroud, *Preaching in Hitler's Shadow,* pp. 158-169.

[9] Ibid., p. 160.

at the highest levels and as taught to the young people, was notorious. "Honor your parents"? German youth were taught to put the Fuhrer and the state above their parents. "Remember the Sabbath day to keep it holy"? The Nazis cared nothing about this, and deliberately scheduled youth activities to conflict with church activities. "You shall not take God's name in vain"? Hitler broke that every time he said "God" or "the Lord."

The specific and practical nature of von Jan's, Schneider's and Galen's opposition should be noted. Merely talking about faith in general was no threat to the regime. Saying in the pulpit that Jesus was a Jew, that there would be a day of judgment and we needed forgiveness for sin, that the Jewish people did not hear the call of the prophets and their nation fell – these and other biblical truths did not get anyone into trouble. They were looked on as Christians talking about theology, which they were allowed to do. As long as the application to present circumstances was lacking, there was no need for the government to be concerned.

Saying "You shall not kill" and saying "You shall not kill and the Nazi state is violating this commandment in such and such a way," naming places and individuals as Galen did – those are two very different things. Saying "God judged Israel for its disobedience and sins" and "God will judge Nazi Germany for its disobedience and sins," followed by a specific naming of those sins, are two very different things. Just talking about the lordship of Christ over all of life means nothing if violations of this are accepted and tolerated. This is one of the many serious problems in American churches today – spiritual truths that float in the air with no relevant application. This is safe preaching that will never get anyone into trouble with the world.

Michael Burleigh referred to this sermon by Galen and quotes a passage from it, yet states the sermon was "not without ambiguities." The "ambiguities" he referred to were not in the sermon itself – there was nothing ambiguous about it. They had only to do with the timing of the sermon. First, it was (according to Burleigh at any rate) given a year after Galen had been informed about the euthanasia program – and who knows why this was? Perhaps he needed more confirmation; perhaps he had a strange unwillingness to risk his life, as Burleigh concedes that he did (he says Martin Bormann wanted Galen executed for the sermon).[10]

The second alleged ambiguity has to do with the fact that the sermon coincided with a Gestapo decision to eject some Jesuits and some nuns from their property in Galen's city of Muenster. This, along with the danger to inmates of an asylum in Galen's diocese, were supposedly "the immediate catalysts"[11] for Galen's sermon. Really? The Nazis had been harassing the

---

[10] Michael Burleigh, *Ethics and extermination: Reflections on Nazi genocide* (Cambridge: Cambridge University Press, 1977), pp. 139-140.

[11] Ibid., p. 140.

Catholics and confiscating their property for years, long before 1941 – and doesn't that make Galen seem to be a rather petty man, to attack the Nazis under the cover of supposed moral concern for innocent lives when in effect he was really equally concerned about the loss of some property? Does this reflect the blinkered Marxist view of people as driven by material considerations?

What if Galen, in spite of undoubted human faults and errors, had been motivated by genuine moral concern for suffering people? This does not mean we have to put him on a pedestal as a hero. It should mean something, though, that the only people in the entire Reich to publicly protest the crimes of the Nazi euthanasia program were religious leaders. Where were the professors of philosophy, the experts on Kant and Hegel? The biologists? The journalists? The psychologists? Silent – why shouldn't they be? Their callings gave them nothing to risk their lives over. And the historians? Ranke, Mommsen, Winckelmann – Germany had a rich tradition of historical writing yet no historians spoke out.

The three men just referred to (and there were others) represent a deeply spiritual response to the demands of the National Socialist State for unquestioning obedience. Why were there not more religious leaders like these and more common people to support them? This question is easy to ask but not so easy to answer. The first point that needs to be established is that Germany was not a Christian country. The churches were not dominant; they did not hold the fate of the nation in their hands. To state or to imply that the churches could have stopped Hitler shows a profound ignorance of modern German culture.

The irrelevance of Christian teaching to most Germans in the Weimar period can possibly be illustrated by the following fictional scenario. Imagine that a devout, genuinely Bible-believing Christian wandered into a gathering of the new Nazi party when it was still a small group meeting in a single room. Imagine further that, after listening to their discussion for a while, he asked for permission to speak, and when this was granted rose and made the following comments:

> Gentlemen! I am glad to be here and have been interested to hear your conversations, but I fear you are on the wrong track. That Germany was defeated in the war and lost some territory isn't as important as you think it is. First, this was God's judgment. He decides the outcomes of these great affairs and we must accept his judgment with patience and humility, confessing our national wrongdoings of pride and militarism. True, our situation is not so good now, but hatred and revenge will only make things worse.

Secondly, what is really important is where you spend eternity. We will all die, some of us sooner than we think, and then we must go to God to be judged. There it will be decided if we go to Heaven or to Hell, for an eternity of punishment and separation from God, or an eternity in the new creation Christ has promised us after the restoration of all things.

What will it profit you, if Germany is a great and mighty nation but you die and are sent to Hell? What will it harm you, if Germany is weakened but you die and God accepts you into Paradise? We can die at any time, and we should be concerned about the reality of the world to come – and although I do not know any of you, I can say that because you are human beings, you have all sinned in some ways, you have all done wrong things. Some of these you know are wrong and would ashamed if others knew them. Others you may think are acceptable but in fact are an affront to a holy and infinite God and a violation of his standards. So, you need forgiveness for your sins. This is found only in Christ. He died on the cross as a sacrifice for you and if you believe in him God can forgive your sins – however: it will not profit you to receive forgiveness if you just go out and repeat the same sins again.

What is also needed is a change of nature, a change of heart. This is promised by Christ through faith in Christ. Without this, we cannot live as we ought, in genuine faith, patience, quietness, and righteousness as God said we should do. This is what the Bible teaches – and don't listen to any of those fake pastors and so-called theologians who tell you the Bible is spiritually true but historically false. They are deceiving you with merely human philosophies dishonestly disguised as religion.

Furthermore, my friends, you are mistaken about the Jews. There is no such thing as a "world Jewish conspiracy." Germany lost the war because of the incompetence of its leadership and because of the superior might of the Allies. Jews are people like anyone else – and your ideas of Aryan superiority and racial purity are not supported by the Bible. This is not what life is all about. A Jew, a Pole, or a Negro who lives a quiet life in obedience to God is morally superior to a blond, blue-eyed Aryan liar, thief, or murderer. There is no such thing as a "master race." We read in the book of Acts that God has created all the peoples of the earth from one blood . . .

173

We can imagine the natural human response, as well as Hitler's response, to such unworldly ideas. As preposterous as those teachings sound to the natural mind, if enough people in Germany had taught, believed and lived those "non-Aryan" and "Semitic" doctrines, the history of Europe would have been unimaginably different.

Was such a message ever given anywhere in Germany in the 1920s? Paul Schneider, the pastor just referred to, preached in a sermon in 1923 that "No cruel fate of our fatherland, no matter how cruel it may seem to us, should ever be able to rob us of profound joy, the joy that is found in God . . . For what is visible is temporal, but what is invisible is eternal." He also stated in the same sermon that "we have a commission and a calling from another world and our citizenship is there. And we know that in spite of everything this world will one day be victorious: Therefore, we will be cheerful in tribulation."[12]

If enough Germans had understood this basic biblical teaching, Hitler's message of revenge and hate would not have been successful – but general histories of the Weimar period do not present ideas of this sort as having any influence or importance. There were very few people like Paul Schneider in Germany of the 1920s, and such a message was not (and is not) well or widely received. It was then and is now considered to be hopelessly out of date, irrelevant, from a bygone era, contrary to the reigning philosophies and scientific or pseudo-scientific theories which all scorn the possibility of another world to come and rely on human intelligence alone. Freud, Marx, Darwin, Fichte, Schopenhauer, Kant – those were names to conjure with, not Jesus Christ or the apostle Paul.

People who say "Germany was a Christian country! Germany was a Christian country!" understand neither Christian teaching nor German intellectual and cultural history. Germany was not immune to the modernist revolution of the eighteenth and nineteenth centuries. This revolution included a massive turning away by much of Europe's intellectual elite from revealed, traditional religion. Peter Watson writes that "With the Mass in B Minor and Bach's death, a whole artistic, spiritual, cultural, and intellectual world was at an end."[13] The influence and prestige of the churches had been steadily declining in Europe ever since the "Enlightenment," and the churches in Germany were deeply influenced by this trend.

This included, of course, the loss of traditional ethics which had been derived either from Christianity or from cultural adaptations of Christianity. New understandings of ethics and morality followed, based on speculative philosophy, on Darwinian science, on feeling and intuition – not on any

---

[12] Wentorf, *Paul Schneider*, p. 51 (both quotes).

[13] Peter Watson, *The German Genius: Europe's Third Renaissance, The Second Scientific Revolution, and the Twentieth Century* (New York: Harper Perennial, 2011), p. 43.

supposed laws of God which we were all universally obligated to obey. The divine origin of the human soul was lost in the turbulent floods of modernism, to be replaced by – by what? By the beliefs that we were nothing but animals; that conventional morality was a hindrance to the full development of the personality; that we could do whatever seemed right in our own eyes with no regard to any higher authority, except perhaps for the state.

It should not be necessary to mention this, and is not necessary most of the time – only when people want to blame Christianity for modern sins. Some people actually seem to believe that there was a Protestant Reformation in 1517, then there was World War I and the Weimar era and Hitler came to power. Have these people heard of Nietzsche, of Wagner, Schopenhauer, Beethoven, Goethe, Kant, Fichte, Hegel and Schiller? Or, if they have at least heard of those names, do they believe that one of those key figures in modern German history believed that the Bible was the word of God? That there would be a resurrection from the dead, and we would stand before the judgment seat of Jesus Christ? The belief that this present, visible world is all we can know is one of the foundational blunders of modernism.

Goethe laughed at Christianity. He wrote a phenomenally successful book, *The Sorrows of Young Werther*, in which the protagonist fell deeply in love with a married woman – and what did Werther do? Discover while reading the Bible that his passion was sinful, and so repent and seek forgiveness for his illicit lusts? No, he killed himself. The god of Goethe's *Faust* is not "the petty-minded jealous God of the Israelites" either, but "more generous . . . even witty." Goethe's idea of the purpose of life, in the words of one scholar, was "that we develop that higher human being within ourselves."[14]

Such attitudes were typical of the mainstream of German cultural development at that time. Does Beethoven's Ninth Symphony represent Christian values? No, it is a celebration of mankind on the mountaintop, glorying in his power. Beethoven used Schiller's lyrics in the choral movement – "Joy! Spark of the gods! Daughter of Elysium! Drunk with fire, we approach your holiness! Your magic binds mankind together!" What does this foolish and empty nonsense have to do with the teachings of Christ? The Nazis could enjoy Beethoven in a way they could never enjoy the refined spirituality of Bach or Handel.

The "Enlightenment" of Kant and many others, that denied revelation and relied on autonomous human reason; Romanticism, with its emphasis on feeling and intuition, and its rejection of conventional morality; the idealistic philosophy of Hegel, which presented a higher spiritual reality totally different from that of orthodox Christianity, one discovered by reason alone and only a figment of human imagination; Fichte, who made the nation into a substitute

---

[14] Ibid., pp. 121, 120 respectively. The second quote is taken from Bruford's *Culture and Society*.

god, the source of our meaning and purpose; the emphasis on the classics and the Greek revival, which taught that the Jews were barbarians, and "only the Greeks and Romans possessed 'a higher *Geisteskultur* (intellectual culture),'"[15] that only the Greek and Roman civilizations were "the source and basis of culture" – an understanding of these things is not necessary if one's sole purpose is to attack Christianity in an ignorant and badly educated way.

In a treatise entitled "On Classical Studies," Hegel authoritatively decreed from his philosophical perch on high in his study that "Greek literature in the first place, Roman in the second" were the true foundations of higher learning. He further exclaimed in secular humanist rapture that "The perfection and glory of those masterpieces" would provide a "spiritual bath" and a "secular baptism that first and indelibly attunes and tinctures the soul." The world of Greece and Rome was "the fairest that has ever been . . . The works of the ancients contain the most noble food in the most noble form."[16] In the school where Nietzsche studied as a teenager "the students breathed the air not of modern Europe but of ancient Greece and Rome and of the Germany of Goethe and Schiller."[17]

What does this have to do with Hitler? First, if we want to understand what happened in the Third Reich we need to stop talking about "Christian Germany." In the entire history of Christianity, there has never been an authentically Christian country, and that includes earlier periods when a generally Christian cultural ethos was the dominant one simply for lack of any other alternative. But modern Germany? Stating that the Germany of Hitler's time "was almost entirely Catholic and Lutheran . . . If you wanted a lever to shift public opinion on anything in the 1930s, religion was where you applied your force" is such a profound mischaracterization of twentieth-century Germany that one begins to wonder about the author's motives and qualifications.[18] The despair and emptiness of modern Germans who had lost their chief supports of national pride and material prosperity and had nothing higher to believe in, these created a deep hunger that Hitler promised to satisfy – and he offered solutions in this life only, not in the unseen spiritual world to come. This in itself was a direct denial of the teachings of Jesus Christ.

---

[15] Ibid., pp. 107, 93.

[16] Stephen N. Williams, *The Shadow of the Antichrist: Nietzsche's Critique of Christianity* (Grand Rapids, MI: Baker Academic, and Milton Keynes, UK: Paternoster, 2006), p. 31 [citing Hegel, *Early Theological Writings* (Chicago, 1948), pp. 325-36].

[17] R. J. Hollingdale, *Nietzsche: The Man and His Philosophy (Revised Edition)* (Cambridge: Cambridge University Press, 1999), p. 19.

[18] Jerry Bergman, *Hitler and the Nazi Darwinian Worldview* (Kitchener, Ontario: Joshua Press, 2012), p. 301 (quoting P. Z. Myers' "Hitler was a True Christian" website). Few today would blame a handful of first-century Palestinian Jews for twentieth-century European horrors.

Secondly, we need to be more mindful of "the relationship of Hitler's world-view to broader currents of nineteenth and early twentieth-century thought."[19] There are some "awkward questions about the genealogy of his beliefs or their place within the intellectual traditions of western modernity" and a study of Matthew, Mark, Luke and John will not yield any constructive new insights. The nineteenth century A.D. is vastly more relevant to an understanding of Hitler than the first century A.D.

For example: if we agree with Hegel (and many people did back in those days) that mankind is led by some impersonal unseen force on an upward path of evolution and progress; and that this progress is spearheaded by great nations (like the Greeks, the Romans, the French, and now the Germans); if we accept that the artistic, philosophical, literary, and political glory and magnificence of Germany is at the cutting edge of human progress; that the blessing of posterity depends on German progress and achievement; and that the state is instrumental in this, meaning that our true freedom lies in obedience to the state – then we have entered into a sickly and deluded mindset that is easily open to further abuses.

In Hitler's words, "However weak the individual may be when compared with the omnipotence and will of Providence, yet at the moment when he acts as Providence would have him act, he becomes immeasurably strong. Then there streams down upon him that force which has marked all greatness in the world's history."[20] Such a reference to the great men of history as moved by some vague higher power represents Hegelian, not biblical philosophy. Hitler borrowed from many sources, and some of his basic ideas came in their first origins not from the gutter but from respectable thinkers (though they later became simplified and popularized). And it must be said that this glorying in human beauty, human intelligence and human greatness with no thought for God or his laws is one of the most essential, basic and fundamental aspects of National Socialism.

It is perhaps noteworthy that Hitler referred to the Greek combination of ideal physical beauty and intellectual brilliance in *Mein Kampf*.[21] Not many pages later he stressed the importance of maintaining the Hellenic cultural ideal, and added in this context that German culture was a combination of Germanism and Hellenism.[22] And of course the Nazi statues of idealized nude figures were cheap and lifeless imitations of classical, not of Christian, ideals and art. Hitler thought he was creating a nobler and more beautiful humanity

---

[19] Neil Gregor, *How to Read Hitler* (New York: W. W. Norton, 2005), pp. 10, 14.

[20] John Snell, ed. *The Nazi Revolution: Germany's Guilt or Germany's Fate?* (Lexington, Mass.: D. C. Heath, 1959), p. 7.

[21] Adolf Hitler, *Mein Kampf,* trans. Ralph Manheim (Boston: Houghton Mifflin, 1999), p. 408.

[22] Ibid., p. 423.

by purifying the highest race and eliminating sources of degeneracy – but the Bible teaches that merely human glory is ephemeral, that we are physically like the flower of the grass that flourishes and then quickly fades. Therefore, our highest fulfillment is not of this world, but elsewhere.

We should not forget Social Darwinism, the belief that Darwin's theory should be applied to people in a new ethic of life in which mercy and compassion had no reality and no place; Marxism; Freudianism; empiricism; materialism; pantheism; extreme nationalism, that saw the German nation and race as agents of a Hegelian World Spirit; modern movements in art, literature and music; the racist, antisemitic and militaristic Folkish movement from which National Socialism directly emerged – all of this was predicated on the irrelevance of the Bible. Hence, it is not in Christianity, but in rebellion against Christianity, that we must seek an understanding of the origins of National Socialist ideology.

Even in the first half of the nineteenth century, the German-Jewish poet Heinrich Heine saw the dangers inherent in the new ideas that emerged subsequent to the "Enlightenment's" declaration of independence from God. Heine foresaw that "Kantian criticism, Fichtean transcendental idealism, and even Naturphilosophie [nature philosophy],"[23] with their repudiation of traditional ethics and values, were extremely dangerous. "Because of these very doctrines," he elaborated, "revolutionary forces have developed which are simply biding their time to break out and to be able to fill the world with horror and admiration"[24] – and many people did admire Hitler. Heine predicted that people armed with these new ideas "will mercilessly tear up the soil of our European life in order to destroy the past to its very roots. Armed Fichteans will come onto the scene, who, with fanatic will, will be untamable by self-interest or fear." They will be "inflexible in a social upheaval" and "not moved by any traditional reverence."[25]

People wonder how the Nazis could have emerged out of German culture. It is too little considered that German culture was part of the problem, and in fact provided fertile soil for ideas that were later to prove integral and foundational to National Socialism. Peter Watson's detailed survey of modern German culture, *The German Genius*, has little to say about traditional Christianity (except for a brief discussion of Pietism that emerged in the late seventeenth century). The greats of nineteenth-century German philosophy, science, music, literature – none of them are presented as devout Christians.

Watson goes so far as to state that even as early as the first half of the nineteenth century "neohumanist *Bildung*," a secular search for inner

---

[23] Heinrich Heine, *On the History of Religion and Philosophy in Germany*, trans. Howard Pollack Milgate (Cambridge: Cambridge University Press, 2007), p. 115.

[24] Ibid.

[25] Ibid.

fulfillment by education, without depending on religion, was "the cultural philosophy of the Prussian state."[26] There was a common belief "that spiritual emancipation through education in the humanities was the true path to (inner) freedom." The belief in submission to divine authority as expressed in the Bible and interpreted by the church was a rapidly fading memory. Those who think that the leading lights of German philosophy, history, art, music, literature, and science were inspired by belief in the Bible, or that Prussian domination of Germany was the result of Bismarck's faithful adherence to the teachings of Jesus Christ only reveal their complete ignorance of this subject. That Christianity should be rejected as false and out of date, and then be blamed when things later go wrong, is more than a little ridiculous. Some people are incapable of admitting that the modernist experiment was, in the case of Germany, a disastrous failure.

Gordon Craig's in-depth history of Germany from 1866 to the end of World War II contains ample evidence of the secularization of German society. An overview of the educational system emphasizes the humanistic content, especially the classics and the natural sciences. Philosophical trends in German universities did not reflect Christian values. Husserl's phenomenology, the increasing importance of the behavioral and social "sciences," Darwin, Comte, materialism and mechanism, revived and updated Kantianism, the study of German history and literature as "a handmaid for the salvation of the nation"[27] – it would be possible I believe to write a detailed book about German universities in the second half of the nineteenth century without even using the name of Jesus once. No doubt such books have been written.

The history of Germany just cited shows that even before 1900 Germans themselves were concerned about the increasingly evident signs of moral decline and decay. Incidents of rape doubled in Berlin during the six years of 1872-1878, along with a significant increase in crime in general. Prostitution and public drunkenness increased, along with "a relaxation in public morals" and a "massive preoccupation with sex" in the theater as seen in "the crudest kind of bedroom farces."[28]

When it comes to the Weimar Republic, the premature experiment in democracy that was terminated by Hitler in 1933, its secular nature should not need to be even mentioned. The chapter title in one cultural history of Germany reads "Weimar: The Golden Age of Twentieth-Century Physics, Philosophy, and History."[29] This chapter and the one preceding deal with Niels Bohr, Werner Heisenberg, breakthroughs in modern cinema, Expressionist

---

[26] Watson, *German Genius*, p. 109 (all quotes this paragraph).

[27] Gordon Craig, *Germany 1866-1945* (Oxford: Clarendon Press, 1978), pp. 190, 194-197.

[28] Ibid., p. 82.

[29] Watson, *German Genius*, Part IV chapters 31 & 32.

painting, Walter Gropius and the Bauhaus, Marx and Freud, Herbert Marcuse, the music of Schoenberg and the poetry of Brecht, Marlene Dietrich and *The Blue Angel* – I may have missed something but I did not see one word about Jesus, the Bible, Heaven, Hell, a day of judgment or forgiveness of sins in the two chapters.

There was a consistent decline in the idea of God from the end of the eighteenth century to the end of the nineteenth. From the transcendent, truly divine God of the Scriptures to the theoretical, inactive and profoundly worthless God of Kant and the many other deists; to Hegel's nebulous and impersonal World Spirit; to Schopenhauer's blindly striving cosmic Will; to the "Creator" of the Darwinist Ernst Haeckel, the "Almighty," a vague cosmic something that worked according to scientific law and was understood by human reason alone (which was close if not identical to Hitler's conception); to the feverish pronouncement of the death of God by Nietzsche – the idea of God faded and finally died in the minds of many. The churches, Protestant and Catholic, had long since lost their dominant position and were incapable of significantly influencing the course of German history.

Intriguingly, these declining concepts of God have been summed up in a remarkable passage in Goethe's *Faust*. Suggesting that the well-known Bible verse "In the beginning was the Word" was inadequate, Goethe proposed replacing "Word" (traditional, revealed religion) with "Mind" (human wisdom, whether religious or secular). This didn't seem adequate, so he suggested replacing "Mind" with "Power." Finally he suggests "Deed," "In the beginning was the Deed."[30] From divine revelation to human wisdom to power and action unrestrained by any concept of divine law – this follows a spiritual law of descent just as real as any law of Newton's. Without God, we decline, and this descent ended, after many unpredictable windings and turnings, in National Socialism. This does not mean a general cultural awareness of God and earlier strong religious cultural influences were sufficient to create paradise on earth, they were not – but they did exercise some real and badly needed restraint. It took modern ideology based on human wisdom to set up the signposts and pave the way to Auschwitz.

These changes were accompanied by an increasing hostility to Christianity. Nietzsche is the most well-known example of this, but – while more extreme in his hatred than others (some might even say fanatical) – he was by no means alone. That traditional, orthodox Christianity was contrary to reason, as determined by philosophy; that it was contrary to science, and especially to the supposed truth of Darwinism; that Christianity was unGermanic, unhealthy, an alien Semitic import not suited to the warlike German spirit; that Christianity had originated in India but was later corrupted by Semitic influences; that Paul

---

[30] Gene Edward Veith, Jr. *Modern Fascism: Liquidating the Judeo-Christian Worldview* (St. Louis: Concordia, 1993), pp. 143-144.

had distorted, falsified and Judaized the teachings of an Aryan Christ; that Christian ethics were contrary to the realities of life – these and other ideas were increasingly current in influential circles among the German intelligentsia long before 1933.

Thus, Hitler's hostility to Christianity was not an aberration, but consistent with a long tradition of first rejection of Christianity, and then contempt for it. The following summary of Hitler's views of Christianity could also be applied (in varying degrees) to Wagner, Schopenhauer, Nietzsche, Lagarde, Langbehn, Haeckel, and numerous German thinkers, writers, educators, scientists and other influential intellectuals:

> It was the Judaeo-Christian ethic that had alienated humanity from the wholeness of the natural order in pursuit of the 'lie' of a transcendent God. Judaeo-Christianity in its secularized form had, he [Hitler] believed, given birth to contemporary teachings of pacifism, equality before God and the law, human brotherhood and compassion for the weak, which the Nazis were determined to uproot. They no longer made any secret of their contempt for Christian ideals of charity, meekness, and humility, inimical as they were to the German warrior ethos . . . it had seemed to Hitler that the churches were allies of Judaism rather than of National Socialism.[31]

This led Hitler to adopt policies aimed at first limiting and then over time eliminating the influence of the churches in Germany – but if Hitler was really so opposed to Christianity, why then didn't the Christian resist him? It is very commonly reasoned nowadays that the churches did not mount any serious opposition to Hitler because they shared significant common ground – an argument bolstered by the many "Christians" who not merely failed to oppose Hitler, but actively supported him.

There are a number of reasons for the failure of the churches in the Third Reich, but before considering them it is necessary to point out that in Germany of that time, as in America today, there were many different kinds of Christians. Some, not too many, were seriously trying to walk in the straight and narrow way of Christ. Others were nominal Christians, cultural Christians who had been born into the church, baptized and registered as infants, but were not very serious about it. They went to church two or three times a year and had some fond memories of childhood experiences in a church environment, but were in no sense committed to following the teachings of Christ.

---

[31] Robert S. Wistrich, *Hitler and the Holocaust* (New York: Modern Library, 2003), p. 135.

There were orthodox Christians who adhered to the creeds as a matter of doctrine and philosophy, but their faith lacked warmth, enthusiasm, and vitality. Christianity was seen more as a set of beliefs to assent to, rather than as a way of life demanding the highest seriousness. There were liberal Christians who sought to amalgamate Christianity with the philosophies of Hegel, Kant, or even Darwin. They accepted the primacy of human reason and denied divine revelation, continuing to use religious language but in a very different context.

Then there were those who openly embraced Naziism. For them, Christianity was what Hitler said it was. These Germanic Christians, these Aryan Christians effortlessly accommodated their faith to the new times, and thought the "gospel" was Hitler's salvation of Germany. They wanted to scrap almost all of the Old Testament, and denounced teachings about original sin, repentance, and the need for salvation as Semitic and non-Aryan. They provided a lot of ammunition for those today who want to claim that the Nazis were Christians, but who seem not to have the faintest idea of what Christianity actually teaches.

"The majority of the people who supported the national socialists were orthodox Christians."[32] If someone says "The Jews control all of the world's banks" or "AIDS was created by the CIA," can they be refuted? Are there not positions that are resolutely held with impregnable indifference to reason, logic, facts, evidence? To attempt even a brief definition of traditionally orthodox Christianity, whether Protestant or Catholic, would be too much of a digression here. Suffice it to say that introducing new ideas of Aryan supremacy and racial antisemitism unheard of before the modern era and directly related to modern secularism, not to the Bible, is not a sign or a proof, or even a hint of orthodoxy.

More can be said about the Germanic Christians in another place. For the present, the question remains – why did not the churches in Germany speak more boldly against Hitler? Keeping the many different sorts of Christians in mind, we can offer the following general reasons. Incidentally, it should not have to be stressed that nobody else stood up against Hitler either. The universities, the news media, the military, big business, the medical and legal professions, scientific associations and research institutes – they all caved in, and some of the explanations for the Christian failure apply to them as well.

---

[32] John Warwick Montgomery, *The Suicide of Christian Theology* (Minneapolis, MN: Bethany Fellowship, Inc., 1971), p. 151. The quote is from Thomas J. J. Altizer, in debate with Montgomery, who says to Altizer later "I can only conclude that nineteen and a half centuries of church history are totally new to you" (p. 159). Ignorance of church history is a common characteristic in many attempts to discuss these topics – ignorance compounded by hostility and contempt.

The most obvious explanation is fear. Even before Hitler came to power, those who were too outspoken in their opposition to him placed themselves in real danger. Assaults and murders by Nazi thugs were common in the years before 1933. Regrettably, in America today pastors who are too outspoken in their opposition to homosexuality are liable to be threatened or have their property vandalized – and we can be sure that more violence is coming. Even where there is no real danger, there are also Christians (including church leaders) who are afraid merely of controversy, or of the world's disapproval.

After Hitler became Chancellor, the possibility of being arrested and sent to a concentration camp was enough to keep people silent. True, Christ did say that we should not fear those who can only kill the body but after that have nothing more that they can do. That is a command of Christ, disobedience to which is sin. Unfortunately, too many Christians – even those who are doctrinally sound in theory – do not have enough confidence in God's providential ordering of their lives or in the reality of the world to come to faithfully follow Christ here.

The fear of Christians in Germany was the result of sin and lack of faith. This is not to condemn them, though. Who knows how we would have behaved in such a situation? It is to state that, to the extent that this was a factor in Christian silence, it shows a failure to live up to the Christian ideal. In this respect, as in too many others, nominal Christians are often no different from the world. They have an ordinary fear of death and of suffering like anyone else. As for those who do not even claim to be Christians at all, keeping silent and going along is the normal and ordinary thing to do – and most of those who so lightly criticize the Christians in Nazi Germany, seemingly without any awareness of the grim realities of life in the Third Reich, would themselves have done exactly the same thing.

Someone blamed the churches for making their baptismal records available to Nazi officials verifying people's racial backgrounds. It is a rare individual who would refuse to cooperate with the Gestapo and risk further observation, maybe even interrogation and incarceration, for strangers of any sort. The right thing to do would have been to deny them access – failure to do so is a failure of human nature, not of biblical teaching. If on the other hand someone willingly cooperated out of support for government policies, then they were following a very different belief system than that of Christ and the apostles. By the way, the New Testament churches kept no such records, and many Christians believe that infant baptism has no validity whatever.

One highly revealing event showing the fear of Christians took place in 1943. The Evangelical bishop of Bavaria was approached by a group of laymen who had written a bold statement condemning the persecution of the Jews. It said that the church should "ardently withstand" the state's attempts to slaughter the Jews. It asserted that the duty of the Church was to present the truths of Christ to the Jews, but could not do so credibly while ignoring Jewish suffering.[33]

The statement also referred to Paul's warning that the Gentiles should not be proud against the Jews but should fear God (Romans 11:20), and said that the church should resist the use of God's curse over Israel as an excuse for passivity in the face of evil. It even asserted the indissoluble bond between the church and the Jews, and stated that the Church "can no longer attempt to save herself by avoiding the attacks made on the Jews,"[34] but needed to recognize that the assault on the Jews was an attack on Christianity as well.

This bold statement is quite impressive – however, when the bishop asked for at least two people to put their names to the document, no one volunteered. This is a clear case of people who were silent not because of antisemitism, but because of fear. It is consistently said that the Christians were silent about the Jews because of biblical teaching, but here were some who clearly understood that biblical teaching did not mean National Socialist racial antisemitism, yet still kept silent.

The failure of Christians to prophetically and publicly condemn Nazi race doctrines was not mainly because of their traditional theological understanding of Judaism. It was perfectly possible for people to have a conventional dislike for Jews, yet still not want to see them exterminated. Many people in America today would like to see large numbers of illegal aliens expelled, but they do not want them to be sent to slave labor camps and gas chambers. To the extent that the old-fashioned religious antisemitism did enter into this, I would say it was a complicating factor, not a primary one. It may at times even have been an excuse for avoiding what one knew in one's heart to be the right thing to do.

Also, the Christians did not speak out for the Jews, but they did not speak out for the Social Democrats, or for the Communists, or for the trade unionists when they were smashed by Hitler. Neither did they speak out for their own friends, relatives, family members and neighbors who were taken away in the middle of the night. A few brave individuals did publicly protest the extermination of the handicapped and the mentally ill in Hitler's euthanasia program. The aforementioned Bishop Galen and a Lutheran Bishop, Theophil Wurm, were two of the most well-known, and there were others. This required real courage, but they were only able to hinder the killing somewhat, not to stop it. Moreover, euthanasia was not as central to Hitler's program as antisemitism, and it was possible to speak out on behalf of German life (not Slavic or Jewish life) without being disloyal to the government.

---

[33] John Conway, *The Nazi Persecution of the Churches 1933-1945* (Vancouver: Regent, 1968), pp. 264.

[34] Ibid.

Michael Burleigh scoffs at Wurm's efforts, describing them as a strategy of "private appeals to the better nature of individual National Socialist ministers . . . appealing privately to the moral sensibilities of Nazi leaders."[35] Surely Wurm did not believe they would receive his letters and stop the program. He was making an official statement, in writing. It was not just a "private appeal," as in personal conversation. One Pastor Braune, Director of the Evangelical Hoffnungstal Institution, was arrested after he personally complained at four ministries in Berlin. Ernst Wilm, another pastor, gave a lecture on the subject to some colleagues and was sent to Dachau where he stayed until the end of the war.[36] No doubt most or even possibly all modern critics of Christianity would have gone to great lengths to avoid a stay in Dachau.

Burleigh finds it "rather worrying" that Wurm should have conceded in his statement that the idea of putting an end to the existence of "such regrettable people" did naturally occur.[37] It was after all an obvious idea many had suggested, though Wurm did not go along with it. Did Burleigh find it worrying that secularists and social Darwinists who did not believe in the Bible had been openly calling for such procedures for many years? Whatever the case may be there, I do not recall having read of any distinguished research professors of modern European history in any German universities drawing attention to themselves in a brutal totalitarian state by making official protests against government policy.

Given an ordinary understanding of human nature, the response of the Christians in Germany was predictable. The great majority said nothing – but to keep silent for the sake of self-preservation is not a peculiar defect of Christians (using the term loosely). People also kept silent under Stalin and Mao, and said nothing when millions were destroyed. The teachings of Christ call us to something higher than ordinary human nature, but those who are not greatly concerned about Christ in times of peace and prosperity are not going to risk their lives for him in times of crisis. Neither are Jews exempt from the natural human desire for self-preservation, and they are capable of behaving like anyone else in times of crisis.

Robert Wistrich makes the point that American Jews did not make any real effort to put public pressure on the American government to accept more Jewish refugees. Their reason for not making more waves was fear of stirring up American antisemitism.[38] It is quite remarkable that German Christians were supposed to speak out for the Jews in the face of death, torture, or concentration camps, while American Jews did not speak out only because they were afraid people might not like it! A more aggressive public relations

---

[35] Burleigh, *Ethics and extermination*, p. 137.

[36] Conway, *Nazi Persecution of the Churches*, pp. 270-271.

[37] Burleigh, *Ethics and extermination*, p. 137.

[38] Wistrich, *Hitler and the Holocaust*, pp. 23, 191-192.

campaign in conjunction with relief groups already trying to help European refugees might have met with more public support than anticipated. Thousands of lives could conceivably have been saved – but the Jewish community in America had a comfortable situation and (allowing as always for exceptions) did not want to rock the boat.

More significantly, Saul Friedländer documents that the leaders of French Jewry "pointedly continued to ignore the fate of the foreign Jews and to plead for the French Israelites only." In dealing with the Vichy authorities, "Time and again some of the most prestigious names of French Jewry confirmed that, in their view, the fate of the foreign Jews was none of their concern."[39] The Jews in Germany too manifested this tendency. Friedländer also shows that "In late 1939 and early 1940, in order to keep all emigration openings for German Jews only, German Jewish leadership attempted to bar endangered Polish Jews from emigrating from the Reich to Palestine."[40]

Come to think of it, there were Jews living in the American south in the days of Jim Crow and lynching. Did they speak out for persecuted blacks? Did they risk their lives and their positions to speak out for strangers? If not, why not? Because of Torah, or some defect inherent in Judaism? Or because they were ordinary people behaving as ordinary people usually do? Frankly, some of those who denounce the Christians for being silent are moral frauds who would have done the very same thing, and who will do the same thing if our present society ever takes a significant turn for the worse. They will look out for themselves first, silent and cold, indifferent to the sufferings of strangers.

Michael Burleigh referred to the "undeniable pressures" with which the totalitarian Nazi government could oppress religious communities, but only specifically mentioned "threats to alter charitable tax status, expropriation or charges of sexual impropriety."[41] He neglected to mention cancellation of salaries, with no hope of other employment. This is no slight thing for a man with a family to support. Then, there were also Sachsenhausen, Buchenwald, Oranienburg, arrests, beatings, tortures and murders, all of which were far more effective in keeping people in line than the comparatively minor measures mentioned by Burleigh.

In 1935, one Pastor Kloetzel (his first name is not given) spoke out in his sermons against "despotism" and "racial insanity."[42] He did not have his tax status altered, or suffer accusations of sexual wrongdoing. He was arrested, and a few weeks later died in a concentration camp. A Catholic priest, Provost

---

[39] Saul Friedländer, *The Years of Extermination: Nazi Germany and the Jews 1939-1945* (London: Weidenfeld and Nicolson, 2007), pp. 177-178.

[40] Ibid., p. 192.

[41] Burleigh, *Ethics and extermination*, p. 4.

[42] Bernt Engelmann, *In Hitler's Germany: Everyday Life in the Third Reich,* trans. Krishna Winston (New York: Pantheon Books, 1986), p. 59.

Lichtenberg, publicly expressed concern for the Jews. He was later arrested and died in captivity. A Protestant pastor named Grueber set up an office to help Christian Jews. He and his assistant, one Dr. Sylten, were both arrested— the latter died in Dachau.[43]

Certainly as a historian Burleigh knew about such things – perhaps the omission was a just a simple oversight. It might after all be taken for granted that anyone who knows even a little about the Third Reich knows about the Gestapo and the concentration camps. Yet, it does seem that such unpleasant realities are consistently forgotten by some who from their positions of comfort and safety blame the churches for not having done more. It is worth repeating that very few if any of those who criticize the Christians for not speaking out would prove to be heroes themselves in a similar situation.

In addition to the simple and obvious motive of fear, a second obvious explanation for early Christian support for Hitler (or at least failure to forthrightly oppose him) is gullibility and naivety. No one imagined what Hitler would finally become. He promised to restore order and stability, promised to respect the churches, said some nice words about religion on occasion, and for many that was enough. He even played down his antisemitism when necessary, and of course gave no direct indication to the public of anything like a Final Solution. He made a point of appearing more respectable than he was, and could be very convincing.

German error here was human error. American Christians have also supported political candidates who said nice things about religion and morality but after coming to power showed no regard at all for Christianity. It should be pointed out that German businessmen and military leaders as well as trained diplomats were also deceived by Hitler's promises. Similarly, many American and British leftists were deceived by Stalin, and actually saw the Soviet Union as the hope of mankind. Historian Paul Johnson gives many examples of the praise for Chairman Mao showered on him by Western intellectuals who had not the faintest idea of what he really represented, but only projected onto him their own ideas.[44]

Along with fear and naivety, we can add the third related cause of love of the world. The Bible tells us not to be too concerned about things that will pass away, but many Christians in Germany were more concerned with political stability and economic prosperity than they were with spiritual truth. Thus, they ignored many danger signals in the hope that Hitler would bring them affluence and an end to years of political turmoil. They were more concerned with this life than the next. This can be (and often is) true even of those who are doctrinally conservative and outwardly adhere to traditional theology.

---

[43] Conway, *The Nazi Persecution of the Churches*, p. 262.

[44] Paul Johnson, *Modern Times: The World from the Twenties to the Nineties* (New York: Perennial Classics, 1992), pp. 544-545 (Mao) and 276 (Stalin).

Does it need to be explained that failure to understand or to oppose Hitler were not faults of Christians alone? Many people who were by no means enamored of Hitler and National Socialism still felt that there was no other alternative, that no one else could restore and revive Germany. And it is significant that Hitler's party did not begin to make great gains until the Great Depression hit. As long as the Germans were doing tolerably well they were not interested in National Socialist solutions and Hitler seemed like a minor figure. Thus, the problems we are speaking of here are problems not of Christianity, but of human nature anywhere. There can be no doubt that if America ever experiences enough economic hardship most Americans will sacrifice their liberty in exchange for a return to prosperity.

A fourth explanation is that many Christians, including pastors, church dignitaries, and theologians, had long ago abandoned biblical Christianity. It is unfortunate that so many of those who like to point to Christian support for Hitler have no understanding of this topic whatsoever. It should be a fact well-known to everyone who tries to discuss the relationship of the churches to Hitler, that the "Enlightenment" hit Germany with great force in the eighteenth century and spread rapidly. The idea that human reason, not divine revelation, provided the key to understanding deeply affected the churches, and it became increasingly believed that Christianity had to be conformed to the demands of the unbelieving world.

Long before 1900, a great number of seminaries and churches were staffed and pastored by people who did not believe in the Bible as the divinely inspired and inerrant word of God. They called themselves "Christians" and were so considered in the eyes of the world, but they had, in effect, invented a new religion which was essentially worldly philosophy in a religious disguise – and their views were often expressed in an evasive and misleading way so as not to upset common people who (they felt) were not sophisticated enough to understand. Kant suggested that pastors who accepted the new ideas but wanted to continue in their present occupation could have it both ways:

> In the same way [as a military officer may obey an order out of necessity while personally finding fault with it], a clergyman is bound to instruct his pupils and his congregation in accordance with the doctrines of the church he serves, for he was employed by it on that condition. But as a scholar, he is completely free as well as obliged to impart to the public all his carefully considered, well-intentioned thoughts on the mistaken aspects of those doctrines . . . there is nothing in this which need trouble the conscience.[45]

---

[45] Immanuel Kant, *An Answer to the Question "What is Enlightenment?"* (London: Penguin Books 2009), pp. 4-5.

Apart from illustrating Kant's contempt for traditional religion and his ignorance of the nature of the church, this raises questions about his own grasp of ethical principles. For example, did he deny the right of a people to rebel against the government because he knew it would make the Prussian authorities happy, while at the same time he had sympathy for the French Revolution? If by clever explanations he can somehow be extricated from the charge of naked hypocrisy, does that show that his principles were so flexible and so subjective as to be readily adaptable to any situation? That all of his lofty talk about ethics was nothing but hot air, and totally useless as a guide to real life in times of crisis?

The extent to which even the churches contributed to the secularization of Germany (and of Europe) by turning away from traditional, orthodox Christianity is little known by people who enjoy belittling Christianity – hence, a quote from Prof. Gene Veith might be appropriate. Speaking specifically of Germany, he says:

> The attack on the Bible within Protestantism was the work of both textual scholars and theologians. By the 20th century, the "higher criticism" of the Old Testament, which undercut traditional ideas about the authorship and composition of the Bible, had already weakened the doctrine of biblical authority. By assuming that the biblical text and the events it describes are to be explained in naturalistic, scientific terms, historical-critical scholarship vitiated the Bible's status as supernatural revelation.[46]

Nineteenth-century church historian Philip Schaff wrote that Germany's renowned Tuebingen school of theology, a fountainhead of new ideas in Christianity, "proceeds from disbelief in the supernatural and miraculous as a philosophical impossibility, and tries to explain the gospel history and the apostolic history from purely natural causes like every other history."[47] To quote another source on this highly important aspect of Christianity in the Third Reich and in the preceding decades, "Because of the influence of modern philosophy and modern science, and particularly because of the philosophy of Immanuel Kant and his followers, modern Protestantism rejects traditional Protestantism."[48]

---

[46] Veith, *Modern Fascism*, p. 53. He says "weakened" when "denied" or "nullified" would be more accurate, in my opinion.

[47] Philip Schaff, *History of the Christian Church, Vol. 1: Apostolic Christianity from the Birth of Christ to the Death of St John A.D. 1-100* (Peabody, Mass.: Hendrickson Publishers, 2011), p. 208.

[48] Cornelius Van Til, *The Reformed Pastor and Modern Thought* (Phillipsburg, NJ: Presbyterian and Reformed Publishing Company 1980), p. 106.

The problem of theological liberalism has greatly confused the question of Christianity and the Third Reich – especially since secular historians who approach this subject (not to mention even less well-informed people) are all too often ignorant of the subject. It is incredible to them that a pastor, a bishop, a theologian, could speak of "God," "Christ," "faith," yet nevertheless be very far removed from the teachings of Christ and in fact introducing a new religion using familiar Christian vocabulary for different ends.

This new religion was based not on divine revelation but on human reason, and was nothing but humanistic philosophy using religious words and still trying to cling to some sort of groundless hope. In this new religious system, Christ was merely a great moral teacher with a "sublime" ethical system, nothing more. He did not die on the cross for the sins of the world, was not born of a virgin, and was not literally God in human form. The biblical Heaven and Hell and the Day of Judgment were dismissed as pre-scientific myths. If there was such a thing as heaven, surely all that was needed to get there was sincerity. Feeling, a vague sense of the infinite, was more important than doctrine, and "faith" was limited to what might seem plausible to an unbelieving world. The buildings, hymns, vestments and ceremonies remained, but much of the church was lifeless and dead.

More needs to be said about the philosophical underpinnings of a radically new approach to the interpretation of Scripture. It was assumed that the four gospels were not historically accurate, and of course not divinely inspired. The early Christians had preserved some of Christ's sayings and given their impressions and hopes concerning him, but the authentically historical Jesus was lost in the mists of antiquity. Higher truth was discovered by the exercise of human reason alone, especially human reason operating according to the highly creative speculations of Hegel and/or Kant. Later in the century Darwinism and other manifestations of scientism also had a great influence on the churches.[49]

For the new theologians, "The Hegelian method had proved itself to be the logic of reality."[50] Of David Friedrich Strauss, who thought that Christianity contained spiritual truths presented in the form of myths and legends, we read "Hegel's philosophy had set him free, giving him a clear conception of the relationship of idea and reality, leading him to a higher plane of Christological speculation, and opening his eyes to the mystic interpretation of finitude and infinity, God and man"[51] (whatever that means). Strauss maintained that Jesus

---

[49] For examples of Christian pastors who believed in Darwinism see Jerry Bergman's *Hitler and the Nazi Darwinian Worldview*, pp. 301-302.

[50] Albert Schweitzer, *The Quest of the Historical Jesus: A Critical Study of its Progress from Reimarus to Wrede*, trans. W. Montgomery, (Tarlton, OH: Suzeteo Enterprises, 2011), p. 109.

[51] Ibid., p. 78.

never rose from the dead at all, but nevertheless the myth of his resurrection carries a deep spiritual meaning that we can somehow derive benefit from. In a book written in 1872, *The Old Faith and the New*, Strauss asserted that Christianity was only a past cultural legacy, and that Germans today should place their faith in the laboratories, factories, and military power of the Reich.[52] What a stupid fool.

The "peculiar kind of rationalism inspired by Kant"[53] was also deeply influential. We cannot have direct experience of God or of the supernatural; supposedly miraculous events all had natural causes, and we can accept no miraculous event until those natural causes have been found; the Bible must be treated like any other ancient book; a real knowledge of the divine is forbidden to us. So Christoph Friedrich von Ammon reasoned "on the lines of Kant's *Kritik der reinen Vernunft*." "As a disciple of Kant," Ammon also explained that there was no miracle of Jesus turning water into wine at Cana. The wine was a gift which Jesus had secretly brought, and the legend of the miracle was based on a misunderstanding.[54]

Brian Magee wrote of Kant that "he wrought more destruction against established religious ways of thinking than any other philosopher has ever done."[55] This seemingly extravagant statement is probably true, given Kant's deep influence on liberal Protestantism in Germany, which then spread to America and to England. That "the empirical world is all there is," while "spirits, God, magic, the occult" belong to a world off-limits to reason, and beyond what we can truly know – such beliefs of the so-called Enlightenment as exemplified by Kant's simple-minded trust in the power of his own intelligence did immense damage to the German church. Not that we blame the churches' problems all on modern attempts at philosophy. The blame lies with people within the church who chose to accept such ideas, or at least passively tolerated those who did.

People with these clever new ideas stood in the pulpits and talked about "the Gospel" and "Christ" and "salvation." They spoke of "faith" and "the Word of God," celebrated Christmas and Easter, took communion, and sang hymns – but it was all emptiness. These deceptions – derived from unbelief, and finding expression in useless and worthless pseudo-religious philosophies – ate out the very heart of the church. Who is going to suffer martyrdom for a Christ we do not know much about, but who was not born of a virgin and did not rise from the dead? Who is going to suffer for a book of myths and legends? Our innate need for higher reality cannot be met by human philosophy using borrowed religious terminology to make itself seem spiritual.

---

[52] Craig, *Germany 1866-1945*, p. 181.

[53] Schweitzer, *The Quest of the Historical Jesus*, p. 103.

[54] Ibid., pp. 103-104 (both quotes).

[55] Magee, *Wagner and Philosophy*, p. 160 (all quotes).

The churches based on this were shallow and weak, and Hitler (and many others) sensed this weakness. These churches were also irrelevant. They had nothing to offer to lost and confused people seething with resentment, fear, hatred, pride, and revenge. Given that they had already abandoned the essentials of the faith, how could such church leaders withstand Hitler? Their hearts were in the world, they had been following the world for a long time, and there was no reason why they should not continue to follow it – especially in the beginning, when Hitler's true nature was completely unknown.

The malleable, flexible and merely human God of liberal so-called Protestantism is easily accommodated to any and every worldly philosophy, as we can see not merely in Germany, but in America today. Schaff wrote that a leading liberal German "theologian" of the nineteenth century tried to explain the gospel of John as the result not of eternal truth and divine revelation, but of a process of merely human literary evolution.[56] There is no need to be puzzled by the collapse of the German churches before Hitler. Their imposing edifices, their seminaries and church buildings were for the most part whitewashed tombs.

When Christ was on earth, his severest criticisms were directed not at thieves, drunkards, murderers, prostitutes, homosexuals or plain people living normally without God. They were directed at religious leaders that used a lot of religious language but placed a barrier between people and God. It was the theologians and the pastors and the bishops who taught the German people that wherever the answer to their problems might lie, it was not in the church. Who can derive any strength, comfort or meaning from the belief that Jesus did not rise from the dead at all, it was just a story invented by the apostles because of their messianic hope?

The abject surrender of the "theologians" and the "scholars" to the forces of secularism had a serious impact on German culture. Near the end of the nineteenth century R. L. Dabney wrote, "While German scholarship has been busy with its labors, it has suffered almost a whole nation to lapse into a semi-heathenish condition."[57] The idea that Germany was a Christian country is a myth perpetrated by those who understand neither Christianity nor Germany. Many people who called themselves "Catholics" or "Protestants" were referring to infant baptism, childhood education, and vague cultural associations – not to a real commitment to following Christ.

Historians who say that such and such a percentage of "Protestants" voted for Hitler are not concerned with how many of those alleged Protestants thought that the biblical miracles never occurred, that Darwin was right about

---

[56] Schaff, *History of the Christian Church*, p. 409. He adds that this concept was followed by "the whole Tübingen School."

[57] Iain H. Murray, *Evangelicalism Divided: A Record of Crucial Change in the Years 1950 to 2000* (Edinburgh: The Banner of Truth Trust, 2000), pp. 270-271.

the origins of life, and that Christ was a religious genius but a mere man nevertheless, who did not die for the sins of the world, and did not rise from the dead. Even a secular historian who discusses the German church only in passing wrote of German church membership in 1890 that "many who maintained their church membership did so from custom rather than from conviction," adding that such Christians were "apt to be susceptible . . . to the challenge of science and the tendency toward modernism that had resulted from textual criticism of the sacred writings." He adds that church membership "was decreasing year by year."[58]

This rejection of scripture led the "Christians" in Nazi Germany into two directions. Some tried to maintain their outward appearance of Christianity, even as they were careful never to cross any red lines and directly challenge the power or the doctrine of the state. Many of them even thought that the undeniable vitality of the Nazi movement would somehow redound to the benefit of Germany and the churches. They thought Hitler would bring about a national renewal from which all could gain. Needless to say, if they could have seen how things would end, they would have wanted nothing to do with Hitler.

Others whole-heartedly embraced Naziism and openly conformed their belief to the Nazi ideology. These were the so-called "Germanic Christians" who declared (among other things) that God had created separate races, and that it was their Christian duty to follow Hitler and to keep the German race pure. Groups such as the Federation for a German Church, the Thuringian German Christians, and the German Christian Movement had been espousing Nazi-like ideas long before 1933. They eagerly turned to Hitler. Blaming the Jews for Germany's defeat in World War I; rejecting democracy and calling for a strong leader; seeking to remove Jewish influences from the Bible; rejecting the "Jewish" doctrine of original sin; redefining the cross as a symbol of struggle for National Socialism or human political sacrifice; stating that God had sent Hitler and that a new revelation was to be found in him – with these and other ideas they provided many "Christian" quotes that have been confusing to those who try to talk about Christianity in the Third Reich with no real knowledge of a complex situation too hard for them to understand.

When we read about clever legitimizations of euthanasia and sterilization by so-called Protestants and so-called theologians who advocated ideas unheard of in previous centuries of Protestantism and in over 1800 years of Christianity, it is easy for people who are hostile to Christianity to say how bad the Christians are. We are told how many people were sterilized in "Protestant" facilities. This is presented as evidence of the evils of religion. Let us not forget who it was that first invented those ideas that the "Christians" were abandoning their faith to follow. If we are not told of the secular authorities in the field of public health who enthusiastically endorsed such

---

[58] Craig, *Germany 1866-1945*, p. 181 (all quotes).

measures long before anyone ever was compelled to practice them; if we are not told of similar practices carried out in secular institutions – then we can conclude we are dealing not with history but with propaganda.

Institutions set up by Christians performed valuable and necessary humanitarian services for many years before 1933. They cared for the mentally ill, the chronically ill, and the aging, in the belief that even those who seemed worthless to the world were still human beings. The social Darwinists believed that to abandon such people to die or simply kill them was healthy and natural. If these charitable institutions later succumbed to Naziism, what then? Does this show the evils of religion? Or does it show the surrender of religion to the evil forces of secularism? If a Protestant pastor apes Nazi rhetoric and conforms to Nazi ideology that is bad, but where did this ideology come from? Does the belief that we are only animals and have no immortal soul not enter into the picture anywhere? If we condemn a supposedly religious person for following evil, what about those non-religious people who invented the evil in the first place?

The Germanic Christian Bishop of the Protestant Church in the Rhine Province, Dr. Heinrich Oberheid, thanked "the living God" who has "given us the Fuehrer," and stated that "the National Socialist movement under our leader Adolf Hitler"[59] was bringing new strength and order to the German churches. This does not – contrary to the ill-informed opinions of some – reveal the Christian origins of National Socialism. It reveals the surrender of Christianity to a worldly philosophy on the part of those who already before Hitler had decided in their hearts to turn from Scripture and follow their own understanding apart from divine revelation. They did not consider or understand what James meant when he wrote "Ye adulterers and adulteresses, know ye not that the friendship of the world is enmity with God? Whosoever therefore will be a friend of the world is the enemy of God" (4:4). This applies to all "Christians" who first adopt some sinful and unbiblical idea from the world around them, and then use the Bible to try and justify it.

This same "Bishop" Oberheid also spoke of the churches' mission to proclaim "Jesus Christ, the Crucified and Risen One," and stated his concern that "the full gospel may be purely preached."[60] That someone could speak about "the full gospel" while at the same time accepting Hitler will not seem too incredible to those who are aware of Christians in America today who speak about "the gospel," and yet at the same time accept abortion, embrace homosexuality, reject large parts of the Bible as unscientific, and consider the gospel to be nothing more than a vague and nebulous appeal to something they're not quite sure what. Bible-believing Christians have been very much to blame in failing to speak out against such flagrant perversions of Christianity.

---

[59] Wentorf, *Paul Schneider*, p. 107.

[60] Ibid., pp. 107-108.

When Christian leaders, bishops, pastors, and "theologians" endorse homosexuality, abortion, role reversal and unisex feminism, this does not demonstrate the Christian origins of those things. It illustrates Christians abandoning their principles to follow ideas that emerge out of the unbelieving world. Similarly, when a Germanic Christian document states that "faith in Christ does not destroy our race, but enhances and sanctifies it . . . marriage between Germans and Jews must be forbidden,"[61] this does not show the Christian origin or nature of those totally unbiblical concepts. Unfortunately, such a distinction is too difficult for some people to comprehend.

These "enemies of the cross of Christ" (Philippians 3:18) masquerading as Christians were useful allies and Hitler was careful not to alienate them. It was for this reason that – as we saw earlier – Hitler expressed his preference for Protestantism over Catholicism because of its "later tradition"[62] of abandoning essential doctrines. When the Germanic Christians were no longer needed, however, and even came to be something of an embarrassment, they were severely restricted, and the Germanic Christian symbol of a cross together with a swastika was officially banned.[63] They too found – as did so many others – that a promise from the Fuehrer meant nothing. Needless to say, the Germanic Christians had no crisis of conscience when it came to speaking out for the Jews. They saw Hitler as their messiah and followed him eagerly.

Incidentally, when people see crosses used by the Nazis, on graves or monuments for example, or in some form of propaganda, most mistakenly think of them as Christian symbols – but actually the Christian symbol of the cross was borrowed and given a new meaning. To Nazis with a religious bent, a cross could also represent struggle to the death, as Jesus, the bold Aryan warrior, struggled against Judaism unto death. The cross to them did not represent the Lamb of God dying as a sacrifice for the sins of the world. In exactly the same way, there are some today who take Christ's death on the cross to represent whatever their current philosophy of the moment happens to dictate. For example, the crucifixion may be used to represent victory over evil by non-violence. It may represent the highest altruism, giving of oneself for others; or "the abusive nature of structures of oppression"; or only God's identification with our suffering and nothing more.[64]

---

[61] Ibid., pp. 69-70, citing F. Wieneke, *Die Glaubensbewegung "Deutsche Christen"* (*The "German Christian" Faith Movement*) (Solin, 1933).

[62] Hitler, *Mein Kampf,* p. 112.

[63] Conway, *The Nazi Persecution of the Churches,* pp. 58-59. Conway's study also contains a detailed description of these Germanic Christian groups and their teachings and doctrinal statements.

[64] Paul Wells, *Cross Words: The Biblical Doctrine of the Atonement* (Fearn, Scotland: Christian Focus, 2006), p. 20.

When Joseph Goebbels referred in his novel *Michael* to Jesus as a socialist who sacrificed himself for mankind, this shows only the borrowing of Christian themes for some other very different end. Goebbels used the word "Christ" rather freely. He referred to Horst Wessel, an S.A. man murdered by a Communist, as "A socialist Christ! One who appealed to others through his deeds!"[65] Richard Evans writes that "Wessel was hardly cold in his grave before Goebbels began work on blowing his memory up into a full-scale cult." At the funeral, "Goebbels praised Wessel in terms that deliberately recalled Christ's sacrifice for humankind – 'Through sacrifice to redemption . . . Wherever Germany is,' he declared, 'you are there too, Horst Wessel!' "[66]

Secularists who are inclined to look on such things with disgust as examples of the worthlessness of religion and religious people need to consider that what we have here is not a case of people who claim to believe in God inventing irrational and ridiculous ideas. It is a case of them abandoning biblical teaching, but still using religious words with deep connotations to justify new and modern ideas invented by people who did not believe in the Bible. Modern racism and hyper-nationalism came from those who rejected divine revelation and sought to invent their own values.

Aryan Christianity is an excellent example of this. It was not politically contrived by the Nazis, but was the logical and consistent result of more than a century of surrendering basic doctrines in order to follow the world. Friedrich Delitzsch, a German biblical "scholar," wrote before World War I that Jesus had not been Jewish; that the Old Testament was derived from Babylonian mythology and culture and was full of deceptions; that Christianity needed to be detached from the Old Testament which was a "dangerous" book. It should be evident to any Bible-believing Christian that his fake scholarship was a complete waste of time. There is entirely too much reverence in the church today for scholars. Adolf von Harnack, another theologian, also wanted the Old Testament removed from the Bible.[67]

The same could be said of many other German so-called scholars and theologians (often quoted by people whose hobby is linking Christianity to Naziism). Gerhard Kittel managed to write a massive *Theological Dictionary of the New Testament* but was deceived by Hitler and embraced National Socialism. All of his time spent studying "theology" was time lost. Not surprisingly, he taught at Tuebingen University.[68] Much of the German

[65] John Toland, *Adolf Hitler (Volume I)* (New York: Doubleday & Company, 1976), p. 250.

[66] Richard Evans, *The Coming of the Third Reich* (New York: Penguin, 2005), pp. 267-268.

[67] Veith, *Modern Fascism*, pp. 53-54 (for Delitzsch and Harnack).

[68] Richard L. Rubenstein and John K. Roth, *Approaches to Auschwitz: The Holocaust and its Legacy* (Louisville KY 2003), p. 257.

Protestant Church was riddled with such heresies and false teachings masquerading as Christianity. Sadly, the same can be said of much of the American church today. How many seminary professors, and pastors and theologians openly deny the faith and replace biblical teachings with modern philosophy, immorality, and social activism?

This is not merely a matter of German history. The ongoing depth of liberal influence in our own time is indicated by the fact that Dietrich Bonhoeffer, a hero to many American evangelicals, not only studied under Harnack, but praised him. Speaking at Harnack's funeral, Bonhoeffer described the man who wanted to abandon the Old Testament as "the champion of the free expression of a truth once recognized . . . we knew that with him we were in good and solicitous hands, we saw him as the bulwark against all trivialization and stagnation . . . ." [69] Bonhoeffer "agreed profoundly with the underlying assumptions that guided Harnack," and asserted that Bonhoeffer saw Harnack as being "on the side of truth," and "a compatriot to be lauded."

Bonhoeffer himself wrote, "I feel obliged to tackle these questions as one who, although a 'modern' theologian, is still aware of the debt that he owes to liberal theology."[70] This debt is evident in Bonhoeffer's questioning of the virgin birth and of the resurrection; his statement that the gospels contain texts "whose authenticity has been destroyed by historical research"; his opinion that Christ partook so fully of our human nature as to be not sinless but flawed and erring.[71]

"The fundamental eros of the leading contemporary theological traditions of Bultmann, Tillich, Bonhoeffer, Whitehead, and Rahner is accommodation to modernity."[72] Can we uncritically embrace such people without being influenced by them? Is it any wonder that faith is fading even from many of the so-called Bible-believing churches? Isn't it obvious that people who will embrace a modern theologian like Bonhoeffer without even knowing or caring what he believed are ripe for further deception? This liberal theology may have an initial appearance of Christianity, but at its heart it is a denial of everything uniquely and distinctively Christian, and an assault on Christianity itself. Those for whom hero-worship takes priority over essential doctrines are in deep trouble spiritually. Many modern Bible-believing Christians have been

---

[69] Eric Metaxas, *Bonhoeffer: Pastor, Martyr, Prophet, Spy* (Nashville: Thomas Nelson, 2010), p. 95 (four quotes).

[70] Dietrich Bonhoeffer, *Letters and Papers from Prison,* ed. Eberhard Bethge (New York: Touchstone, 1997), p. 378.

[71] Dietrich Bonhoeffer, *Christ the Center,* trans. Edwin H. Robertson (New York: HarperOne, 1978), pp. 105 (the virgin birth), 112 (the resurrection), 73 (authenticity of Scripture), 108-109 (Christ's flawed humanity).

[72] Thomas C. Oden, *After Modernity . . . What? Agenda for Theology* (Grand Rapids, MI: Zondervan, 1992), p. 33.

far too quick to embrace anyone who uses religious language without really understanding the different meanings that may lie beneath the surface.

Many Christians do not know what is going on with liberal "theology." The belief that the Bible is spiritually true but not historically true allows for a great deal of religious sounding language that points people in the wrong direction. That Jesus rose from the dead for example is a central fact of Christian teaching. The Bible affirms that – but what does it all really mean? What happened exactly? Was it an actual physical resurrection of a dead body, a revived corpse? Or was it not an historical event at all but rather a symbolic expression of a deeper spiritual reality that does not depend on historical veracity to be valid? Something that was real in the hearts and minds of the believers but not real in the ordinary world of daily experience?

In liberal theology, "faith" does not have to be chained to historical fact. For example, Jesus told the parable of the good Samaritan. Whether or not the good Samaritan was an actual person and Jesus was talking about a historical incident is totally irrelevant. If it actually happened, or if it was only a parable, we still get an important spiritual message, and that is the main thing. And what if we apply this sort of thinking to the resurrection of Christ? The Christian community somehow believed Christ arose, but what is important for us today in these sophisticated modern times is newness of life and revived hope. Belief in the resurrection of Christ is important as a symbol, but this can exist independently of history. Similarly, the creation; the Day of Judgment; the fall; the virgin birth – these are for the new theologians important spiritual truths expressed in mythology that do not need historical veracity for their validity.

That we can derive hope from something that maybe never happened is pure nonsense and atheists are justified in scoffing at it – but liberal theologians (whether in nineteenth-century Germany or today) thought they were saving Christianity. They were "trying to preserve the faith, not destroy it."[73] They felt that if Christianity did not conform itself to the realities of modern science and philosophy it would be left behind – but their proposed synthesis of biblical and secular truth was nothing but capitulation and led in the end to "the collapse of theology."

"We have been told that modern ears simply cannot hear classic Christian language, cannot bear to hear of sin, incarnation, atonement, sacrifice, resurrection, or salvation."[74] This misguided premise, which goes back to the "Enlightenment," has led to the capitulation of establishment churchianity to every major challenge, be it never so evil and never so contrary to the

---

[73] David F. Wells, *No Place for Truth: or Whatever Happened to Evangelical Theology?* (Grand Rapids, MI: William B. Eerdmans, 1993), pp. 116-117 (both quotes).

[74] Oden, *After Modernity*, p. 128.

teachings and the Spirit of Christ. Accommodation to modernity requires abandonment of vital principles, and once that process is begun there is no telling where it will stop.

Responding to the accusation that Christians who insisted on vital doctrines were irrational, the old English Puritan John Owen responded that it is better for us to "suffer the imputation of so doing [going against reason], than by renouncing the Scripture turn infidels, that we may be accounted rational."[75] But, many did just that – renounced the Scripture so that they might be considered "rational." Things reached such a state in Germany that someone like Rudolf Bultmann could openly deny the fundamentals of the faith yet still be a Lutheran pastor – and today he is called "neo-orthodox."

A substantial excerpt from an essay by Bultmann called "New Testament and Theology" gives us some of his basic ideas: that the New Testament's triple-decker cosmos of earth, heaven, and hell, with a world in which supernatural forces often intervene, "is essentially mythical in character."[76] Christ as God's Son sent to earth, dying for our sins, rising from the dead, and other aspects of traditional Christianity are dismissed with the question – "Can Christian preaching expect modern man to accept the mythical view of the world as true? To do so would be both senseless and impossible . . . It is simply the cosmology of a pre-scientific age."

If Bultmann is neo-orthodox then the term "orthodox" has no meaning at all. We might just as well call Elvis Presley and Marilyn Monroe "neo-orthodox." Why didn't the churches oppose Hitler more effectively? Because to a large extent they were dead, dead and decomposing. That Bultmann and others like him were even allowed to remain in the church is a sign of spiritual death. His vague and empty "sermons" never got him into any trouble in Hitler's Germany. In one such "sermon" "preached" in Nazi Germany – a lecture any Gestapo agent or police spy could have safely dozed through and probably did – Bultmann asked why Christian influence had declined so sharply in the country. He was one of the reasons.

Some historians nowadays seem to enjoy linking the "Protestants" to Hitler. The "Protestants" voted for Hitler, Hitler did well in this "devoutly Protestant" area; even the pro-Nazi philosopher Heidegger (who did not believe in the Bible by the way) has been linked to his "Protestant" background. We are not informed as to how many of those alleged Protestants went to church once or twice a year, discounted the first three chapters of Genesis as myth, believed in evolution, and thought they would go to heaven (if there was a heaven)

---

[75] John Owen, *The Holy Spirit: His Gifts and Power* (Ross-shire, Scotland: Christian Heritage, 2007), p. 36.

[76] Montgomery, *The Suicide of Christian Theology*, p. 518.

because they were baptized as infants, paid their mandatory church tax, and never robbed a bank or murdered someone.

One historian wrote that "even Protestant pastors" joined the Nazi party. Why shouldn't they join the Nazi party, or any other party, if they didn't believe in the Bible? Significantly, this same author forgot to state that "even some professors of biology who believed in evolution joined the Nazi party" – although the word "even" would be out of place there, as there is nothing in Darwinism to contradict Naziism. Darwinists could and did become Nazis without having to violate any essential teachings of evolutionary theory. This cannot be said of Christians. These numerous little barbs shot at Christianity by those who are supposedly objective historians are one of the many signs of the increasingly dark post-Christian era.

Parenthetically, Bultmann's attempts to remove the outdated and unscientific mythology from the New Testament included a lecture duplicated for former pupils serving as chaplains in Hitler's armies.[77] I have no doubt they found his denial of the literal and historical sacrificial death, resurrection, and return of Christ to be very helpful in their work. Concerning Protestant and Catholic chaplains in the armies of the Reich, their appointment depended on approval by the Gestapo, and " 'Insufficient antisemitism' was cause for rejection."[78] Their failure to represent Christ faithfully is hardly surprising. What is surprising is that Dietrich Bonhoeffer while in prison expressed more than once his willingness to serve in such a dishonorable capacity.[79]

American evangelist Francis Schaeffer wrote that "the higher critical methods of the study of the Bible . . . destroyed the authority of the Bible for the Protestant church in Germany." He adds "there was a span of approximately eighty years from the time when the higher critical methods originated and became widely accepted in Germany to the disintegration of German culture and the rise of totalitarianism under Hitler."[80] Of course, there were many factors behind the rise of Hitler, but the destruction of biblical authority was one of the main reasons for the failure of the churches to speak out against him. Many churches in America today cannot and will not stand for Christ, because they are not of Christ, but they have a different spirit entirely.

Similarly, one might even say ominously, it has been approximately eighty years since destructive liberal theology gained control of the mainline denominations in America. This, along with other factors, has contributed

---

[77] David L. Edwards, "Rudolf Bultmann: Scholar of Faith." *Christian Century*, September 1-8 (1976), 728-730. Religion Online; www.religion-online.org/showarticle.asp?title=1827   accessed May 2014.

[78] Rubenstein and Roth, *Approaches to Auschwitz,* p. 258.

[79] Bonhoeffer, *Letters and Papers from Prison,* pp. 57-58, 60, 174, 198.

[80] Francis Schaeffer, *The Great Evangelical Disaster* (Westchester, IL: Crossway Books, 1984), pp. 37, 35.

greatly to our pronounced national decline – and many seminaries and churches are now in such a state that we can confidently predict there will be no resistance from them should the forces of evil manage to get control of the levers of power. Is the collapse of the churches before National Socialism any different from the beginning collapse of the churches before the gay-rights movement today? Wouldn't Christians who effortlessly accommodate their faith to meet the demands of abortionists, radical feminists, and homosexual rights activists also have willingly embraced the equally false philosophies of Aryan supremacy and racial antisemitism? In denying Scripture, they open the door to any and every idea that might emerge out of the unbelieving world.

Thomas Oden's book *Requiem: A Lament in Three Movements* gives a striking picture of seminaries and church bureaucracies that have largely and even completely abandoned biblical Christianity and embraced the world. He speaks of "unprecedented mutations" in the church; of mockery of the Trinity and dismissal of the need for Christ's sacrificial death; of "overt advocacy of lesbianism as an acceptable and commended practice for Christian women"; of a communion service dedicated to the feminist goddess Sophia.[81] Does anyone imagine these people will stand for Christ in times of persecution? If we want to understand the strange silence of the German churches under Hitler we need only to look around us.

People who want to discuss these things should read more German history. Craig's history of modern Germany contains a brief yet insightful description of German Protestant theology towards the end of the nineteenth century. He writes that the leading theologians of Germany had yielded to the pressures of modernism, and "had long since abandoned the dogmatic rigour of an earlier age." Christianity was no longer considered to be divinely revealed, and scholarship that undermined the Bible led to "an incautious eagerness to adapt the beliefs of the Church to the latest fashions in scientific speculation."[82]

Protestantism in the end became "nothing but a bundle of ethical rules, inspired not by divine authority but by social utility."[83] And, if the main benefit of religion is not forgiveness of sin and eternal life but rather social utility, it is not hard to see what might happen when someone came along who promised to solve Germany's severe economic and political problems. It would naturally be the duty of religion to support him, for the good of the people. After all, if true religion is doing good, and tearing up the Versailles Treaty and restoring economic stability and national honor are good, there is no need for deeper reflection about vexing questions of right and wrong.

---

[81] Thomas Oden, *Requiem: A Lament in Three Movements* (Nashville: Abingdon Press, 1995), pp. 109, 48, 27.

[82] Craig, *Germany 1866-1945*, p. 182 (both quotes).

[83] Ibid., pp. 182-183.

This is not to blame the collapse of the churches solely on theological modernism. Christians who are theoretically orthodox can also be part of the problem. There is after all such a thing as lifeless, spiritless, powerless orthodoxy. Much of today's theoretically orthodox evangelical and fundamentalist Christianity lacks power, commitment and authority. D. Martyn Lloyd-Jones wrote of this, saying, "Correct doctrine can leave the church dead; you can have dead orthodoxy, you can have a church that is perfectly orthodox but perfectly useless."[84] Christ said, "Ye are the salt of the earth: but if the salt have lost his savour, wherewith shall it be salted? It is thenceforth good for nothing, but to be cast out, and to be trodden under foot of men" (Matthew 5:13). It must be said with sadness that there were churches in Nazi Germany, and there are churches in America today, that were and are good for nothing, that were and will be trodden under foot by men.

A Nazi census of 1939 revealed that 95% of Germans polled stated they were Protestants or Catholics. It was not mentioned that the people were asked if they were seriously committed to living by the teachings of Christ, or if they had been among the millions of Germans who voted for Communist candidates before Hitler came to power, but now wanted to conceal their past. I am sure it was not asked if their Protestantism or their Catholicism were vague cultural concepts having to do with childhood education but not with adult belief. Plus, if someone had answered "Neither" without being able to prove a real commitment to National Socialism, it might have led to a dangerous suspicion of Communism.

In August 1914 one Pastor Ernst von Dryander, speaking in a worship service in the Berlin Cathedral, promised that God would support the German cause, and referred to "the fatherland in which the roots of our strength lie."[85] If this man actually believed that the roots of the German people's strength lay in Germany, then he did not have the faintest understanding of Christ's teachings concerning the kingdom of God. Is this a case of how religious people harm society with their bad ideas? No. Since the idea of the fatherland as providing us with strength, meaning, and purpose emerged out of German Romanticism and idealistic philosophy, this is a case of a religious person abandoning biblical teaching and following false worldly ideas that emerged out of an entirely different tradition. It is a case of the world setting the agenda, and the church once again tagging along timidly behind, trying desperately to win acceptance and prove its relevance.

On a different occasion – March 15, 1933 – President Hindenburg spoke at the ceremonial opening of the new Reichstag (the German parliament). The

---

[84] D. M. Lloyd-Jones, *The Puritans: Their Origins and Successors* (Edinburgh: Banner of Truth Trust, 1987), pp. 13-14.

[85] Wentorf, *Paul Schneider*, p. 39. Hitler spoke in *Mein Kampf* of God smiling on the Germany army in World War I – hardly a biblical concept (p. 199).

ceremony was held at the Garrison Church in Potsdam, a national shrine where Frederick the Great was buried, a historic place redolent of the glories of Bismarck, the Kaiser, and the old Prussian kings. In his speech to an audience including many military leaders of the old Imperial Germany, Hindenburg invoked "the old spirit of this celebrated shrine," and expressed the hope that said spirit would "permeate the generation of today . . . liberate us . . . bring us together . . . to bless a proud and free Germany, united in herself."[86] The Spirit of Jesus has nothing to do with national spirits of power and vainglory, and any reference to the Sermon on the Mount would have been ludicrously out of place. To my knowledge no historian has yet referred to this as a "Protestant" gathering, as much as they like to fling that adjective around like kids in school shooting spitwads.

This is related to the fifth reason for the failure of the churches – a seriously defective and unbiblical understanding of the church's relationship to the state. For generations, for centuries, the churches had been too dependent on the state, and had a long history of relying on it for support. In the 1870s, "the Protestant establishment was merely an instrument of the authoritarian state."[87] This is very far from what Luther and the other reformers had in mind, although it was only natural for them to value the support of sympathetic rulers at a time when they were under direct physical threat.

Rudolf Wentorf stated that "Church and state were linked together too closely . . . the fears of the state were also the fears of the church." As an example he gives the following statement by one R. Moeller, President of the German Protestant Church Congress convened in 1919. Concerning recent political developments, he stated that "By losing a church government upheld by the ruler of the state, the churches have had their chief support taken from them."[88] Describing the Kaiser and his government as the church's "chief support" is a sign of serious spiritual disorientation. Is it any surprise such people were receptive to Hitler's promises – all of them later broken – to restore and protect the churches?

Referring to Hitler's rise to power, Shirer noted "the inexplicable weakness, that now bordered on paralysis, of existing institutions – the Army, the churches, the trade unions, the political parties – or of the vast non-Nazi middle class and the highly organized proletariat . . . ."[89] It is easily understandable that people should have been incapable of resisting Hitler at the cost of their own lives when they believed in nothing except comfort and

---

[86] William L. Shirer, *The Rise and Fall of the Third Reich: A History of Nazi Germany* (New York: Simon and Schuster, 2011), p. 197. Hitler stated in his speech that President Hindenburg was the agent of a "protective Providence" (also p. 197).

[87] Craig, *Germany 1866-1945*, p. 77.

[88] Wentorf, *Paul Schneider*, pp. 44-45.

[89] Shirer, *Rise and Fall*, p. 185.

prosperity, national glory, human science and philosophy, or a nebulous religion grounded shakily on empty liberal pseudo-religion and fake scholarship. We can see the same thing in America today – the weakness and helplessness of traditional conservatives who don't really believe in much and have passively allowed forces diametrically opposed to them to gain control of all of the most influential vantage points of political and cultural influence.

ii.

In spite of their evident and long-standing weaknesses, the churches still remained a potentially serious problem for Hitler after he came to power. On the one hand, he could not tolerate any rivals for the allegiance of the German people. The goal was not merely to gain territory or make Germany great. It was to completely reorient the entire German people to the ideology of National Socialism, and to exalt and preserve the German race by the practice of doctrines gradually brought to fulfillment in over one hundred years of German secularism. This required total national unity, with no place for dissenting doctrines.

On the other hand, a direct assault on religion would have created great havoc in Germany. Hitler understood this well, and in fact had already considered at some length in *Mein Kampf* the problem of how a future government should deal with the churches. In volume I chapter 5, Hitler questioned whether opposing philosophies could be combatted by force alone (170). He stresses two lines later that he is concerned with the issue "particularly on a religious basis." He answered his own question by stating that mere persecution had two serious drawbacks. This was discussed in chapter 4 but, I think, merits repetition because of its importance to an understanding of Hitler's church policies.

First, "force alone . . . can never lead to the destruction of an idea . . . except in the form of a complete extermination of even the very last exponent of the idea" (170). This of course was Hitler's policy with the Jews and to a lesser extent with the Communists. To have tried the same with the Christians would have been a "blood sacrifice" that would strike "the best part of the people" (170). The Christians in Germany (using the word "Christian" only in a general cultural sense) were of Aryan blood, and an attempt to simply wipe out the Christians and the churches would have done immense damage to the race and to the nation. There would have been unacceptable chaos and disruption, completely inimical to Hitler's plans for re-armament and conquest. This was of course very different from the situations under Lenin, Stalin, and Mao, where a much weaker Christian presence allowed for more overt persecution.

Secondly, not only would the mere application of force have been impractical, it would have led not to the disappearance of Christianity, but rather would strengthen it. Hitler understood that overt persecution would only

204

create more sympathy for the churches, and be counterproductive (170). He had observed that von Schoenerer's assault on the Catholics in pre-World War I Austria had only strengthened them in their conviction and cost him much valuable support. Hitler knew that creating Christian martyrs would not be to his advantage. Even weak and nominal Christians could be driven back to the church by resentment against the government.

Excessive persecution would be harmful and counterproductive – but the churches could not be left alone to propagate un-Germanic values either. If a direct assault was untenable, so was too much liberty – so Hitler sought a middle way. This also is explored at length in the same passage in *Mein Kampf* just referred to. In planning the marginalization of the churches (with a view to their final disappearance), Hitler speculated that two things were necessary. First, the aim was not merely to eliminate the old idea, but to offer something positive in its place. "Conceptions and ideas, as well as movements with a definite spiritual foundation . . . [can] only be broken with technical instruments of power [i.e., secret police and concentration camps] if these physical weapons are at the same time the support of a new kindling thought, idea, or philosophy" (170).[90] The idea was not merely to eliminate the old idea, but to replace it.

This is illustrated by a quote from Rudolf Hess:

> A religion which has influenced, indeed dominated, the life of a people for two thousand years cannot be destroyed or overcome by external measures . . . The more we National Socialists avoid religious disputes and stay away from church ceremonies, and rather earn the loyalty of the people through fulfilling our duties, so men will be drawn more and more to National Socialism.[91]

So, force and repression were necessary, but they needed to be applied in a controlled fashion. "Only in the steady and constant application of force lies the very first prerequisite for success" (171). This refers not to seizing more territory in the east, but to making National Socialism the sole belief of the German people. This was the policy Hitler later followed: steady and consistent repression short of excessively violent conflict, and a sustained effort to indoctrinate all Germans with the new ideas. Those who talk about

---

[90] Since some people seem to be unclear about the use of brackets [ ] in quotes, perhaps it should be explained that these do not represent additions to the quote itself. They represent clarifications by the person citing the quote, and are understood to be attempted explanations to give the proper context, not misleading alterations of the quote.

[91] John Conway, *The Nazi Persecution of the Churches,* p. 167. This was from a speech to Nazi leaders in 1938, and expressed Hitler's ideas exactly.

Hitler's Christianity consistently ignore or misrepresent what actually happened to the churches in Germany – as they must in order to maintain their fictions.

Why have Hitler's clear statements about his plans for the churches been so consistently ignored? Who are these people who talk about Hitler and Christianity at such length but seem not to have even read his book? Hitler was planning for an assumption of power long before 1933. Even in the 1920s he provided his party with departments of justice, labor, agriculture, and foreign affairs so as to be ready when the time came. He did not have a detailed blueprint, but he did have ideas – including ideas for the churches – and he put them in writing. After coming to power Hitler, feeling his way and adapting himself to circumstances as required, pursued the general goal he had set down in *Mein Kampf* of replacing an old philosophy with a new one by a combination of indoctrination and controlled force. After coming to power, Hitler therefore implemented a three-pronged policy designed first to limit, and then to eliminate the influence of the churches.

The first aspect of this policy was bureaucratic control, an attempt to bring the church bureaucracies under the complete control of the state. The second was indoctrination, a prolonged ideological struggle to replace Christianity, especially among the youth, with a new faith, a new idea. The third was carefully calibrated persecution. This was severe enough to discourage independence of thought, but not so severe as to turn large numbers of people into martyrs, thereby strengthening people's religious commitment and turning them against the state. These policies are described at length and in scholarly detail by John Conway in his book *The Nazi Persecution of the Churches 1933-1945*.

Before looking at this triple assault, it is important to repeat that Hitler had come to power without ever having received a majority vote in any election. Many Germans were not sympathetic to Naziism, and had either voted against Hitler, or else supported him without complete conviction for lack of a better alternative. Thus the churches needed to be dealt with carefully, and Hitler – especially in the beginning of his regime – had to be mindful of them. It quickly became apparent, however, that his promises to respect and support the churches had been lies. He sought to reduce them to a position of complete subservience and marginalize them as much as possible from all important aspects of German life. In this struggle, the Nazis did not much differentiate between Protestant and Catholic, the only question being whether they submitted to Hitler or not.

It is also worth noting that the top Nazi leadership was divided when it came to the question of official church policies. Himmler, Bormann, and Heydrich were openly hostile to the churches, and wanted to break them as quickly as possible, even by overt persecution if need be.[92] Others, such as Rudolf Hess and Religious Affairs Minister Hans Kerrl, thought that too much persecution would be counter-productive and favored a more gradual approach. Some thought that appealing to the churches and winning them over would strengthen Hitler's regime – others thought that there was no benefit to the Reich in any sort of church entity whatever.

Hitler steered a course between the two extremes of outright assault and too much toleration, sometimes having to restrain his more zealous subordinates. In June of 1941, for example, shortly before the invasion of the Soviet Union, Martin Bormann released a statement to party officials stating "Never again must influence in the leadership of the people be yielded to the churches. This (influence) must be broken completely and finally."[93] A few days later the statement was officially withdrawn – Hitler did not need more internal dissension over secondary issues on the eve of the invasion.

Concerning administrative control, this was more of a Protestant issue than a Catholic one. The Concordat had legitimized the most important Catholic ecclesiastical structures, and the Catholic Church had never been so closely tied to the state. Catholics were subjects to the same pressures, harassments, and persecutions on other fronts as were the Protestants, but their ecclesiastical structure at least was centralized under the Vatican, and less open to manipulation. When it came to the mainline Protestant churches, the Nazis had more room for maneuver (smaller independent groups were simply banned, as was mentioned in chapter 4).[94]

There was at first an ambitious attempt to forcibly unify all of the Protestant churches into one National Evangelical Church. This led to such strong dissent and turmoil that the project was abandoned. Incidentally, this attempt does not indicate Hitler's religious belief, as has been recklessly claimed. It indicates a totalitarian desire to ensure that no aspect of life was outside of the government's control. Chairman Mao also centralized the much weaker Christian churches in China in order to bring them under more effective government control. To reason from government control to government sympathy and support is quite a gymnastic feat.

The Nazis also sought to gain control of existing structures through manipulating elections. Non-Nazi candidates were harassed, ballots were confiscated, unsympathetic church officials were fired and replaced with more suitable candidates, and Hitler's approved candidate for the new post of Reich

---

[92] Ibid., p. 287.

[93] Ibid., p. 260.

[94] Ibid., pp. 370-374. A few of those groups were Bible Faith Fellowship; Free Pentecostalists of Berlin; Mission for Awakening in Germany; Bible Community, and the Union of Free Religious Communities in Germany. A number of others were mentioned in the Gestapo document cited by Conway.

Bishop, Ludwig Mueller, won the election when his more traditionally Christian candidate Pastor Friedrich von Bodelschwingh was compelled to withdraw due to intense government pressure. Photographs of Nazi Brownshirts attending church in formation come from this period, when the Brownshirts were being used to intimidate opponents of the government and also influence church elections. Baptized into the church in infancy, they were members and eligible to vote regardless of their beliefs or actions, and were ordered to attend by their superiors.[95]

John Owen wrote in the 1600s, "it is so come to pass, that let men be never so notoriously and flagitiously wicked, until they become pests of the earth, yet are they esteemed to belong to the church of Christ."[96] We read in I Corinthians that openly sinful people were to be put out of the church (5:11, 13). Not understanding that certain standards were required both for entering the church and for remaining in it was one of the most serious flaws of the German churches. It showed they did not take the Bible seriously.

One German pastor, Paul Schneider, attempted to impose church discipline on three pro-Nazi members of his congregation. This meant not that they were to be burned at the stake or tortured, but that they should not be allowed to partake of communion, and were no longer to be considered members of the church. Church members were advised not to shun them, but "to treat them kindly in all necessary things,"[97] so that if possible they might be won back to the church. This was done in accordance with established church practice after previous conversations and attempts at correction. The response of one of the disciplined members was to report his pastor to the police.

A Gestapo document lists this attempt to exercise church discipline as one of the reasons for the pastor's arrest. Other reasons were: publicly and on the spot objecting to Nazi propaganda at a church funeral; stating that "The brown crowd [the SA] does not belong in the church"; disparaging *Mein Kampf* in a sermon; calling National Socialism a work of the devil in conversation; and stating in another sermon that German youth belonged to Christ, not to Adolf Hitler.[98] Such incidents were more troubling to the authorities and hence more dangerous than many Barmen Declarations or philosophical statements about the lordship of Christ over all of life.

Schneider's attempt to actually discipline Nazi church members was so shocking that it reached the attention of Heinrich Himmler himself. In response to a letter from Church officials in 1939 commenting on Schneider's

---

[95] Wentorf, *Paul Schneider*, p. 81.

[96] John Owen, *The True Nature of a Gospel Church and Its Government* (Works of John Owen (Vol. XVI), ed. William H. Goold (Edinburgh, UK: Banner of Truth Trust, 2009), p. 11.

[97] Wentorf, *Paul Schneider*, pp. 236, 296.

[98] Ibid., pp. 325-328 (for the full report).

death in confinement and respectfully asking the authorities to "ensure that constantly increasing actions taken against Protestant pastors and church members are stopped," Himmler referred to some details of the case. He described the attempt at discipline as "far exceeding the sphere of the church and amounting to the complete boycott of a national comrade," and closed with the words "I do not have to take any measures against pastors if they stay within the framework of current laws."[99] This by the way was concerning the pastor of a small rural community.

Given that so many church members cared little or nothing about the commandments of Christ and had no business in the church at all, the church elections were not surprisingly a victory for the Germanic Christians. These were eager to cooperate with Hitler in every way, and were perfectly willing to make the churches merely an arm of the state. Reich Bishop Mueller used his authority to forcibly impose Nazi doctrines and sympathetic install church functionaries, attempting to rule the church in a dictatorial manner in defiance of established church rules and procedures. Attempts to reorient the churches to fit the new times met with increasing resistance on the part of more traditional Christians who were willing to support Hitler – or at least refrain from opposing him – but still wanted the churches to have some independence. This group developed into the Confessing Church, or *Bekennende Kirche*.

This unwillingness on the part of the churches to cooperate fully was not overt opposition to National Socialism. The vast majority of Protestants gave their allegiance and support to Hitler (whether willingly or out of fear)—hence their attempts to maintain at least some sort of theoretical doctrinal and administrative independence from the state were not seen as a direct threat. Given loyalty to the Fuhrer, administrative squabbles over church organization seemed not worth pursuing. It was also felt that these intensifying conflicts were damaging to Germany's image abroad. For example, in 1934 Reich Bishop Mueller's assistant August Jaeger (backed by the Gestapo) decreed that the Protestant churches of Bavaria were to be arbitrarily placed under his authority. He placed an uncooperative Bishop under house arrest and commanded that all disobedience to government control of the church must cease. This was done in spite of earlier promises from the government that force would not be used.

Jaeger's actions caused such hostility that public demonstrations in which thousands of people participated occurred in Bavaria and also in Wuerttemberg, where another Bishop, Theophil Wurm, had been similarly

---

[99] Ibid., pp. 362 (both quotes) and 297 (rural location). Himmler's letter further stated that Pastor Schneider could possibly have been released if he would have agreed to obey the deportation order forbidding him to speak in his church, but he refused to accept this "and thus had only himself to blame for his continued stay in the camp."

deposed. These very rare mass public demonstrations against government policy generated much unfavorable publicity overseas. This contrasted so dramatically with Nazi propaganda about a Germany unified in its support for the new government that the Nazi Foreign Minister personally informed Reich Bishop Mueller that he would lose Hitler's support if he could not successfully resolve the church problem.[100] Even the Pope expressed his concern over the treatment of the Evangelicals, realizing that the Catholics might get the same treatment. Conway relates that the Archbishop of Canterbury also protested to the German ambassador, and states that because of all of the negative publicity, Hitler was left in no doubt that Jaeger's activities were proving to be a liability, damaging to the Reich's image abroad.[101]

This is dismissed by people as not very important and not very interesting, given the assumed irrelevance of the churches to modern life, but this was the only substantial public opposition to Hitler's policy in the entire Third Reich. Every other important part of society fell without a whimper into the arms of Hitler. This does not mean the churches as a whole heroically opposed Hitler's basic doctrines, they did not. It should mean something, however, that the churches alone had any form of contrary belief significant enough to arouse even this limited and ineffectual opposition to Hitler.

The government sought to minimize the problem by avoiding unnecessary conflicts and forbidding all discussion of church issues in the press. The two deposed Bishops were reinstated, which was hailed as a victory but merely reflected a change of tactics on Hitler's part. He was by no means resolved to leave the churches even the small amount of independence desired by the Confessing Churchmen, but found that a gradual approach would be more effective in breaking down the already feeble resistance of the churches.

As a result, yet another attempt was made to bring a government-imposed unity to the divided churches. This was the establishment of a Ministry of Church Affairs in 1935. The head of this ministry was one Hans Kerrl, Reich and Prussian Minister for Ecclesiastical Affairs. His tasks were to ensure that the Catholics followed the Concordat (that is, were submissive to the government); bring the divided Protestant groups into unity and into conformity with the demands of the state; and to oversee all administrative and legal problems pertaining to the churches.

Kerrl personally believed in "Positive Christianity." He felt that a Christianity purged of its Jewish elements – meaning the Old Testament and the corruptions of Paul, a Jew – was not only compatible with National Socialism, but necessary to it. He believed that God was leading and guiding the German people to greatness through his messenger Adolf Hitler, and hoped that a unified German church in agreement with his doctrines and loyal to the

---

[100] Conway, *The Nazi Persecution of the Churches*, p. 100.
[101] Ibid.

government would be an important aspect of the Third Reich. Once again, people who are tempted to scorn Christianity and religion in general for this sort of thing would do well to read more about the Soviet Union, or about Western blindness concerning Stalin's real nature. They might also consider much more important figures in the Nazi hierarchy who did not share Kerrl's views. He was a comparatively minor official.

Trying to start out on a positive note, Kerrl amnestied pastors who had been convicted or in some way disciplined for opposition to administrative measures attempting to subjugate the churches. He also established some commissions to try and straighten out the by then extremely confused legal situation in the Protestant churches, but he was trying to do the impossible and ran into trouble from the outset. High-ranking Nazis such as Rosenberg, Himmler, and Bormann opposed Kerrl's efforts. They felt that the desired end was not the unification of the church but its replacement.

Christians who had not gone completely over to German or Positive Christianity were not receptive to Kerrl's plans or ideas either. Members of the Confessing Church refused to accept Kerrl's program. Their leader, Martin Niemoller, eventually became too outspoken and was arrested. One Bishop, Otto Dibelius, wrote an open letter to Kerrl stating that, in Conway's words, Christianity "was based on the historical personality of Jesus Christ, the crucified and resurrected. It was not subject to new revelations or interpretations according to political expediency. Any attempt to make it so constituted an invasion of the church's autonomy by the state."[102]

Hanging Nazi flags in sanctuaries, giving the Hitler salute, singing Nazi songs along with hymns, never publicly contradicting the basic tenets of Naziism, and repeatedly expressing loyalty to the Fuhrer were not enough. What was required was total obedience to the government, and even safely theoretical theological disagreement was viewed as a threat. Some Christians even went so far as to contest the Nazi plan of forbidding non-Aryans (meaning Jews) from serving as pastors. Saying nothing while Jews were taken away, even supporting the removal of Jews from German life were also not enough – the idea that a Jew who converted to Christianity could serve as a pastor in a church, as if faith and religious belief were more important than race, was a direct contradiction of Nazi doctrines.

Kerrl had told Hitler that he could bring the churches into line within two years, yet troublesome dissension continued with no end in sight. This dissension was in no sense a threat to the government, but still there remained a disquieting lack of the total unanimity demanded by the Fuhrer. There was so much opposition to Kerrl's attempts to force the churches into line (both administratively and doctrinally) that Kerrl eventually abandoned persuasion and resorted to force. In 1937 Bishop Dibelius was put on trial for his open

---

[102] Ibid., p. 208.

letter—it violated a law against "conspiracy." Obviously, anyone who criticized the government was conspiring against it.

More repression followed. A church council meeting in Berlin was broken up by the Gestapo and some of the members were arrested. Other dissenting church leaders were also arrested, including Pastor Niemoller – the most visible opponent of total state domination of the church (one who learned to regret his earlier blind and foolish enthusiasm for Hitler, and spent years in captivity). Hundreds of pastors were arrested. Other repressive measures included: forbidding certain pastors to preach; expulsion of pastors from their parishes; cancellation of salaries (the Lutheran Church was a state church); banning of private seminaries; seizing an Evangelical publishing house; and destroying a large church in Berlin on the pretext of urban renewal.

Not only did Kerrl fail to bring about the desired harmony of the churches; he also was unable to keep all handling of church affairs in his control. Attacks on the churches from Himmler and others who were vastly more influential than he was, and much closer to the Fuhrer, continued. In fact, Kerrl's position was hopeless. He could not restrain the radical anti-church elements of the party, nor could he reduce the Confessing Church to docile and unthinking obedience. It became evident that his Ministry was failing, and Kerrl's influence quickly waned. In the end, he was not even able to get a personal audience with the Fuhrer, and he died in 1941 without having achieved his objective of a genuinely German church.

In spite of Kerrl's inability to reduce the churches to complete compliance, the individuals who spoke out and directly and publicly contradicted Naziism were rare. The Confessing Church tried to avoid becoming merely a bureaucratic extension of the state, and wanted to affirm historic doctrines without adopting the views of the Germanic Christians, but its leaders were careful not to cross the government's red lines. For example, in 1933, a few weeks after the founding of the Pastors' Emergency League that later was to coalesce into the Confessing Church, its representatives (including Pastor Martin Niemoller) sent Hitler a telegram congratulating him for the "manly deed" of withdrawing from the League of Nations, and pledging "faithful allegiance" to their Fuhrer.[103] Even the well-known Barmen Declaration, which sought to assert the churches' theological independence from the state, was a safely abstract document that did not confront Hitler directly.

If John the Baptist had merely written an intellectual and theological document about the nature of marriage, he would never have gotten in trouble with Herod. It was saying "It is unlawful for you to have your brother's wife" that cost him his life. If Luther had written a theological treatise on salvation but never objected to the selling of indulgences, there would have been no Reformation. The Barmen Declaration asserted in theory that all of our

---

[103] Wentorf, *Paul Schneider,* pp. 79-80.

allegiance was owed to Christ, but in allowing this to co-exist with loyalty to the Reich and obedience to Hitler, and in keeping silent in the face of Hitler's false teachings about the meaning of life and the nature of God and of Christ, the authors of that theoretical statement nullified their fine but useless theology, in my view.

Nevertheless, it should be recognized that even a tamely theoretical statement like the Barmen Declaration contained the seeds of future conflict with the state, and denied the subordination of the church to the state. For this reason the government confiscated copies of it where possible, and possession of it could lead to complications, even arrest. It did not develop into a major confrontation with Naziism, however, and the Confessing Church never openly challenged the legitimacy of the Nazi government.

Wentorf writes that "the Confessing Church collapsed in the mid-1930s," and any pastors who wanted to stand against Naziism were left to do so on their own.[104] This is hardly surprising, since many of its adherents, including Karl Barth, the principal author of the Barmen Declaration, were "neo-orthodox" in their theology, "neo-orthodox" meaning "not orthodox." Neo-orthodoxy is in fact a branch of liberalism that denies the historical truth of scripture, but conceals this denial behind a fog of theological rhetoric that sounds religious but is often intentionally ambiguous. Most of the Confessing Churchmen would I fear have been satisfied if Hitler had just left them alone in their churches to play at theology while the world burned around them and lost people were deceived into an eternity of separation from God by the lies of National Socialism – lies that they never confronted.

This was not a matter of politics, of saving Germany or reforming the government. It was a matter of evangelism, of representing Christian teaching for the eternal life of those who chose to believe. This necessitates opposition to false ideas that lead men astray. It is spiritual, not political, warfare. It involves teaching biblical truths, not violence, not fighting, revenge, or undercover assassination plots. It would mean saying, for example, that the Germans were not the master race, and that where we spend eternity is more important to us as individuals than how great or powerful our country is. It would mean saying publicly that there would be a resurrection from the dead and a day of judgment, and that liars, thieves, drunkards, murderers, and other sorts of evildoers would be sent to a place of eternal punishment unless they found forgiveness in Christ.

But, this message did not appear, and in spite of ongoing problems, it became apparent that the churches were for the most part co-operative, or at least docile. For this reason, church politics were never anything more than a minor headache for Hitler. The second prong of Hitler's campaign, however, that of indoctrinating the nation, was central to his program in a way that

---

[104] Ibid., p. 12.

controlling church bureaucracies were not, and it was pursued with great rigorousness. The government's ideological campaign to indoctrinate the German people with Nazi doctrines continued with unabated intensity throughout the whole of the Third Reich.

The extremely anti-Christian ideology of Alfred Rosenberg, a high-ranking Nazi official, was disseminated freely, while rebuttals were forbidden and critics were silenced (either by jail or by fear of jail). We are commonly informed that Hitler never bothered to read Rosenberg's book, *The Myth of the Twentieth Century*, but he appointed Rosenberg to important positions, and a Catholic university chaplain who criticized Rosenberg's teachings was sentenced to eighteen months in prison.[105] State control of the press meant that the teachings of National Socialism were incessantly broadcast, while church publications and publishing houses were strictly censored and even banned. Any attempt whatever to publicly disagree with Nazi doctrines was deemed "political" and hence an offense against the state. Churches were criticized in the press by high officials, even Goebbels and Goering, but were not allowed to respond.

This campaign was of course not confined to the press. Religious organizations (Catholic or Protestant) that might compete for the allegiance of the people were limited and finally banned. The churches were to be strictly confined to their sanctuaries, and any means of outreach or public service – orphanages, rest homes, youth groups, professional associations – were either banned, seized, or forcibly amalgamated with Nazi organizations. Group outings, sports events, parades, political parties, publications, kindergartens, schools, public lectures, were all restricted or forbidden. Christians were supposed to do nothing more than sit in their church buildings, sing "A Mighty Fortress is Our God," and discuss theology (Christ's lordship over the whole of a Christian's life, for example) or maybe collect contributions for charity.

A vital sector of this campaign was of course the schools. Although Hitler had promised to support and protect the churches, a systematic campaign was begun to eliminate religious education. Hitler repeatedly stressed the importance of educating the youth in the spirit of National Socialism, and Christian education was an obstacle to this goal. It was felt that children needed instruction in moral values – the values of Aryan supremacy, antisemitism, German domination, and loyalty to the Fuhrer. In a similar fashion, modern American schools also seek to teach children new concepts of morality – concepts acceptable to the state, but often completely contrary to biblical Christianity.

The process by which church influence on education was eliminated, not overnight but slowly and by degrees, could be described at great length. Church schools were harassed and restricted, if not seized outright. Parents

---

[105] Conway, *Nazi Persecution of the Churches*, p. 112.

were subjected to extreme pressures, including the threat of loss of employment, if they continued to send their children to religious schools. Uncooperative people were considered enemies or potential enemies of the state. Any attempt by the churches to defend their schools was forbidden. Rigged elections in which 97% of the voters called for public schools rather than religious ones were used to justify the authorities' arbitrary measures. Clerics who called for the continuance of church schools were denounced for their "political" interference.

So effective was this campaign that all church schools had been completely abolished by 1939. Religious schools were either closed or converted to public schools. Public schools were of course quickly and easily brought into harmony with National Socialist practices. Religious classes in those schools were either canceled or made to conform to National Socialism. Jesus was presented as a Nordic fighter against Jewry; Christmas was transformed to a secular holiday; students were discouraged from saying grace. Religious pictures of Christ or saints were removed, openly Christian teachers who did not conform to Nazi doctrines were fired, and students were taught about Adolf Hitler during the religious period.

The Nazification of the educational system was not confined to the lower levels. Opponents of Naziism were dismissed from institutions of higher learning and theological schools were subjected to government pressures of various sorts. Some were closed, others had their staffs reduced, and vacancies were left unfilled. Nazis or people sympathetic to Naziism were appointed to key positions, and excessive criticisms of the regime were not tolerated.

Great attention was paid to winning the youth. Membership in the Hitler Youth was made a job requirement for high school graduates. Hitler Youth were taught that Christianity, Judaism, and Masonry were enemies of Germany, and Hitler Youth activities were timed to coincide with church activities so as to keep young people away from the churches. Prayers were forbidden at school assemblies – no chance was missed to remove Christianity from public life.

From the actions of the Nazi government, from official documents, from public statements in the press by Nazi officials, the Nazi vision for the future of the churches was plain: they should be isolated from the public arena and totally subordinated to the state. They should remain silent while their rights, properties, and organizations were systematically limited or eliminated – until such time as their non-Germanic and Semitic Jewish-inspired religion would die out and be replaced by a new idea, a new philosophy of race and nation.

Not content with organizational and educational efforts designed to bring about the slow death of the church, Hitler also applied steady and relentless pressure of a more physical sort, as he had advocated earlier in *Mein Kampf*. Anyone who drew the attention of the government as hostile or even potentially hostile was liable to physical assault, arrest, a term in a concentration camp (the horrors of which were widely known or at least rumored), even murder. Church property (including orphanages, hospitals, monasteries and schools) could be seized on any pretext.

In occupied Poland the policy of the government toward the churches was one of open persecution. Thousands of priests were sent to concentration camps or executed for any reason, even trivial ones. They were assigned to the harshest and most degrading work in the camps, along with the Jews. Other Catholics were sent to Germany as forced laborers, and many church buildings were closed or destroyed. The much smaller Protestant Church in Poland also received harsh treatment. Karol Kulisz, the director of an Evangelical charity organization died in Buchenwald. A professor of the University of Warsaw's Evangelical Faculty of Theology, Edmund Bursche, died in Mauthausen. ". . . virtually the whole of the Evangelical clergy in the Teschen (Cieszyn) area of Silesia were consigned to the concentration camps of Mauthausen, Buchenwald, Dachau and Oranienburg, their places being taken by Germans who conducted their services in German only."[106]

Some comments from Conway on this are so significant as to merit quoting more fully:

> In the Warthegau, the model Nazi region that had been carved out of conquered Polish territory, the apotheosis of Nazi Church policy can be seen. The draconian measures introduced there can leave little doubt of what would have happened elsewhere had Hitler been able to carry out his frequently repeated threat 'after the war, to deal decisively with the churches.'[107]

In Germany itself (both before and during the war), such a policy of outright destruction was not adopted. Many Catholics and Protestants were serving in Hitler's armies, some of them in the belief that they were fighting to defend their country from Bolshevism. If their priests, pastors, or relatives back home were being thrown into jail, the devotion of even nominal Christians to the Fuhrer would have been diminished, and the internal situation in Germany would have been greatly complicated. Yet, while Hitler was constrained to be cautious, it is necessary to stress again the climate of fear, the constant pressure from knowing that the churches were spied on, watched, observed. Any criticism of the government or even disagreement with fundamental Nazi doctrines was considered dangerous. Any offense, real or imagined, could lead to arrest, with no legal recourse.

The danger of being arrested was very real. Conway relates that in May of 1935, the President of the Confessing Church Synod asked member churches to pray for sixteen pastors who had been sent to concentration camps or to

---

[106] Ibid., pp. 296-297.

[107] Ibid., p. 292.

prison, or had been expelled from their parishes.[108] With a diligent desire for information unknown to some who enjoy babbling witlessly about Hitler's imagined Christianity, Conway quotes in this context a bulletin from the Bavarian Political Police. Taken from government archives, it states that action would not be taken against churches holding such intercessory services. "However the personal details of such priests who conduct these services are to be sent in. Any attempt to publicize the prayers of intercession in the press, in leaflets or in parish magazines, is to be prevented . . . ."[109]

People look at photographs of church dignitaries shaking hands with Hitler or giving the Hitler salute and say "Aha!" There are no photographs of those sixteen pastors being taken away from their families, or doing heavy labor in a concentration camp. There isn't a photo of a pastor being dragged out of bed in the middle of the night and beaten by a gang of thugs. Photographs of Paul Schneider, the previously mentioned pastor who died in Buchenwald after disobeying an order from the Gestapo to leave his parish, are not prominently displayed by enemies of Christianity.

Schneider's great sufferings in the camp, including being lashed for refusing to salute a Nazi flag, were reported by fellow prisoners. An official Buchenwald document sent to the camp headquarters and signed by an SS-Oberscharfuhrer stated that Paul Schneider began preaching from his cell window to the inmates lined up for morning roll call. He ignored the SS man's command to stop and had to be taken away from the window by force.[110] The document described this as "unbelievable behavior," and it certainly must have been unique in the entire history of the Third Reich.

Walter Poller was a political prisoner in Buchenwald. He ended up working in the medical records department and after the war wrote a book about his experiences, *The Medical Recorder of Buchenwald* (*Der Arztschreiber von Buchenwald*).[111] He stated that after Schneider preached from his solitary confinement cell to prisoners lined up for roll call "he was brought to the central square where roll call was taken. There he was whipped until the blood oozed through his clothes. And then he was dragged back to the solitary confinement building half-conscious."[112] He also described Schneider shortly before his murder by lethal injection in 1939: "The body was nothing but skin and bones, the arms were unshapely and swollen, on the wrists were bluish-red, green and bloody cuts. And the legs – they were no longer human legs but elephant legs . . . How was it possible that this man was still living?" Then the

---

[108] Ibid., p. 113.

[109] Ibid., p. 422.

[110] Wentorf, *Paul Schneider*, p. 307.

[111] The following description of Schneider's last days is taken from a lengthy excerpt from Poller's book, in Wentorf, *Paul Schneider*, pp. 340-346.

[112] Ibid., p. 341.

camp physician, one Dr. Ding, said to him, "Why didn't you let us know that you were sick, Schneider?"

Schneider was given decent treatment for eight to ten days, during which time he "recovered surprisingly fast." The doctor said to him, "'Stop this nonsense, Schneider. You can see that you are treated properly when you fit into camp discipline.' Paul Schneider does not answer, he only smiles, but his eyes are sparkling." The doctor then offered to have Schneider released from solitary confinement, where (as he was able to relate to some orderlies during his treatment), he had been chained "for two weeks, day and night, without interruption, as if he had been nailed to a cross." This would explain the swollen legs. An SS-guard named Sommer, whom Schneider had called "a murderer and a torturer" to his face, had abused him the whole time.

Not long afterward, he was murdered by injection. Poller did not directly witness it, but he saw the doctor with the injection needle and expected from past experience that Schneider was going to be killed. In the report on Schneider's death, the doctor subsequently dictated "a completely false medical history he simply made up." Possibly he was killed because this last attempt to reform him failed, or else because his death had been decided on earlier and the treatment was only intended to improve his appearance, since the wife was allowed to view the body (the face and hands only were visible, the rest being covered by a blanket) and take it away in a casket for a full funeral ceremony.

Another of Schneider's fellow-prisoners, Alfred Leikam, wrote: "In my opinion he is the only one in Germany who so consciously took upon himself the cross of Christ to the point of death, overcoming all human fear and who was so deeply influenced by this word of faith: 'Our faith is the victory that has overcome the world.'"[113] While of course there were others in Germany whom Leikam had no knowledge of, we can I believe look on Paul Schneider as an example of the proper biblical response to governmental tyranny over the church. But we also recognize him as an unprofitable servant, a sinful human being, who with God's help only did that which it was his duty to do – and also as a man who now has no need of human praise or honor.

Shirer's *Berlin Diary* has an entry dated June 15, 1937, that speaks volumes: "Five more Protestant pastors arrested yesterday, including Jacobi from the big *Gedaechtniskirche*. Hardly keep up with the church war anymore since they arrested my informant, a young pastor; have no wish to endanger the life of another one."[114] It is true that the great majority of pastors and priests never went to prison or a concentration camp. Some of them sincerely supported National Socialism, or just kept their anti-Nazi feelings to

---

[113] Ibid., p. 363.

[114] William L. Shirer, *Berlin Diary* (New York: Alfred A. Knopf, 1941), p. 76.

themselves. The few that did speak out, and did suffer, however, are given far too little attention.

The situation of the churches deteriorated as the war progressed. Blatant nationwide persecution was avoided, but every pretext was used to continue harassment and limitation of the churches. Monasteries, hospitals, convents, and other institutions – so many of them were seized that one church official, Cardinal Bertram, wrote of "a systematic campaign" of persecution.[115] The Vatican sent an official protest to the German Embassy in January 1942 stating that the great numbers of seizures or closings of Catholic institutions (including convents, monasteries, and abbeys) revealed "a deliberate intention of rendering impossible the very existence of the Orders and Congregations in Germany."[116] Prior to this the papal Nuncio had sent frequent protests – all of them to no avail.

There was not only the confiscation of buildings. There was a consistent policy of repression in every area of life. It is difficult for us to imagine a situation in which failure to obey the government in even the slightest matter could lead to loss of a job, denial of promotion, beating, or arrest. In considering the responses of the Christians it is necessary to remember the ever-present reality of prisons and concentration camps. Too often people with no real feeling for the situation say or imply that the entire nation of Germans (all of them devout, Bible-believing Christians who began their day with an hour of prayer, naturally) were joyfully following Hitler. Others mention Hitler's policy of repression as an obvious fact, but don't seem to grasp the implications or sense the human dimension.

Murder was also an option. During the Blood Purge of 1934, not only SA leaders but other opponents, real or imagined, were gunned down. Fritz Gerlach, editor of a Catholic weekly critical of the Nazis; Adalbert Probst, Director of the Catholic Youth Sports Association; and Erich Klausner, General Secretary of Catholic Action (that attempted to coordinate the activities of Catholic organizations) were all murdered. The Catholic Bishop of Berlin, Bishop Bares, wrote to Hitler personally about Klausner's death. Rejecting the official statement that Klausner had committed suicide, Bishop Bares sought some explanation, but was careful to stress that his death was surely unintended, and not the result of deliberate policy.[117]

In his book *Metapolitics*, Peter Viereck quotes the following Nazi propaganda song, stating that students at the University of Munich were forced to write down and learn the song at compulsory lectures. He explains that the "black band of rascals" refers to Catholic priests:

> The old Jewish shame is at last swept away;

---

[115] Conway, *The Nazi Persecution of the Churches*, p. 258.

[116] Ibid., p. 257.

[117] Ibid., p. 94.

The black band of rascals rages on.
German men, German women, beat the black band to a jelly.
Hang them on the gallows. . . . Ravens have been waiting.

Plunge the knives into the parson's body.
We'll be ready for any massacre.
Hoist the Hohenzollerns high on the lamp-post!
Hurl the hand-grenades into the churches.[118]

In the same vein, a Nazi propaganda poster from the 1932 Reichstag election shows a black Catholic priest bound to a red Marxist, both of them being smashed by the power of National Socialism.[119] The persecution that German Christians experienced was the direct result of the incompatibility between Christianity and Naziism. Some can imagine that hostile acts were carried out against the wishes or without the knowledge of a Fuhrer who admired the churches and respected them, but how much their imaginations have to do with historical realities is another question. Hitler stated that "the pious Catholic Christian Center [Party] always had the Jewish-atheist Marxists as beloved allies."[120]

Both in words and in deeds, Hitler was hostile to Christianity. It not only directly contradicted his own view of life as struggle – it also had infested Germany (and Europe) with Jewish values. These "Jewish" values included pacifism, democracy, and liberalism which had emerged out of a Christian background. That he should seek to eliminate this alien world view was inevitable, but practical constraints required him to move slowly. Goebbels referred to the need for caution in a diary entry of 1942:

> For the present, he [Hitler] does not want to become very active in the church question. He would like to save that up for the end of the war . . . [Goering] agrees with me completely that it won't do to get started now, in wartime, on so difficult and far-reaching a problem. The Fuehrer, too, expressed that viewpoint to him as he has often expressed it to me.[121]

---

[118] Peter Viereck, *Meta-politics: The Roots of the Nazi Mind* (New York: Capricorn Books, 1965), p. 259. Lutheran ministers also wore black robes.

[119] "Pre-1933 Nazi Posters, *German Propaganda Archive*, http://www.bytwerk.com/gpa/posters1.htm (poster # 39) accessed May 2014.

[120] Adolf Hitler, *Hitler's Second Book: The Unpublished Sequel to Mein Kampf*, trans. Krista Smith (New York: Enigma Books, 2006), p. 60.

[121] Joseph Goebbels, *The Goebbels Diaries 1942-1943*, trans. Louis P. Lochner (Westport, CT: Greenwood Press, 1948), p. 142.

That Hitler "often" spoke of dealing with the church after the war is significant. Fortunately, the Christians did not need to find out what that would have involved. Nazi Plans for a future national church are indicated by a program consisting of thirty points for the National Reich Church. These points included: the replacing of all crosses with swastikas; copies of *Mein Kampf* on the altars instead of Bibles; no more Bibles to be published or distributed in Germany; the extermination of "the strange and foreign Christian faiths imported into Germany" in 800 A.D.; the replacement of pastors and priests by national orators.[122] It is also significant that Section IV B of the Gestapo was divided into four sections: B. 1 dealt with Catholics; B. 2 with Protestants; B. 3 with Freemasons: and B. 4 with Jews. IV B. 4 was headed by Adolf Eichmann.

And what was the Christian response? We have already referred to a few individuals. We might also remember hundreds of Lutheran pastors who were arrested in 1935 for reading a Confessing Church statement denying Nazi racial ideology.[123] This statement was a direct contradiction of the Nazi world view as expressed by Alfred Rosenberg. It said that the Nazis violated the first of the Ten Commandments by putting blood, race, and the nation in the place of God, and rejected Rosenberg's ideology as the ideology of the anti-Christ (it was possible to criticize Rosenberg's book, but not Hitler's). The government banned the statement, but hundreds of pastors ignored the ban. There were no such protests by hundreds of people in any other area of German life, only in the churches. The very idea of such a protest from people who believed they were in essence only advanced animals is ridiculous.

In that same year, Confessing Churchmen who wanted to speak out yet still remain loyal wrote a personal protest to Hitler (approaching him through his Presidential Secretary). They asked if hostile actions against the churches by the state were the result of official policy, contrary to Hitler's earlier promises to support the churches and maintain their status and privileges. The Church leaders also rejected the Nazi concept of "Positive Christianity" (Christianity with all teachings contrary to Naziism removed) and protested against police measures taken against the churches. The state's policy of closing church schools and limiting church activities in the fields of press and radio was criticized, and antisemitism was rejected. Nazi ideology was specifically described as being "against the Christian commandment to love one's neighbor."[124]

The churchmen went on to condemn the concentration camps and the lawlessness of the Gestapo, as well as the elevation of the nation to the place of God. More astonishingly, they even objected to the glorification of Hitler,

---

[122] Shirer, *Rise and Fall*, p. 240.

[123] Conway, The Nazi Persecution of the Churches, p. 122.

[124] Ibid., p. 162.

who was allowing himself to be presented and adulated as much more than a merely human political leader. This appears at first glance to have been a very courageous act, but Conway suggests that the memorandum was an expression not of courage but of naivety. It appears that the church leaders believed that calling Hitler's attention to these abuses would in some way help the situation. Subsequent developments support this view, although it is also possible that this was on the part of some a statement for conscience' sake from which no real results were expected.

Sending the memorandum to Hitler privately instead of publicly disseminating it allowed the churchmen to avoid a head-on confrontation with the government. It also allowed Hitler to ignore the message, which he did. A copy was sent to Switzerland, however, where it was published, and discussed in the foreign press. This led to accusations of "treachery" and "conspiracy" against the Confessing Church leaders. Instead of standing behind the statement and distributing copies to their congregations, which would have created a political firestorm, the churchmen backed down. Wanting (sincerely or fearfully) to be loyal supporters of the state yet unable to deny the document, they sought a way out by issuing a drastically diluted version.[125]

The revised version omitted objections to the concentration camps, to antisemitism, and to the excessive elevation of Hitler and the nation. Instead, it confined itself to protesting attacks on the churches, and explaining that Rosenberg's ideology (not Hitler's) was incompatible with Christian teaching.[126] Even this was too daring for some of the bishops, however – they thought such an approach would damage church-state relations. A few months later this same group of bishops offered a much more helpful statement, expressing their total support for the Fuhrer in his struggle against Bolshevism.

The government's reaction was restrained. A Dr. Weissler who was responsible for publishing the first full version of the memorandum in Switzerland was arrested and sent to Sachsenhausen. He died there within a few months.[127] No direct action was taken against the churches, however. Conway suggests that this was possibly due to a desire to avoid negative publicity during the Olympic Games – the image of national unity would have been tarnished. Another possibility is that the capitulation of the churchmen meant that this was not a direct threat to Hitler's power and so required no significant response.

On July 16, 1943, Lutheran Bishop Wurm wrote a letter to Hitler, stating that the "persecution and extermination" of non-Aryans were crimes that "stand in sharpest contradiction to the law of God and violate the foundation of all Western thought and life – the elemental God-given right to human

---

[125] Ibid., p. 164.
[126] Ibid.
[127] Ibid.

existence and human dignity."[128] Possibly (or probably) Hitler never received the letter. It could have been received by a sympathetic official and covered up – but it could also have easily led to complications and the bishop took some risk in writing it. The Bishop also wrote to the Church Ministry (again in 1943) stating:

> The measures taken against the Jews . . . have for a long time been depressing many circles in our nation, particularly the Christian ones . . . the question automatically arises whether our nation has not made itself guilty of bereaving men of their homes, their occupations and their lives without the sentence of a civil or military court.[129]

This quote states that the Bishop was speaking for a larger number of people. It also shows that someone might acquiesce in the Nuremberg laws yet still recoil at extermination. The same statement of Bishop Wurm's to the Church Ministry declared that, "in view of a possible political exploitation of a public protest by the enemy countries, the Christian Churches have exercised great restraint in this respect." Even in his protest he sought to reassure the government of the church's loyalty – but the bishop went on to state that Christians "cannot, however, possibly be silent when lately even Jews living in mixed marriage with Christian Germans, some even being themselves members of Christian Churches, have been torn from their homes and occupations to be transported to the East."[130]

Bishop Wurm wrote other letters to government officials. These were circulated secretly among the churches, and expressed the sentiments of those who still saw Jews as human beings. Ultimately, correspondence between Bishop Wurm and the Reich Chancellery was officially banned. Hans Lammers, the chief of the Reich Chancellery, forbade him to write further. In the words of Diephouse's study, "Wurm himself interpreted his silencing as a pre-emptive move by Lammers and other moderates in the Fuhrer's circle designed to protect him from possible detention and trial, sanctions that Hitler may indeed have considered and elected to defer out of concern for their effect on wartime morale."[131]

---

[128] David J. Diephouse, "Antisemitism as Moral Discourse: Theophil Wurm and Protestant Opposition to the Holocaust," paper presented to the 30th Annual Scholar's Conference on the Holocaust and the Churches, Philadelphia, March 2000, p. 6 [page numbers are from document sent by Prof. Diephouse as an e-mail attachment]. Diephouse cites the *Landeskirchliches Archiv Stuttgart* and also *Landesbischof Wurm*, ed. Gerhard Schaefer.

[129] Conway, *The Nazi Persecution of the Churches*, pp. 264-265.

[130] Ibid., p. 265 (both quotes).

[131] Diephouse, "Antisemitism as Moral Discourse," p. 6.

Friedländer suggests that Wurm was silenced too easily.[132] This is a difficult criticism to evaluate. If I rebuke a man for his wrongdoing and he responds with hostility, even threatening my life, am I obligated to keep chasing after him? Certainly, the churches should have said far more than they did, yet I think Wurm deserves some credit for possibly risking his life. Wurm's early support for Hitler, as well as negative statements made about Jews even after the war, greatly detract from his stature. Nevertheless, his willingness to protest government policies shows the power of biblical truth to help us transcend (however imperfectly) our environment and our biases.

It is unfortunate that Wurm was such a rare exception, in no sense representative of German Christians as a whole. It is also worth pointing out that he respectfully framed his protests so as to avoid crossing a certain line. If, for example, he had openly proclaimed that National Socialism was a false philosophy, that the Germans were not the master race and that Hitler was in danger of eternal punishment for his crimes, he would surely have been swiftly silenced without regard for possible political fallout.

The Catholic leaders also made some effort to express themselves. In 1941, the Catholic bishops protested against the violation done to the sanctity of marriage by the deportation of Jews married to Catholics, but the Nazis could easily afford to ignore such protests. Like those of Bishop Wurm, they had no significant impact. More instances could be given to show that the German people were not solidly united behind Hitler in his fiendish plans, but only one more will be mentioned.

In 1943 the Prussian Synod of the Confessing Church sent a pastoral letter to the Confessing Churches. Dealing with the biblical commandment, "Thou shalt not kill," it stated that the state's power to take life was limited to criminals or to war-time enemies. The letter further stated that Nazi terms such as "eradication," "liquidation," and "unfit to live," were not part of God's law. Finally, it asserted that "The murdering of men solely because they are members of a foreign race, or because they are old, or mentally ill, or the relatives of a criminal, cannot be considered as carrying out the authority entrusted to the state by God."[133]

The government's response is not recorded. No doubt the Nazi government had long since learned that occasional objections by the churches were insignificant, led to no further action, and did not demand immediate response – though if the doctrines had become widespread enough to be perceived as a threat, the government would not have tolerated such heresies. The government sought to avoid creating martyrs, but enough people were arrested at times to serve as examples, and there was always danger in any kind of deviation from the required ideological norm.

---

[132] Friedländer, *The Years of Extermination*, p. 517.

[133] Conway, *The Nazi Persecution of the Churches*, pp. 266-267.

In Nazi occupied Europe, where there was more possibility of action, there were more examples of Christians whose obedience to the teachings of Christ led not to persecution but to the reverse. One example is that of Pastor Andre Trocme. He and his wife Magda, and others in the small French village of Le Chambon, helped to save many Jews, providing them with food, lodging, and false documents. They felt it was their Christian duty to help anyone, Jewish or not. A moving account of this spiritual heroism is found in Philip Hallie's book *Lest Innocent Blood Be Shed*.[134]

Christian groups such as the YMCA, the American Friends Service Committee, and others tried to help the Jews. I have not yet found reference to groups of Darwinists in America or England saying that their philosophy compelled them to be concerned about suffering and starving people in other parts of the world. This is not to say that only Christians took risks to help others. There were Christians who did nothing, and non-Christians who helped at great risk to themselves – but the non-Christians followed a basic human impulse that was inarticulate, without foundation. The Christians were acting according to a fixed moral principle, rooted in God and independent of human circumstances.

There are other instances. Stephen of Sofia, the Greek Orthodox Metropolitan of Bulgaria, publicly declared it was wrong to torture and persecute Jews, and Boris III, king of Bulgaria, had popular support in his resistance to German demands that the Jews be deported. The Dutch, Norwegians, and Danes also did not find that Christian teaching led them to support Naziism's bizarre racial policies. I believe there were also Germans who would have done the same, had it been possible.

In his study of life in the *Third Reich Germany: Jekyll and Hyde*, Sebastian Haffner (himself a German and a refugee from Hitler) stated that for a time in the 1930s there was a significant increase in attendance in the Confessing (or Confessional) Church. This was due to people who were not particularly religious, but were encouraged by that church's attempts to maintain some independence from the government. They started going to church, Haffner said, "because they scented possibilities of struggle and resistance against the Nazis, and for no other reason." Unfortunately for them, they were disappointed. "The leaders of the Confessional Church wanted no political struggle."[135]

There is that well-known saying of Christ's, that we should render to Caesar the things due to Caesar, and to God the things due to God. That the kingdom

---

[134] Philip Hallie, *Lest Innocent Blood Be Shed: The Story of the Village of Le Chambon and How Goodness Happened There* (New York: Harper and Row, 1979). See also Rubenstein and Roth, *Approaches to Auschwitz*, pp. 284-286.

[135] Sebastian Haffner, *Germany – Jekyll and Hyde: A Contemporary Account of Nazi Germany*, trans. Wilfrid David (London: Abacus, 2009), p. 160 (both quotes).

of God in Christ is radically different from political power and earthly kingdoms has long been a basic teaching of Christianity. For this reason, the pastors in the Third Reich had no spiritual obligation as church leaders to comment on Hitler's remilitarization of the Rhineland, or his disarmament negotiations with the British (although they should have been free to do so if they chose).

They did have an obligation, however, to offer the Christian message about the continued existence of the soul after death, and the Day of Judgment at which our eternal destines will be decided. They did have a spiritual obligation to oppose the false teachings of Hitler about the importance of race, the meaning of life, the nature of Jews and Judaism, and the love of earthly power, conquest, and glory. They had the obligation to state that basic concepts of right and wrong do not originate with any human leader, but are grounded in the nature and character of God as revealed to us in Scripture. This, with rare exceptions they failed to do – because of ordinary human failings, because of cowardice, or because they did not even believe in the Bible themselves and so had nothing to say.

As to the plot to assassinate Hitler, that does not belong (as I see it) in a chapter about Christians in the Third Reich, not having been a specifically Christian activity. Major-General Henning von Tresckow, one of the leaders of the conspiracy, stated his reasons for wanting to assassinate Hitler: "It's not a matter anymore of the practical aim, but of showing the world and history that the German resistance movement at risk of life has dared the decisive stroke. Everything else is a matter of indifference alongside that." He was motivated by pride and by national honor. The poor man was still thinking about Germany's "honor" in 1944! Moreover, Claus Graf von Stauffenberg, the man who actually placed the bomb that nearly killed Hitler, has been quoted as saying "Long live holy Germany" just before he was shot.[136] If he did in fact say this, he had very confused notions of holiness, certainly not biblical ones.

I see no biblical justification for assassination of wicked leaders. Since many innocent people died as the result of Hitler's fury at the failed attempt, the conspirators caused more suffering and death, not less. We need to be careful of trying to take matters into our own hands without really knowing what we are doing. Furthermore, if an attempt to kill Hitler had succeeded before D-Day or Stalingrad, but the regime had survived intact (to be led by Goebbels or Himmler), many of Hitler's military mistakes would have been avoided and it is easy to imagine the war ending not in the spring of 1945, but in the spring of 1946. If the Final Solution had been pursued during that time, a million more people could have died.

Hitler was brought down by the authorities of England, America and Russia as allowed for by Paul in Romans chapter 13, not by undercover conspiracies.

---

[136] Ian Kershaw, *Hitler* (London: Penguin Books, 2008), p. 818, 841 (both quotes).

The responsibilities of individual Christians were to oppose Hitler openly with the truths of the Bible and to disobey all laws and commands contrary to Christ. Almost all of them failed to do this for various reasons. Yet, in spite of the manifest inability of the German churches to wage a genuinely spiritual warfare, and to stand in quiet and confident righteousness against evil, it should be evident, and will be evident to impartial people, that a great gulf separated traditional, orthodox and historic Christianity from Hitler's world view. The failure of the churches was a failure not of Christianity, but of dubious if not openly unbelieving twentieth-century German versions of it.

Afterword

Discussing the Holocaust, Christian author Tony Pearce writes:

> It is significant that such an extreme manifestation of evil in the human heart took place in a century which began with many people putting their trust in the innate goodness of humanity, the perfectibility of human nature and the coming of a Golden Age of peace, prosperity and tolerance through advances in science, education and politics.[1]

Does any informed person care to deny this? It is a simple fact of Western European cultural history that in 1900 multitudes and myriads of optimistic starry-eyed secularists believed that science and education, as established by emancipated human reason, were the guides that would lead us to a happier tomorrow. This, of course, was to be done without the irritating and stifling constraints of outdated religious beliefs.

They were all wrong. Their misty pink fantasies, inspired by vanity, superficiality and conceit, were confronted by the First World War. They managed to hang onto their faith in mankind in spite of all the evidence, but then, a short time later, there was yet a second world conflagration. In this one modern technological advances were harnessed to the service of a murderous ideology. This ideology emerged out of a culture that had widely rejected traditional religion, and relied on humanistic philosophies and science for guidance. None of Hitler's basic ideas can be found in the Bible. All of them can be found in various forms and degrees in the writings of eighteenth- and nineteenth-century French and German thinkers.

These pioneers of the emancipated human intellect did not believe in the Bible but invented instead new ideas of nation, of race, of ethics and especially of human life as the result of an impersonal process explainable in terms of scientific law, or of great philosophical schemes, or in a combination of both philosophy and science. This was replete with rhetoric about "the Divine," "Providence," "the Almighty," and so on, which is very confusing to those whose ignorance of German philosophy leads them to conclude that such terms must necessarily be Christian

What we have in the crimes of the Third Reich is the complete failure and collapse of all of the humanist dreams of building a brave new world by reason alone – and yet many people find this difficult to face. Therefore, they insist on the validity of the humanist project and try to blame the disasters of modern secularism on religion instead. They reason, "It can't possibly be human nature

---

[1] Tony Pearce, *The Messiah Factor* (Chichester, England: New Wine, 2004), p. 26.

that is to blame. It can't be science or human reason that led people astray. Those things are good and rational. But Hitler was bad and irrational. And religion is bad and irrational. Therefore, it is self-evident that Hitler must be linked to religion."

This is the simple-minded logic (with purely subjective and highly dubious definitions of "good" and "bad," "rational" and "irrational") that often lies concealed behind outwardly much more sophisticated attempts at explaining the Holocaust, and it manifests itself in countless little ways. For example, a generally reputable historian claimed that enthusiastic Nazis reminded him of some "holy rollers" he had once seen in America. This sort of comment is deeply gratifying to many. It absolves them of the necessity of having to give their own comfortable and complacent presuppositions a hard look. Whether or not it is accurate, however, is an entirely different question.

I have met Christians of various sorts, including those who (like myself) believe in the literal truths of the Genesis account and of the rest of the Bible, in its entirety; who see Christ as God come to earth in human form; who feel there will be a day of judgment followed by heaven or hell. They believe that they are supposed to follow Christ's commandments, and make sincere if fallible efforts to do so. They believe that if they are sinful, evil, wicked people, liars and murderers, thieves or sexually immoral, they will be sent to hell, since such activities were totally incompatible with the forgiveness for sins and the victory over sins offered by Christ. They have a healthy and constructive fear of God that is totally absent from the sophisticated moderns who think that they can do whatever they please with no future accountability after death.

Some of the Christians I have met even spoke in tongues, or claimed to, and could definitely be considered "holy rollers," yet they were harmless and inoffensive people. They did not believe that traditional concepts of ethics, of right and wrong, were irrelevant. They did not believe people were merely animals without a conscience and without a soul. They did not believe that Jews were subhuman vermin who were undermining American racial purity, and that conventional morality was only a devious Jewish trick.

They did not believe that historical progress was a grand impersonal scheme in which only the great men and nations counted, while the sufferings of insignificant common people were irrelevant. Unlike Kant, Hegel, Nietzsche and Hitler, they did not believe that war was healthy and natural, while too much peace led to decline. They did not believe that America should invade Canada or Mexico for the sake of *Lebensraum*, or that democracy was harmful, that only the elite few should rule over the inferior masses. They did not believe that lying, cruelty and murder were acceptable and normal instruments of state policy, or that life was nothing but an impersonal and ruthless struggle in which victory was all that mattered.

Some of these people have an enthusiasm for religion that seems improper to me – anything can be abused – but to compare them to Nazis is, to my mind, unreasonable, unfair, and ignorant. This sort of lack of comprehension is, however, a sign of the times. The ideal of the autonomous human intellect remains so attractive, while belief in God and in the reality of a spiritual world to come is so repellent, that blame is much more commonly attributed to the latter.

Countless examples of this tendency to link secular modern excesses to religion could be given. One very informative and useful book about Americans trapped in Stalin's Russia does a real service in recording their experiences in the Soviet nightmare. Yet, in spite of its historical value, it contains the now standard modern anti-religious bias. For instance, the author says that Stalin's personality cult "had taken on a fervor and fanaticism seen only in the early stages of mass religious movements."[2] He went on to say in this context that Stalin had created a socialist religion with himself as a god.

I am not sure what early mass religious movements he is referring to. I don't know too much about Hinduism and Buddhism, but I doubt that in their early (or later) stages those religions were in any way comparable to Stalinism and to the Soviet Union. As to Christianity, in its early stages – for approximately three centuries – it was a persecuted movement with no political power whatever. There were no massive pictures of Jesus placed in public locations, with secret police, torture, and slave labor camps for those who disbelieved, or who believed but not precisely in the right way. As to the horrors of the Inquisition, they never even remotely approached the crimes of Stalin, and anyway have nothing to do with Christianity's early stages.

The conquests of early Islam were an extraordinary phenomenon, but of course the people of that era lacked the blessings of modern technology necessary to set up a totalitarian slave state, and there was never anything like the institutionalized, industrialized slavery of Stalin's Russia. As to Judaism, I have not yet seen any informed comparisons between Stalin and Moses, but the Bronze Age Hebrews did not have slave labor camps and secret police to torture anyone who was suspected of insufficiently honoring Moses. Neither were they atheists who believed that matter was the only reality, that they would be able to create a paradise on earth without God.

The Israelite massacres of the Canaanites have been compared to Hitler (though not to Stalin as far as I know), but that is a highly dubious comparison. People who are willing to accept the devastating air raids of World War II accept in principle that there may be some evils so great that extreme violence is necessary to end them. Many today accept millions of dead babies slaughtered in the name of a woman's right to enjoy freedom from natural

---

[2] Tim Tzouliadas, *The Forsaken: An American Tragedy in Stalin's Russia* (New York: Penguin Press, 2008), p. 303.

responsibility, showing that they do not really care about human life at all and are perfectly willing to accept any amount of deaths when it suits them.

But this is a little off-topic. Returning to our subject, Hitler and Stalin both emerged subsequent to the modern rejection of religion. Stalin was an overt materialist and atheist. He denied the existence of God and affirmed that human reason and science were sufficient to build a better society on earth. He saw religion as an obstacle to human progress, and even wrote a book called *Dialectical and Historical Materialism* (1938) which is still available on Amazon. In this book, Stalin states (assuming he actually did write it himself) that the material world is all that there is, and even human consciousness is nothing but a product of matter.

We should not leave Lenin out of this. "As a philosopher, Lenin always insisted on strict materialist monism. Arguing from geology that nature is prior to man, he concluded that man's consciousness is a late evolutionary product of no fundamental significance."[3] Now, Lenin did not create a personality cult behind himself. He did not have images of himself placed everywhere, and was in some ways self-effacing. No one to my limited knowledge has ever said that Lenin was not a *real* atheist – yet he established the foundations of Stalinist tyranny. He was a cruel and heartless mass murderer who used the full apparatus of tyranny – secret police, mass executions, imprisonment and slave labor – in order to enforce his superior and all-knowing will. Similarities between Lenin and Hitler have already been remarked on in this study.

Tzouliadas describes the images of Stalin that were omnipresent in the Soviet Union in the 1930s as having a "sacramental quality, demanding the very greatest reverence from his subjects."[4] Some may understand the term "sacramental" to mean only "sort of religious somehow, coming from a realm of belief without reason," but does that really describe mandatory adulation for Stalin? It certainly has nothing to do with the two Protestant sacraments of baptism and communion. These are not imposed by secret police with threats of slavery, torture, or murder.

Did those pictures of Stalin everywhere really have any kind of a genuinely religious character? True believers in Stalin's life and mission felt they were building a better world without God. No doubt others were motivated by sheer opportunism, and would have been willing to follow anyone who would give them power and special privileges. And how many, the vast majority I believe, were afraid to show any hint of disrespect to an image of Stalin only because they wanted to live, to stay out of a labor camp, to avoid the dungeons of the KGB? How many behaved as was required of them only because any sign of failure to conform could bring them under suspicion, and end in their

---

[3] Jacques Barzun, *Darwin, Marx, Wagner: Critique of a Heritage* (New York: Doubleday Anchor Books, 1958), p. 221.

[4] Ibid., p. 93.

destruction? None of this has anything to do with legitimate faith in God, and no Christian leader, not even the worst of the Popes, has ever set himself as a demigod like the modern totalitarian rebels against God.

But Stalin couldn't have been a *real* atheist. He was irrational, but atheism is rational. And religion is irrational. *Ergo*, Stalin was essentially religious in some way. Of course, one does not need to take a college philosophy course to see that the problem lies with the definition of the word "rational." Many educated Western intellectuals in the 1930s thought it was very rational to try and build a better society by eliminating selfish and greedy capitalism and replacing it with a society controlled by the workers. And, of course, a party needs to represent the workers, and the party needs a leader, and the leader needs power to defend socialism against all of its enemies. And, it is eminently rational to destroy the enemies of the happiness of mankind so that someday we might enjoy a world without injustice, oppression and exploitation. And, if you are going to destroy them anyway, it is rational to get some socially constructive labor out of them before they die.

This is not to deny that there was a very advanced degree of irrationality in Stalin's megalomania. It is to state that "rationality" is a highly subjective term. Hitler, and many others as well, thought it was rational to use force to undo the injustices of the Treaty of Versailles. Jean Paul Sartre was an atheist – in fact, one of the leading atheists in the modern western world – and he supported Stalin's tyranny. His dazzling intellect told him that Stalinist repression was necessary to establish real freedom in the end – hence, in Sartre's words, "Any anti-Communist is a dog."[5] Was Sartre also not *really* an atheist? Other so-called intellectuals also argued that Stalin's camps were necessary to end exploitation, and defended the brutal and inhuman tyrannies of Stalin, Castro, Mao and even of Pol Pot, when the first rumors of the catastrophe there began to come out – because they were intoxicated with the atheist dream of building a better world on earth without God.

One can't help wondering: if life is meaningless and absurd, does this not mean that Sartre's books are also meaningless and absurd? This is a good example of a faulty syllogism that nevertheless yields a valid conclusion. Sartre demonstrates clearly that official and orthodox atheism is perfectly capable of callous insensitivity in the support of tyranny. And who arbitrarily decreed that atheism was "rational" anyway? What if atheism is really not rational after all? What if believing that our world just sort of happened somehow, by accident, with no higher purpose, is in fact profoundly, deeply and darkly irrational? What if it is in fact rational to believe that there is a supreme power behind the universe, and that this power did not just create us and then go off and leave us in cosmic isolation? What if it is rational to

---

[5] Ibid., p. 277 (quoting *The Black Book of Communism: Crimes, Terror, and Repression* by Rigoulet, Courtois, and Malia, Harvard University Press, 1999).

believe, like Socrates, Plato, Seneca and many others, that there is a moral and rational order in the cosmos? What if there really are moral laws built into the very fabric of human existence?

Stalin's crimes and megalomania do not prove he was not really an atheist – they prove that atheists have started out on the wrong path and that if they get their hands on the levers of power there is nothing inherent in their atheism to prevent them from doing all sorts of wrong and destructive things in the misguided belief that it is justified for the future good of humanity. This, however, is humanity only in the abstract. It does not take into account individual suffering, which is and can be of no importance once the divine origin of the soul is lost and people are reduced to mere material objects of no enduring significance. And if the desired end proves to have been nothing but a mirage? That's too bad for the many people who suffered and died for nothing but secularist fantasies.

This is a great evil that sincere religious belief provides a bulwark against. Religion in and of itself is not a panacea, obviously – but the belief that human life is unique and special; that there is a God who is aware of what we do; that we will be judged after this life for what we have done here – these and other related beliefs do add a special quality to life. They place limits and constraints on us which, far from denying us the fullest development of character, provide a framework within which we can truly flourish, while at the same time having a due regard for the rights of others.

Kant wrote about our propensity to evil even as he diligently undermined the most effective safeguards against it. He replaced them with his paper-thin system of ethics, an excessively clever contrivance by which no one has ever really lived and for which no one ever has or ever will die. What a colossal egotist, to imagine he could sit in his study and invent a system of ethics that great numbers of people would seriously follow – as if his thoughts alone could provide a solid basis for existence. Not surprisingly, Kantian ethics proved to be very malleable, and could be used to justify all sorts of things that Kant never imagined in his somnolent complacency. Few Christians publicly protested Hitler's enormities, but no Kantian academic philosophers did.

Hitler understood that Christian values, not empty, pretentious Kantian obfuscations, were an obstacle to his full control of the German people. This is why he persecuted the Christians, not the philosophers. We are constantly told that the churches did not oppose Hitler – and what about university professors of philosophy? Did they oppose Hitler? It was their ideas that contributed to his rise. It was Christianity, not German philosophy, that directly contradicted Hitler – at least when it was sincerely followed, which was unfortunately not very often.

In his study of the Holocaust, Robert Wistrich expressly recognizes that Naziism was "an assault on the ethics of Christianity, as well as the negation of abstract monotheism that Judaism had bequeathed to the West"[6] – though some might say that "Judaism and Christianity had bequeathed to the West." Yet, in spite of saying that Nazi ideology was a direct denial of and assault on Christianity, he still tries to link it to Christianity. Repeating the by now standard theme that "the Holocaust cannot be divorced from the dominant religious tradition of Western civilization"[7] – while at the same time somehow a direct denial of that tradition – he fails to explain that the central Nazi themes of Jews were unheard of in many centuries of Christian cultural predominance, and first emerged subsequent to the modern turning away from Christianity that began with the so-called Enlightenment.

Jews as defilers of racial purity (which the Bible says nothing about); Jews as the source of all social decadence, including democracy, liberalism, and pacifism (which biblical values fostered and facilitated); Jews as plotting to rule the world; Jews as a virus, a bacterium, a disease that needed to be completely eliminated (in direct contradiction to New Testament teachings about God's future plans for the Jews); Christianity as a Jewish plot to undermine stronger and more virile peoples with a fake slave morality – Christianity should not be blamed for those ideas. People who rejected Christianity, people like Kant, Schopenhauer, Fichte, Hegel, Gobineau, Wagner, Haeckel, H. S. Chamberlain and Nietzsche – these and many others should be blamed. But, religion must be put down at every opportunity and autonomous human reason must be protected from searching criticisms that might expose its complete inadequacy.

When Hitler said that Judaism was not even a religion at all, that Jews cared for nothing but material advantage in this world only, he was echoing unChristian themes introduced by Kant, who tried to discuss Judaism without even knowing what he was talking about. When Hitler said that the Old Testament was a historically false book, that conventional ethics were nothing but human inventions with no solid basis in reality and that life was merely a struggle for survival, he was echoing many respected nineteenth-century thinkers who believed that science and philosophy, not the Bible, were the sources of a proper understanding of life.

Yet, Hitler did use religious language. "Heaven . . . Providence . . . the Almighty" – don't such words clearly place Hitler among the ranks of religious believers? Some might try to dismiss Hitler's comments as mere rhetoric, a tactic cynically designed to magnify his influence and inspire devotion among his followers. Others on the other hand believe that Hitler did really see himself as being the agent of some sort of higher power, that he had

---

[6] Robert S. Wistrich, *Hitler and the Holocaust* (New York: Modern Library, 2003), p. 240.

[7] Ibid., p. 239.

a genuine sense of mission and saw himself as the instrument of some sort fate, destiny, providence, one that might even be called "god."

If we take the latter view, as I do, then it seems inarguable that Hitler was indeed motivated on a very deep level by religious concerns – until we consider that vaguely religious language was also used by German philosophers who rejected traditional Christianity. Thinkers who did not accept the Bible as the inspired and authoritative Word of God nevertheless used such words as "Divine . . . Divine Providence . . . the Creator . . . Absolute Spirit . . . Divine governance of the World . . . God" – such rhetoric was very common. In only a few pages of Kant's *Universal Natural History and Theory of the Heavens* we read of an "Infinite Being . . . the great Builder of the universe . . . the Divine Presence . . . the Deity . . . His Infinite Power . . . the revelation of the Divine Omnipotence" – such words were used by German philosophers who were in no sense conventionally Christian.[8]

People like Kant, Hegel, Fichte, Schopenhauer, and numerous lesser thinkers did not accept traditional Christianity. That a higher reality unknowable to reason unaided might nevertheless make itself known to us by revelation was incredible to them, as it is incredible to many today. Nevertheless, they were not materialists, and disdained materialism. They believed that there was a mysterious something above and beyond the world of ordinary experience, but insofar as it was attainable at all, it was attainable by human reason. The most we could know about it was accessible to the human mind unaided. This opened the door to many new ideas of a higher reality, all of which were merely human inventions, and many of which are perfectly compatible with Hitler's concept of "the Almighty."

If Hitler can be linked with this tradition, then we must speak not of Hitler the theologian, but of Hitler the philosopher. The second option will seem incredible to those who assume from the outset that Hitler could not possibly have anything to do with any German philosophers as he was too far beneath them, but several points need to be considered before we confidently jump to hasty and pre-conceived conclusions. The first point is that those philosophers need to be taken off of their pedestals. They had many ideas no one would accept today. They greatly exaggerated the scope and power of speculative philosophy, and often made false and even foolish statements.

Secondly, the ideas of important philosophers were popularized over the decades and moved well beyond the limited confines of academic and

---

[8] Milton K. Munitz (ed.), *Theories of the Universe: From Babylonian Myth to Modern Science* (New York: The Free Press of Glencoe, 1957), pp. 240-246. Kant has been called a "Protestant philosopher," but no serious student of Kant will claim that he believed in the literal truth of the Bible. He was the epitome of "Enlightenment" rationalism and expressly rejected traditional religion.

professional philosophy. Their ideas were deeply influential on the culture at large, if in altered form, and readily available. Antisemitic writers would freely quote the great philosophers' twisted opinions about Jews. Thirdly, while many abstruse and technical aspects of their thought were far removed from Hitler and of no interest or use to him, some of their basic ideas were not at all hard to understand, and very easily adaptable to Hitler's ends. He could sift through summaries, condensations, or even parts of original works, seeking – and finding – not understanding but only confirmation of his own ideas.

Finally, we should not underestimate the importance of philosophers that now seem obscure and remote to us. Their ideas became part of the popular culture and had an influence too many are unmindful of when they try to explain the origins of National Socialism. Kant's idea that Judaism was not even a religion at all, that Jews had no concern at all for higher things but only sought material gain was integral to later secular and racial antisemitism. Hegel's teaching that history was progress, and this progress was spearheaded by great nations and by great men – once the Greeks and the Romans, and now the Germans; that the world historical heroes were too far above the petty and trivial sufferings of ordinary people to worry about them; that the state was the instrument of a higher power and hence demanded the full allegiance of the people – these ideas were sweet music to the ears of Prussian militarists. An academic degree in philosophy was not necessary to grasp them either.

Fichte's writing during the Napoleonic era "contributed to a huge upsurge of nationalist feeling 'and went on being read by Germans throughout the nineteenth-century, and became their bible after 1918.'"[9] His rational and philosophical conviction that the German people because of their purity had a unique bond with the mystical Absolute and this purity needed to be maintained for the German people to fulfill their mission of leading mankind on its upward path, and that the Jews were absolutely incompatible with Germany's call to greatness and had no place in Germany – these earned him a high place in the Nazi pantheon.

Schopenhauer's view that life was essentially a struggle of conflicting wills, and that will was dominant over reason merged seamlessly with the Darwinist Ernst Haeckel's later ideas about life as a pitiless struggle. It was from this amoral and ruthless struggle for survival that the Germans had emerged as the most advanced and highly developed species of humanity. This was also easily harmonized with Nietzsche's (and many others') belief that Christian virtues were false, weak and unhealthy, but vicious brutality and cruelty were healthy, noble, free, warlike. That Christianity was only a Jewish trick; that democracy was bad and the common herd needed to be ruled by their masters, the elite –

---

[9] Peter Watson, *The German Genius: Europe's Third Renaissance, The Second Scientific Revolution, and the Twentieth Century* (New York: Harper Perennial, 2011), p. 196 (quoting Isaiah *Berlin's Freedom and Its Betrayal*).

many of these and yet more ideas can be found in *Mein Kampf* (sometimes in altered form). These were ideas that came not from the gutter, but from some of Germany's finest minds.

Hegel's influence on Marxism is well known; the extent to which he contributed to a proto-fascist mentality in Germany merits more attention. Kant, Schopenhauer and others also had an influence far greater than many realize.[10] The unfortunate importance of Nietzsche today shows that ideas can penetrate very deeply, and be influential on a popular level – even with people who have not deeply studied the philosopher in question. There is a fair amount of philosophy littering the pages of *Mein Kampf*, and the book is by no means as lacking in substance as many think – if by "substance" we mean many false and ugly concepts easily recognized as wrong today, but widespread among certain influential German circles before World War I.

The question of Nietzsche's influence on the Nazi mentality is often debated, as is never done with Kierkegaard, Dostoevsky, or John Stuart Mill. No one has ever said that the Nazis found some agreeable ideas, taken out of context and distorted, in the writings of John Locke. Nietzsche's defenders have their responses and arguments, but many of his comments, taken at face value, did serve to legitimize the National Socialist cultural revolution. Even Nietzsche's condemnations of tame bourgeois German culture could be taken as a call to revolt against the status quo and establish a society based on the new values of cruelty, power, elitism and war so loudly and insistently exalted by Nietzsche. Nietzsche might very well have been thrilled to see Hitler's new Germany, with a hard, dominant and mastering elite ruling the masses with a whip and repudiating tricky Jewish-Christian lies about God, justice, forgiveness, quietness of life, and love (this last a concept of which the confused, lonely and unhappy Nietzsche had not the faintest comprehension).

Along with the popularization and the fundamental simplicity of some philosophical ideas which anyone could easily grasp once paraphrased, we need to consider that Hitler was by no means as stupid as many seem to think. Saying that Hitler was in some ways a highly intelligent man, even a brilliant one, by no means minimizes his evil. On the contrary, it intensifies his evil. He was fully capable of cutting and pasting basic ideas from various sources and working them into a coherent ideology. True, he was working in conditions of social upheaval that the naïve philosophers never dreamed of while sitting in their cozy academic nooks, and he added new elements, but many of his most basic ideas seemed true and reasonable at the time and were perfectly consistent with some basic philosophical principles.

---

[10] For an analysis of Kant's influence on Schopenhauer, and Schopenhauer's influence on Richard Wagner, see Bryan Magee, *Wagner and Philosophy* (London: Penguin Books, 2001). Wagner, of course, as an evangelist for racial antisemitism and for pre-Christian Germanic values has often been directly linked to Hitler.

Consider for a moment the philosophy of Spinoza. This eminent example of autonomous and independent human rationality began not with divine revelation but "clear and distinct ideas, notions which he thought to be self-evidently true."[11] Now, that sounds very good to any self-respecting humanist – but what if it is a clear and distinct idea, self-evidently true, that the Versailles Treaty was unjust, and that Germany needed to regain its lost territories? What if it was self-evidently true that all of the Germans in Europe should be united in one state? That human life emerged out of struggle, and that conventional ethics were a delusion? That Christianity was false and had corrupted pre-Christian Germany's joyful paganism?

One could go on and on. What if it was self-evident that Germany needed to be racially pure in order to prevail in the brutal struggle for survival, and that the Jews corrupted that racial purity? Moreover, Spinoza thought that God was immanent in nature, that nature was an expression of God. But if that is the case, and science later reveals the truth of evolution, then the process of survival of the fittest that weeds out the less fit and brings about the evolutionary advancement of the human race is the work of God. By facilitating the dominance of Germany, by purifying the race, Hitler could be seen as doing the work of a philosophical sort of god – a work of ruthless evolutionary progress that had been hindered by false Christian sentimentality and respect for individuals.

"To Spinoza, 'the universal laws of science' were the decrees of God which followed from 'the necessity and perfection of the Divine nature.'"[12] If nature decrees that the weak and the unfit should perish, this is a decree of God, since nature is a manifestation of God. Thus exterminating the unfit is doing the will of God. Now Spinoza, of course, had no such thing in mind, yet it is remarkable how closely these ideas follow those of Ernst Haeckel. Nineteenth-century Germany's leading evangelist for the new theory of Darwinism, he too saw "the Almighty" as working through scientific law, and understood through scientific law – only for Haeckel, scientific law was survival of the fittest.[13]

It has been claimed that Hitler represented a denial of modernity, but in many ways he merely carried some of modernity's assumptions to their farthest conclusions. Science, not religion, teaches us what life is all about. We need to live scientifically, without any outdated concepts of God, heaven, hell, conscience, guilt, morality. Those are all human inventions, ethical chains that

---

[11] Colin Brown, *Christianity and Western Thought: From the Ancient World to the Enlightenment (Volume I)* (Downers Grove, IL: IVP Academic, 1990), p. 186.

[12] Ibid., p. 187.

[13] In his book *The Scientific Origins of National Socialism* (New Brunswick USA / London: Transaction Publishers, 2004), Daniel Gasman has proven conclusively that many of Haeckel's views were close to and even identical to Hitler's. Richard Weikart has pointed out however that many people besides Haeckel had such views.

hinder the free development of the highest species of humanity in evolutionary struggle. And isn't even a fascination with the primitive as being more authentic than tame bourgeois civilization also a part of the modern experience? Weren't Picasso and other modern artists fascinated with the primitive and the ugly as supposedly closer to real experience?

"It is customary to date the rise of fascist theory from the turn of the century"[14] – but some have seen Hegel as the source of modern totalitarianism. Some have seen glimpses and foreshadowings of Hitler in earlier thinkers. Michael Mack's *German Idealism and the Jew: The Inner Anti-Semitism of Philosophy and German Jewish Responses* and Paul Lawrence Rose's *German Question / Jewish Question: Revolutionary Antisemitism in Germany from Kant to Wagner*[15] are only two of the books that find the ominous stirrings of new and more deadly forms of antisemitism in the murky brains of those ostensibly devoted to reason, yet at the same time driven by unhealthy and dishonest motives.

The French Revolution and its subsequent events, which occurred in a neighboring country less than a century before Hitler was born, also provide some noteworthy parallels. In both National Socialism and in the silly vaporings of the French *philosophes*, we see blind and foolish attempts to replace religion with human reason alone, to create a new man, a new society, a new world – attempts that ended in catastrophe. We see anger at perceived injustice leading to more injustice, and dreams of improving society that somehow went horribly wrong.

"The French Revolution was the first movement in modern times to attempt 'to replace Catholicism, with its supernatural frame of reference, by a secular religion of humanity, which, in various forms, runs through the subsequent history of Europe'."[16] Later there were to be Communism and the German and Italian varieties of fascism, as well as contemporary 21st-century variations of secularism. All of them sprang (or spring) from the same root – defiance of God and rebellion against his laws – and all of them shared (and share) common features of inhumanity and brutality (as in the abortion holocaust), as well as weird ideas divorced from reality (such as the beliefs that homosexuality is healthy and normal, and that women are supposed to be socially identical to men). Hence they were (and are) ultimately doomed to failure.

Conway notes some external similarities between the Nazis and the radical French revolutionaries. They sought to prop up their newly-invented political

---

[14] Barzun, *Darwin, Marx, Wagner*, p. 214. Barzun rejects this view.

[15] See bibliography for full information.

[16] John Conway, *The Nazi Persecution of the Churches 1933-1945* (Vancouver: Regent, 1968), p. 330 [quoting New Cambridge Modern History, vol. IX, *War and Peace in an Age of Upheaval* (Cambridge 1965)].

faith with symbols, songs, new holidays, a flag and distinctive caps to symbolize their movement and create a feeling of community. Significantly, Napoleon felt, like Hitler, that the church should be subordinated to the state, that "religion must be in the hands of the government."[17] People needed religion, so let them have it – the support of the churches lent legitimacy to the state. But of course, religion that places itself in the hands of dictators is not real religion of the heart, the only religion that is of any value.

Napoleon, though, was motivated primarily I think by an old-fashioned love of power and glory. He did not have the benefit of sophisticated modern ideologies to tell him that destroying certain classes of people would further human progress. Nor did he or his revolutionary predecessors have the benefits of modern technology. It would take another century or so for colorless little scientists diligently toiling in the service of the state and of the military to create ever more ingenious means of destruction. New technology and new ideology. Here we have two fundamental ingredients of the Holocaust which, combined with age old human hatred and cruelty, facilitated an explosion of evil such as the world had never seen before. Had any one ever, at any other time in history, written that the suffering and dying of multitudes of weak and inferior people were natural and even a positive good, necessary to the emergence of higher life forms? That cruelty and war were healthy, while peace, mercy and kindness were unhealthy and contrary to real life?

Kierkegaard wrote that "when feeling or understanding or will has become fantastic . . . where the person plunges headlong into the fantastic," then the self is lost, and emotions also become fantastic. Turning from God to follow beliefs of their own contrivance, people lose themselves more and more. They become increasingly detached from deeper spiritual truths which alone are the true source and guarantee of human rights, until finally their trivial and selfish understanding "becomes a kind of inhuman knowledge" in which the self is finally lost, and humanity becomes an increasingly remote abstraction.[18] This is why Kierkegaard so strongly rejected Hegel's vast but cold and inhuman schemes, lofty philosophical abstractions in which the sufferings of trivial individuals were of no importance relative to the great deeds of the conquering heroes.

Through German philosophy, romanticism, empiricism, social Darwinism, nationalism, militarism, imperialism, all of which seemed rational and reasonable at the time, the German consciousness became to a great extent corrupted, inflamed, conceited, deluded, and in the end fantastic. Intensified by the feelings of humiliation, fear, and lust for revenge excited by Germany's political problems, myriads of Germans who did not care about the biblical

---

[17] Ibid.

[18] Soren Kierkegaard, *The Sickness Unto Death*, trans. Alastair Hannay (London: Penguin Books, 2008), pp. 34-33.

solutions to all of these problems were vulnerable to a metaphysical swindler, charlatan, and con man, who promised security and honor, but brought shame and dishonor.

A German nation that was seriously dedicated to preparing for the life to come as instructed by Jesus Christ would never have given birth to a National Socialist movement, and in earlier, more authentically religious periods, Hitler would have been instantly recognized as a fool. It was the corruptions of modernism and secularism that poisoned the minds of the German people with false and exaggerated notions of themselves, and with inhuman ideas of life and society, to the point where they saw good as evil, and evil as good.

I hope in another volume to look more closely into the various roots of Hitler's ideology. For the present, suffice it to say that Hitler and his crimes represent the failure of gullible human reason and of the sinful, corrupt and spoiled human personality. We do not need a glorification of self that tells us how wonderful we are, and tells us we will be happy if only we can pursue our own base desires to the outermost limit. We do not need false and ugly philosophies of lies that tell us we should just be whatever we feel like with no regard for God. We need God's rules and we need God's laws. They are for our benefit, we live most happily within them, and the casting aside of those laws has not led to a higher, nobler, better, freer world. In the case of Germany, it led to social breakdown, and it is doing the same in our own day, although in different forms suitable to our own context.

"Longing to take hold of all beneath heaven and improve it . . . I've seen such dreams invariably fail."[19] Ironic, that an ancient Chinese sage understood more about life than many intellectual leaders and opinion makers in what was considered to be one of the most advanced countries in the world. Lao Tzu went on to say in this context that "you never use weapons to coerce all beneath heaven. Such things always turn against you." This reflects a humane modesty, a healthy humility conspicuously absent from those who thought that their scientific and technological advances equipped them to remake mankind; who thought that nothing was more important than the gratification of their will to power.

There was a profound and lofty conceit underlying much of nineteenth-century German thought. This conceit led people farther and farther from normal human considerations, into a fantasy world of imaginary threats to an imaginary superiority. This conceit was nourished by the denial of God and of His unique creation of man. Contrary to popular misconceptions, this denial of our divine origin did not lead to less pride, it led to more pride. It did not remove man from the center, for man was never at the center of the traditionally theistic world; he could not have been, for God was at the center.

---

[19] Lao Tzu. *Tao Te Ching*, trans. David Hinton (Berkeley, CA: Counterpoint, 2002), pp. 32-33. The italics and ellipsis are Hinton's.

It rather encouraged the vain and destructive belief that there is no one above us; that we are at the apex of creation and hence accountable to no one.

The common boast that science has made us more humble is nothing but a lie. The declaration of independence from higher divine authority was one of the hidden roots of the Holocaust. The crimes of Hitler and his followers become less of a mystery if we accept that people first adopted false ideas of life and then proceeded to act on them. It also helps if we can understand that there are unseen spiritual forces of good and of evil. When people reject the higher forces of good, and embrace and serve the lower forces of evil, it is not surprising if they then act accordingly. If people really are nothing but animals, why should they be treated with humanity and respect? Doesn't nature itself teach that the perishing of multitudes of the weak and the unfit is normal, natural, healthy? And why not use the hair and skin of dead human animals? Why should useful raw materials be wasted? Assigning a special value to people is mere bourgeois sentimentality that has no basis in scientific fact.[20]

But why the hatred of the Jews? They were not killed because of what they had done. They were killed because of what Hitler thought they had done – debasing Aryan blood by inter-breeding, and corrupting humanity with democracy, liberalism, pacifism and humanitarianism. These emerged out of and because of Christian concepts, and Christianity was obviously an invention of the Jews, as Hitler, Nietzsche and many others noted. Here was the source of the corruption that had robbed the Germans of that simple and innocent paganism that allowed them to plunder, fight, wench and kill without having to worry about such sickly Jewish concepts as guilt, conscience, heaven and hell.

There is more than a little truth in Stephen Hicks' assertion that "The primary cause of Naziism lies in *philosophy*. Not economics, not psychology, and not even politics. National Socialism was first a philosophy of life believed and advocated by highly intelligent men and women. Professors, public intellectuals, Nobel Prize-winners . . . ."[21] Like the French revolutionaries, they had hopes and dreams of a better world founded on human reason. What they did not understand was that the corruption, vanity, self-deceit and even cruelty of human reason unrestrained by divine law would lead them to disaster.

Hitler did have a world view, and he was not a stupid man. He was thoroughly in harmony with significant aspects of modernism, and sought to

---

[20] Those who think that the Nazi use of human products taken from the corpses of their victims was repulsive, disgusting, and just plain wrong are in effect showing a conviction that there is something great and profound separating mankind from sheep, cows, horses and goats.

[21] Stephen R. C. Hicks, *Nietzsche and the Nazis: A Personal View* (Loves Park, IL: Ockham's Razor Publishing, 2010), pp. 10-11.

purify a humanity that had emerged out of ruthless struggle and would sink back into decay without that struggle. What he did not understand, and what many modernists also do not understand, is that there is a moral order to the universe. There are concepts of right and wrong that are rooted not in human convention, but in the character and in the truth of God. These are revealed to us in the Bible, and if Germany had not widely rejected the Bible and relied on humanistic principles of autonomous human reason, the Holocaust would never have occurred.

It would be possible to stop here, but let's conclude instead with an imaginative biography of someone born in Austria in the last part of the nineteenth-century. We will start with our subject as an intelligent and sensitive little boy with an angry, harsh, and domineering father. Instead of the warmth, encouragement, and love he needed from his father he received only insensitivity, beating, and a complete lack of sympathy with his budding talents and interests.

This would have a negative impact on anyone. In the case of our subject, it led to three profound personality problems. The first was a deep-seated anger and resentment at a world that was somehow profoundly and confusingly wrong. This was a burden the boy never got over, but carried with him for the rest of his life. The second problem was the development of a rich fantasy life, in which all was as it should be. This comforting fantasy world was sometimes more real than life itself, and certainly much more agreeable. This, too, was a problem he never recognized or resolved, and carried with him to his grave.

The third problem was a deep-seated inferiority complex, a permanent and deeply ingrained sense of worthlessness. This, too, he never understood or resolved, but (in the context of nineteenth-century Austrian culture) he did find some ease for it in the knowledge that he was a superior German, not an inferior and worthless Slav. This widespread belief in German superiority was one of the anchors that helped him to face the world, and (along with fantasy) became his most effective means of self-justification.

This child was also an avid reader, inquisitive and with a high order of intelligence, and books greatly influenced his view of the world.[22] He read widely, over a broad range of subjects. Sometime as a teenager or a young adult, let's imagine he came across Ernst Haeckel's *Die Weltraetsel* (*The Riddle of the Universe*). This best-selling book of popular science was easily comprehensible, and from it, or from other writings in a similar vein, the boy became convinced of the truth that life was only a process of struggle, in which

---

[22] Timothy W. Ryback's book *Hitler's Private Library: The Books that Shaped his Life* (London: Vintage Books, 2010) has some doubtful points, but it does conclusively demonstrate, in my opinion, that Hitler was an avid reader from his youth on.

the dominance of the more fit and the elimination of the less fit led to the development of higher life forms.

He also readily accepted the related idea that traditional religion was out of date, unscientific. There was no immortal soul, no day of judgment, no afterlife, no divine laws that we had to follow, only cold and ruthless struggle – a negative view of life that was deeply congenial to his already deeply troubled personality. This became a foundational belief, one that he never changed or altered, and earnestly and sincerely sought to live by.[23]

At about the same time, our subject became deeply enamored with first the music, and then with the writings of Richard Wagner. The power of Wagner's music lured him, as it did many others, into a new world of myth and fantasy, in which themes of German supremacy and dark forces of negativity were easily blended with the view of life as unrelenting struggle. In Wagner's political writings he was also warned of the importance of racial purity and of the dangers of Judaism, the spiritual disease that threatened to undermine German superiority and plunge the world into a quagmire of distortion and warped values such as democracy, liberalism, pacifism and Christianity in which true Germanic heroism would be impossible.

Hitler's teenage friend Kubizek asserts that Hitler not only read Wagner, he "read avidly everything he could get hold of concerning Wagner . . . He was particularly keen on biographical literature about him, read his notes, letters, diaries, his self-appraisal, his confessions. Day by day he penetrated ever deeper into the man's life." Kubizek further states, "His devotion to, and veneration of, Wagner took almost the form of a religion."[24] That this went far beyond mere music appreciation is seen from Wagner's influence on *Mein Kampf*, which has been noted by more than one writer.[25]

From reading many other authors or at least about their ideas – Lagarde, Langbehn, H. S. Chamberlain, Schopenhauer, Hegel, Fichte – our subject learned that the German people had a unique destiny to lead mankind on its onward and upward path. This required mastery in a world dominated by conflict, and assertion of will in a world in which will predominated over reason. To fulfill its destiny the noble and superior German people needed to purify itself of alien influences, both spiritually and biologically. This included

---

[23] To be sure, many others shared Haeckel's views, but Haeckel very effectively put them into popular and accessible form.

[24] August Kubizek, *The Young Hitler I Knew*, trans. Geoffrey Brooks (London: Greenhill Books, 2006), pp. 84, 187. Kubizek's youthful friendship with Hitler is an accepted fact, and his memoir is believed by reputable historians to contain valid information, though not of course infallible in every detail.

[25] One translator of Hitler's book describes it as being full of "largely unintelligible flights of Wagnerian terminology" – "Translator's Note," Adolf Hitler, *Mein Kampf,* trans. Ralph Manheim (Boston: Houghton Mifflin, 1999), p. ix.

liberation from the spiritually restricting confinements of conventional religion, which by its false values hindered the free play of forces in conflict necessary to the further development of the human race to its fullest potential.

This also meant emancipation from the insidious forces of Judaism which had through Christianity introduced alien values that were wholly contrary to the free and noble German spirit. Such ideas had been common among an influential segment of the German intelligentsia for decades before Hitler was born, and seemed self-evidently true to many. They were greatly intensified by the destruction of the old order by the First World War and its aftermath. This allowed for the replacement of the status quo by a new ideology which consisted of the effective implementation of values and ideas that had previously been only talked about. There was also the greater radicalization of feeling that whipped resentment into hatred and violence.

These issues were manipulated by a political and a criminal genius, a man unique in world history. He effectively organized a party to implement a coherent policy based on the aforementioned principles. What others had only talked about, he did. In more stable times he could never have arisen. In a society dominated by traditional ideas he could never have arisen – but in a society undermined first by over a hundred years of modern thinking, and second by political, military, and economic catastrophes, he found sufficient numbers of empty people in need of a cause, a purpose, and a leader.

He led them to great heights of power and glory, but because his philosophy was untrue, contrary to the world as it really is and a defiance of the moral laws that inform all of life, he fell. He left behind him smoking ruins and piles of corpses, his monument to the sinfulness of human nature, and to the folly of believing that we can make a better world without God, that we have advanced beyond good and evil, and have no need of conscience or regard for the world to come in which all will be judged.

Bibliography

Aristotle. *Physics.* Translated by Robin Waterfield. Oxford: Oxford University Press, 2008.

Aumann, Moshe. *Conflict and Connection: The Jewish-Christian-Israel Triangle.* Jerusalem: Gefen Publishing, 2003 / 5763.

Bartrop, Paul and Steven Leonard Jacobs. *Fifty Key Thinkers on the Holocaust and Genocide.* London: Routledge, 2011.

Barzun, Jacques. *Darwin, Marx, Wagner: Critique of a Heritage.* New York: Doubleday Anchor Books, 1958.

Bauman, Zygmunt. *Modernity and the Holocaust.* Ithaca, NY: Cornell University Press, 2000.

Bentley, James. *Martin Niemoller.* London: Hodder and Stoughton, 1984.

Berdyaev, Nicolai. *Christian Existentialism: A Berdyaev Anthology.* Translated by Donald Lowrie. New York: Harper Torchbooks, 1965.

Bergman, Jerry. *Hitler and the Nazi Darwinian Worldview.* Kitchener, Ontario: Joshua Press, 2012.

Biddis, Michael D. *The Father of Racist Ideology: The Social and Political Thought of Count Gobineau.* London: Weidenfeld and Nicolson, 1970.

Bonhoeffer, Dietrich. *Christ the Center.* Translated by Edwin H. Robertson. New York: HarperOne, 1978.

_____. *Letters and Papers from Prison.* Edited by Eberhard Bethge. New York: Touchstone, 1997.

Brown, Colin. *Christianity and Western Thought: From the Ancient World to the Enlightenment* (Volume I). Downers Grove, IL: IVP Academic, 1990.

Burleigh, Michael. *Ethics and extermination: Reflections on Nazi genocide.* Cambridge: Cambridge University Press, 1977.

Chamberlain, Houston Stewart. *Foundations of the Nineteenth Century (Volume 1).* Translated by John Lees. Lexington, KY: Elibron Classics, 2013.

Chandler, David P. *Brother Number One: A Political Biography of Pol Pot.* Boulder, CO: Westview Press, 1999.

Conquest, Robert. *Reflections on a Ravaged Century.* New York: W.W. Norton, 2001.

Conway, John. *The Nazi Persecution of the Churches 1933-1945*. Vancouver: Regent, 1968.

Craig, Gordon. *Germany 1866-1945*. Oxford: Clarendon Press, 1978.

Craig, William Lane. *Reasonable Faith: Christian Truth and Apologetics*. Wheaton, IL: Crossway, 2008.

Diephouse, David J. "Antisemitism as Moral Discourse: Theophil Wurm and Protestant Opposition to the Holocaust." Paper presented to the 30th Annual Scholar's Conference on the Holocaust and the Churches, Philadelphia, March 2000. CD-ROM Sourcebook, Philadelphia, Geneva: Vista Intermedia, 2001.

Engelmann, Bernt. *In Hitler's Germany: Everyday Life in the Third Reich*. Translated by Krishna Winston. New York: Pantheon Books, 1986.

Evans, Richard. *The Coming of the Third Reich*. New York: Penguin, 2005.

_____. "Nazism, Christianity and Political Religion: A Debate," *Journal of Contemporary History* 42, no. 1 (2007), 5-7.

Ferguson, Niall. *Civilization: The Six Killer Apps of Western Power*. London: Penguin Books, 2012.

Friedländer, Saul. *The Years of Extermination: Nazi Germany and the Jews 1939-1945*. London: Weidenfeld and Nicolson, 2007.

Gasman, Daniel. *The Scientific Origins of National Socialism*. New Brunswick USA / London: Transaction Publishers, 2004.

Gelb, Norman. *Kings of the Jews: The Origins of the Jewish Nation*. Philadelphia: The Jewish Publication Society, 2012.

Gilbert, Martin. *The Holocaust: A History of the Jews of Europe During the Second World War*. New York: Henry Holt and Co., 1985.

Glazov, Jamie. *High Noon for America: The Coming Showdown*. Brantford, Ontario: Mantua Books, 2012.

Goebbels, Joseph. *The Goebbels Diaries 1942-1943*. Translated by Louis P. Lochner. Westport, CT: Greenwood Press, 1948.

Golomb, Jacob and Robert S. Wistrich, Editors. *Nietzsche, Godfather of Fascism? On the Uses and Abuses of a Philosophy*. Princeton: Princeton University Press, 2002.

Gramsci, Antonio. *The Antonio Gramsci Reader: Selected Writings 1916-1935*. Edited by David Forgacs. New York: New York University Press, 2000.

Gregor, Neil. *How to Read Hitler*. New York: W. W. Norton, 2005.

Haffner, Sebastian. *Germany – Jekyll and Hyde: A Contemporary Account of Nazi Germany*. Translated by Wilfrid David. London: Abacus, 2009.

Hallie, Philip. *Lest Innocent Blood Be Shed: The Story of the Village of Le Chambon and How Goodness Happened There*. New York: Harper and Row, 1979.

Hawking, Stephen and Leonard Mlodinow. *The Grand Design: New Answers to the Ultimate Questions of Life*. London: Bantam Books, 2011.

Hayek, F. A. *The Fatal Conceit: The Errors of Socialism*. Chicago: University of Chicago Press, 1991.

Heine, Heinrich. *On the History of Religion and Philosophy in Germany*. Translated by Howard Pollack Milgate. Cambridge: Cambridge University Press, 2007.

Henry, Matthew. *Matthew Henry's Commentary on the Whole Bible (Vol. 5 Matthew to John)*. Peabody, Mass.: Hendrickson Publishers, 1991.

Hicks, Stephen R. C. *Explaining Postmodernism: Skepticism and Socialism from Rousseau to Foucault*. Phoenix, AZ: Scholargy Publishing, 2004.

____. *Nietzsche and the Nazis: A Personal View*. Loves Park, IL: Ockham's Razor Publishing, 2010.

Hitler, Adolf. *Hitler's Second Book: The Unpublished Sequel to Mein Kampf*. Translated by Krista Smith. New York: Enigma Books, 2006.

____. *Mein Kampf*. Translated by Ralph Manheim. Boston: Houghton Mifflin, 1999.

____. *The Speeches of Adolf Hitler (April 1922 – August 1939)* (vols. 1 and 2). Translated by Norman H. Baynes. London: Oxford University Press, 1942.

Hobsbawm, Eric. *How to Change the World: Tales of Marx and Marxism*. London: Abacus, 2012.

Hollingdale, R. J. *Nietzsche: The Man and His Philosophy (Revised Edition)*. Cambridge: Cambridge University Press, 1999.

Holton, Gerald. *Science and Anti-Science*. Cambridge, Massachusetts: Harvard University Press, 1993.

Johnson, Paul. *Modern Times: The World from the Twenties to the Nineties*. New York: Perennial Classics, 1992.

Josephus. *Josephus: The Life & Against Apion*. Translated by H. St. J. Thackeray. Cambridge, Mass: Harvard University Press, 1966.

Justin Martyr. *The First and Second Apologies.* Translated by Leslie William Barnard. Mahwah, NJ: Paulist Press, 1997.

Kant, Immanuel. *An Answer to the Question: What is Enlightenment?* London: Penguin Books, 2009.

_____. *Religion Within the Limits of Reason Alone.* Translated by Theodore M. Greene. Clermont Ferrand, France: Digireads, 2011.

Katz, Steven A. *The Holocaust in Historical Context (Vol. 1).* New York: Oxford University Press, 1994.

Kershaw, Ian. *Hitler.* London: Penguin Books, 2008.

Kersten, Felix. *The Memoirs of Doctor Felix Kersten.* Translated by Dr. Ernest Morwitz. Garden City, NY: Doubleday and Co., 1947.

Kierkegaard, Soren. *The Sickness Unto Death.* Translated by Alastair Hannay. London: Penguin Books, 2008.

Koehne, Samuel. "Reassessing *The Holy Reich*: Leading Nazis' Views on Confession, Community and 'Jewish' Materialism," *Journal of Contemporary History* 2013 48: 423.

Kubizek, August. *The Young Hitler I Knew.* Translated by Geoffrey Brooks. London: Greenhill Books, 2006.

Lao Tzu. *Tao Te Ching.* Translated by David Hinton. Berkeley, CA: Counterpoint, 2002.

Lloyd-Jones, D. M. *The Puritans: Their Origins and Successors (Addresses Delivered at the Puritan and Westminster Conferences 1959-1978).* Edinburgh: The Banner of Truth Trust, 1987.

Luther, Martin. *Martin Luther: Selections From His Writings.* Edited by John Dillenberger. New York: Anchor Books, 1962.

_____. *A Meditation on Christ's Passion: Devotional Writings I.* Translated by Martin H. Bertram. Luther's Works American Edition, vol. 42. Philadelphia: Fortress Press 1969.

_____. *On the Jews and Their Lies.* Translated by Martin H. Bertram. Luther's Works American Edition, vol. 47. Philadelphia: Fortress Press, 1971.

Macfarlan, D. *The Revivals of the Eighteenth Century (Particularly at Cambuslang) With Three Sermons by the Rev. George Whitefield.* Glasgow: Free Presbyterian Publications, 1988.

Machen, John Gresham. *Christianity and Liberalism.* Charleston, SC: Bibliolife, date not given, reprint of the 1923 edition.

Mack, Michael. *German Idealism and the Jew: The Inner Anti-Semitism of Philosophy and German Jewish Responses.* Chicago / London: University of Chicago Press, 2003.

Magee, Bryan. *Wagner and Philosophy.* London: Penguin Books, 2001.

Maser, Werner. *Hitler's Letters and Notes.* New York: Harper and Row, 1974.

McGrath, Alister. *The Twilight of Atheism: The Rise and Fall of Disbelief in the Modern World.* London: Rider, 2004.

Metaxas, Eric. *Bonhoeffer: Pastor, Martyr, Prophet, Spy – A Righteous Gentile vs. The Third Reich.* Nashville: Thomas Nelson, 2010.

Miller, James. *The Philosophical Life: Twelve Great Thinkers and the Search for Wisdom, From Socrates to Nietzsche.* (London: Oneworld, 2013), p. 275.

Monod, Jacques. *Chance and Necessity: An Essay on the Natural Philosophy of Modern Biology.* Translated by Austryn Wainhouse. New York: Alfred A. Knopf, 1971.

Montgomery, John Warwick. *In Defense of Martin Luther: Essays by John Warwick Montgomery.* Milwaukee: Northwestern Publishing House, 1970.

_____. *The Suicide of Christian Theology.* Minneapolis, MN: Bethany Fellowship, Inc., 1971.

Mosse, George L. *The Crisis of German Ideology: Intellectual Origins of the Third Reich.* New York: Grosset & Dunlap, 1971 (and London: Weidenfeld and Nicolson, 1966).

Munitz, Milton K., Editor. *Theories of the Universe: From Babylonian Myth to Modern Science.* New York: The Free Press of Glencoe, 1957.

Murray, Iain H. *Evangelicalism Divided: A Record of Crucial Change in the Years 1950 to 2000.* Edinburgh: The Banner of Truth Trust, 2000.

_____. *Jonathan Edwards: A New Biography.* Edinburgh: The Banner of Truth Trust, 1988.

Nestingen, James A. *Martin Luther: A Life.* Minneapolis: Augsburg Books, 2003.

Nietzsche, Friedrich. *The Antichrist.* Translated by Anthony M. Ludovici. Amherst, NY: Prometheus Books, 2000.

_____. *The Genealogy of Morals.* Translated by Horace B. Samuel. Mineola, NY: Dover Publications, 2003.

Oden, Thomas C. *After Modernity . . . What? Agenda for Theology*. Grand Rapids, MI: Zondervan, 1992.

_____. *Requiem: A Lament in Three Movements*. Nashville: Abingdon Press, 1995.

Owen, John. *The Holy Spirit: His Gifts and Power*. Ross-shire, Scotland: Christian Heritage, 2007.

_____. *The True Nature of a Gospel Church and Its Government*. The Works of John Owen (Vol. XVI). Edited by William H. Goold. Edinburgh, UK: Banner of Truth Trust, 2009.

Pearce, Tony. *The Messiah Factor*. Chichester, England: New Wine, 2004.

Pink, Arthur W. *The Seven Sayings of the Saviour on the Cross*. Hyderabad India: Authentic (by arrangement with Baker Books) 2010.

Prager, Dennis Prager and Joseph Telushkin. *Why the Jews? The Reason for Antisemitism*. New York / London: Touchstone, 2003.

Reck-Malleczewen, Friedrich. *Diary of a Man in Despair*. Translated by Paul Rubens. London: Duck Editions, 1995.

Riasanovsky, Nicholas V. and Mark D. Steinberg. *A History of Russia*. New York: Oxford University Press, 2011.

Rees, Laurence Rees. *Hitler's Charisma: Leading Millions into the Abyss*. New York: Pantheon Books, 2012.

Rose, Paul Lawrence. *German Question / Jewish Question: Revolutionary Antisemitism from Kant to Wagner*. Princeton: Princeton University Press, 1990.

_____. *Wagner: Race and Revolution*. New Haven / London: Yale University Press, 1992.

Rubenstein, Richard L. and John K. Roth. *Approaches to Auschwitz: The Holocaust and its Legacy*. Louisville KY: Westminster John Knox Press, 2003.

Ryback, Timothy W. *Hitler's Private Library: The Books that Shaped his Life*. London: Vintage Books, 2010.

Sachar, Abram Leon. *A History of the Jews*. New York: Alfred A. Knopf, 1966.

Sachar, Howard M. *A History of the Jews in the Modern World*. New York: Vintage Books, 2006.

Sanneh, Lamin. *Whose Religion is Christianity? The Gospel Beyond the West*. Cambridge: William B. Eerdmans Publishing, 2003.

Schaff, Philip. *History of the Christian Church (vol. 1, Apostolic Christianity from the Birth of Christ to the Death of St. John A.D. 1-100)*. Peabody, Mass: Hendrickson Publishers, 2011.

Schaeffer, Francis. *The Church at the End of the Twentieth Century*. Wheaton, IL: Crossway Books, 1994.

____. *The God Who is There*. Dower's Grove, IL: IVP Books, p. 1998.

____. *The Great Evangelical Disaster*. Westchester, IL: Crossway Books, 1984.

____. *He is There and He is Not Silent*. Carol Stream, IL: Tyndale House Publishers, 2001.

____. *No Little People*. Wheaton, IL: Crossway, 2003.

Schweitzer, Albert. *The Quest of the Historical Jesus: A Critical Study of its Progress from Reimarus to Wrede*. Translated by W. Montgomery. Tarlton, OH: Suzeteo Enterprises, 2011.

Scougal, Henry. *The Life of God in the Soul of Man*. Ross-shire Scotland: Christian Heritage, 2005.

Shirer, William L. *Berlin Diary*. New York: Alfred A. Knopf, 1941.

____. *The Rise and Fall of the Third Reich: A History of Nazi Germany*. New York: Simon & Schuster, 2011.

Snell, John. Editor. *The Nazi Revolution: Germany's Guilt or Germany's Fate?* Lexington, Mass.: D. C. Heath, 1959.

Snyder, Louis L., Editor. *Documents of German History*. New Brunswick, NJ: Rutgers University Press, 1958.

Spicer, Kevin P., Editor. *Antisemitism, Christian Ambivalence, and the Holocaust*. Bloomington, IN: Indiana University Press, 2007.

Steigmann-Gall, Richard. *The Holy Reich: Nazi Conceptions of Christianity, 1919-1945*. Cambridge: Cambridge University Press, 2004.

Stroud, Dean G. *Preaching in Hitler's Shadow: Sermons of Resistance in the Third Reich*. Grand Rapids, MI: William B. Eerdmans, 2013.

Tozer A. W. *The Knowledge of the Holy*. Colorado Springs: Authentic, 2008.

Tzouliadas, Tim. *The Forsaken: An American Tragedy in Stalin's Russia*. New York: Penguin Press, 2008.

Van Til, Cornelius. *The Reformed Pastor and Modern Thought*. Phillipsburg, NJ: Presbyterian and Reformed Publishing Company, 1980.

Veith, Gene Edward Jr. *Modern Fascism: Liquidating the Judeo-Christian Worldview*. St. Louis: Concordia Publishing House, 1993.

Viereck, Peter. *Meta-politics: The Roots of the Nazi Mind*. New York: Capricorn Books, 1965.

Watson, Peter. *The German Genius: Europe's Third Renaissance, The Second Scientific Revolution, and the Twentieth Century*. New York: Harper Perennial, 2011.

Weikart, Richard. *From Darwin to Hitler: Evolutionary Ethics, Eugenics, and Racism in Germany*. New York: Palgrave Macmillan, 2004.

Weiss, John. *Ideology of Death: Why the Holocaust Happened in Germany*. Chicago: Elephant paperbacks, 1997.

Wells, David F. *No Place for Truth or Whatever Happened to Evangelical Authority?* Grand Rapids, MI: William B. Eerdmans Publishing Company, 1993.

Wells, Paul. *Cross Words: The Biblical Doctrine of the Atonement.* Fearn, Scotland: Christian Focus Publications, 2006.

Wentorf, Rudolf. *Paul Schneider: Witness of Buchenwald*. Translated by Daniel Bloesch. Vancouver: Regent College Publishing, 2008.

Werth, Alexander. *Russia At War 1941-1945*. New York: E. P. Dutton, 1964.

Wilken, Robert Louis. *The Spirit of Early Christian Thought: Seeking the Face of God*. New Haven: Yale University Press, 2003.

Williams, Stephen N. *The Shadow of the Antichrist: Nietzsche's Critique of Christianity*. Grand Rapids, MI: Baker Academic, and Milton Keynes, UK: Paternoster, 2006.

Wistrich, Robert S. *Hitler and the Holocaust*. New York: Modern Library, 2003.

Internet sources

Edwards, David L. "Rudolf Bultmann: Scholar of Faith." *Christian Century*, September 1-8 (1976), 728-730. *Religion Online*; www.religion-online.org/showarticle.asp?title=1827 *accessed May 2014.*

"Israeli Messianic congregation building burned down," *israel today*, Friday Jan. 18, 2013; http://www.israeltoday.co.il/NewsItem/tabid/178/nid/23628/Default.aspx accessed February 2014.

"Julius Striecher," *Jewish Virtual Library*, www.jewishvirtuallibrary.org/jsource/Holocaust, accessed January 2014.

"Pre-1933 Nazi Posters," German Propaganda Archive; http://www.bytwerk.com/gpa/posters1.htm (poster # 39) accessed May 2014.

Ryback, Timothy W. "Hitler's Forgotten Library: The Man, His Books, and His Search For God." *The Atlantic Monthly*; http:www.fpp.co.uk/Hitler/library/Atlantic_Monthly.html; accessed April 2014.

Index

www.ingramcontent.com/pod-product-compliance
Lightning Source LLC
Chambersburg PA
CBHW080511090426
42734CB00015B/3028